THE BURMA DELTA

Economic Development and Social Change
on an Asian Rice Frontier, 1852–1941

NEW PERSPECTIVES IN
SOUTHEAST ASIAN STUDIES

THE BURMA DELTA

Economic Development and
Social Change on an
Asian Rice Frontier, 1852–1941

Michael Adas

THE UNIVERSITY OF WISCONSIN PRESS

The University of Wisconsin Press
1930 Monroe Street, 3rd Floor
Madison, Wisconsin 53711-2059
uwpress.wisc.edu

3 Henrietta Street
London WC2E 8LU, England
eurospanbookstore.com

Printed in the United States of America

Library of Congress Cataloging-in-Publication Data

Adas, Michael, 1943–
The Burma Delta : economic development and social change on an Asian rice frontier, 1852–1941 / Michael Adas.
p. cm. — (New perspectives in Southeast Asian studies)
Includes bibliographical references and index.
ISBN 978-0-299-28354-4 (pbk. : alk. paper) —
ISBN 978-0-299-28353-7 (e-book)
1. Burma, Lower—Economic conditions. 2. Burma, Lower—Social conditions. 3. Rice trade—Burma, Lower. I. Title. II. Series: New perspectives in Southeast Asian studies.
HC422.Z7B872 2011
338.9591—dc22

2010054359

TO JANE, JOEL, AND CLAIRE

CONTENTS

MAPS

TABLES

PREFACE TO THE 2011 EDITION

Together with many of the area specialists whose research and writing came during the peak years of the misbegotten U.S. intervention in Vietnam in the late 1960s and early 1970s to be increasingly focused on the peasantry of postcolonial nations, I came to view my work on Burma's rice frontier as part of a larger, collective scholarly project. I shared with colleagues working on agrarian change and peasant protest in areas as diverse as South Asia and Latin America a sense of urgency and social responsibility that gave a moral dimension to our work. We hoped—in most cases in vain—that our findings, lectures, and published writings would change minds and even influence policymaking beyond academe. But even my preliminary research on *The Burma Delta* made it abundantly clear that from a long-term historical perspective I had immersed myself in one of the most remarkable episodes in the modern history of colonization. In the half century after its annexation to Britain's Indian empire in 1852, the Irrawaddy delta region, which comprised much of what came to be known as Lower Burma, had been transformed from what its colonizers routinely depicted as an impoverished, sparsely populated backwater region of the Konbaung kingdom into the world's largest exporter of rice. Hundreds of thousands of hectares of what was officially designated "jungle waste" had been cleared and planted by a massive and ever-increasing flow of migrants. This confluence of processes made it evident that Burma could be studied as an Asian prototype of a moving agrarian frontier. And that phenomenon in turn offered abundant opportunities to explore the impact of the commercialization of peasant agriculture under the aegis of European colonial rule.

From another perspective, which has only become apparent in the last two or three decades, these processes also established Burma as a significant participant in the European-dominated wave of globalization that peaked in the half century before the outbreak of World War I in 1914. Though, for example, many of the migrants who cleared and cultivated the fertile, well-watered deltaic plains were drawn from other areas of Burma itself, hundreds of thousands more—enticed by British incentives and indenture recruiters—migrated from near and distant provinces of the Indian empire as well as China, Malaya, and other areas in Southeast Asia. As was the case throughout the European global empires, this massive movement of peasants and urban laborers was paralleled by a far smaller, but vital, influx of merchants and moneylenders—mostly Indian but also some Chinese—as well as Indian policemen, soldiers, civil servants, lawyers, and other professionals. The combination of the migrant influx and the rapid development of processing industries in rice, logging, and mining turned once-sleepy delta villages into boomtowns and the colony's capital, Rangoon, into one of the top trading, financial, and administrative centers of South and Southeast Asia. In the towns and rural areas of Lower Burma, the mixing of the indigenous and immigrant populations gave rise to one of the largest and most complex plural societies (as J. S. Furnivall was the first to label them) to emerge in the modern era. It is not at all surprising, then, to find that reports and memoirs of British colonial officials who served in Lower Burma around this time tend to be suffused by a sense of accomplishment. Many in fact viewed the experiment in economic development and social change that they and their predecessors had overseen in Burma as one, if not the greatest, of the success stories of the modern British Empire.

Yet despite the accelerated growth of the Burma rice export economy in the early 1900s, a number of British officials, especially those in charge of rural areas on the frontier, expressed concern at the scarcity of new cultivable land in the rice-producing districts of the delta. This shortage, which marked the gradual closing of the frontier, was in turn linked to troubling increases in indebtedness, land alienation, and the impoverishment of the cultivating classes, which are explored in depth in the present book. Severe disruptions of transportation and communication networks during World War I exacerbated these problems, and the postwar recovery proved short-lived. By the 1920s, Furnivall, who had served for decades as a commissioner and land settlement officer in the delta, had begun to write his seminal critiques of the economic and social foundations on which the rice export economy and colonial order in Burma had been built. The collapse of world markets for primary products with the onset of the Great Depression in the early 1930s proved devastating to the Burmese economy. Hard times gave rise to widespread peasant unrest and ultimately to a major rebellion in the countryside, as well as to communal tensions that culminated in widespread urban violence early in the decade. The final chapter of *The Burma Delta* is devoted to these disruptions, which set the stage for the collapse of British rule in the face of a full-scale Japanese invasion in late 1941 and early 1942.

Because my long-term interest was in the comparative study of these processes and in broader questions relating to the failure of the British economic experiment, to peasant responses to the market economy, and to the emergence of mass protest, I resisted the temptation to become a full-fledged Burma specialist, which would have confined me to a national framework. The difficulty of mastering the Burmese language was another factor in this decision. But of greater importance was my sense that opportunities to work and live in Burma and to enjoy meaningful contacts with Burmese scholars and students—virtually nil during the years when *The Burma Delta* was the center of my research and writing—would be limited at best for decades to come. Fortunately, the British colonizers regularly shipped the voluminous official correspondence and departmental records relating to Burma, which was attached administratively to their sprawling Indian Empire, home to London where the materials were well preserved and meticulously archived at the Indian Office and Records. Conversations with seasoned Burma scholars, particularly Dorothy Woodman, made it clear that for my purposes, there would be little left in Rangoon, where white ants and monsoon rains had made short work of most of the documents left behind by the retreating British. It was also dishearteningly evident that any relevant materials that had somehow been preserved would be accessible only if I secured the approval of the army officers whose control over the Burmese heartlands was already pervasive. That I lacked this sort of connection, and was delving into issues regarded as off limits by the authorities, was made clear in the curt rejections I received from Burmese embassy officials in both Washington and London in response to applications for permission to conduct research in Rangoon.

In the years after my book and early articles on colonial Burma appeared, I drew on additional sources in London, as well as some of the materials archived in Amsterdam, to write a comparative study, *Prophets of Rebellion*, as well as numerous essays on peasant protest and millenarian movements in colonial sites ranging from German East Africa to New Zealand. As my work on both Burma and these widespread peasant rebellions revealed, the upheavals in Vietnam, which were often the exclusive focus of so much of the research on agrarian societies at the time, had counterparts over much of the rest of the postcolonial world. In fact, in many ways Vietnam was atypical in the excessive repressiveness of the French regime there, its lower levels of commercialization in the agrarian sector (excepting the plantation enclaves), and the predominance of communist-led, cadre-based guerrilla warfare in resistance to foreign occupiers and in building an independent nation. Market-oriented, expansion-minded frontier societies—ranging, besides Burma, from Thailand, the Philippines, and the Panjab in India to Ghana and Côte d'Ivoire and throughout Latin America—had historically tended to emerge under the aegis of European colonial regimes. In large part this was due to the fact that European colonizers viewed the spread of commercialized agriculture as the key to making overseas colonies productive and profitable.

From the mid-nineteenth century, wet rice agriculture in the Irrawaddy delta region was transformed from what had been primarily subsistence to market-based production, geared toward export. By the end of the century the once-quite-diversified economy of the area, where there was in fact a good deal more land under cultivation before colonization than the British acknowledged at the time, had become a monoculture, heavily dependent on growing, processing, and exporting rice to seemingly insatiable market outlets around the Indian Ocean and throughout Europe. For several decades, Lower Burma funneled more rice into the global system than any other region. The environmental, entrepreneurial, and demographic engines and repercussions of these transformations epitomized those we have come to associate with globalization, which has often been shortsightedly deemed a late-twentieth-century phenomena. The increasingly rapid opening of new lands to rice cultivation, for example, had within decades all but eliminated the rain forest and coastal swamplands that had covered much of the lower delta when it came under British control in the 1850s. Though the restrictions imposed by the current military regime have made it difficult to study with any precision the effects of the tropical cyclone that hit Lower Burma in the spring of 2008, the clearing of the great *kanazo* forests and particularly the mangrove swamps, which stretched across the coastal fringe of the delta, may well have contributed substantially to the devastating damage inflicted by torrential winds and extensive flooding.

The prospect of owning individual plots of land and the steady growth of consumer attractions, from kerosene lamps to bicycles, drew hundreds of thousands of peasant migrants from other regions of Burma into the delta between the 1850s and World War I. This internal migration was matched by an even greater cross-cultural influx of the sort often highlighted in discussions of globalization. Though Chinese and other foreign groups were present, the great majority of these immigrants were impoverished Indian laborers who were transported to Rangoon and, to a lesser extent, other port cities, as well as to areas newly opened to rice production throughout the delta frontier. A sizeable portion of these laborers, who accounted for most of the million Indians residing in Burma by the time of the Great Depression, were indentured workers who endured the harsh working conditions and low wages associated with the *maquiladora* enclaves that have come to dominate globalized commodity production in the late twentieth and early twenty-first centuries.

Indian merchants and moneylenders, particularly Chettiars from Madras in south India, provided most of the capital needed for clearing the land, settling it, and establishing wet-rice cultivation. Indian, and to some extent Chinese, merchants were also the main source of the consumer goods that increasingly provided small landowners and tenant farmers with an incentive to produce surpluses for local urban and overseas markets. Burmese moneylenders also played a significant role, and Burmese entrepreneurs, managers, and workers were present in some sectors, including local transport and processing, as well as skilled labor in the Burmese oilfields. Nonetheless, Burmese colonial society came to be dominated by the British at the top and the Indians at the middle levels of the economy and colonial administrative system. As long as new land was plentiful and jobs could be found in the port towns, the dominance of foreign officials and investors and the competition of migrant laborers do not appear to have been major sources of tension. But when economic growth slowed markedly in the years after World War I and especially when global depression threw the highly vulnerable, export-oriented, monocrop economy into disarray beginning in 1929, Burmese resentment and inter-ethnic tensions generated a decade of protest and violent strife.

In many ways, the highly touted British experiment in (what would later be termed) development economics centered on the Irrawaddy delta had been, from the outset, flawed in ways that slowly became apparent in the first decades of the twentieth century. Sustained growth in the cultivation and export of rice, on which the whole edifice depended, had begun to slow precipitously by this time. As open land suitable for settlement and rice production became increasingly scarce, the share of tenants and landless laborers among the cultivating classes grew steadily. And because the colonial administration had done little to introduce new techniques and tools to improve productivity, yields stagnated or fell over most of the delta. A surfeit of rice on the global market led to declining prices, which in turn caused widespread insolvency among smallholders and further swelled the ranks of the landless. As the crisis deepened, it became clear that government checks on exploitative moneylenders, and the resources at its disposal for relief or to provide much-needed agrarian credit, were woefully inadequate to stem the tide of indebtedness, displacement, and abject poverty.

These setbacks made all too evident the dominance that immigrant groups had come to exert in both the economic and political sectors of the colony as a result of its incorporation into the global capitalist system. As local officials and policemen, merchants, and moneylenders, as well as laborers competing for increasingly scarce employment, Indians interacted far more on a day-to-day basis with the Burmese than the British. Consequently, they frequently became the main focus of popular resentment and very often the chief targets of Burmese nationalist agitators. In the early 1930s, widespread anti-Indian sentiment sparked communal riots and contributed to a major rebellion, both of which spread widely in the Lower Burma districts where the rice-export economy was centered. A decade later, fears of Indian domination did much to account for the Burmese refusal to support British efforts to resist the Japanese invasion and conquest and for the extensive Burmese collaboration with the Japanese regime during the war. Although the British briefly reoccupied their former colony following the defeat of the Japanese, Burma's plural society had in effect been dismantled by the flight of the great majority of Indians and other immigrant groups in the late 1930s and early 1940s.

The self-inflicted marginalization of Myanmar—as the country has been known since 1989—in the late-twentieth-century phase of globalization has drastically reduced the amount of even reasonably accurate information available about postcolonial Burmese society. Nevertheless, given the sorry state of British Burma in its latter days, it is not surprising that those who seek to account for its rather precipitous and extreme withdrawal from the global system often cite the traumatic effects of the collapse of the global export economy in the 1930s and Burmese determination to ward off a return of Indian domination in the postcolonial era. This concern with the return of foreign domination was compounded by the decades-long occupation of Burmese territory by Nationalist Chinese forces fleeing the Communists after the latter emerged victorious from the long civil war in China in 1949. Though the importance of such factors cannot be discounted in explaining Burma's retreat into isolation, they should not be allowed to obscure the self-serving motivations of the corrupt and dictatorial military regimes that followed. The legacies of the colonial era have included the military's obsessive preoccupation with monopolizing power and concentrating wealth in the hands of the elite, repressing all forms of dissent, and forcibly denying autonomy to non-Burmese ethnic minorities.

The fallacy of placing most of the blame for Burma's isolation on the effects of British rule is underscored by the fact that the colonial experience of numerous other Asian and African societies, which have been far more fully integrated into the world economy since World War II, was often far more humiliating, exploitative, and brutal than anything the Burmese experienced. Moreover, millions of Burmese peasants, urban workers, and members of the educated classes eagerly participated in the globalized market economy that undergirded Burmese colonial society for nearly a century. No one has even attempted to assess popular attitudes toward the postindependence regimes' dismantling of the export economy and the consequent decline in living standards for all but the military elite. Certainly, the Burmese people have been given little say in determining that outcome. And the globalizing majority of humanity has evinced scant concern for the pervasive denial of basic human rights—including the chance to attain a decent standard of living—that has been the defining feature of Burma/Myanmar for the better part of the postcolonial era.

Michael Adas
August 2010

ACKNOWLEDGMENTS

I wish to acknowledge the assistance given by a number of institutions and individuals in the preparation of this study. Research funds were provided by a Fulbright Fellowship and the University of Wisconsin under the auspices of a Ford Foundation grant. The Danforth Foundation provided support during the period when I was writing the original dissertation draft, as well as during the early years of my graduate study. The Research Council of Rutgers University supplied funds for support while I was revising the manuscript. The staffs of the India Office Records and Library, the British Museum, and the libraries of the University of Wisconsin, Cornell University, and Yale University assisted my research efforts. In this respect, I would particularly like to acknowledge the invaluable services of Martin Moir of the India Office Records staff. I would also like to thank C. D. Cowan, Dorothy Woodman, and K. N. Chaudhuri for their assistance while I was working in London. Michael Wiseman, Arnold Sherman, and J. Joseph Brennig contributed stimulation and insight during the period when I was preparing the first draft. David Ringrose, John Cady, Traian Stoianovich, Rudolph Bell, Dorothy Guyot, and Peter Stearns offered useful criticisms and suggestions for revision. Robert Frykenberg co-supervised the writing of the dissertation and directed my graduate study in Indian history. I would also like to thank Philip D. Curtin for his careful reading and valuable criticisms of the first draft and for developing the

Comparative Tropical History Program at the University of Wisconsin, which made a study of this nature possible. A special debt is owed to John Smail, whose graduate seminar inspired this study, who rigorously supervised its preparation, and who proved the main source of stimulation and exchange during my years of graduate study. My parents provided support and encouragement during my years of undergraduate and graduate study. Finally, the assistance as critic, editor, and typist provided by my wife, Jane, was essential. The responsibility for the content of the study is my own.

M. A.
Somerset, New Jersey
September 1973

CITATION OF SELECTED GOVERNMENT REPORTS

1. Census reports will be cited by *Province, Census, date,* page numbers.
2. Government of Burma, *Reports on the Administration of the Province of Pegu, 1853/54–1860/61,* will be cited by *RAP, date.*
3. Government of Burma, *Annual Reports on the Administration of the Province of Burma, 1861/62–1939/40,* will be cited by *RAB, date.*
4. Government of Burma, *Reports on the Land Revenue Administration of Burma, 1901/2–1939/40,* will be cited by *Land Revenue Report, date.*
5. Government of Burma, *Season and Crop Reports, 1901/2–1939/40,* will be cited by *Season and Crop, date.*
6. Citations of individual settlement reports will include only the district name, year, and page number: for example, *Myaungmya Settlement Report (1916–19),* p. 49. Series of settlement reports will be cited as, for example, *Settlement Reports–Tharrawaddy (1901–2),* p. 7; *Henzada (1900–1901),* p. 4; etc.
7. All gazetteers will be cited by *District, Gazetteer.*

THE BURMA DELTA

Economic Development and Social Change
on an Asian Rice Frontier, 1852–1941

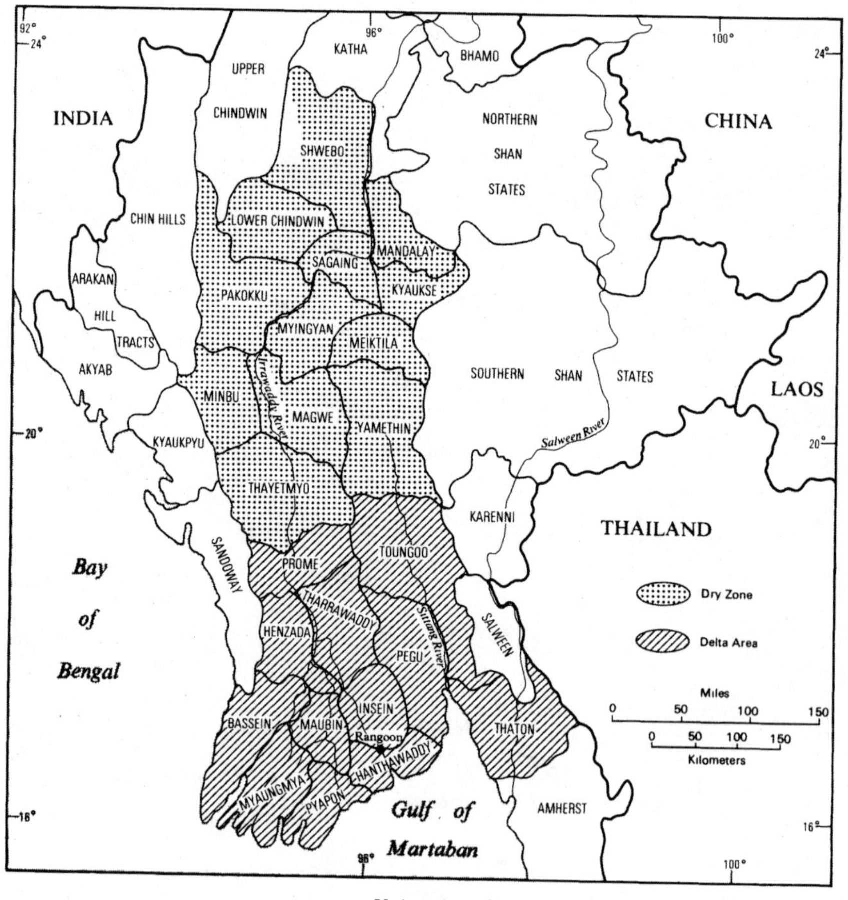

University of Wisconsin Cartographic Laboratory

Map. 1. Political Divisions of the Province of Burma in the Twentieth Century. Source: J. R. Andrus, *Burmese Economic Life* (Stanford, 1948).

INTRODUCTION

With the rise of the Konbaung dynasty in the last decades of the eighteenth century, the Burman[1] people reasserted their hegemony over the various ethnic groups whose territories bordered on their traditional heartland, the Dry Zone of the region later known as Upper Burma. After several years of bitter warfare between 1752 and 1757, the Burmans defeated the Mons and added their lands in the Irrawaddy-Sittang delta regions and Tenasserim to the growing Burman empire. The rulers of the Shan kingdoms to the north and east of the Dry Zone proffered their allegiance to the Konbaung monarchs and supplied troops for their armies. Following a number of victorious campaigns against the Siamese kingdom of Ayuthia and a successful struggle to repulse a Chinese invasion from the north, Burman armies overran Arakan on the western littoral in 1784–85. The Konbaung monarchs also demanded tribute and *corvée* labor from the various peoples who inhabited the rugged hill and forest regions which fringed the plains of the Dry Zone and the Irrawaddy delta. The most important of these peoples were the Karens, who were scattered along the Pegu Yoma and throughout the Irrawaddy delta and the Sittang River valley, and the Chins and Kachins, who inhabited the mountainous terrain to the west and

1. Following current usage, the term "Burman" is used throughout this study to refer specifically to the major ethnic and linguistic group of modern Burma. The term "Burmese" denotes all the groups which presently constitute the population of Burma, including the Burmans, Mons or Talaings, Chins, Shans, Karens, and Kachins.

northeast of the Dry Zone. These groups avoided contact with Burman forces whenever possible, and thus offered little challenge to Konbaung supremacy. Within a matter of decades the Konbaung rulers had restored the Dry Zone to its traditional position of pre-eminence, and it became once again the political, economic, and cultural center of the region which presently constitutes the nation of Burma.

The Burmans' defeat in the first Anglo-Burman war in 1824–26 and their loss of the outlying provinces of Arakan and Tenasserim did little to erode the predominant position of the Dry Zone within the Burman empire. However, British victory in the second Anglo-Burman war and the subsequent annexation of the Irrawaddy-Sittang delta region, or Lower Burma,[2] to the Indian Empire in 1852, initiated a number of developments which resulted in a dramatic shift in the center of influence and control away from the Dry Zone to the Delta area. For several decades political power was shared by the Konbaung monarch at Mandalay and the British Commissioner at Rangoon, with the latter clearly dominant. Following the final Anglo-Burman conflict and the annexation of the remaining portions of the Konbaung Empire in 1886, the royal palace at Mandalay was made into a British club, while Rangoon became the capital of the Province of Burma within the Indian Empire.

British efforts to develop the Delta region into a source of raw materials and a market outlet in the decades after 1852 insured the dominant economic position of the area during the period of colonial rule in Burma. Within fifty years Lower Burma was transformed from an underdeveloped and sparsely populated backwater of the Konbaung Empire into the world's leading rice-exporting area. This transformation resulted in a shift in the demographic balance within Burma. The growth of an export economy in the Delta attracted large numbers of migrants from the Dry Zone and the Indian subcontinent. By 1891, the year of the first British-administered census in Upper Burma, the population of the districts which made up the Delta area was greater than that of the Dry Zone, which had historically surpassed the population of surrounding regions.[3] In addition, the growth of processing, port, and rail centers in Lower Burma, particularly Rangoon and Bassein, far

2. The British initially called the area which they annexed in 1852 Pegu, a name which reflected its traditional position as the heartland of the Mon people. In this study I shall refer to this region as either the Delta (capitalized to distinguish it from the Irrawaddy or Sittang deltas which form only part of the whole) or Lower Burma. The latter designation is something of a departure from conventional usage, since many authors have included Tenasserim with Pegu in their references to Lower Burma.

3. *Burma Census, 1921,* Tables, p. 6. The Dry Zone contained the districts of the Magwe and Meiktila divisions, Mandalay District, and the Sagaing Division minus the Chin Hills and Upper Chindwin. The Delta and the districts which composed it for the purposes of this study are delineated below.

exceeded that of the old court towns which were the chief urban concentrations in the Dry Zone. The population of Rangoon grew from 182,000 to almost 342,000 between 1891 and 1921, while the inhabitants of Mandalay decreased from 189,000 to 149,000 in the same period.[4] By the end of the nineteenth century the economic and demographic balance had clearly shifted in favor of the Delta area.

Although Mandalay remained the main religious center and repository of traditional Burman culture, the introduction of Western education and the formation of an English-trained, Burmese elite provided Lower Burma with a counterbalance. Rangoon's university and private schools became the major centers for Western-educated Burmese intellectuals. During the period of British rule, the Burmese nationalist movement was concentrated in the urban centers of Lower Burma, especially Rangoon, where potential support was available and the political and economic presence of both the British and Indians was the most pronounced. Since independence in 1948, the dominant position of the Irrawaddy delta region and Rangoon in the affairs of the Republic of Burma has been still more firmly established.[5]

The central theme of this study is the rise of the Delta in the British period to a position of pre-eminence within Burma, with emphasis upon the economic basis and the social ramifications of that process. In analyzing this process my major objectives are twofold and interrelated. The first is to present a detailed history of agrarian development in Lower Burma during the period of British rule. The growth and ensuing crisis of the rice industry on the Delta frontier provides a superb case study which may be used to test many of our standard assumptions concerning official policies and the nature of colonial economies in the era of "high imperialism," as well as theories concerning the responses of agriculturists to new economic opportunities and incentives. My second major objective is to develop an approach to the modern history of Burma which is neither politically oriented nor elite-centric. My intent is to provide a framework of analysis which makes it possible to fully integrate the much neglected history of the "peasant masses" with the much studied history of the traditional rulers, the colonial overlords, and the nationalist elite which emerged in the British period.

Like Cheng Siok-Hwa,[6] I confine my discussion of economic develop-

4. Ibid., Report, p. 76. For a discussion of the factors behind these opposite growth trends see E. H. Vadja, "Burmese Urban Characteristics" (Ph.D. diss., University of Chicago, 1960), table, p. 66, and pp. 64–68.

5. On post-1947 developments see, for example, Nathan Keyfitz's article on "Urbanization in South and Southeast Asia," in *The Study of Urbanization*, ed. P. M. Hauser and L. F. Schnore (New York, 1965), pp. 265–311, esp. pp. 274–79, 298–301.

6. In her recent study *The Rice Industry of Burma, 1852–1940* (Kuala Lumpur-Singapore, 1968).

ment primarily to the rice industry which dominated the economic life of Lower Burma in the British period. Unlike Cheng and J. S. Furnivall,[7] I focus on a single region within Burma, the Delta region annexed by the British in 1852. In addition, I concentrate on two sectors of the rice-export economy which evolved in Lower Burma, agricultural production and agricultural credit provision and finance. I deal with the other sectors of the rice industry (transportation, marketing, and processing) only insofar as they relate to the social themes which I consider in achieving my second objective, and as they provide essential background for examination of developments in production or credit provision.

In this study I examine many of the general patterns introduced by Furnivall and earlier writers from the perspective of the local or regional unit. The settlement reports which the revenue department compiled periodically for each district during the period of British rule serve as the main source of statistical data and information on local conditions which make this approach possible. Hitherto historians of Burma have made little use of this superb series of documents. Undoubtedly Furnivall read many, perhaps all of them; but he used them primarily to form general impressions rather than to supply specific details regarding conditions and events at different times. Cheng has used very few of these reports in her recent work, and this more than any other factor may explain the absence of a historical dimension in her discussion of agrarian development. I have supplemented the information found in the settlement reports with data from the annual *Reports of the Land Revenue Administration,* the *Season and Crop Reports,* and general reports on the administration of Burma. I have also made extensive use of a wide range of special reports relating to economic and agrarian conditions which were produced by the governments of India and Burma in the first decades of the twentieth century. In addition, I have consulted the proceedings and correspondence of both governments which relate to the developments examined in this study.

I devote a considerable portion of this study to the early stages of the evolution of an export-oriented, market economy in Lower Burma. Earlier authors have tended to reduce their discussions of this period, which extends from 1852 through the last half of the nineteenth century, to general impressions and debates over a standard set of specific points, such as the impact of the opening of the Suez Canal in 1869 on economic growth in

7. Furnivall has produced most of the basic secondary works on Burmese social and economic life in the colonial period. His major contributions may be found in *An Introduction to the Political Economy of Burma,* 3d ed. (Rangoon, 1957), hereafter cited as *Political Economy*; and *Colonial Policy and Practice,* 2d ed. (New York, 1956). For a fine bibliography of his other articles and writings see Frank Trager's *Furnivall of Burma: An Annotated Bibliography of the Works of John S. Furnivall* (New Haven, Conn., 1963).

Burma. I stress the contrasts between this early period of growth and the 1920s and 1930s in terms of the impact of the spread of a market economy and the condition of the agrarian classes in Lower Burma. The emphasis placed in earlier works on the Depression and the economic crisis of the 1920s and 1930s has largely obscured the rapid and for the most part healthy economic growth which occurred in the first decades of British rule and the general prosperity of the agrarian classes throughout most of the late nineteenth century. I also deal in depth with the factors which undermined this general prosperity and increasingly impeded economic advance in the early decades of the twentieth century. These factors lay behind the social and economic dilemmas which played such a large role in the history of Burma in the last decades of British rule. For each period or phase of Lower Burma's development I focus on the condition of the agrarian classes measured in terms of the population-to-land ratio, the availability and cost of credit, the level of rural indebtedness, standard of living estimates, consumption trends, and tenancy and land alienation patterns. I also give particular attention to agricultural technology and its evolution, or lack of same, during each of the phases in question.

Despite an abundance of census data and related materials, historians of Burma have dealt with demographic trends in only the most general and fragmentary fashion. In this study I give considerable attention to basic demographic questions, particularly as they relate to migration which shaped the course of Lower Burma's historical development and in a very real sense made its economic evolution possible. I examine at length the determinants of the great influx of both Indian and Burmese migrants into Lower Burma. Insofar as the sources permit, I also analyze the composition of these different migrant streams and the impact of these movements on population growth and the composition of Lower Burma's population as a whole.

Relative to statistics compiled elsewhere in the "Third World," those available for Burma dealing with demography and economic growth in the period of British rule are quite comprehensive and reasonably reliable. For a number of reasons (see the appendix, section 1), the statistics collected from the late 1870s on tend to be far more accurate than those compiled in earlier decades. However, even those for the post-1880 period are subject to considerable errors. For this reason, I have included discussions of the reliability of specific sets of important statistics in the appendix. I have also rounded off figures cited in the tables in the following chapters. In addition, in calculating averages or percentages I have excluded figures which I felt, on the basis of the available evidence, were clearly inaccurate. In all cases, unless otherwise noted, I have calculated the totals, percentages, and averages listed in the tables and cited in the text of this study from the raw data found in census, settlement, and administrative reports. In the source notes I merely indicate the reports where the original data may be found.

My concentration on economic growth and rural society naturally furthers my attempts to achieve my second objective, a non-elite-centric history of modern Burma. However, this emphasis alone would not allow me to provide a viable alternative to the imperialist establishment-nationalist response perspective which has so dominated recent historical writings on Burma. A study which dealt only with agrarian development would merely serve to reinforce the compartmentalized treatment that characterizes many scholarly works on Burma. Furnivall's writings, particularly *Colonial Policy and Practice,* provide major exceptions to the tendency to study the economic and social or "peasant" history of Burma as something separate from its political or "elite" history. More than any other historian of Burma, Furnivall has managed to bridge the gap between "elite" and "mass," between political events and the social and economic developments which shape them. It is from Furnivall that I derive the concept of the plural society as the basis for an alternative perspective for the study of the history of Burma during the period of British colonial rule.

The plural-society approach performs a number of vital functions. It provides a framework in which to consider social structure and group interaction in Lower Burma during the period under study. It allows me to fully integrate the role of the Europeans, Indians, and Chinese into my discussion of Burma's social and economic development. Most important, the plural-society approach makes it possible for me to relate the specific events and themes I am dealing with, which are mainly social and economic, to broader patterns and other events which may be political, as well as social or economic. The plural-society framework encompasses both minority elite groups and the "masses" of Burmese and Indian agriculturists and urban laborers. It provides a far more comprehensive and dynamic approach to the history of modern Burma than the standard "imperialist versus nationalist" format.

The geographic scope of this study corresponds roughly to the territory annexed by the British in 1852 after their victory in the second Anglo-Burman war.[8] Initially, this area was divided into seven districts which were based largely on the provincial divisions of the Konbaung period. By 1912 the Delta had been divided into the twelve district units that composed it until the end of the period of British rule. These were: Prome, Tharrawaddy, Henzada, Bassein, Myaungmya, Maubin, Pyapon, Insein, Hanthawaddy, Pegu, Toungoo, and Thaton (see maps 2a–2c). This region, covering an area of over

8. The southern half of the area later known as the Thayetmyo District was also annexed in 1852. Because the history and geography of this area are more closely related to those of the Dry Zone of Upper Burma, it is not included in this study. In addition, part of the Thaton District, which *is* included in this study, was taken by the British along with Tenasserim in 1826.

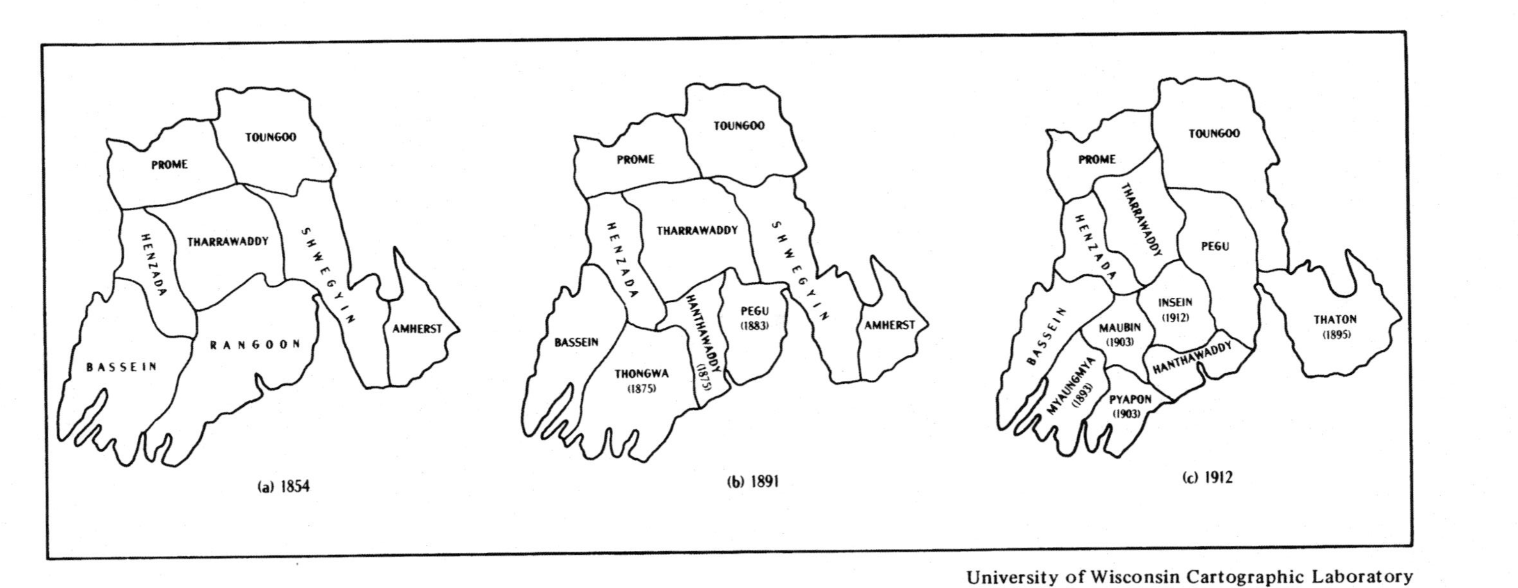

University of Wisconsin Cartographic Laboratory

Map 2. Changes in the Political Divisions of Lower Burma between 1854 and 1912. Sources: Map 2a—*Syriam (Hanthawaddy) Gazetteer*, app., map of the Rangoon District; Map 2b—Government of Burma, Revenue and Agriculture Proceedings, vol. 2887, February 1886, no. 2, map of the Delta in 1885-86; Map 2c—Andrus, *Burmese Economic Life*, end map.

38,000 square miles, includes several different geographical zones.[9] It is dominated by the great alluvial plain which makes up the delta of the Irrawaddy River, and extends over an area of more than 20,000 square miles from the Henzada and Tharrawaddy districts in the north to the nine mouths of the Irrawaddy in the south. The whole of this area is extremely flat, but in the lower delta the continuous plain of the northern districts breaks into a maze of islands of widely varying sizes which are separated by major rivers and myriad *chaungs* or tiny creeks. These islands are generally fringed with thickly vegetated mangrove swamps, and prior to their settlement in the late nineteenth century they were covered with *kanazo* forest and open stretches of *kaing* grass. Most of these islands are shaped like saucers with belts of high land encircling low-lying hollows which are flooded in the monsoon season.

The western edge of the Irrawaddy delta is flanked by the Arakan Yomas, a series of rugged hills covered with evergreen tropical and deciduous monsoon forests. To the east, the Pegu Yoma separates the Irrawaddy delta from the fertile valley of the Sittang River, which forms the second major cultivable zone of Lower Burma. The delta of the Sittang River and the Martaban plain complete the coastline of the area under consideration. Except for the Pegu and Arakan Yomas and several laterite ridges or *kondans* in the southeastern corner of the Irrawaddy delta, the whole of Lower Burma is uniformly flat and fertile. As numerous authors have observed, a high-quality soil combined with the rainfall patterns and climatic conditions found in Lower Burma render the area "almost ideal for rice cultivation on a large scale."[10]

Throughout the period of British rule, the Delta area formed an economic, social, and demographic unit. It contained twelve of the thirteen principal rice-growing districts in Burma,[11] and land under rice cultivation accounted for nearly 90 percent of the cropped area in each of its districts. In Lower Burma the transformation from a subsistence, natural economy to a market-oriented, cash economy was carried further than in the other areas of the Province of Burma. Throughout most of the British period a high percentage of the rice mills of Burma were located in the Delta. In addition, its two major urban centers, Rangoon and Bassein, were the chief ports for Burma's rice-export trade and the main entry points for Indian immigrants and consumer goods from the West. The flow of both Indian and Burmese

9. The following description of the geography of Lower Burma is based primarily on K. E. Bruen, "The Agricultural Geography of the Irrawaddy Delta with Special Reference to Rice" (Ph.D. diss., University of London, 1939); and the sections on geography in the early settlement reports and gazetteers.

10. Ibid., p. 83.

11. Amherst was the thirteenth. Although economically, socially, and demographically similar to the districts included in this study, it was annexed in 1826, and consequently had a longer and somewhat different history under British rule.

migrants in the 1852–1941 period was primarily into Lower Burma, and most of the Indians who lived and worked in Burma were concentrated in this area. This meant that the plural society was the most developed in the Delta, and also that the communal conflicts which raged in the last decades of British rule would be the most pronounced there.

Despite the unity displayed by the development of Lower Burma vis-à-vis the other regions of Burma, there was considerable variation within the Delta itself. Some areas were more populated and cultivated than others in 1852; the growth of the rice industry and the movement of migrants centered in different districts in different decades; and patterns of agrarian change varied in form and intensity from district to district. Because earlier writers have attempted to deal with all of the principal regions of Burma, they have at best treated the Delta as one of a number of regional units. This approach has obscured the diversity of the Delta's history. In this study differential rates of change and internal variations in the social and economic development of Lower Burma are considered in some depth. These differences are important because they have great bearing on the intensity of social and economic dislocations and the incidence of violent protest movements which dominated the last decade of nearly a century of British rule in the Delta.

Part I

THE FOUNDATIONS OF SOCIAL ECONOMIC DEVELOPMENT

1
THE DELTA RICE FRONTIER UNDER KONBAUNG AND EARLY BRITISH RULE

THE KONBAUNG DELTA

Historians of Burma have presented the century of Burman rule in the Delta which preceded the British conquest of 1852 as an era of suffering and strife. They have also agreed that the Burman-Mon wars of the mid-eighteenth century, the subsequent Burman oppression of the vanquished Mons, and general Burman misrule were the main factors responsible for the underpopulated and underdeveloped state of Lower Burma in the Konbaung period.[1] A closer examination of the available sources suggests, however, that Lower Burma was not as desolate or strife-torn in this period as scholars have assumed. Factors such as disease, marriage patterns, infant mortality, the level of agricultural technology, and the nature of the Konbaung economy had a far greater impact on conditions in the Delta than the small and poorly equipped armies of the Konbaung monarchs or the rapacious conduct of their officials.[2]

1. For examples of these views see Furnivall, *Political Economy,* p. 41; G. E. Harvey, *History of Burma . . .*, 2d ed. (London, 1967), pp. 234–36, 241, et passim; Cheng, *Rice Industry of Burma,* pp. 3–5.

2. For a detailed critique of the traditional view of conditions in Lower Burma in the Konbaung period and a reassessment of the factors responsible for the low level of development in the area, see my article, "Imperialist Rhetoric and Modern Historiography: The Case of Lower Burma before and after Conquest," *Journal of Southeast Asian Studies* 3, no. 2 (September 1972): 175–92.

If the evidence provided by European travelers is combined with that found in the *Hanthawaddy Sittans* (Burman revenue rolls) and the more detailed statistical data contained in British reports compiled in the first decades after 1852, an alternative to the standard "devastated Delta" approach to the history of Lower Burma in the Konbaung era emerges. The region can be viewed as a frontier area on the southern periphery of a slowly expanding traditional society concentrated in the Burman heartland, the Dry Zone. Although it was not fully drawn into the Burman orbit until after the Burman-Mon wars of the mid-eighteenth century, the events which led to the decline of the Delta as the nucleus of an independent Mon society and culture belong to a much earlier period.

Mon civilization in Burma reached the peak of its power and prosperity in the early sixteenth century under the aegis of the kingdom of Pegu. The accounts of the merchants and missionaries who visited Pegu at this time indicate that the kingdom was based on a combination of trade and wet-rice agriculture, with emphasis strongly on the former.[3] The urban trading centers, which dominated the political, social, and economic life of Pegu, carried on extensive commerce with the ports of the Indian subcontinent to the west and Malacca and the Indonesian archipelago to the east. Although this flourishing Mon kingdom came under the control of the Burman Toungoo dynasty in the mid-sixteenth century, its cities initially prospered under the rule of the Toungoo monarchs, Tabinshwehti and Bayinnaung.[4] In the last decades of the sixteenth century, however, internal strife, several unsuccessful campaigns in Siam, and a series of foreign invasions proved disastrous for the urban trading culture of the Mons. Armies from Ava, Prome, and Arakan captured Mon cities and leveled them, or sacked them and turned them over to adventurers like Philip de Brito. Mon rebels and Siamese invaders ravaged the Martaban littoral and the Pegu-Sittang River valley, where the bulk of the nonurban Mon population was concentrated. Thus, over a century and a half before the armies of Alaungpaya, the founder of the Konbaung dynasty, entered the Delta, the Mon people had suffered reverses from which they never fully recovered.[5]

3. For a more complete description of Pegu see my article "Imperialist Rhetoric and Modern Historiography" or the travel accounts written in the sixteenth and early seventeenth centuries, particularly those by Gasparo Balbi in Samuel Purchas, *Hakluytus Posthumus or Purchas His Pilgrims,* vol. 10 (Glasgow, 1905); and Cesar Frederick in Robert Keer, *A General History and Collection of Voyages and Travels* (Edinburgh, 1812).

4. Excepting Martaban, which was destroyed after a long seige during the Burman conquest.

5. D. G. E. Hall has also seen the late sixteenth century and not the Konbaung period as the time when the Delta was most seriously devastated and depopulated. See *A History of South-East Asia* (London, 1964), pp. 362, 736.

Although some of the Delta's urban centers were partly restored prior to the Burman-Mon wars of the 1750s, the surviving Mon population was less concentrated and more agrarian than it had been in the sixteenth century. The Delta which the Burmans annexed after their victory over the Mons in the 1750s was not the densely populated and prosperous region many writers have pictured. It was for the most part a sparsely settled wilderness covered with *kanazo* forests, mangrove swamps, and *kaing* grass plains. Under Burman rule, Lower Burma served as a frontier outlet for the Dry Zone, where the population was far more dense and the monsoon rains and adequate crop production far less certain. The Delta would continue to play this role, on a much expanded scale, throughout the British era.

Despite technological limitations, a low level of incentive resulting from the nature of the Konbaung economy, and the hostile Delta environment, there was considerable change and some significant developments during the century of Burman rule. Because this growth occurred within the framework of a traditional society centered on the distant Burman court cities in the Dry Zone, it was far slower and more limited than that which occurred after 1852, when the Delta became a major area of expansion for a dynamic, capitalist, and development-oriented European imperial establishment. Growth prior to 1852 has also been obscured by historical accounts which have emphasized Burman misrule and neglected evidence of important changes which were to become major themes of development in the British period.

The most far-reaching changes in the Konbaung period were those related to demography. When Alaungpaya's armies conquered the Delta in the 1750s, the population of the area was predominantly Mon. In the following century, migrations and the policy of Mon acculturation fostered by Burman rulers radically altered the composition and distribution of Lower Burma's population. There were three main movements, each by different ethno-linguistic groups—Burman, Mon, and Karen.

Although a number of Burman settlements were established for strategic reasons during the Burman-Mon wars,[6] the Konbaung monarchs did not regularly use military or penal colonies to extend their control over the Delta region, such as those which spearheaded the Vietnamese drive south from Tonkin to Annam and Cochinchina.[7] Through most of this period the migration of Burmans into the Delta appears to have been voluntary and on

6. Arthur Phayre, *History of Burma* (London, 1883), pp. 155–57; *Bassein Gazetteer,* p. 25; *Henzada Gazetteer,* p. 18.

7. See Le Thanh Khoi, *Le Viet-Nam: histoire et civilisation* (Paris, 1955), pp. 202, 223–24, 228, 265–68, 358–59, et passim; Michael Cotter, "Towards a Social History of the Vietnamese Southward Movement," *Journal of Southeast Asian History* 9, no. 1 (March 1968): 12–24.

an individual or family basis. In the last decades of the eighteenth century, Burman settlement was concentrated along the Irrawaddy River between the towns of Prome and Henzada. Hiram Cox reported in 1796 that Burman migrants had occupied most of the towns along and near the river, and that the original Mon inhabitants had moved away.[8] By the 1850s Burmans were the dominant ethnic group in the Prome and Tharrawaddy districts of the upper Delta and constituted approximately one-half of the population of the Henzada District.[9] In the lower Delta early Burman settlement was virtually confined to the largest towns such as Bassein and Rangoon. Burman migrants were for the most part soldiers and administrators or the retainers of these two groups. By the end of the Konbaung period, however, Burmans made up nearly one-third of the population of the Rangoon District and were the major ethnic group in the Bassein District to the west. In the Toungoo District in the northeast Delta, the Burmans retained their centuries-old predominance.[10]

During the century of Konbaung rule the Mon population of Lower Burma was diminished by wars, emigration, and assimilation by the Burmans. At least eight Mon rebellions broke out in the period of Konbaung rule. Each was followed by Burman reprisals and Mon emigration to Siam.[11] In addition, Burmans conscripted Mons for their armies, which periodically invaded the kingdoms to the east, and they transported some Mons to Upper Burma. Although there are no reliable estimates of the size of Mon migrations or of Mons killed in Burman reprisal raids and foreign campaigns, most authors have tended to exaggerate the numbers involved. Cheng Siok-Hwa pictures a "mass emigration into Siam" and "vast numbers" of Mons being sold into slavery, while D. G. E. Hall refers to the "great exodus" of the Mons.[12] J. S. Furnivall has demonstrated that the earlier estimates, upon which these assertions are presumably based, are gross overstatements. He points out, for instance, that contemporary records list only about 10,000 immigrants in Arakan and Tenasserim from Burman territories between 1826 and 1852. Earlier writers, he notes, had calculated that as many as 257,000 persons migrated in this period.[13]

8. *Journal of a Resident in the Burmhan Empire, and More Particularly at the Court of Amarapoorah* (London, 1821), pp. 426–28.

9. These statements are based on the figures in Appendix W of the *RAP* for 1856–57. They are useful only as estimates (see the appendix to this book, pts. 1 and 2). For a map of the approximate political divisions in the Konbaung period, see Map 2a.

10. Ibid.

11. Phayre, *History of Burma,* pp. 167, 186, 206, 210, 219; John Cady, *A History of Modern Burma* (Ithaca, N.Y., 1958), p. 79; Robert Halliday, *The Talaings* (Rangoon, 1917), p. 1. Mon migration into Siam began as early as the time of troubles in the late sixteenth century.

12. Cheng, *Rice Industry of Burma,* p. 3; Hall, *History of South-East Asia,* p. 388.

13. *Colonial Policy and Practice,* pp. 59–60.

It is probable that much of the decrease in the Mon population can be attributed to the Burman policy of suppressing the Mon language, rather than to an increase in the Mons' death rate or mass emigration. Since language was the major difference between the two groups,[14] many Mons would have been listed as Burmans once they spoke Burmese. The number of Mons who were Burmanized cannot be determined, but by the first decades of British rule the Rangoon and Henzada districts were the only areas where Mons were still in the majority.[15]

Karens made up the remainder of Lower Burma's nonurban population in Konbaung times. The Karens had originally migrated from the Salween-Sittang area, the mountainous belt east of the Delta which separates it from Siam. By the end of the Konbaung period they were spread in small groups over most of the Delta. Most Karens preferred to live in the interior away from the towns and main river arteries.[16] Although the Bassein District was farthest from the source of Karen migration, nearly half of the Karens in Lower Burma were located there by the end of the Konbaung period. The district must have been favored because of its combination of inaccessibility and paucity of population. The other main areas of Karen settlement were the Rangoon and Henzada districts.[17]

Although the great majority of the inhabitants of Lower Burma in the Konbaung period were subsistence cultivators, there were also settlements of fishermen, salt manufacturers, and *dhani* palm gatherers, as well as a number of urban trading and administrative centers. The fishermen, who were mainly Mons, were concentrated along the lower portions of the Bassein River, on the shores of Maubin island, and along the rivers and creeks of the Rangoon District.[18] The manufacture of salt was the chief occupation of the population in the Syriam and Angyi townships which lay south of Rangoon.[19] Whole settlements north of Rangoon lived primarily by the sale of *dhani* palm leaves, which were used for thatching roofs.[20]

The towns of Lower Burma prior to 1852 were little more than oversized

14. Halliday, *Talaings*, pp. 16–17; *Burma Census, 1881*, pt. 1, p. 64.

15. *RAP, 1856–57*, app. W. See also the appendix to this book, pt. 2.

16. John Crawfurd, *Journal of an Embassy from the Governor-General of India to the Court of Ava in the Year 1827* (London, 1829), pp. 6, 22, 421; Cox, *Journal of a Resident*, p. 430; *Bassein/Thongwa Settlement Report (1888–89)*, p. 23; *Maubin Gazetteer*, p. 14.

17. *RAP, 1856–57*, app. W. See also the appendix to this book, pt. 2.

18. Henry Yule, *A Narrative of the Mission Sent by the Governor-General to the Court of Ava in 1855 . . .* (London, 1858), p. 255; *Maubin Gazetteer*, p. 26; J. S. Furnivall, "Some Historical Documents," *Journal of the Burma Research Society* 6, no. 3 (December 1916): 217–18, 9, no. 1 (April 1919): 35–37.

19. Government of India, Political and Foreign Proceedings, range 201, vol. 63, 8 August 1856, no. 157, par. 11, India Office Records, London, Eng.

20. *Insein Gazetteer*, p. 60.

villages. They were usually surrounded by wooden stockades and made up of haphazardly arranged thatch and bamboo dwellings interspersed with a few brick warehouses and pagodas. The largest urban centers were Rangoon and Prome. John Crawfurd estimated that in 1826 each had about ten thousand inhabitants.[21] Other centers, like Bassein and Henzada, had from two to three thousand persons,[22] while the population of towns like Myaungmya and Pegu numbered only in the hundreds. Although most of the towns were primarily administrative centers, both Rangoon and Bassein served as outlets for overseas trade. The merchants engaged in external commerce were predominantly foreigners. Michael Symes described the merchant community of Rangoon at the end of the eighteenth century as a mixture of Muslims (both Persian and Indian), Parsis, Armenians, and a few Christians (Portuguese, English, and French).[23] By the 1850s the foreign population of Lower Burma was almost wholly Indian and Chinese and was located mainly in Rangoon and Bassein.[24]

In the century prior to 1852 most of the Delta's inhabitants lived in small settlements of bamboo and thatch houses which were grouped into *taiks* (circles) which formed the basic unit of administration. Officials known as *thugyis,* who were normally local notables, were placed in charge of the *taiks.* The *taiks* were in turn grouped into larger provincial units which were run by *myowuns,* who were drawn from the higher officials of the Konbaung central bureaucracy.[25]

Various travelers attempted to estimate the total population of the Konbaung empire, but none provided separate figures for Lower Burma.[26] However, the approximate population of the Delta in the last years of Konbaung rule can be measured by use of the statistics compiled just after 1852. Contemporary British administrators agreed that the totals listed in the official reports for the 1850s were far too low (see the appendix, section 1).

21. *Journal,* pp. 35, 346; H. Gouger, *A Personal Narrative of Two Years Imprisonment in Burma* (London, 1864), pp. 6–7.

22. Crawford, *Journal,* pp. 22, 462.

23. *An Account of an Embassy to the Kingdom of Ava . . . in 1795,* 3 vols. (London, 1800), 2: 4–5.

24. *RAP, 1856–57,* app. W.

25. Daw Mya Sein, *Administration of Burma: Sir Charles Crosthwaite and the Consolidation of Burma* (Rangoon, 1938), pp. 34–47; Furnivall, *Political Economy,* p. 204.

26. Symes, *Account of Ava,* 2: 353; William Francklin, *Tracts, Political, Geographical, and Commercial; on the Dominions of Ava . . .* (London, 1811), pp. 32, 140; Crawfurd, *Journal,* pp. 464–66; Howard Malcolm, *Travels in South-Eastern Asia . . . ,* 2 vols. (Boston, 1840), 1: 168; Henry Burney, "On the Population of the Burman Empire," *Journal of the Royal Statistical Society of London* 4, no. 4 (1842): 335–47. Tun Wai has attempted to derive a separate estimate from Burney's tables, but his interpretation of Burney's rather vague regional divisions is questionable. See Tun Wai, *Economic Development of Burma* (Rangoon, 1961), pp. 4–5.

After correcting these figures for undercounting and omissions, Arthur Phayre, the first Chief Commissioner, concluded that the population in the 1850s was between one and one and a quarter million people.[27]

The population of the Delta was concentrated in several main areas which can be determined through a comparison of the observations of European travelers with the evidence provided by the Burman *Sittans* and British officials in the decade after 1852. A topographical map of Lower Burma by Ferdinand Fitzroy dated 1862 is the chief source of information relating to settlement patterns in the early British records. If corrections, based on Konbaung sources, are made to allow for the fact that the map was drawn ten years after the British annexation, it serves as a fairly accurate guide to patterns of population distribution in the late Konbaung era.[28] Major concentrations of population were located in the upper circles of the Bassein District and around Myaungmya town in the west Delta, near Dallah and Pyapon in the south and Toungoo town in the northeast. The population of the Delta was also clustered along the Irrawaddy River in the northern circles of the Prome District, in central Henzada, and in the vicinity of Danubyu just above the confluence of the Irrawaddy and the Hlaing rivers. Since the environs of Rangoon town were heavily settled in the years just after the British annexation, the sizable concentrations of population in the area indicated on the Fitzroy map were probably considerably larger than those found there in the Konbaung period.[29]

Although the available sources indicate that Lower Burma was more heavily settled prior to 1852 than the general statements of most writers would lead one to assume,[30] there is no record of how extensively each of the tracts shown on the Fitzroy map was cultivated, nor are there estimates of how much land was occupied in Lower Burma as a whole. If one assumes, however, that the area worked in the first years of British rule was roughly

27. *RAP, 1855–56,* par. 234. F. Mason, who compiled a bulky tome on *Burmah, Its People and Natural Productions . . .* (Rangoon, 1860) at this time, also estimated that the population of the Delta was about one million (pp. 603, 610).

28. The Fitzroy map may be found in the map collection of the India Office Records, no. A.I.(4), India Office, London, Eng. As Furnivall has pointed out (*Colonial Policy and Practice,* p. 59), there was little economic growth in Lower Burma until after 1861, when pacification was finally completed. Therefore, the ten-year interval does not seriously affect the map's value as an indicator of settlement distribution in Konbaung times.

29. For a detailed comparison of the map and the observations of Cox, Crawfurd, Malcolm, Symes, and early British administrative reports, see Michael Adas, "Agrarian Development and the Plural Society in Lower Burma, 1852–1941" (Ph.D. diss. University of Wisconsin, 1971), pp. 37–39, and app., Map II-A. The approximate political divisions in the Konbaung period are shown in Map 2a in this book.

30. See, for example, Furnivall, *Political Economy,* p. 41; Hall, *History of South-East Asia,* p. 736; Cheng, *Rice Industry of Burma,* p. 4; or J. R. Andrus, *Burmese Economic Life* (Stanford, 1948), p. 14.

equal to that cropped in the decades before 1852, the extent of cultivation in the late Konbaung period can be estimated. The most reliable district figures of the area occupied in the first decades of British control were those compiled in 1856–57.[31] In that year over 662,000 acres of land in the Delta were listed as cultivated, of which 616,000 acres were planted in rice.[32] If corrections are made for undercounting (see the appendix, section 1) and the cultivated tracts which lay in the area which later constituted the Thaton District are added, the total area under rice cultivation would have been at least 700,000 to 800,000 acres.

This was a small amount compared to the area occupied in later decades. By 1871–72, 1,146,000 acres were cropped in Lower Burma, and by the mid-1930s, when the area occupied reached its greatest extent, 8,702,000 acres were under cultivation.[33] Vast tracts of fertile land on the Henzada-Tharrawaddy plain, in the Pegu-Sittang River valley, and in the central Delta region remained uncultivated in Konbaung times. Owing to the absence of embankments, much of Lower Burma, especially the central Delta, was flooded during the monsoon season and unfit for habitation for several months of the year.[34]

Although it is impossible to estimate the size of the area involved, there is evidence which indicates that considerable amounts of unoccupied land were brought under cultivation in the Konbaung era. The movement of settlers into various parts of the Delta has been detailed above. In addition, local Burman functionaries reported their attempts to develop tracts in the area around Pegu, and stated that they were ordered to do so by high-ranking Burman officials.[35] Evidence of economic growth is also suggested by the fact that many European travelers, including those who were antagonistic to the Burman regime, reported that in the last decades before the British conquest Lower Burma was regarded as the granary of the Konbaung empire.[36]

Despite these signs of growth, however, development in the century prior to 1852 was slow and sporadic compared to that which occurred in the

31. Enough time had passed by 1856–57 for most refugees and men conscripted into the Burman army to return to their homes and for most of Lower Burma to be "pacified." In addition, a larger percentage of the land listed was actually measured than in earlier surveys, where it was largely estimated.

32. *RAP, 1856–57,* app. F.

33. *RAB, 1871–72,* app. cix; *Season and Crop, 1935–36,* acreage use tables.

34. Robert Gordon, *The Irrawaddy River* (London, 1885), p. 5, reprinted from the Royal Geographical Society.

35. Furnivall, "Historical Documents," 6, no. 3: 218–19; 8, no. 1: 40, 43, 46, 49; 9, no. 1: 41.

36. H. L. Maw, *Memoir of the Early Operations of the Burmese War* (London, 1832), p. 83; T. A. Trant, *Two Years in Ava* (London, 1827), pp. 29, 235; Gouger, *Personal Narrative,* pp. 19–20.

British period. This gradual pace of development resulted less from Burman misrule or deliberate repression than from the traditional context in which change took place. The limitations placed on growth by the subsistence-oriented policies and practices of the Burman government can best be seen in the effects of the Konbaung prohibition of the export of rice from the empire. Although this policy was probably viewed by government officials as humane and farsighted, it was one of the central factors impeding rapid economic expansion on the Delta frontier. Following a practice quite typical of pre-industrial regimes, the Burmans stored most of the surplus grain produced in Lower Burma in granaries and used it to supply areas where there was a food shortage or where famine threatened. Much of this store of rice, which supplied most of the revenue which the government received from the Delta provinces, was carried annually to Upper Burma by great fleets of river vessels.[37] Although there was a foreign demand for Delta rice, government restrictions insured that exports of paddy were practically nonexistent. In addition, the limited domestic market was regulated and stabilized by the great quantities held by the government. Consequently, the price of the grain was very low in the Konbaung period. Many writers, like Cheng Siok-Hwa,[38] have sought to demonstrate the low returns received for surplus rice production by comparing the value of rice in the Konbaung period with its value in the years after the British annexation of 1852. Such comparisons clearly do not demonstrate the value of rice relative to other products in the Konbaung period itself. However, Howard Malcolm, who visited the Delta in the 1830s, supplies figures that illustrate the low price received for rice on the domestic market. He estimated that the average price for one hundred baskets of paddy at Rangoon was only about five rupees (Rs. 5). The same amount of wheat, on the other hand, sold for Rs. 40.[39]

The low return which the cultivator received for the extra labor required to produce a surplus provided little incentive for him to harvest more than he needed for food, seed, and taxes. There was no reason for him to bring new areas under cultivation. Even if he were able to harvest a sizable surplus for market, the cultivator would have little to buy with the bullion[40] he received for his produce. Consumer goods imported into Burma prior to 1852 were

37. Symes, *Account of Ava,* 2: 166-67; Maw, *Memoir,* pp. 83–84; Gouger, *Personal Narrative,* pp. 19–20. The boats were said to range from twenty to forty tons capacity and number in the hundreds. Salt, *ngapi* (fish paste), and dried fish were also transported on these vessels to the Upper Provinces.

38. *Rice Industry of Burma,* p. 3n.

39. *Travels,* 1: 75. Crawfurd (*Journal,* p. 449) claimed at an earlier date that the price for rice was about 50 percent higher on the Upper Burma market.

40. The Konbaung economy was predominantly natural. No coins were in circulation prior to 1852 in Lower Burma. However, lumps of gold, silver, and lead were used as a medium of exchange on a limited basis. Henry G. Bell, *An Account of the Burman Empire* (Calcutta, 1852), p. 12; Crawfurd, *Journal,* p. 433; Malcolm, *Travels,* 1: 227.

limited in quantity and quality and subject to heavy duties.[41] In addition, there were many sumptuary laws in Konbaung society. The type and size of a man's house, the domestic implements he was permitted to use, his clothing and jewelry were all rigidly regulated by his position and social standing.[42] The cultivator was low on the social scale and thus his options as a consumer were very limited.

The absence of market incentives to promote agrarian development was complemented by the obstacles and hazards facing the cultivator who sought to open new lands. Most of the available land in the Delta was covered with jungle and swamp. Considerable capital and labor were required to bring this land under cultivation. Because monetary and market systems were poorly developed, there were few sources of credit in Konbaung times and the rates of interest were high.[43] There was virtually no labor available for hire. In addition, the malarial conditions which prevailed in newly cropped areas severely limited the productivity of the labor which the cultivator could generate from within his own household.

Malaria was (and is) endemic to most of the Delta. It was particularly intense in those areas which were being settled for the first time. S. Grantham reported in 1920 that colonies attempting to open jungle tracts in the Myaungmya district were debilitated and even wiped out by malaria epidemics. He observed that after an area had been worked for some time the death rate and general malaise of the population declined. He attributed this drop to immunities developed by settlers who survived and a decrease in the number of mosquito vectors.[44] More recent research bears out Grantham's observations. It has shown that the *Anopheles hyrcanus* mosquito, which is the principal vector in Lower Burma, becomes extremely prolific in areas where forest has recently been cleared. If such areas are in tropical climates, the species has been known to produce serious malaria epidemics.[45] Officers in many other Delta districts in the British period concurred with Grantham's claim that malarial conditions had greatly hindered efforts to bring fertile tracts into production.[46] In Konbaung times there was little incentive for

41. For a list of imports (and exports) see B. R. Pearn, *History of Rangoon* (Rangoon, 1939), p. 67; and on the "exactions" of customs officials see Crawfurd, *Journal,* pp. 428–29, 439–41.

42. Mya Sein, *Administration of Burma,* pp. 73–74; Symes, *Account of Ava,* 1: 353–54, 2: 60–62, 189–90, et passim.

43. U Tun Wai, *Currency and Credit in Burma* (Bombay, 1953), p. 1; Crawfurd, *Journal,* p. 434. Crawfurd listed the current rates at 24 percent per annum with "pledge" and 60 percent per annum without "pledge."

44. *Myaungmya Settlement Report (1916–19),* p. 19.

45. See the various sections on the *Anopheles hyrcanus* in M. F. Boyd, *Malariology,* 2 vols. (Philadelphia, 1949), 1: 316, 433, 619, 2: 815.

46. *Settlement Reports–Henzada (1900–1901),* p. 2; *Pegu (1900–1901),* p. 2; *Tharrawaddy (1900–1901),* p. 3; *Pegu (1911–13),* p. 4; C. W. Dunn, *Studies in the History of Tharrawaddy* (Cambridge, 1920), p. 57.

settlers to move into virgin areas where malaria was likely to be endemic. Both migrants from the Dry Zone and the indigenous inhabitants tended to cluster in areas which had long been occupied. Thus, malaria was not only a major obstacle to agrarian development, it was also a prime determinant of settlement patterns on the Delta frontier, just as it has been in Java, Vietnam, and other tropical areas.[47]

Since agriculturists could gear production to suit their nutritional needs and malaria was not a major problem in traditionally settled areas, one might assume that there was a high rate of population increase in the pre-British period. Although there is no data available to determine even approximate birth or mortality rates in Konbaung times, a number of factors probably served as checks to significant population growth. In the 1850s British officials concluded on the basis of a special survey that high infant mortality was one of the main factors responsible for the underpopulated state of the Delta.[48] Contemporary evidence supports this conclusion, for Burma's infant mortality rate is currently one of the highest in the world,[49] and it was probably higher in Konbaung times. In addition, there were a number of factors which might have depressed the birth rate during the Konbaung period. On the basis of anthropological and demographic research conducted in Upper Burma, June and Manning Nash have discerned three practices which hold down the Burman birth rate because "they delay or withdraw women from the breeding population." These are the late age of marriage, a high percentage of unmarried persons, and the fact that widows and widowers often choose not to remarry. Since illegitimacy is very low in rural Burma, these factors have a significant impact on population growth.[50] Although rural society in Burma has changed considerably since the Konbaung period, it is likely that these familial practices represent traditional norms rather than products of the modernizing process. In this respect, the fact that they characterize familial patterns in Upper Burma is particularly significant because social and cultural institutions and practices in the Dry Zone were much less affected by outside influences in the British period than their counterparts in the Delta. Therefore, it is very likely that these practices, which retard population growth in Burma today, retarded it at least among the Burmans and Mons in the Konbaung era.

47. See, for example, Clifford Geertz, *Agricultural Involution* (Berkeley, Calif., 1966), p. 45; Pierre Gourou, *L'utilisation du sol en Indochine Française* (Paris, 1940), pp. 140, 165–77.

48. *RAP, 1855–56,* par. 236; Government of India, "Report by Lt. Williams on the Survey of Pegu," in Political and Foreign Proceedings, range 201, vol. 25, 13 July 1855, no. 95.

49. Norton Ginsburg, *Atlas of Economic Development* (Chicago, 1961), p. 66.

50. "Marriage, Family and Population Growth in Upper Burma," *Southwestern Journal of Anthropology* 19, no. 3 (Autumn, 1963): 251–66.

The effects of the ban on the export of rice reached far beyond its impact on the expansion of cultivation. More than any other factor, the cultivator's inability to take advantage of foreign outlets for rice shaped the nature of the agrarian economy in Konbaung times. Although some cultivators who lived near towns like Rangoon or Bassein harvested surplus rice for the domestic market,[51] paddy was produced primarily for subsistence. If a cultivator planted more rice than his family required, he seldom harvested the surplus.[52] The basic unit of production was the family, which was largely self-sufficient. The cultivator built his own house from materials which he obtained free in a nearby forest. He grew fruit and vegetables to supplement his rice staple, and caught fish in neighboring streams from which his wife made the family's supply of *ngapi* (fish paste). His wife and daughter wove and dyed the family's clothes. They also hand-milled the household's rice supply.[53] If agricultural implements, pottery, or cotton yarn were needed, the cultivator would harvest extra grain and exchange it for the required item. He rarely hired labor because the members of his family were normally sufficient for his limited needs. In fact, familial labor was generally under-employed because subsistence production in the fertile Delta region required only minimal inputs of time and effort once the land had been cleared.[54] If extra labor was required, it was provided by the cultivator's neighbors on a mutual assistance basis.[55]

The size of the holding worked by the cultivator's family varied from region to region. In the first years of British rule, holdings in the Rangoon District averaged ten acres, while those in Henzada and Prome were only six and five respectively.[56] The manner in which these holdings were cultivated also varied widely. Three main cropping patterns were followed in different areas of Lower Burma in the Konbaung period: shifting/broadcast sown, sedentary/broadcast sown, and sedentary/transplanting. Shifting cultivation with broadcast sowing resembled in many respects the slash-and-burn agriculture practiced by many hill peoples in South and Southeast Asia. The cultivator burnt off the *kaing* grass or forest growth before planting. After

51. *Insein Gazetteer,* p. 63.

52. Furnivall, *Political Economy,* p. 43.

53. *Thaton Gazetteer,* p. 44; *Burma Gazetteer,* 1: 410; Cox, *Journal of a Resident,* pp. 23–24.

54. Hla Myint, *The Economics of the Developing Countries* (New York, 1964), pp. 42–43. Myint's statements are generally in line with his intent to develop a theoretical model of growth, but the "Peasant Exports" portions of his theory are clearly based on Burmese and like precedents.

55. Government of India, Foreign Proceedings (Revenue), range 205, vol. 39, January 1865, no. 13, India Office Records, London, Eng; Furnivall, *Political Economy,* pp. 118–19.

56. *RAP, 1855–56,* par. 142.

several years he would abandon one area and bring another under cultivation. This form of cropping was practiced mainly by the Karens and was quite widespread in the first decades of British rule.[57] There are no direct references to the second mode of cultivation, sedentary/broadcast sowing, in either Konbaung or early British sources. In view of its predominance in the lower Delta in the last decades of the nineteenth century, however, it is probable that this pattern was followed in tracts in the southern portions of the Rangoon and Bassein districts.

The third form of cropping, sedentary/transplanting, was dominant in the upper Delta and the Toungoo area of the Sittang valley. John Crawfurd noted that it was also practiced near and above Danubyu in the central Delta.[58] Since sedentary/transplanting was the dominant mode of cultivation in the rice-growing areas of Upper Burma,[59] it would be logical to assume that Upper Burman migrants who settled tracts in the Delta practiced this form of cropping. If the pattern followed was the same as that dominant in the last half of the nineteenth century, however, it is possible that migrants from the Dry Zone who settled in the lower Delta changed to the sedentary/broadcast sown pattern. Mon cultivators transplanted their rice crops.[60] Therefore, in regions like the Pegu-Sittang River valley, where Mons formed a sizable proportion of the population, sedentary/transplanting was the dominant method of rice cultivation in Konbaung times.

Whatever his mode of cropping, the cultivator had only a few primitive implements with which to work his land. Although a plow similar to that found in the Dry Zone was occasionally employed, the soil was normally turned by a crude wooden harrow. A number of hand implements were used for clearing forest, weeding, and harvesting. These included wooden hoes, crude axes of various kinds, and the *dah* (Burmese knife).[61] In many cases individual rice fields were enclosed by bunds, called *kazins.* In addition, a few clay embankments were constructed which protected whole tracts from flooding. The largest of these stretched for almost two miles south of Henzada.[62] These implements and embankments proved sufficient for

57. Crawfurd, *Journal,* pp. 6, 421, 448; Symes, *Account of Ava,* 2: 15–16; *RAP, 1854–55,* par. 26; Government of India, Foreign Proceedings (Revenue), range 205, vol. 31, November 1862, nos. 7, 10, 11.

58. *Journal,* p. 7.

59. Ibid., p. 448.

60. J. S. Furnivall, *The Fashioning of Leviathan . . .* (Rangoon, 1939), p. 105; Government of India, Foreign Proceedings (Revenue), range 205, vol. 31, November 1862, no. 11.

61. Crawfurd, *Journal,* p. 448; Trant, *Two Years,* p. 235; Than Tun, "Agriculture in Burma: A.D. 1000–1300," typed (India Office Library, London, Eng., 1961), p. 7.

62. *Maubin Settlement Report (1925–28),* p. 38.

subsistence production, and given the absence of both population pressure and a market demand for surplus rice there was little impetus for technological innovation.

There was also little or no competition for land. As in India and other areas of the Afro-Asian world,[63] there were no concepts of private property or proprietory rights as these were understood in Western Europe. In Konbaung times villagers in the Delta usually held land in common. A person established his right to occupy a particular piece of land by cultivating it. If he abandoned the land, it reverted to the common land held by the village as a whole. If another cultivator chose to take it up, he could do so with or without the permission of its original occupant, depending on local custom. Because land was so plentiful and its potential productivity meant little in the absence of market outlets for surplus rice, holdings were seldom sold.[64] Even in exceptional cases where sales transactions took place, the vendor had the right to repurchase the land should he decide to do so within ten years of the sale. The buyer could not ordinarily resell the land without the original owner's permission.[65]

CONQUEST AND EARLY BRITISH MEASURES TO PROMOTE ECONOMIC GROWTH

In the traditionally structured Konbaung context there was little incentive for agriculturists to risk the hazards involved in opening new lands on the Delta frontier. As a result, economic growth was limited. Following the British conquest, the political and economic institutions of Lower Burma were transformed as the area was rapidly drawn into a capitalistic, commercially oriented global economy. These transformations resulted in outlets for the surplus production of Burmese agriculturists and consumer rewards for their efforts. These returns proved sufficient incentive for cultivators to brave the obstacles which had long impeded the extension of settlement in the Delta. Political and economic change led to the emergence of a new society in Lower Burma which was radically different and far more complex than that which had existed in the Konbaung period.

British diplomats and merchants who visited Burma in the Konbaung period clearly recognized the great economic potential of the Delta region.

63. One of the best recent discussions of differences in approaches to land tenure in Western and non-Western societies can be found in Walter C. Neale's "Land is to Rule," in *Land Control and Social Structure in Indian History,* ed. R. E. Frykenberg (Madison, Wis., 1969), pp. 3–15.

64. The best researched and most convincing of a number of conflicting descriptions of pre-British tenure systems in the Delta is set forth in J. S. Furnivall's "Land as a Free Gift of Nature," *Economic Journal* 19 (1909): 552–62.

65. *Henzada Gazetteer,* p. 56.

They noted the fertility of the soil and pointed out that the flat and open nature of the terrain was well suited to the cultivation of a wide range of market crops, including rice, cotton, tobacco, indigo, sugar, and coffee. Some observers felt that Lower Burma would provide both an excellent source of foodstuffs and raw materials, and a fine market for British manufactured goods. A number of officials also suggested that the Delta might serve as a "safety valve" for densely populated and famine-prone areas in the Indian Empire like Bengal.[66]

Although the British were well aware of Lower Burma's potential, they were seldom able to take advantage of the possibilities for commercial expansion which the area offered prior to its conquest in 1852. Burman rulers imposed many duties and restrictions on foreign merchants who traded at Rangoon. The Konbaung monarchs also banned the export of rice, bullion, and a number of other commodities which European merchants sought to purchase in the Burman empire.[67] British hopes of developing a market in Burma for their manufactured goods were also frustrated. As early as 1795 the Governor-General of India complained that despite a demand in the Konbaung dominions for products from England and India, the "machinations" of Burman officials had impeded the importation of these goods.[68]

The reluctance of the Konbaung monarchs to open Burma to foreign economic enterprise complemented their refusal to cooperate with the political designs of East India Company officials who ruled the vast empire Britain was building in the Indian subcontinent. Successive Burman kings rejected alliances proffered by British ambassadors and denied the British permission to station Residents in the Konbaung capital. Even after the Burman defeat in the first Anglo-Burman war (1824–26) had made the technological and organizational superiority of the British obvious, Konbaung rulers continued to resist British efforts to establish permanent political contact or to develop trade in their dominions.[69]

66. Henry G. Bell, *A Narrative of the Late Military and Political Operations in the Burmese Empire . . .* (Calcutta, 1852), pp. 57, 62; Crawfurd, *Journal,* p. 6; Symes, *Account of Ava,* 2: 363; William Griffith, *Journals of Travels in Assam, Burma, Bootan, etc. . . .* (Calcutta, 1847), p. 151; Francklin, *Tracts,* pp. 31, 34; J. J. Snodgrass, *A Narrative of the Burmese War* (London, 1827), p. 287.

67. Francklin, *Tracts,* pp. 72, 97–98; Crawfurd, *Journal,* pp. 240–42, 428–29, 440–41; Pearn, *Rangoon,* p. 67; *RAP, 1855–56,* par. 139.

68. "Instructions from the Governor-General to the Bengal Deputation to Ava, 1795," in India Office Records, MSS. European, E. 63, Political, no. 7, pp. 100–101, India Office, London, Eng.

69. Anglo-Burman relations in the pre-1852 period from the British viewpoint are best handled in the writings of D. G. E. Hall. See his *History of South-East Asia,* pp. 554–78. For treatments of the events described by Hall from a Burman perspective, see Dorothy Woodman, *The Making of Burma* (London, 1962), pp. 41–121; and Maung Htin Aung, *The Striken Peacock: Anglo-Burmese Relations 1752–1948* (The Hague, 1965), pp. 12–51.

Burman responses to British overtures furnish a superb example of how a kingdom which failed to provide "satisfactory conditions for commercial or strategic integration" could frustrate the informal controls which John Gallagher and Ronald Robinson have argued the British preferred to outright annexation until the last decades of the nineteenth century.[70] The Maung Ok incident and the aggressive actions of Commodore Lambert, which precipitated the second Anglo-Burman war of 1852,[71] can best be seen as the end result of decades of failure on the part of the British to establish "informal paramountcy" over the Konbaung domains. The refusal of the Burmans to cooperate with the British cost them their fertile southern provinces and their access to the sea. On December 20, 1852, Lower Burma was annexed to the Indian Empire by proclamation of the Governor-General, Lord Dalhousie.

In the first decade after the annexation British officials were more occupied with military and administrative problems than with measures to promote economic growth. Their first concern was to establish control over yet another addition to the Indian Empire. Prolonged military operations were required to suppress the armed resistance of local Burman officials and their retainers in several areas and to put down a serious Karen uprising which broke out in 1858.[72] Even before the Delta had been completely pacified, however, the British were reversing the policies and dismantling or altering the traditional institutions which had impeded economic growth in the Konbaung era. Among the first measures taken by the new regime were the abrogation of the ban on the export of rice and the removal of restrictions on free trade which early nineteenth-century travelers and merchants found so pernicious.

Lifting the ban on paddy exports would, of course, have been of little consequence if there had been no foreign demand for Burma rice. Although paddy exports from the Delta went primarily to Upper Burma in the first two years of British rule, by 1855–56 over half of nearly 127,000 tons of rice exported from Lower Burma was shipped overseas.[73] In the following year the Sepoy Mutiny in India forced rice millers and merchants in England and elsewhere in Europe to turn to alternate sources for their supply. The obvious alternative was the newly acquired Province of Pegu. The outbreak of the

70. "The Imperialism of Free Trade," *The Economic History Review,* 2d ser., 4, no. 1 (August 1953): 1–15.

71. For descriptions from varying perspectives of the events which led to the 1852 war and the conflict itself, see Hall, *History of South-East Asia,* pp. 578–82; and Woodman, *Making of Burma,* pp. 122–53.

72. Albert Fytche, *Burma Past and Present,* 2 vols. (London, 1878), 1: 128–37; D. G. E. Hall, *The Dalhousie-Phayre Correspondence* (London, 1932), pp. 90, 97, 165–66, et passim; Cady, *Modern Burma,* pp. 89–90.

73. *RAB, 1856–57,* par. 69. This total excludes paddy (unhusked rice) exports which went mainly to Upper Burma.

Civil War in the United States and the subsequent decline of the Carolinas as a source of rice for Europe further enhanced Burma's position as a major supplier for London, Liverpool, and continental milling centers like Hamburg and Bremen. In the early 1860s Europe became the principal market outlet for the Delta's rice exports, a position it was to retain until 1910.[74]

With a strong demand from Europe and more and more Europeans investing in processing and transport facilities in the Delta's port centers, the price of rice rose sharply and the volume of exports kept pace. By the mid-1860s the price of one hundred baskets of paddy on the Rangoon market had reached Rs. 50. In the year prior to the British annexation of the Delta, the same amount of paddy had been worth only Rs. 15.[75] In 1867–68 exports of rice from Lower Burma totaled nearly 235,000 tons. In the 1870s the Delta's position as an exporter of rice was firmly established, and by 1872–73 over half a million tons of rice was shipped annually from the ports of Burma.[76]

Although no formal measures were taken with regard to Konbaung sumptuary laws, they were abrogated by the fact that the new government no longer enforced them. On the diplomatic level, in 1862 the British negotiated a treaty with Mindon Min, who ruled the remaining portions of the Konbaung kingdom. The agreement stipulated that neither party would interfere with migration in either direction across their common frontier.[77]

Aside from the abrogation of the ban on rice exports, perhaps the single most important administrative decision in the early years of British rule concerned the type of land revenue settlement which was to be established in Lower Burma. As was the case with most of the policies the British applied and the institutions they established in the Delta, this decision was based on a blend

74. F. B. Leach, "The Rice Industry of Burma," *Journal of the Burma Research Society* 27, no. 1 (April 1937): 61–62; Cheng, *Rice Industry of Burma*, pp. 8–10, 200–202.

75. Cheng, *Rice Industry of Burma*, p. 73; *RAP, 1855–56*, app. 1.

76. Cheng, *Rice Industry of Burma*, pp. 73, 237. These totals exclude paddy exports. All statistics cited for split-year intervals (for example, 1856–57) are based on reports or series which were compiled during a twelve-month period running from July 1 to June 30 of the following year, rather than a normal calendar year.

This early growth bears out both Cheng's (*Rice Industry of Burma*, pp. 12–14) and Aye Hlaing's ("Trends of Economic Growth and Income Distribution in Burma, 1870–1940," *Journal of the Burma Research Society* 47, no. 1 [June 1964]: 91–94) assertions that there was considerable development in Lower Burma prior to the opening of the Suez Canal in 1869. Furnivall (*Colonial Policy and Practice*, p. 50) and other earlier writers have generally regarded this date as the beginning of the full-scale development of a rice-export industry in the Delta area.

77. C. U. Aitchison, comp., "Treaty with the King of Burma," 10 November 1862, in *A Collection of Treaties, Engagements and Sanads Relating to India and Neighboring Countries*, vol. 12 (Calcutta, 1931), art. 9.

of Indian precedents, contemporary British social and economic theory, and indigenous Burmese patterns.

A number of different approaches to land revenue collection had developed in India since the end of the eighteenth century. In the early 1850s those policies which called for direct dealings between government officials and the "cultivator" were in favor. In the decades before the Mutiny of 1857–58, the influence of the English Utilitarian philosophers on Indian revenue systems reached its height. Thinkers like James Mill had been strongly opposed to settlement agreements which favored a landed aristocracy and thus had been critical of the Whig-oriented Permanent Settlement which was dominant in the Bengal Presidency. Mill believed that profits which accrued from agrarian production in the form of rents should go to the state and not to intermediaries like the *zamindars* in Bengal or the *taluqdars* in Oudh. His writings, as well as the works of Utilitarians such as David Ricardo, deeply influenced men like Holt Mackenzie and George Wingate. These men worked for the introduction of systems under which revenue was collected directly from the cultivator or the communal village.[78] One of these systems was the *ryotwari,* which was found mainly in the Madras and Bombay presidencies. It was established in Lower Burma in the decade after 1852.

Although Thomas Munro had not been the first to apply the *ryotwari* system, he had become its chief proponent in the first decades of the nineteenth century. He was mainly responsible for the fact that it had become the dominant land revenue arrangement in the Madras Presidency. Munro believed that the *ryotwari* system would best promote the interests of the state. He contended that the small landholder was more likely to improve and extend his holdings than the large landholder. Munro reasoned that since the small landholder personally supervised the working of his own land, he would strive for maximum crop output.[79]

Burma seemed an ideal province for the introduction of a settlement geared to the interests of the small landholder. In fact, the nature of the pre-British agrarian system and the structure of rural society probably had a far greater effect on the decision to introduce the *ryotwari* settlement in Lower Burma than did the writings of Utilitarian thinkers or contemporary attitudes regarding settlements in other areas. In the Konbaung period most of the land in the Delta was held and worked in small units by the actual cultivators of the soil. There was no "landed" class, comparable to the *zamindars* of Bengal, in Lower Burma. The available evidence indicates that Konbaung officials, such as the *myowun,* were primarily administrators and not large landholders. Local leaders, like the *taikthugyi* or *ywa-ok* (hamlet

78. Eric Stokes, *The English Utilitarians and India* (Oxford, 1959), pp. 76–78, 87–99, 104–9, 122–28.

79. T. H. Beaglehole, *Thomas Munro and the Development of Administrative Policy in Madras, 1792–1818* (Cambridge, 1966), pp. 28–29, 80–81, 133.

leader) did not come to form a landed class.[80] In addition, there was apparently very little tenancy or land alienation in the first decades of British rule.[81] The absence of caste in Burmese society meant that there was no danger that high caste groups could frustrate the intent of the *ryotwari* system by acting as intermediaries between the government and the mass of cultivators. In India, high caste groups, like the *mirasidars* of the Bombay and Madras presidencies, had gained great advantage from the *ryotwari* arrangement by exercising their traditional control over low caste cultivators and laborers.[82] Since there was not a well-established landed group in Lower Burma, it appeared possible to develop a rural economy in which the small proprietor received the profits of his labors and the rent surplus went to the state rather than to intermediaries. The vision of such a system lay behind the establishment of the *ryotwari* settlement in the Delta.[83]

The government strove to make rights to land easily attainable and at the same time to insure that holdings came to be controlled by agriculturists and not by speculators and moneylenders. Several forms of land tenure were experimented with, but two types were dominant in the decades of rapid expansion. British officials initially favored the *patta* system under which the government granted tenure *before* the cultivator cleared his land. Grants were made by local *thugyis,* or district officers, depending on the size of the holding. Only persons who were able to prove that they were bona fide agriculturists could obtain *patta* grants, which averaged fifteen to twenty acres.[84]

The amount of land brought under cultivation by means of the *patta* arrangement was small compared to the amount claimed by virtue of "squatter" tenure.[85] Most cultivators, following pre-British precedents, became landholders by the act of clearing and cultivating a patch of jungle or

80. Government of India, Land Revenue and Settlement Proceedings of the Department of Agriculture, Revenue and Commerce, vol. 679, 22 July 1871, no. 29, India Office Records, London, Eng.; Mya Sein, *Administration of Burma,* pp. 34–47, 64–71.

81. Anonymous, *A Few Words on the Tenure and Distribution of Landed Property in Burma* (Rangoon, 1865), p. 5.

82. See Nilmani Mukherjee and Robert Frykenberg, "The Ryotwari System and Social Organization in the Madras Presidency," in *Land Control,* ed. Frykenberg, pp. 220–25; and Ravinder Kumar, *Western India in the Nineteenth Century* (London, 1968), pp. 94–112.

83. "Memorandum by the Financial Commissioner H. P. Nodd-Taylor," in Government of Burma, Revenue and Agriculture Proceedings, vol. 8633, November 1911, pp. 311, 316, India Office Records, London, Eng.; Government of Burma, *Report of the Land and Agriculture Committee* (Rangoon, 1938), pt. 1, p. 2, pt. 2, pp. 35, 42, hereafter cited as *RLAC.*

84. John Nisbet, *Burma Under British Rule and Before,* 2 vols. (London, 1901), 1: 271; *RLAC,* pt. 2, p. 40.

85. See the tables on land tenure in the settlement reports for Lower Burma until about 1905, and *Settlement Reports–Myaungmya-Bassein (1901–2)*, p. 11; *Hanthawaddy (1907–10)*, p. 12.

scrub. After 1876 the government recognized the squatters' tenurial rights once they had occupied and paid revenue on their holding for twelve years. Until the twelve years had passed, squatters were listed as temporary occupants whom the government could, but very rarely did, evict. Either form of tenure gave the cultivator a permanent and heritable title to his land which he could sell, mortgage, or transfer.[86] To encourage the cultivator to extend his holdings and migrate to unsettled areas, the government exempted newly occupied lands from taxation for periods ranging from one to twelve years and kept the rates of assessment on fallow lands extremely low. To promote immigration into the Delta, the government waived payment of the capitation tax for the first two years after a migrant's arrival.[87]

The concern to develop land revenue systems which would advance the interests of both the cultivator and the state was only one example of the many initiatives taken by the Government of India to promote economic growth within the empire. In the first half of the nineteenth century, when the liberal economic doctrines of free trade and *laissez-faire* were ascendant in Europe, British officials in India were actively working for social reforms and seeking measures that would lead to economic development. The premise that governments should do no more than "maintain order, administer the law and collect their revenues" and leave the rest to "individual enterprise"[88] had little meaning in the Indian context. It was to be ignored many times by the new administrators of Lower Burma. Government officials promoted public works and revenue concessions to attract migrants, provided relief measures for agriculturists who had been forced to abandon their land during the second Anglo-Burman war, and supported schemes to develop new products for export and new sources of labor.[89]

Although early British administrators were well aware of the Delta's potential as a rice-growing area, they sought to introduce additional crops which might be sold and exported. Most of these attempts ended in failure. In some cases, such as the government's projects to induce the Burmese to grow cotton and tobacco,[90] the ecology of the Delta proved unsuitable. Basically,

86. *RLAC,* pt. 2, p. 39; B. H. Baden-Powell, *Land Systems of British India,* 3 vols. (London, 1892), 3: 498.

87. *RAP, 1856–57,* par. 66; Aye Hlaing, "Trends of Growth," p. 94; Furnivall, *Political Economy,* p. 50. The capitation tax, a carry over from Konbaung times, was a small sum levied annually on all permanent residents of the Delta.

88. F. S. V. Donnison, *Public Administration in Burma* (London, 1953), p. 15.

89. See, for examples, Government of India, Political and Foreign Proceedings, range 201, vol. 21, May 1855, no. 165; Hall, *Dalhousie-Phayre Correspondence,* p. 93; *RAP, 1855–56,* par. 32; Government of India, Secret and Political Correspondence, vol. 23, November 1856, no. 66, India Office Records, London, Eng.

90. Government of India, Political and Foreign Proceedings, range 200, vol. 1, nos. 119, 128–30, vol. 60, nos. 136–38; Range 202, vol. 18, no. 114; *RAP, 1859–60,* p. 32, *1860–61,* p. 26.

the preference of the cultivators themselves was decisive. They favored rice, for which conditions in Lower Burma were ideal and which, compared to other export crops, was "easily raised, require[d] little labor, and above all, [was] the most profitable crop" they could produce.[91] Hence, rice production came to dominate the Delta's economy even more than it had in Konbaung times.

The government also financed public works to facilitate the movement of labor and export products and to make cultivation of empty lands possible. The Governor-General, Lord Dalhousie, was a strong advocate of public works and technological innovations.[92] He pressed for their introduction into the area which he had done so much to make part of the Indian Empire. Dalhousie stressed the need for a network of roads. As river transport in the Delta was superb, however, officials in Burma tended to give the completion of the road network low priority. As a result, only about eight hundred miles of roads had been completed by 1873, none of which were main trunk roads.[93] Railroads, which were first introduced in India in the 1850s, were not constructed in Burma until the 1870s. The first was completed in 1877, and by 1914 railway connections had been established between most of the important rice-growing areas and the port centers.[94] The greatest improvement in river communications resulted from the founding of the Irrawaddy Flotilla Company in 1868. Although a private firm, its operations were encouraged and subsidized by the government. By 1932 the company controlled a fleet of over six hundred vessels.[95] The government also financed the construction or improvement of a number of canals. The most important of these were the Twante, the Pegu-Sittang, and the Pegu-Kyaikto canals in the east Delta.[96] These improvements in transportation encouraged the movement of seasonal laborers, permanent settlers, moneylenders, and merchants into the frontier areas of the Delta. They also facilitated the collection of paddy at inland market towns and its transport to Rangoon, Bassein, or Moulmein for milling and shipment overseas. In addition, they made possible a great extension of rural retail networks, specializing in cheap, imported consumer goods, which were to prove a major stimulus to production for the market on the part of the Burmese peasant.

91. *RAB, 1861–62,* pp. 15, 33.

92. George D. Bearce, *British Attitudes Towards India 1784–1858* (Oxford, 1961), pp. 220–21; W. W. Hunter, *The Marquess of Dalhousie* (Oxford, 1890), pp. 27–29.

93. Maung Shein, *Burma's Transport and Foreign Trade, 1885–1914* (Rangoon, 1964), pp. 37–38.

94. J. W. Grant, *The Rice Crop in Burma . . .* (Rangoon, 1932), p. 2; Maung Shein, *Burma's Transport,* pp. 40–42, and map opposite p. 40.

95. Grant, *Rice Crop,* p. 2; George W. Bird, *Wanderings in Burma* (London, 1897), pp. 112–16; *RAB, 1880–81,* p. 123; Tun Wai, *Economic Development,* p. 45.

96. Grant, *Rice Crop,* p. 2; Government of Burma, Revenue and Agriculture Proceedings, vol. 4023, November 1892, nos. 1, 6.

Since Lower Burma received ample and reliable rainfall annually from the southwest monsoon, there was no need for government irrigation projects to promote agrarian expansion. Embankments were required, however, to protect those areas of the Delta which were inundated annually by the flooding of the Irrawaddy River. The embankment which had been built south of Henzada in the Konbaung period was badly damaged during the monsoon rains in 1860. In the dry season of 1860–61 it was rebuilt and extended. In the following decades major embankments were constructed along stretches of the Irrawaddy River from Henzada to Thongwa island, and one was built along a portion of the Sittang River in the 1880s. In some areas whole townships and large portions of settlement tracts were protected by government embankments. The total area which they rendered suitable for cultivation amounted to nearly a million acres by the 1920s.[97]

Measures taken by the government to promote economic growth were supplemented by the activities of private firms and individual merchants and financiers. In the decades after 1852 European investors provided capital for many improvements in transport and in the rice-processing industry which were essential to agrarian development. As noted above, European merchants purchased most of the surplus rice produced in Burma. European merchants also imported consumer goods which served as incentives for indigenous cultivators to produce large surpluses and extend their holdings. During the last half of the nineteenth century, consumer products such as cotton piece goods, cotton twist and yarn, and "sundries" (kerosene lamps, processed foods, cheap furniture, and so on) topped the list of imports into Burma.[98]

The imposition of British rule also led to the creation of a new administrative framework in Lower Burma. In the first decades after 1852 structural change was the most pronounced at the upper levels of the political system, while Konbaung institutions at the subdistrict level were largely preserved. The central administration was reordered, largely on the basis of Indian precedents, and staffed by British and Indian officials who were drawn from the Indian Civil Service and the Indian Army.[99] Indian influence was also apparent in the division of Lower Burma into districts which corresponded to

97. *RAP, 1860–61,* p. 27; Grant, *Rice Crop,* pp. 2, 3; *Settlement Reports–Bassein (1912–14),* pp. 5–6; *Bassein-Henzada (1883–84),* p. 3; *Maubin (1925–28),* pp. 38–40.

98. *RAP, 1855–56,* app. K; Government of Burma, Revenue and Agriculture Proceedings, vol. 4043, November 1892, nos. 1, 6.

99. Hall, *Dalhousie-Phayre Correspondence,* p. lxii; Donnison, *Public Administration,* p. 22; Furnivall, *Political Economy,* p. 206. For the purposes of this study only the local, rural administrative structure need be described at any length. A detailed description of the central administrative system may be found in Alleyne Ireland's *The Province of Burma* (Boston, 1907), 2 vols.; and a fine analysis in James Guyot, "Bureaucratic Transformation in Burma," in *Asian Bureaucratic Systems Emergent from the British Imperial Tradition,* ed. Ralph Braibanti (Durham, N.C., 1966), pp. 354–443.

the units of the same name in India. Each was placed in the charge of a Deputy Commissioner whose powers and responsibilities were similar to those of the District Officer in India. Below the district level, the political structure of the Konbaung period was retained with only minor modifications.[100] The district was divided into *myo-oks* or townships which were placed under the overall supervision of European Assistant Commissioners. The head of each township unit was known as the *myothugyi* and was normally a Burman or a Mon. The townships were in turn divided into *taiks* (circles) under the direction of *thugyis* drawn from the local notables, just as they had been in Konbaung times. For purposes of revenue administration, the *taiks* were divided into *kwins* which usually comprised the holdings of a single large hamlet or several smaller ones.

Far-reaching social and economic change in the first decades after 1852 made the need for a major overhaul of local political arrangements increasingly apparent. The inaction or impotence of most of the *thugyis* and the vulnerability of the *taiks* during the period of unrest which followed the British annexation of Upper Burma in 1886 precipitated the transformation.[101] In accordance with the Lower Burma Village Act of 1889, circles in the Delta were arbitrarily divided into village units similar to those found throughout most of the Indian subcontinent. Also as in India, a headman was placed in charge of each village. Police powers, which had been taken from the *thugyi* in 1861, were granted to the headmen. In addition, revenue collection was gradually turned over to the village headmen as the remaining *thugyi* posts fell vacant.[102]

Beyond specific measures enacted to stimulate or accommodate economic growth, the establishment of British rule meant that Lower Burma received a number of general benefits which were already in effect throughout most of the Indian subcontinent. M. D. Morris has summarized these, speaking of India generally, in the following passage:

> The British *raj* introduced the political framework of the nineteenth-century liberal nation state with its virtues and its limitations. Public order was established on a scale never before achieved in India. Taxation and commercial regulations were rationalized, and the arbitrary features of traditional government were largely eliminated. A high degree of

100. The following description of subdistrict administration is based primarily upon *RAP, 1855–56*, pars. 34–36; Mya Sein, *Administration of Burma*, pp. 81–82; Cady, *Modern Burma*, pp. 89–93; and the *Henzada Gazetteer*, pp. 101–6.

101. Ireland, *Province of Burma*, 2: 712–17.

102. Donnison, *Public Administration*, pp. 31–32; Mya Sein, *Administration of Burma*, pp. 90, 110, 167–69; Cady, *Modern Burma*, pp. 143–44; Government of Burma, Revenue and Agriculture Proceedings, vol. 4277, December 1893, nos. 15–17.

> stability, standardization, and efficiency was achieved in administration.[103]

These and the other innovations introduced by the British rendered Lower Burma a safe and profitable place for foreign investment. Equally important, they freed the Burmese agriculturists from restrictions and obligations, common to traditional societies, which had limited their mobility and productivity in the Konbaung era. These factors, combined with the great fertility of the Delta and a rising foreign demand for the area's chief product, rice, resulted in economic growth and social change on a scale and at a speed unequaled in Southeast Asian history.

103. "Towards a Reinterpretation of Nineteenth-Century Indian Economic History," *Journal of Economic History* 23, no. 4 (December 1963): 611.

Part II

THE EARLY PHASE OF GROWTH, 1852–1907

2

INTERNAL MIGRATION IN THE LAST HALF OF THE NINETEENTH CENTURY

More than any other factor, the favorable response of Burmese agriculturists to the incentives provided by the British and the potential which the Delta offered made possible the rapid growth of the Burma rice industry after 1852. The responsiveness of the Burmese agriculturist was most strikingly manifested in large-scale internal migration,[1] both from Upper Burma and other provincial divisions outside the Delta and from one region to another within the Delta itself. In-migrants played a major role in the extension of paddy cultivation into wild and sparsely inhabited areas of Lower Burma. In the first decades of British rule, Burmese migrants were also dominant among the laborers who built the embankments which made settlement in many areas possible and who manned the wharves and rice mills of Rangoon and Bassein.[2] In addition, Burmese in-migrants were active in internal trade and transportation, marketing, and credit provision

1. In this study I treat all movement from one area to another within the present-day boundaries of Burma as internal. Since Upper Burma was ruled by the Konbaung monarchs until 1886, migration between this region and the Delta prior to that date was not technically internal. I consider it that, however, to distinguish it from migration involving Indians, Chinese, or other groups from abroad and to lend cohesion to the discussion of internal population movements as a whole.

2. *RAB, 1870–71,* p. 32; Government of India, Political and Foreign Proceedings, range 202, vol. 18, 17 March 1857, no. 103, sec. B; J. S. Furnivall, "Safety First–A Study in the Economic History of Burma," *Journal of the Burma Research Society* 40, no. 1 (June 1957): 29.

Table 1. Internal Migrants in the Population of Lower Burma, 1881–1901

Date	(a) Total population of Lower Burma	(b) Number and percentage of persons enumerated who were born outside of the Delta	(c) Number and percentage of persons who were born in the Delta but enumerated in districts other than those of their birth
1881	2,626,000	310,900 (12%)	145,600 (5.5%)
1891	3,301,000	393,100 (12%)	153,800 (4.6%)
1901	4,107,000	411,400 (10%)	255,100 (6.0%)

Sources: *Burma Census, 1921,* Imperial Table 2; and the place-of-birth tables in the 1881, 1891, and 1901 censuses.

Note: It is important to point out that these totals and percentages considerably understate the impact of internal migration on population growth in the last decades of the nineteenth century. The figures in columns b and c are based on place-of-birth rather than transit statistics. Thus, they record migrants in terms of the number of persons who were enumerated outside the area of their birth on a given census date rather than counting the actual number of persons who migrated. Consequently, the totals listed in Table 1 do not include the number of in-migrants who died before a census was taken, nor do they account for seasonal migrants who may have returned to their areas of origin prior to the census enumeration. In addition, it is impossible to determine what percentage of the migrants listed were double counted or listed on several successive census dates. These statistics give no indication of what percentage of the total population of the Delta were descendants of in-migrants from the Dry Zone and other provincial divisions. They also do not record circular or multiple movements. Consequently they do not indicate the number of in-migrants from outside the Delta (column b) who also moved one or more times within Lower Burma after their initial migration to the area. This means that internal migrants from one district to another within the Delta (column c) would be even more undercounted. For further discussion of the problems involved in the use of place-of-birth data, see the appendix, section 3.

throughout the period covered by this study.[3] The importance of in-migrants in the population of Lower Burma from 1881 to 1901[4] is illustrated by the figures set forth in Table 1.

Due to the nature of the available data, the following discussion of the determinants of internal migration in this period is conducted largely within what has come to be known as the "push-pull" approach first introduced by E. G. Ravenstein.[5] The first chapter of this study was devoted in part to the "pull" factors which developed after the British annexed the Delta in 1852, while this chapter concentrates on factors which tended to push migrants from the Dry Zone and other areas into Lower Burma. The cost-and-returns approach to migration introduced by L. A. Sjaastad[6] is difficult to apply because there is little data pertaining to wages, the cost of living, and so on for the largely natural, rural economy of the Dry Zone during the period in question. In addition, there are few statistics relating to the money costs of travel to the Delta, and it is impossible to gauge the importance of the nonmonetary costs of migration.

Some aspects of the group-selectivity approach developed by Simon Kuznets and others will be dealt with in the following discussions of the composition of the migrant flow.[7] This framework, however, yields only marginal returns in analysis of internal migration in Burma for the c.1870–1901 period. Most of the migrants to the Delta were agriculturists with a common cultural heritage, religion, and monastic educational background, and most migrated from villages which were similar in social and political structure. Although it is possible to determine sex ratios on the basis of the available data, there is little information relating to other compositional aspects, such as the percentage of migrants who were urban and rural dwellers or agriculturists and nonagriculturists. The problems of the selectivity approach are also compounded by the fact that rural society in the Dry Zone was not highly or rigidly stratified. There are no class or caste labels to enable one to distinguish between one peasant migrant and another.

The volume of in-migration to the Delta increased steadily during the first phase of agrarian development. This trend is indicated by the rise in the

3. For more detailed discussions of Burmese involvement in these activities, see Chapters 5 and 7 on the plural society in the Delta.

4. Because no systematic or comprehensive statistics relating to internal migration in British Burma were compiled until the census of 1881, it is impossible to estimate the number or importance of in-migrants in the population of the Delta before that date.

5. In his articles on "The Laws of Migration," *Journal of the Royal Statistical Society of London* 48 (June 1855): 167–227, 52 (June 1889): 241–301.

6. See "The Costs and Returns of Human Migration," *Journal of Political Economy* 70, no. 5, pt. 2 (October 1962): 80–93.

7. Simon Kuznets et al., *Population Distribution and Economic Growth–United States, 1870–1950,* 3 vols. (Philadelphia, 1957, 1960, 1964).

number of persons born outside of, but enumerated in, Lower Burma from 311,000 in 1881 to 411,000 in 1901. This increase meant that the flow of migrants to the Delta in the last decades of the nineteenth century was sufficient to replace earlier migrants who died and to add substantially to the total migrants in the area. Throughout these decades the great majority of in-migrants to Lower Burma came from the Dry Zone region in Upper Burma. The Dry Zone's percentage of total in-migrants ranged from 93 percent in 1881 to 87 percent in 1901. The number of migrants from the Shan States, the next largest supplier, reached 6 percent by 1891, while the percentage from Tenasserim (Amherst, Tavoy, and Mergui districts) rose from 2 to 5 percent in the two decade interval. The proportion of migrants from Arakan (Akyab, North Arakan, Sandoway, and Kyaukpyu districts), the Trans-Salween (Karenni and Salween), the Chin Hills, and the other hill areas of northern Burma ranged from 2 percent to negligible amounts.[8]

The statistics set forth in Table 2 relating to the area and population of the divisions which supplied out-migrants to the Delta explain in part why the Dry Zone predominated as a source of migrants. Although it was only the

Table 2. Area and Population in 1901 of Provincial Divisions Supplying Out-Migrants to Lower Burma

Provincial divisions	Area (sq. mi.)	Total population	Density (pop./sq. mi., in rural areas)
Arakan	18,500	762,100	38
Tenasserim	22,100	498,900	15
Trans-Salween	12,400	83,000	14[a]
Shan States	57,900	1,137,500	20
Chin Hills	8,000	87,200	10
Dry Zone	41,200	3,281,500	83
North Tier	46,400	565,400	14

Sources: *Burma Census, 1901,* Imperial tables; *Imperial Gazetteer of India,* 9: 236–37.
[a] Karenni not included.

8. For the location of the provincial divisions cited see Map 1. The northern hills or North Tier consists for the purposes of this study of Katha, Bhamo, Ruby Mines, Myitkyina, and Upper Chindwin. For the composition of the Dry Zone, see the introduction, note 3.

third largest unit in terms of area, the total population and population density of the Dry Zone far exceeded those of other divisions. The population of the Dry Zone was greater than that of all the other divisions combined, while the density per square mile was more than twice that of the closest competitor, Arakan. These figures alone, however, are not sufficient to explain why the Dry Zone, with slightly over one-half of the population of divisions contributing in-migrants to the Delta, should supply almost 90 percent of the total in-migrants during the last decades of the nineteenth century. The Dry Zone's predominance was due to a number of geographical and historical factors in addition to the demographic patterns set forth above.

The contrast between the climate of the Dry Zone and that of the Delta was the most marked of any of the provincial divisions of Burma. Rainfall in the former area, as its name implies, was scanty compared to that in other divisions. The average annual rainfall in the Dry Zone ranged from 32 to 38 inches compared to over 168 inches in Tenasserim, 187 inches in Arakan, and 71 inches in the North Tier.[9] Although the Dry Zone received an amount of rainfall that was adequate for agriculture, its supply was extremely uncertain. The monsoon rains that insured stable and sufficient productivity in coastal areas, in the mountainous north, and in the Delta, were largely blocked from the Dry Zone by the Arakan Yomas. Consequently, the region was prone to drought, food shortages, and periodic famines. The peasants of the Dry Zone usually rotated their crops and double- or triple-cropped in order to stave off the threat of famine. In addition, many areas of the Dry Zone were irrigated by elaborate canal systems which had provided the economic base of Burman kingdoms from the time of the Pagan dynasty (1044–1287). In other areas in the late nineteenth century, however, there was little or no irrigation and the failure of the rains led to distress such as that which occurred in 1856–57:

> The rains failed and the rice withered in the fields. There were no steamers to bring rice up from Lower Burma; there was no railway to carry immigrants down; there were no roads. *Bajra* [millet] was scarce and *jowar* [another form of millet] not known. The rice failed and the people died. They died in the fields gnawing the bark of trees; they died on the highways while wandering in search of food; they died in their homes . . . .[10]

Food shortages were usually not as widespread nor as severe as that of 1856–57, but several major famines threatened the Dry Zone during the last half of the nineteenth century. Following the 1856–57 famine, serious food shortages occurred in one or more Dry Zone districts in 1864, 1866,

9. *Imperial Gazetteer of India,* 9: 234.

10. Government of Burma, *Report on the Famine in Burma in 1896–7* (Rangoon, 1898), p. 28.

1889–90, 1891–92, 1895–96, and 1899–1900.[11] In addition, a severe drought struck the Yamethin, Meiktila, Mandalay, Myingyan, Minbu, and Thayetmyo districts in 1896–97. By the last decades of the nineteenth century improved transportation had greatly diminished the danger of famine in the Dry Zone. Rice was imported into threatened areas,[12] and more important, the inhabitants of affected districts could migrate to the Delta, where employment or cheap land promised temporary or permanent relief.

The volume of out-migration to Lower Burma was directly proportional to the severity of food shortages in the Dry Zone. The Commissioner of Myingyan noted in the 1890s that it had long been the practice of agriculturists in the district to emigrate to Lower Burma when drought and food shortages threatened. He also noted that many of these migrants returned when the drought had ended and they could again earn a livelihood in their home villages.[13] The recurrent threat of scarcity also led many Burmans to migrate to and settle permanently in Lower Burma. When new Burman settlers in Pyapon were asked in the 1920s why they had left the Dry Zone, they complained of crop failures and pointed out that they were certain to have a "full stomach" in the Delta.[14]

The influence of drought on the volume of out-migration from the Dry Zone was most pronounced in the 1896–97 cropping season. Once it was clear that the rains would fail, the roads and railways leading south from the affected districts were crowded with migrants in search of employment or new lands to settle. Many of these migrants were seasonal laborers who regularly harvested crops in the Delta, but in 1896–97 their numbers were swelled by agriculturists in search of sustenance for their families. During the period of the drought the total number of out-migrants from Yamethin, Meiktila, and Myingyan, the three districts most affected, was estimated at 200,000 persons, or nearly one-third of the population. At times whole families moved south with their cattle and goods, but more often single males migrated, leaving their wives and children behind.[15] In contrast to the Dry Zone, no major food shortages were recorded for any of the other divisions sending migrants to the Delta during the last half of the nineteenth century.

The tendency for Burmans "pushed" from the Dry Zone by overpopulation or drought to migrate to the Delta was reinforced by the fact that

11. *Magwe Settlement Report (1897–1903)*, pp. 22–23; Government of Burma, Revenue and Agriculture Proceedings, vol. 3814, October 1891, no. 6, vol. 4043, November 1892, nos. 1, 6, vol. 4886, May 1896, no. 13; *Minbu Settlement Report (1893–97)*, p. 12.

12. Government of Burma, *Report on the Famine*, pp. 4–5; T. W. Holderness, *Narrative of the Famine in India in 1896–7* (London, 1897), p. 9.

13. *Burma Census, 1901*, p. 23. See also *Burma Census, 1911*, p. 69; *Pegu Settlement Report (1897–98)*, p. 9; Government of Burma, *Report on the Famine*, p. 29.

14. *Pyapon Settlement Report (1921–22)*, p. 9.

15. Government of Burma, *Report on the Famine*, pp. 4, 30.

long-range movement of the Burman population in the Konbaung period had been southward. Persons who wished to migrate from the Dry Zone had a cultural and linguistic affinity with these earlier settlers, as well as with the indigenous Mons. Improved river and rail transportation facilitated north-south movement between the Delta and Dry Zone. It also reduced the obstacles provided by the considerable distance which separated districts like Mandalay and Pakokku from Lower Burma.[16] Movement from Arakan or the Shan States, on the other hand, was greatly impeded by geographical barriers. The population of Arakan was concentrated mainly in the Akyab district, which was located a considerable distance from the Delta. The small number of persons who migrated from Akyab tended to move south along the Arakan littoral into Kyaukpyu or Sandoway, rather than across the mountain range which separates Arakan from Lower Burma.[17]

Despite special government measures to encourage Shan in-migration, it played only a minor role in the Delta's development. Distance, reliable agricultural yields, Shan political and social institutions, and the rugged terrain which separates most of the Shan kingdoms from the Delta in part explain the relatively weak Shan response to British incentives.[18] The small percentage of in-migrants from Tenasserim, on the other hand, was a function of both the low population density of the area and the fact that Amherst District was developing in this period along the same lines as the Delta. Cultivable lands and opportunities for employment in agriculture and industry were sufficient in Amherst to satisfy migrants from Tavoy or Mergui, and to occupy most of the district's own population. A number of conditions account for the fact that only negligible numbers of in-migrants came from the Chin Hills and the Trans-Salween districts of Karenni and Salween. Low population density was, of course, the chief determinant. In addition, the nature of Chin and Karen social structure, the slash-and-burn agricultural patterns practiced by these groups,[19] and the hostility which they have traditionally felt toward the lowland dwellers may explain the low level of their response to British incentives.

As Table 3 illustrates, the more populous districts of the Dry Zone—Mandalay, Myingyan, and Pakokku—provided the highest percentage of

16. River transportation was improved through the introduction of steamboats on the Irrawaddy while Upper Burma was still under Burman control. Rail links between Upper and Lower Burma began to play a major role after the completion of the Rangoon-Mandalay line in 1894.

17. *Burma Census, 1881*, p. 73.

18. See Cheng, *Rice Industry of Burma*, p. 115; and *RAP, 1857–58*, par. 176.

19. Some groups of hill-dwelling Chins in the province of Burma practice wet-rice agriculture in valley bottoms, but the dominant form of agriculture for both hill-dwelling Chin and Karen groups is slash-and-burn. See F. M. LeBar et al., *Ethnic Groups of Mainland Southeast Asia* (New Haven, Conn., 1964), pp. 42, 60.

Table 3. Internal Migration from the Districts of the Dry Zone to Lower Burma in the Last Decades of the Nineteenth Century

(1) Dry Zone districts, ranked according to the volume of migrants supplied to the Delta	(2) Percentage of total migrants from the Dry Zone to the Delta supplied in		(3) Total district population in 1891	(4) Population density, measured in terms of the average number of cultivated acres per person (1901)
	1891	1901		
Mandalay	22	15	375,000	0.6 acres
Myingyan	13	12	318,000	3.0
Minbu	11	12	215,500	1.6
Pakokku	9	10	312,900	1.2
Thayetmyo	8	10	250,200	0.9
Shwebo	6	10	223,700	1.6
Lower Chindwin	8	8	240,500	1.9
Magwe	6	8	256,800	2.9
Meiktila	4	6	217,900	2.4
Sagaing	6	6	241,700	2.5
Yamethin	6	2	205,900	1.5
Kyaukse	1	1	126,800	1.7
Total	100	100		

Sources: *Burma Censuses*, 1891, 1901, 1921, Imperial tables; *Season and Crop, 1901–2*, acreage land use tables.

migrants to Lower Burma in the last decades of the nineteenth century.[20] Although there was a strong correspondence between total population and the number of migrants supplied, there seems to have been little connection between the volume of out-migration and population density measured in relation to cultivated area (compare columns 2 and 4 in Table 3). Distance from Lower Burma also had little effect on the volume of migrants supplied.

20. Since Upper Burma was still ruled by the Konbaung monarchs in 1881, no breakdowns by individual Dry Zone districts are available until the 1891 census.

Districts, like Mandalay and Pakokku, which were far from the Delta supplied large numbers of migrants, while nearby districts, like Yamethin and Magwe, provided much lower percentages of the Dry Zone's total. The fact that all of the leading districts of out-migration were on the Irrawaddy River seems to indicate that the availability of water transportation was a more important determinant of the level of migration than sheer distance. In addition, there was an inverse relationship between irrigated acreage and the volume of out-migration. The most heavily irrigated Dry Zone districts, like Magwe, Meiktila, Yamethin, and especially Kyaukse, supplied the lowest percentages of migrants to the Delta.

The nature of rural society in the Dry Zone enhanced the mobility of the Burman agriculturist. The average Burman family was (and is) nuclear and neolocal. Therefore, a peasant's decision to migrate did not depend on a consensus of the male family heads in an extended household. It would not be reversed by the opposition of his father or an elder brother. The peasant's ability to migrate was also enhanced by the strong position of women in Burman society. He could leave his wife in charge of his household in the Dry Zone while he traveled to the Delta to establish a new home or work as a seasonal laborer. This pattern was the most pronounced during times of drought and food shortage in Upper Burma. During the famine of 1896–97, many of the men in the affected districts migrated to Lower Burma in search of temporary employment. In most cases, their wives and children were left behind to take care of their villages in the Dry Zone.[21]

Although village society in Upper Burma was often tightly knit, there were no institutions comparable to the caste system in India which might bind a peasant to a particular locale. The caste-based *jajmani* arrangement, for instance, which is found in many areas of India, enmeshed the village dweller in a web of interdependent and ritually sanctioned exchanges of goods and services.[22] Burman villagers exchanged products and assisted each other in crop production, but there was no formal or rigid system of interchange like the Indian *jajmani.*

The mobility of the Burman household was apparent even in Konbaung times. Lower Burma attracted numerous migrants seeking to better their social and economic position by claiming unoccupied land or by moving into new professions, such as trade.[23] The Burman agriculturist's recognition of

21. Government of Burma, *Report on the Famine,* p. 30.

22. For a detailed discussion of the *jajmani* system, see William H. Wiser, *The Hindu Jajmani System* (Lucknow, 1936), or Thomas O. Beidelman, *A Comparative Analysis of the Hindu Jajmani System* (Locust Valley, N.Y., 1959).

23. Fine expressions of the Burman view of the Delta as a land of opportunity in Konbaung times may be found in the tracts translated by U Htin Aung in *Epistles Written on the Eve of the Anglo-Burmese War* (The Hague, 1968), pp. 5, 9–11, 14–15, 32–33, et passim.

the potential which migration offered is illustrated by the traditional proverb, "Without transfer to another village a person cannot become great."[24]

Although there were many factors which enhanced the potential mobility of the Burman peasant, there were also a number of serious obstacles which might deter his migration beyond the Dry Zone to Lower Burma. To begin with, the Delta was traditionally the heartland of the Burmans' long-standing adversary, the Mons. Even after the Konbaung conquest, Lower Burma remained a frontier region where in many areas Burmans formed a minority, living among often hostile Mons and Karens. In the British period the dangers of inter-ethnic conflict abated, but the feeling lingered among Burmans that the Delta was a wild and uncivilized region. Village society was less cohesive and Buddhist culture less refined and revered on the Delta rice frontier than it was in the Dry Zone.[25] The Burman peasant may also have preferred the dryer climate of the Dry Zone to the alternating hot and wet seasons of Lower Burma. Seasonal migrants would have returned to Upper Burma with tales of wild animals, floods, disease, and the other hazards which confronted peasants who settled in the fertile but thinly populated tracts of the lower Delta.

If a migrant were a mixed-crop farmer in Upper Burma, he would face the problems involved in shifting to wet-rice cultivation in Lower Burma. Even if he grew wet rice in the north, the migrant would have to adjust to different techniques of rice-cropping in the Delta, where holdings were far larger and water regulation, not irrigation, was the major preoccupation of the rice producer. In addition, migrants from Upper to Lower Burma moved from a natural, subsistence economy where social standing was largely ascriptive to a semi-cash nexus, market-oriented economy in which one's position in society was determined to a far greater degree by initiative and manipulative skill.

These obstacles notwithstanding, thousands of Burmans migrated to the Delta in the Konbaung era. In the British period a combination of conditions in the Dry Zone and opportunities for advancement in a society dominated by a growing export economy caused hundreds of thousands of Burman agriculturists to migrate to Lower Burma, either as seasonal laborers or as permanent settlers.

Although the mobility of Burmese agriculturists as expressed in extensive migration is stressed for the purposes of this study, it is also important to point out that a high rate of fertility played a large role in population increase

24. Thein Maung, *Immigration Problem of Burma* (Rangoon, 1939), p. 6. It should be noted that there were also adages which ran counter to the sentiments of that cited by Thein Maung, such as "The foolish ducks abandon the stream and go to the river, only to discover that although there is more water, there are no fishes." Htin Aung, *Epistles*, p. 12.

25. For examples of these views see Htin Aung, *Epistles*, pp. 1–2, 4–6, et passim.

in Lower Burma. If one assumes that there were approximately one million inhabitants in the Delta in 1852,[26] the area's population increased at a very high rate of 3.4 percent per annum between 1852 and 1881. Between 1881 and 1901 the annual growth rate, though still high, dropped to 2.3 percent. The nature of the census data for this period renders it impossible to determine precisely what percentage of the Delta's population growth was due to natural increase and what percentage to migration into the area.[27] However, a rough estimate of the relative importance of fertility and migration can be derived from the observations of census officials and the statistics available after 1881. Although no percentage breakdowns were provided in the 1872 Burma census, its authors concluded that a high rate of fertility was the major factor responsible for a high rate of population growth in British Burma. They noted that over one-third of the province's population was under fifteen years of age.[28] Between 1881 and 1891 Burmese in-migration and Indian immigration combined accounted for nearly 22 percent of the net increase in the Delta's population. Even if one attributes as much as 10 or 15 percent of the natural increase in this decade to births within these migrant groups, the fertility of the indigenous inhabitants was responsible for well over 60 percent of the Delta's net increase. Between 1891 and 1901 the increase due to all migration directly fell to 19 percent, and thus fertility accounted for at least 70 percent of Lower Burma's net increase.[29]

Despite the absence of specific information, it seems fairly safe to assert that the high fertility rate of the Delta population in this period was largely a function of the large amounts of available fertile land, the great demand for labor, and the general prosperity of the agrarian classes in Lower Burma. Net population increase might also have resulted from the decline in deaths due to malaria and other diseases once large tracts in the Delta had been opened and settled (see above, Chapter 1). Whatever the factors which stimulated a higher

26. See Chapter 1, p. 21.

27. No regular vital statistics were recorded prior to 1881, and those for the post-1880 decades are often of poor quality. In addition, as noted above, all migration statistics were recorded in place-of-birth rather than transit terms. In addition to the problems involved in the use of these statistics discussed above, there are no data which would allow one to determine the degree to which births to Burmese in-migrants or Indian immigrants affected the fertility rate though these births must have had a substantial impact throughout this period.

28. *Burma Census, 1872,* pp. 1–2. These observations included Tenasserim and Arakan in addition to the Delta area.

29. These percentages were derived from the statistics listed in Table 1 and the census tables on Indian immigration for this period. The 1901 census estimate (Report, p. 22) for the Province of Burma as a whole was 87 percent due to natural increase and 13 percent to migration. Since most migration was into the Delta, it is consistent that the share of net increase due to migration would be somewhat higher for that area.

fertility rate, it was to have important effects in the future. The children born in the decades of prosperity at the end of the nineteenth century would not enter the labor market until the first decades of the twentieth century when land was running out on the frontier and labor was increasingly in oversupply.

In the first decades after the annexation of 1852, most in-migrants from divisions outside Lower Burma settled in or near areas where population had been concentrated in Konbaung times. In-migrants from the Dry Zone, both permanent and seasonal, favored the heavily settled tracts along the Irrawaddy River and the area around the towns of Toungoo and Yedashe in the upper Delta and the tracts surrounding Rangoon city in the lower Delta.[30] There was a significant influx of migrants from Tenasserim into the fertile areas on the Gulf of Martaban littoral and along the Salween River in the Shwegyin (later Thaton) District.[31] There was also considerable movement of in-migrants into the growing urban port centers of the Delta. Burmans from the Dry Zone made up most of Rangoon's labor supply in the early 1860s,[32] and substantial numbers of seasonal migrants from Upper Burma worked in the rice mills of Bassein town as late as the 1880s.[33] Until the last decades of the nineteenth century, the influx of Burmese migrants was the main factor behind the fairly rapid growth of towns like Bassein and Rangoon. There was little migration into the heavily flooded and sparsely settled tracts of the Tharrawaddy District or the areas that were later to form the Pyapon, Maubin, and Myaungmya districts.[34]

In the last decades of the nineteenth century, the direction of migratory movements into Lower Burma altered substantially, reflecting a shift in the areas where the expansion of the Delta's rice frontier was concentrated.[35] The upper Delta declined as an area of heavy settlement, while the wilderness of the central and lower Delta was brought under cultivation on a large scale. Migration into Toungoo and Thaton also declined. In addition, there was a substantial drop in the percentage of in-migrants whose destination was Rangoon. Whether the low level of Burmese movement into urban areas was a cause or result of the growing influx of Indian laborers into port centers like

30. *RAB, 1867–68*, pp. 146–47, *1870–71*, p. 32, *1872–73*, p. 162; *Hanthawaddy Settlement Reports (1879–83)*, Maps and Descriptions of Areas Cultivated (*1881–82*), p. 8; *Pegu Gazetteer*, p. 47; *Henzada Gazetteer*, p. 34; *Insein Gazetteer*, pp. 46–47.

31. *Thaton Gazetteer*, p. 32.

32. Government of India, Foreign Proceedings (General), range 205, vol. 10, June 1862, no. 60, India Office Records, London, Eng.

33. *Burma Gazetteer*, 1: 97.

34. *Settlement Reports–Tharrawaddy (1913–15)*, p. 7; *Maubin (1925–28)*, p. 15; *Tharrawaddy Gazetteer*, p. 82; *RAB, 1885–86*, p. 63.

35. For a more detailed discussion of in-migration patterns in this period, see Adas, "Agrarian Development," pp. 119–22.

Rangoon and Bassein cannot be determined, but by the 1890s Rangoon was well on its way to becoming an Indian city.

Most Burman in-migrants who settled permanently in the Delta lived in small villages just as they had in the Dry Zone. In Lower Burma, however, the physical layout of the Burman village was radically different from that normally found in the north. The large nucleated villages of Upper Burma, self-contained and surrounded by hedges of thorn or cactus,[36] gave way in the Delta to linear settlements. In some areas, such as along the Pegu Yoma, nucleated villages were common, but throughout most of the lower Delta linear villages predominated. Houses were strung out in single or double file on the edges of rivers or stagnant *chaungs,* along roads and railway lines, on the margins between uplands and paddy plains, on the edges of the saucer-like islands that made up most of the tidal Delta, and on old beach ridges that had been left by the seaward advance of the Irrawaddy delta.[37] Village houses were normally wooden-framed, with walls of woven bamboo and roofs thatched with *dhani* palm or palmyra grass. Prosperous villagers often built their houses with wooden walls and corrugated iron roofs. In most areas houses were raised off the ground from two to five or more feet by wooden piles. The open area underneath the houses was used to store implements and grain.[38] In some areas each house was set within its own compound, which contained a garden and several shade trees. In other areas houses were crowded together on the fringe of rice fields, and the villages which they made up were unsanitary and fire-prone.[39]

Due primarily to restrictions which the Konbaung regime placed on migration from Upper Burma, the composition of the stream of in-migrants to the Delta differed in a number of respects in the pre- and post-1886 periods. Despite the provisions of the 1862 treaty, Burman border officials refused to allow women or children to leave the Konbaung domains.[40] Although numerous settlers managed to slip undetected with their families across the long Konbaung-British border, the ratio of males to females among in-migrants to the Delta was considerably higher before 1886. In 1881 there were 170 males per 100 females among migrants from the Dry Zone enumerated in Lower

36. For descriptions of Dry Zone villages see the *Sagaing Settlement Report (1915–18),* p. 6; *Shwebo Gazetteer,* p. 66; *Thayetmyo Gazetteer,* p. 18.

37. O. H. K. Spate, "The Burmese Village," *Geographical Review* 35 (1945): 532–40; *Settlement Reports–Myaungmya (1916–19),* p. 21; *Maubin (1925–28),* p. 2; *Insein Gazetteer,* p. 52; *Tharrawaddy Gazetteer,* p. 41; *Bassein Gazetteer,* p. 26.

38. Bruen, "Agricultural Geography," p. 57; *Settlement Reports–Hanthawaddy (1879–80),* pp. 8–9; *Thaton (Pa-an) (1928–30),* p. 8.

39. Compare, for example, *Thaton (Pa-an) Settlement Report (1928–30),* p. 7, or *Bassein Gazetteer,* p. 26, with the *Pegu Gazetteer,* p. 52.

40. *RAB, 1870–71,* p. 32.

Burma, while in 1891 and 1901 there were respectively 144 and 138 males per 100 females. The sex ratios for in-migrants from all Burma divisions into the Delta for these years were 163, 138, and 133 males per 100 females.[41] Because the censuses from which these ratios are derived were taken after the cropping season was over in most areas of Lower Burma,[42] the majority of seasonal migrants had returned to their homes and thus were not counted. Since seasonal migrants were normally males, the ratios of male to female migrants were, probably, somewhat higher than those cited.

The fact that migration statistics for Burma are place-of-birth rather than transit means that it is impossible to determine the percentage of seasonal to permanent migrants with any precision. It is probable, however, that the percentage of permanent migrants after 1886 rose substantially above the 20 to 25 percent estimated by census officials in 1872.[43] Since agricultural labor in Lower Burma was considered too strenuous for persons over forty,[44] it can be assumed that most seasonal laborers were young males between the ages of fifteen and forty. It is also probable that permanent in-migrants to the Delta were drawn from younger age groups. They would have been less attached to their areas of origin and more willing to endure the hardships of travel and would have received greater returns from migration because a greater portion of their productive years still lay before them.

Beyond the fact that the majority of migrants were agriculturists, little is known about the occupational composition of the stream of in-migrants to the Delta. The available sources suggest that peasant migrants were generally from the poorer classes of agriculturists in their districts of origin.[45] Traders and cattle drovers are also mentioned as temporary, and at times permanent, migrants to the Delta.[46] In addition, artisans and domestic servants from the declining court towns of Upper Burma probably migrated in search of more lucrative employment in the Delta's growing urban centers. Finally, *pongyis* (Burmese Buddhist monks) must have migrated to Lower Burma in

41. I have calculated all of the sex ratios cited from the place-of-birth tables in the Burma censuses for 1881, 1891, and 1901. For provincial divisions other than the Dry Zone, see Adas, "Agrarian Development," p. 125.

42. The dates for the three censuses were 17 February 1881, 26 February 1891, and 1 March 1901.

43. *Burma Census, 1872,* p. 15. This estimate is lower than the 35 percent which I have calculated from the transit statistics available only for the Henzada District between 1867 and 1876. See *Burma Gazetteer,* 2: 167.

44. *Hanthawaddy Settlement Report (1907–10),* p. 27.

45. *Henzada Gazetteer,* p. 34; *Pegu Gazetteer,* pp. 56–57; *Settlement Reports–Hanthawaddy (1881–82),* p. 8; *Bassein-Thongwa (1888–89),* p. 3.

46. *Settlement Reports–Bassein (1881–82),* p. 16; *Myaungmya-Thongwa (1902–3),* app. B; *Bassein (1912–13),* p. 6; *Pyapon (1921–23),* p. 23; *Burma Census, 1921,* p. 94; A. McKerral, *The Supply of Plough Cattle in Burma* (Rangoon, 1929), pp. 22–23; Cheng, *Rice Industry of Burma,* p. 46.

considerable numbers because *pongyis* from Upper Burma took charge of the *kyaungs* (monasteries) and pagodas in many areas of Lower Burma.[47]

Migration into the Delta from other divisions within the Province of Burma was paralleled by considerable migration within Lower Burma itself. Many of the same social and psychological factors which lay behind the great mobility displayed by the rural population of the Dry Zone also promoted migration on the part of agriculturists in the Delta. The cultivator in Lower Burma was even less bound by ties to a particular village or locality than was his counterpart in the Dry Zone. In pre-British times households were known to move to escape the jurisdiction of unpopular *myothugyis.* The low population density in the Delta facilitated such movement and served as a check on the power of local officials.[48] In the British period officials reported that the Delta agriculturist showed little attachment for ancestral holdings.[49] In fact, the familial inheritance patterns followed in Lower Burma stimulated the migration of many agriculturists. According to Burman Buddhist law, the children, both male and female, of a deceased landowner divided his holdings equally. This practice led to the fragmentation of holdings and often resulted in prolonged legal disputes and the financial ruin of the parties concerned.[50] In many instances, however, one of the heirs would buy up the others' shares of the holding and thus prevent fragmentation. This pattern promoted migration, for those who had lost their land gained the capital necessary to clear and cultivate a new holding.[51]

Another factor which contributed to migration within the Delta was the spread of agrarian indebtedness in the last decades of the nineteenth century. Cultivators in tracts where the soil was infertile or those who suffered heavy losses from flooding, cattle disease, or other calamities often became heavily indebted to local moneylenders or merchants. If their debts became so serious that they were in danger of losing their land, many cultivators chose to escape their obligations by moving to distant circles where they would clear and claim new holdings.[52] In this manner agrarian debt led to the extension of

47. *Pyapon Settlement Report (1921–22)*, p. 10.

48. Mya Sein, *Administration of Burma*, p. 71.

49. Government of Burma, Revenue and Agriculture Proceedings, vol. 8633, November 1911, p. 651.

50. For example, see O. H. K. Spate, "Beginnings of Industrialization in Burma," *Economic Geography* 17, no. 1 (January 1941): 90–91.

51. A number of other patterns were adopted to prevent fragmentation. The heirs would agree to hold the land in common and work it individually on a rotation basis. The person who worked the land in any given year would give part of his surplus toward the support of the other heirs. In some cases the joint-owners rented the land to an outsider.

52. Government of Burma, Revenue and Agriculture Proceedings, vol. 4487, August 1896, no. 13, p. 14, vol. 6743, July 1904, nos. 1355–61, p. 84; *Bassein Settlement Report (1880–81)*, p. 10; Nisbet, *British Burma*, 2: 296–97.

cultivation on the Delta rice frontier. For displaced heirs and debtors, as well as migrants in search of a new beginning, large tracts of fertile, unoccupied land were available in Lower Burma throughout the first phase of agrarian development.

The main movement of migrants within the Delta in the last decades of the nineteenth century was from heavily settled areas like Prome, Henzada, and the environs of Rangoon city into the frontier areas of the central and lower Delta.[53] There were also sizable migrations of Karens, who descended from the Pegu and Arakan Yomas and clustered in the interior portions of tracts in Henzada, Pegu, and the wilderness of the central Delta.[54] In addition, there was considerable local migration throughout the period covered by this study. During certain seasons large portions of the population of many Delta villages traveled to other areas to plant or harvest rice, to trade, to fish, or to cart timber and paddy. Often peasants' fields were located some distance from their villages. It was common practice for them to move to the area outside their village and live in a field hut during the cropping season.[55]

Population movements within the Province of Burma in the first half-century of British rule were generally continuations of earlier migration patterns rather than new trends. Burman migration into the Delta from the Dry Zone was one of the dominant demographic themes of the Konbaung period. The Karen movement onto the plains of the Irrawaddy delta began long before the Burman conquest and continued throughout the century of Konbaung rule in Lower Burma. Population movement within the Delta itself was also substantial. Burmans brought new tracts under cultivation, Mons abandoned traditional areas of settlement for tracts more remote from the centers of Burman colonization, and Karens moved about the Delta in search of fertile, but inaccessible, areas to cultivate. Due to the prevalence of the shifting method of cultivation in many areas of Lower Burma, local migration may have been even more pronounced in pre-British times than in the last decades of the nineteenth century. Thus, in terms of migration, major change in the British period was not in direction or composition, but in volume. Since most of the factors which "pushed" migrants from areas like the Dry Zone were present in pre-British times, the great acceleration of internal migration must

53. For a detailed discussion of interregional movement see Adas, "Agrarian Development," pp. 120–24.

54. *Bassein Gazetteer,* p. 23; *Pegu Gazetteer,* p. 47.

55. According to the Village Act of 1907, peasants were required to live within village limits. However, if a peasant's fields were a considerable distance from his village, he could obtain permission to build a field hut where he could live during the cropping season. See Government of Burma, *The Burma Village Manual and Village Act* (Rangoon, 1907), sec. 18.

be attributed primarily to the "pull" factors which developed after the annexation of the Delta. Rapid economic growth, improved transportation facilities, the promise of abundant and fertile land, and incentives such as low taxes and consumer rewards drew increasing numbers of potentially mobile Burmese into Lower Burma between 1852 and 1900.

The influx of Burmans from the Dry Zone was clearly the most important internal movement of population in the first phase of agrarian development. Ironically, British conquest accelerated the process of Burman expansion into Lower Burma and their absorption of the Mons. By the last decades of the nineteenth century most of the Mons in the Delta had been Burmanized and considerable numbers had intermarried with Burmans. Burmese had replaced the Mon language in most areas of Lower Burma, thus removing the main distinction between the two ethnic groups. Throughout most of the Delta contemporary observers found it impossible to distinguish between Burman and Mon.[56] By the end of the nineteenth century the Burman heartland had grown to include most of Lower Burma.

56. *Settlement Reports–Hanthawaddy-Pegu (1881–82)* p. 3; *Bassein (1882–83)*, p. 2; *Thongwa (1889–90)*, p. 3; *Hanthawaddy (1897–98)*, p. 4; *Henzada (1899–1900)*, p. 7; *Pegu (1899–1900)*, p. 12.

3

AGRARIAN DEVELOPMENT ON THE ADVANCING RICE FRONTIER

The expansion of the Delta rice industry in the last half of the nineteenth century represents one of the most impressive examples of sustained economic growth under the aegis of a European colonial regime. A steadily rising overseas demand for rice was fed by an increase in the amount of rice and paddy exported from Lower Burma from 162,000 tons in 1855 to 2,000,000 tons in 1905–6.[1] This was accompanied by a rise in the price of paddy in the same period from Rs. 45 to Rs. 120 per 100 baskets.[2] These increases were paralleled by an expansion of the area under rice cultivation from about 700,000–800,000 to nearly 6,000,000 acres.[3] This growth was supported by and in turn stimulated an increase in the Delta's population from approximately one million in 1852 to over four million in 1901.[4] The rise of the rice industry was also the basis for the mushrooming growth of port and processing centers in Lower Burma, especially Rangoon and Bassein.

The very real benefits which the Burmese received from this process in

1. Grant, *Rice Crop,* p. 56. Paddy refers to rice which has not been husked. There are several forms of "rice" depending on the degree to which it has been processed. See Cheng, *Rice Industry of Burma,* pp. 9–10 ff.

2. The prices quoted are those on the Rangoon market; see Cheng, *Rice Industry of Burma,* p. 73.

3. See Chapter 1; and *Season and Crop, 1905–6,* statistical tables on acreage use.

4. See Chapter 1; and *Burma Census, 1921,* Imperial Table 2.

terms of higher living standards and consumption levels is reflected in the expansion of rice cultivation, which in the first phase of development was due mainly to the efforts of Burmese peasant proprietors. In the first decades of British rule agrarian expansion was concentrated in the districts of the upper Delta and the tracts around Rangoon. Between 1856 and 1872, 131,000 acres of additional land were brought under rice cultivation in the districts of Prome, Henzada, and Tharrawaddy.[5] In the same time span 262,000 acres were added in the circles in the vicinity of the towns of Rangoon and Pegu. In the vast wilderness of the central and western portions of the Delta less than 80,000 additional acres of paddy land were brought into production in this period.[6]

In addition to the clearing of new tracts near established paddy concentrations and urban centers, the increase in cultivated area prior to 1872 was due to growth in the size of individual holdings. In response to market rewards, cultivators worked longer hours and made use of formerly under- or unemployed familial labor in order to increase the area which they cultivated and could thus claim.[7] In the early decades of expansion, however, cultivators generally regarded surplus production as a spare-time operation. The peasant household continued to produce most of the food and goods required for its subsistence, but extra man hours were spent clearing waste land and harvesting paddy that might formerly have been left to rot for want of market outlets.[8]

As the limits to expansion in most areas of the upper Delta and around Rangoon town were reached in the 1870s, migrant agriculturists began to move in large numbers into the tidal Delta districts to the west and south of Rangoon. Beginning in the late 1880s there was also a considerable influx of settlers into south Toungoo and the interior of the Thaton District. These shifts in the direction of migration and new settlement can be traced in Table

5. As noted in Chapter 1 most of this expansion was in Prome and Henzada, but since Tharrawaddy was joined with Henzada to form the Myanoung District in these decades, no separate statistics of acreage increase are available.

6. These totals were calculated from the figures in *RAP, 1856–57,* app. F, and *RAB, 1871–72,* appendix on area cultivated by districts. See also the maps appended to the settlement reports for Hanthawaddy and Pegu from 1879 to 1884. Thaton was not listed in the 1856–57 report. The increase for Toungoo in these decades was only 13,000 acres.

7. Between the early 1850s and the 1880s the average holding size in the three districts of the upper Delta rose from 6.5 to 9.5 acres, in the tidal Delta frontier (Bassein, Pyapon, Myaungmya, and Maubin) from 8 to 16 acres, and in the districts around Rangoon town from 10 to over 30 acres. See *RAP, 1855–56,* par. 142; and the settlement report tables on average holding sizes for the 1880s.

8. For a more detailed discussion of these changes see Myint, *Economics of Developing Countries,* pp. 42–47.

Table 4. The Increase in Acres under Rice Cultivation between 1876 and 1906 (actual increase in thousands; percentage increase in parentheses)

Region	1876–82		1882–92		1892–1902		1902–6	
Upper Delta	129	(27)	332	(56)	191	(21)	30	(3)
Prome								
Henzada								
Tharrawaddy								
Tidal Delta frontier	275	(133)	344	(113)	768	(146)	151	(15)
Bassein								
Myaungmya								
Pyapon								
Maubin								
Rangoon and hinterland	248	(39)	363	(41)	398	(32)	252	(16)
Pegu								
Insein								
Hanthawaddy								
Sittang-Salween fringe	35	(38)	153	(121)	493	(176)	111	(15)
Toungoo								
Thaton								
Total	687	(43)	1,192	(52)	1,850	(53)	544	(10)

Sources: 1871/2–1891/2: *RAB, 1871/2–1891/2,* appendices on area cultivated by district; 1901/2–1905/6: *Season and Crop,* 1901–2, 1905–6, tables on area under rice cultivation.

4, which shows the growth in acreage under rice cultivation in various Delta regions from 1876 to 1906.[9]

Prodigious hazards and obstacles confronted the migrant agriculturists who settled in frontier areas in the last decades of the nineteenth century. Large areas of the lower Delta were flooded annually for several months during the monsoon season. Although the government constructed embankments and individual cultivators built *kazins* to protect their paddy fields, these barriers were often breached by the flooding of the Irrawaddy River or one of its branches. On the coast, the monsoon tides often inundated paddy fields with salt water, which destroyed the crop if it were not quickly

9. The substantial rise in the area occupied in the upper Delta in the 1880s was due almost wholly to settlement in the Tharrawaddy District, which had been bypassed in earlier decades.

drained.[10] As late as 1925, after nearly seventy-five years of embankment and *kazin* construction, hundreds of thousands of acres of Delta paddy land were still liable to damage from flooding.[11] Tides also carried tens of thousands of *kunpaga* crabs onto the rice fields along the littoral. If the paddy crop were sown or planted before the adult crabs returned to the sea, they would devour the paddy seeds or the young paddy shoots.[12]

Before the last decades of the nineteenth century most of the lower Delta was covered with *kanazo* forest and *kaing* grass. In many tracts *kanazo* trees, which grew to a height of one hundred and fifty feet in fresh-water areas of Lower Burma,[13] had to be cut down and burnt before a settler could begin cultivation. The labor involved in clearing *kanazo* forest was so arduous and time-consuming that new settlers often cultivated only the less fertile, but *kanazo*-free, high ground that fringed the *kanazo* swamps. Several years were required to prepare land covered with *kanazo* forest for paddy cultivation. The trees were cut down and the undergrowth burnt off in the first year. At times, the cultivator would flood the area and wait several years for the roots to rot away. More often, however, he would plant sugar cane between the roots for one or two years. In the third or fourth year, having cleared the roots with fire and *dah,* the cultivator would plow the land and plant paddy for the first time.[14] Clearing land covered with *kaing* grass was considerably easier. The grass was burnt off and remaining roots or growth were hoed or harrowed under.[15] *Kanazo* tracts did not normally reach full productivity until the seventh or eighth year of cropping, while *kaing* land did so in the third or fourth year.[16]

The struggle to transform jungle and swamp into paddy fields on the rice frontier of the Delta entailed many dangers and frustrations. Tigers and elephants roamed the wilderness of the lower Delta, and poisonous snakes abounded in its swamps and grassy plains. Maung Kyaw Din, one of the few settlers for whom detailed biographical information is available, recalled that in the fourth year after his arrival in the Myaungmya District, his brother was

10. *Settlement Reports–Bassein (1881–82),* pp. 3–4; *Thaton (1897–98),* pp. 7–8; *Myaungmya-Thongwa (1902–3),* p. 6; *Pyapon (1921–22),* p. 15.

11. Government of Burma, *Report of the Floods Enquiry Committee, 1924–5,* 2 vols. (Rangoon, 1927), 1: esp. 6–11.

12. C. C. Ghosh, *Insect Pests of Burma* (Rangoon, 1940), p. 58; *Settlement Reports–Myaungmya-Thongwa (1902–3),* p. 6; *Pyapon (1921–22),* pp. 14, 18.

13. Bruen, "Agricultural Geography," pp. 33–34, 37–38. For further description and pictures of *kanazo* forest growth, see L. D. Stamp, *Vegetation of Burma* (Rangoon, 1926).

14. *Settlement Reports–Thongwa (1890–91),* p. 5; *Myaungmya-Thongwa (1902–3),* p. 5; *Myaungmya (1924–25),* pp. 1–2; *Myaungmya (1916–17),* p. 48.

15. *Settlement Reports–Thongwa (1890–91),* p. 5; *Myaungmya-Thongwa (1902–3),* p. 5.

16. *Thongwa Settlement Report (1890–91),* p. 5.

killed by a tiger.[17] Cultivators in newly settled areas often built palisades around their thatch houses to ward off wild animals that prowled in the nearby forest.[18] Their paddy fields, however, lay open to raids by monkeys, elephants, deer, wild pigs, rats, and many types of birds.[19] In addition, a wide variety of insects threatened the cultivator's growing crop. The most serious insect pests were the rice-swarming caterpillar and the rice case-worm, which attacked paddy shoots in the seedbed, and the rice *Hispa* (beetle), rice ear-bug, and the rice grain-nibbling caterpillar, which did considerable damage to maturing rice plants.[20]

The cultivator's ability to prepare his land for planting and to resist the threats posed by wild animals and insects was often impaired by malaria, dysentery, and other diseases which were particularly virulent in newly settled areas. Settlers were sometimes so weakened by disease that they could not work their holdings. They were then forced to borrow money to hire laborers or to purchase food and seed paddy for the next season.[21] Disease also struck the cultivator's livestock. The climate of the lower Delta was unhealthy for buffalos and bullocks, which supplied the source of motor power for rice production and land transportation in Burma. Mortality among draft animals was high and epidemics of rinderpest, anthrax, and hoof and mouth disease were frequent.[22]

In-migrants from Upper Burma or migrants from the more populous areas of the Delta normally possessed little or no capital when they arrived on the rice frontier.[23] In the early decades of British rule (and presumably in the Konbaung period) when there were few sources of agricultural credit, migrants would assist and live with established cultivators who were sometimes friends or relatives. New settlers continued to work the land of another until they had acquired the capital which they needed to clear their own holdings.[24] In later decades population growth and the rising value of

17. *Myaungmya-Thongwa Settlement Report (1902–3)*, app. A, p. 118.

18. *Myaungmya Settlement Report (1916–19)*, p. 26.

19. *Settlement Reports–Thaton (1897–98)*, pp. 7–8; *Pegu, Bawni Circle (1900–1901)*, p. 5; *Myaungmya-Thongwa (1902–3)*, p. 6; *Pyapon (1921–22)*, pp. 15, 18; Government of Burma, *Agricultural Leaflets*, 2 vols. (Rangoon, 1927), 2: 9–10.

20. Ghosh, *Pests*, pp. 53, 59, 60, 67–68; D. Hendry, "Rice in Burma," *Tropical Agriculture* 5, no. 1 (January-March 1928): 15.

21. *Myaungmya Settlement Report (1916–19)*, pp. 26–27.

22. Government of Burma, *A Hand-Book of Agriculture for Burma* (Rangoon, 1898), pp. 73–79; Government of Burma, *Circulars of the Director of the Department of Land Records and Agriculture in Burma, 1888–1889* (Rangoon, 1899), no. 4 of 1888, pp. 237–39; Government of Burma, Revenue and Agricultural Proceedings, vol. 4886, March 1896, pp. 25, 40, 48, et passim.

23. *Settlement Reports–Hanthawaddy (1881–82)*, p. 8; *Bassein-Henzada (1884–85)*, pp. 26–27; *Bassein-Thongwa (1888–89)*, p. 3; *Toungoo (1898–99)*, p. 20; *Pegu Gazetteer*, pp. 56–57, or *Henzada Gazetteer*, p. 35.

24. Aye Hlaing, "Trends of Growth," p. 96. A variant of this pattern is still followed by migrants in the Dry Zone today. In his study of Nondwin village near Sagaing,

paddy land greatly intensified the struggle for cultivable land. A new settler had to begin working his own holding soon after his arrival on the frontier or he would find that the best land had already been occupied by others.[25] The growing availability of agricultural credit made it possible for the migrant to begin clearing and planting his own fields in the first year after his arrival. He used as little hired labor as possible, and in order to save the expense of buying or hiring plows and cattle he often hoed his fields rather than plowing or harrowing them. The settler also sowed the paddy broadcast instead of transplanting it. Haste and the migrant's reluctance or inability to obtain large amounts of capital greatly limited the productive capacity of newly occupied tracts.[26]

Despite efforts to save on cultivation costs, migrants rarely succeeded in bringing waste land under cultivation without borrowing. The high cost of clearing jungle growth and low productivity in the first years of cropping meant that it was usually necessary for the cultivator to borrow to feed, clothe, and house his family and/or to purchase *wunsa* (seed paddy) or agricultural implements. If he lost part or all of his crop through flooding or the depredations of animal or insect pests, or if he was afflicted with malaria, the settler almost invariably was forced to borrow.[27]

Once settlers were established their method of paddy cultivation was fairly standard throughout the Delta. Although these techniques are well documented,[28] some aspects require specific comment because of their important impact on the general economic development of British Burma. The tools employed by the great majority of Burmese cultivators showed little advance in design or construction over those used in the pre-British period. The crude harrow (*htun*) found throughout the Delta was much like that employed by the Burmans who settled in the Dry Zone at the end of the first millennium A.D.[29] In the Konbaung period the plow (*hte*) was not widely used in Lower Burma, but by the end of the nineteenth century it was a

Manning Nash observed that during their first years of residence migrants who move into the village usually share the compounds of relatives. See *The Golden Road to Modernity* (New York, 1965), p. 49.

25. Ibid., p. 96. The need to claim land quickly also applied to the established cultivator who wished to extend his holdings. See Furnivall, *Political Economy*, p. 104.

26. *Settlement Reports–Hanthawaddy-Pegu (1883–84)*, p. 5; *Pegu (1897–98)*, p. 9; *Myaungmya (1924–25)*, pp. 2, 7–8.

27. *Settlement Reports–Toungoo (1898–99)*, p. 20; *Thongwa (1890–91)*, pp. 5, 7; *Myaungmya (1916–19)*, p. 27; *Myaungmya (1924–25)*, p. 7; Government of India, Emigration Proceedings of the Department of Agriculture, Revenue and Commerce, vol. 693, May 1875, no. 13, India Office Records, London, Eng. For credit sources and borrowing patterns, see below.

28. See, for example, Cheng, *Rice Industry of Burma*, pp. 32–36; Grant, *Rice Crop*, pp. 12–23; and Adas, "Agrarian Development," pp. 155–60.

29. G. H. Luce, "The Economic Life of the Early Burman," in *Fiftieth Anniversary Publication of the Burma Research Society* (Rangoon, 1960), p. 331.

standard tool in most Delta areas. The cultivator strongly preferred the traditional Burman plow to the newer varieties which government officials attempted to introduce. The government also sought to promote the use of a number of other farming implements, but its efforts met with little success in this period.[30]

Cultivators in Lower Burma used little fertilizer of any kind. The ash of burnt-off stubble and weeds or *kaing* grass that were plowed under provided some nourishment for the soil, but in most areas little else was done to replenish heavily cropped lands. In tracts where paddy was transplanted, nurseries were generally fertilized with cattle manure, and in certain townships of a few districts (Prome, north Henzada, and north Bassein) cattle manure was also spread thinly over the cultivator's entire holding.[31]

The shifting/broadcast method of cultivation which was widely followed in Konbaung times was replaced in the first decades of British rule by sedentary/transplanting and sedentary/broadcasting techniques. Transplanting was dominant in the upper Delta and in the northern circles of the Bassein and Maubin districts, where agricultural labor was readily available, water conditions favorable, and the size of holdings not too large. It was also dominant in areas where the soil had been repeatedly planted for many decades and its fertility was on the decline. Broadcast sowing was particularly popular in the newly settled and fertile areas of the lower Delta frontier and in the districts around Rangoon town.[32]

The cultivator in Lower Burma seldom took time to select better seeds for use in his fields. Almost all paddy grown in the Delta was "winter" (*kaukkyi*) or "autumn" (*kauklat*) rice. Toward the end of the nineteenth century a special deep-water paddy called *tadaungbo* was introduced in limited areas of some districts. According to the classification used by rice millers and traders, most of the rice grown in Lower Burma was either of the *ngasein* or *midon* varieties.[33]

In the first decades after 1852, sources of agricultural credit were few and capital for agrarian development in Lower Burma was limited. The descrip-

30. *Settlement Reports–Bassein-Henzada (1883–84)*, p. 3; *Hanthawaddy (1897–98)*, p. 9, (*1898–99*), p. 10; *RAP, 1855–56*, par. 240; Nisbet, *British Burma*, 2: 315; *Imperial Gazetteer*, 3: 189.

31. *Settlement Reports–Bassein (1879–80)*, p. 3, (*1897–98*), p. 16, (*1898–99*), p. 14; *Thaton (1896–97)*, p. 6; *Pegu (1897–98)*, p. 9; *Toungoo (1898–99)*, p. 6; *Henzada (1899–1900)*, p. 9; *Prome (1900–1901)*, p. 10, (*1903–4*), p. 5; Nisbet, *British Burma*, 2: 318.

32. See especially *Pyapon Settlement Report (1921–22)*, p. 18; and Map IV-A in Adas, "Agrarian Development," p. 158.

33. *Settlement Reports–Bassein (1879–80)*, p. 3; *Hanthawaddy (1880–81)*, p. 3; *Toungoo (1898–99)*, p. 6; *Tharrawaddy (1903–4)*, p. 2; *Maubin (1904–5)*, p. 3; Nisbet, *British Burma*, 2: 318; Cheng, *Rice Industry of Burma*, pp. 36–39.

tions of credit institutions, which have appeared in recent works on the Burmese economy in the British period,[34] have dealt almost entirely with conditions in the twentieth century, particularly the 1920s and 1930s. The different government and private agencies, the various types of loans and the rather well-defined procedures for borrowing and repayment which characterize this period were nonexistent or embryonic in the early years of agrarian development. Since there had been little need for credit or capital accumulation in the predominantly subsistence and natural economy of the Delta in Konbaung times, there were few bankers or moneylenders in Lower Burma at the time of its annexation to the Indian Empire. The capital of existing creditors was devoted primarily to trade, and only marginally, if at all, to agricultural production.[35]

Sources of agricultural credit emerged gradually after the ban on rice export was lifted, and a cash-nexus, market-oriented economy began to develop in Lower Burma. Before the 1880s most cultivators borrowed from friends and relatives, local shopkeepers, or indigenous moneylenders. The interest rates on loans from a cultivator's neighbors or family ranged from 2.5 to 3.33 percent per month, which was considerably below the 4–5 percent normally charged by moneylenders in this period. Lending transactions between friends or family were verbal and usually no security was required.[36]

Because of their overlapping activities, it was often difficult to distinguish between shopkeepers, moneylenders, and rice traders in the first decades of agrarian development. Local shopkeepers made loans according to the *sabape* system, which meant that they advanced goods or cash to cultivators in the monsoon season and received paddy in repayment after the harvest. *Sabape* interest rates far exceeded the normal rates charged by professional moneylenders. The value of the paddy given in repayment usually equalled three to four times the value of the goods originally borrowed. After several years of successful lending at these high rates, the shopkeeper often purchased a boat which he used to transport paddy that he had received as interest to the closest market town.[37]

Most of the persons listed as moneylenders in the first decades after 1852 were Burmese. They usually resided in towns or in the largest villages, and their operations were confined mainly to tracts that were heavily cultivated and near population centers. Moneylenders normally gave *ngwedo* loans, which meant that the loan was given in cash and that both the principal and interest were repaid in cash. They charged interest rates which ranged from

34. See, for example, Cheng, *Rice Industry of Burma*, pp. 171–93; and Tun Wai, *Currency and Credit*, pp. 42–82.

35. Tun Wai, *Currency and Credit*, p. 1.

36. *Settlement Reports–Tharrawaddy (1880–81)*, pp. 9–10; *Hanthawaddy (1880–81)*, p. 7; *Bassein (1881–82)*, p. 7.

37. *Bassein Settlement Report (1881–82)*, p. 3.

1.5–2.5 percent per month on gold security to 4–5 percent on land security. The cultivator's land was the most common form of security, but gold, jewelry, cattle, and houses were also accepted. Although friends and relatives might accept a cultivator's current rice crop as security, moneylenders almost never did.[38] Although there are no direct references to moneylenders engaging in the rice trade until the 1890s, it is probable that many, like the shopkeepers, were involved in paddy marketing long before. Their participation was to become more pronounced as their control over their clients' surplus production increased.

Prior to the 1880s Nattukottai Chettiar moneylenders from the Madras Presidency, who played such a dominant role in credit provision in the twentieth century, confined their activities mainly to Rangoon and other urban centers. Although there is no record of cultivators taking loans directly from Chettiars in the settlement reports for the 1880s, agriculturists who lived in the neighborhood of Rangoon and other large towns probably did so. In some areas, Chettiars financed agricultural production indirectly through loans to indigenous moneylenders, who in turn lent to cultivators at higher rates.[39] Burmese moneylenders also obtained capital from paddy brokers and rice millers which they repaid in paddy.[40]

The number of moneylenders, both Indian and Burmese, increased considerably in the last decades of the early phase of agrarian development. In 1881 only 587 professional moneylenders were enumerated in Lower Burma, of whom most were located in Rangoon and Bassein or in the districts nearby. By 1901 nearly 3,200 bankers and moneylenders were found in the Delta, and they were far more evenly distributed than twenty years earlier.[41] With the exception of remote and undeveloped tracts where relatives remained the chief source of credit, Burmese moneylenders played a dominant role in the provision of credit at the village level by the 1890s. Their operations were usually supplemented by those of paddy brokers and village shopkeepers, whose lending activities increased greatly around the turn

38. *Settlement Reports–Hanthawaddy (1880–81)*, p. 7; *Bassein (1881–82)*, p. 7; *Tharrawaddy (1882–83)*, p. 3; *Bassein-Henzada (1883–84)*, p. 7, *(1884–85)*, pp. 9, 27; *Bassein-Thongwa (1881–89)*, p. 11; *Thongwa (1890–91)*, p. 18; *Toungoo (1898–99)*, p. 20; *Maubin (1904–5)*, p. 17; A. F. English, *A Handbook of Co-operative Credit for Burma* (Rangoon, 1911), p. 4; Government of Burma, Revenue and Agriculture Proceedings, vol. 4886, March 1896, p. 97.

39. *Hanthawaddy Settlement Report (1880–81)*, p. 7.

40. *Thongwa Settlement Report (1890–91)*, p. 18.

41. I have calculated these figures and percentages from the tables on occupations in the Burma censuses of 1881 and 1901. Since the 1901 tables include bankers, they overstate the increase in moneylenders. These totals do not include paddy brokers, merchants, and landowners who advanced large sums of capital to agriculturists.

of the century.[42] The distinction between indigenous moneylender, shopkeeper, and paddy broker remained vague.

In the 1880s agents of Chettiar firms began to fan out over the Delta from Rangoon and other urban centers. They established branches in the larger villages of rural tracts and in towns along the railway line. Chettiar moneylenders supplied credit directly to the cultivator on a much larger scale, and enlarged their role as a source of capital for indigenous moneylenders. It became common practice for Burmese moneylenders to borrow from Chettiar firms at 2 percent per month and to lend to cultivators at 3 or 4 percent per month.[43] In addition, the lower rates of interest charged by the Chettiars forced Burmese moneylenders in many areas to scale down their rates.[44] From the 1890s until 1907, the normal *ngwedo* interest rate for loans on land security was 3 percent or less per month.[45]

In addition to professional moneylenders, established cultivators and large landholders gradually replaced friends or relatives as credit sources in newly settled areas. After building up his holdings for ten years, Maung Kyaw Din, a successful landlord in the Myaungmya District, began to lend money to new settlers moving into the area. His involvement in moneylending was paralleled by that of numerous other large landholders and established cultivators who often acquired their working capital from Chettiars.[46]

The Government of Burma also established facilities to provide credit for agriculturists beginning in the 1880s. Under the Land Improvement Loans Act of 1883 and the Agriculturists' Loans Act of 1884, funds were made available to cultivators at the low interest rate of 5 percent per year. Little use was made of these opportunities, however, because cultivators could obtain only limited amounts of capital after considerable inconvenience and delay.[47] Cooperative societies and a privately owned joint-stock bank for

42. *Settlement Reports–Hanthawaddy (1897–98)*, p. 16; *Bassein (1897–98)*, p. 14; *Toungoo (1898–99)*, p. 20; *Henzada (1900–1901)*, p. 10; *Pyapon (1906–7)*, p. 6.

43. Government of Burma, Revenue and Agriculture Proceedings, vol. 7237, May 1906, pp. 25–26; *Settlement Reports–Hanthawaddy (1897–98)*, p. 16; *Pegu (1898–99)*, p. 11; *Maubin (1904–5)*, p. 17.

44. R. E. V. Arbuthnot, "Note on the Burma Land Alienation Bill" (18 January 1910), in Government of Burma, Revenue and Agriculture Proceedings, vol. 8633, November 1911, p. 4; *Settlement Reports–Tharrawaddy (1901–2)*, p. 7; *Maubin (1904–5)*, p. 17.

45. *Settlement Reports–Tharrawaddy (1900–1901)*, p. 7; *Myaungmya-Thongwa (1903–4)*, p. 39; *Hanthawaddy (1903–4)*, p. 27. In some areas rates were considerably higher. See, for instance, *Toungoo Settlement Report (1898–99)*, p. 20.

46. *Myaungmya-Thongwa Settlement Report (1902–3)*, p. 118; Government of Burma, Revenue and Agriculture Proceedings, vol. 8633, November 1911, p. 496; *Pegu Settlement Report (1898–99)*, p. 11.

47. Government of Burma, Revenue and Agriculture Proceedings, vol. 8633, November 1911, pp. 497, 514, et passim; *Imperial Gazetteer of India* 9: 156. For a

agriculturists were also founded near the end of the first phase of development. Since their role prior to 1907 was minimal, they will be discussed in later chapters on the periods of transition and crisis in Burma's rice industry.

Short-term or crop loans which were normally repaid after the harvest became increasingly essential to agricultural production in Lower Burma. These loans, which may have been taken in several installments in this period just as they were in the 1920s and 1930s,[48] were used to meet cultivation costs, which included the wages and food of hired laborers, the costs of cattle replacement or cattle hire, and the depreciation on or purchase of agricultural implements. These costs and the amount taken for crop loans rose steadily in this period as the use of hired labor increased and the cost of goods and services rose in the expanding Delta economy.[49] The cultivator also borrowed on a long-term basis, which meant that he was not expected to repay the loan within five years, in order to expand his holdings.[50] Medium-term loans, which were repaid in two to five years, were taken to extend or repair *kazins,* to build granaries or a new house, to improve drainage works, or to purchase new or additional cattle.[51]

Despite the cultivator's need to borrow and the high rates of interest charged, agrarian debt was not a serious problem during the first phase of economic growth. Settlement officers estimated in both the 1880s and 1890s that over 70 percent of agricultural debts could be repaid within one year or at the end of the cropping season. At the same time, the percentage of indebted cultivators who were classified as "hopelessly" involved, or so heavily in debt they were likely to lose their land for failure to repay, was estimated to be only 3.7 and 5.4 percent in each decade. In the 1900–1907 period the proportion of debtors who could pay in a single season had fallen to 60 percent, and those hopelessly involved had risen to 9.5 percent, but these percentages were still far below those recorded in later decades.[52]

Agrarian debt tended to be the highest in tracts near large towns where

---

detailed list of the procedures required to obtain a loan under these acts see Government of Burma, Revenue and Agriculture Proceedings, vol. 7800, January 1908, pp. 5–6.

48. Government of Burma, *Report of the Burma Provincial Banking Enquiry Committee, 1929–30,* 3 vols. (Rangoon, 1930), 1: 76–77, hereafter cited as *Banking Enquiry Report.*

49. For cultivation costs by acre and holding for the various regions of Lower Burma between 1880 and 1910, see Adas, "Agrarian Development," p. 162, Table IV-E.

50. B. O. Binns, *Agricultural Economy in Burma* (Rangoon, 1948), p. 27.

51. Ibid., pp. 34, 36.

52. I have calculated these percentages from the averages in the sections on indebtedness in the district settlement reports for the periods in question. The average for the 1880s is based on a rather small sample because this information was not frequently given in the early settlement reports. For a discussion of the problems involved in the use of these statistics, see Adas, "Agrarian Development," app. 7, pp. 554–55.

moneylenders, paddy brokers, and other credit sources were more accessible and where holdings were generally larger.[53] Some revenue officials felt that another reason for the higher incidence of debt near urban areas was the fact that consumer goods were more readily available there and consequently cultivators generally attempted to maintain a higher standard of living.[54] The percentage and average amount of agrarian indebtedness was also high in areas where unoccupied lands were being brought under cultivation on a large scale,[55] and in more fertile tracts because moneylenders and paddy brokers were willing to lend large amounts to persons who could offer highly productive paddy land as security.[56] The amount owed also increased in direct proportion to the wealth of the borrower. J. S. Furnivall has suggested that debt in Lower Burma was an index of prosperity, not poverty, for:

> . . . the richer a man is, the more money he wants to borrow. A cultivator with a hundred acres who owes Rs. 10,000 is richer than a peasant who cultivates five acres and owes Rs. 20, just as a Company with a capital of ten crores of rupees is richer than a bazaar seller with the capital of a few hundred rupees.[57]

At times, however, the high percentage of indebtedness in an area reflected the cultivators' inability to work their holdings consistently at a profit. In some tracts large debts were incurred because of periodic flooding which destroyed crops and forced cultivators to turn to moneylenders for assistance.[58] In tracts in the upper Delta districts, holdings were too small to be worked at a profit in the highly competitive Delta economy. In these areas, if subsidiary occupations such as agricultural labor or carting were not resorted to, cultivators often fell heavily in debt.[59]

The dominant characteristic of rural social structure in Lower Burma during the first phase of agrarian development was its great fluidity. Not only was there a high degree of mobility between different social strata, but the social strata themselves were difficult to distinguish and highly mutable. For the

53. *Settlement Reports–Prome (1884–85)*, p. 3; *Thongwa (1890–91)*, p. 18; *Bassein (1897–98)*, p. 121; Government of Burma, Revenue and Agriculture Proceedings, vol. 4886, March 1896, p. 6.

54. *Bassein Settlement Report (1897–98)*, p. 12.

55. See Table IV-G in Adas, "Agrarian Development," p. 172.

56. *Settlement Reports–Bassein (1881–82)*, p. 8; *Bassein-Henzada (1884–85)*, p. 8; *Toungoo (1898–99)*, p. 20; *Toungoo (1899–1900)*, p. 36; *Prome (1900–1901)*, p. 10.

57. Furnivall, *Political Economy*, pp. 107–8. See also *RLAC*, pt. 3, p. 77.

58. *Settlement Reports–Tharrawaddy (1880–81)*, p. 8; *Thaton (1897–98)*, p. 25.

59. *Bassein Settlement Report (1882–83)*, p. 7; and a "Note" by W. T. Hall appended to Philip Nolan's *Report on Emigration from Bengal to Burma and How to Promote It* (Calcutta, 1888), p. 2.

purpose of analysis, persons involved in paddy production can be divided into four main groups: landlords, cultivator-owners, tenants, and landless agricultural laborers. In the last half of the nineteenth century, it was possible for an individual beginning as a landless laborer to work his way upward until he eventually attained the status of a large landholder. The number of persons who began as laborers and rose to become landlords was small, but large numbers of agriculturists moved one or two notches up or down the social scale. Tenants became cultivator-owners, and laborers aspired to become tenants. Some cultivator-owners extended their holdings until they achieved the status of landlords, while others who were less fortunate lost their lands and were forced to rent or move about the Delta in search of employment as seasonal laborers.

The activities and class attributes of persons who were theoretically classified in different social groups varied from region to region and often overlapped. Large landholders in some areas worked a portion of their holdings along with their hired laborers and let the rest to tenants.[60] The holdings of persons classified as cultivator-owners in many of the districts of the lower Delta and the large amounts of hired labor which they employed would have elevated them to the status of landlords in many areas of India or elsewhere in Southeast Asia.[61] Some cultivator-owners worked both their own holdings and land rented from others, while others worked as agricultural laborers. Some owners participated in cropping operations, while others merely supervised their laborers.[62] Tenants worked in neighboring fields as hired laborers when they had finished a particular operation on the holding which they were renting. They also saved to purchase their own holding or to enable them to clear and cultivate land on the rice frontier.[63]

Until the first years of the twentieth century the area held by persons classified as large landholders, or those who owned more than 100 acres, made up only a small percentage of the total occupied area in Lower Burma. In fact, in 1905–6, at the end of the first phase of development, only 18

60. *Settlement Reports–Thongwa (1889–90)*, p. 16; *Thaton (1894–95)*, pp. 42–43; *Myaungmya (1897–98)*, p. 15; *Hanthawaddy (1898–99)*, pp. 16–17; *Myaungmya-Thongwa (1902–3)*, p. 10; *Myaungmya (1903–4)*, p. 13.

61. Compare, for example, the average holding of 60 acres in the Hanthawaddy District in the early 1900s with the 71 acres of large estates of Oudh in North India (J.S. Furnivall, "Industrial Agriculture," *Journal of the Burma Research Society* 48, no. 1 [June 1965]: 93).

62. J. P. Hardiman, *Compilation on Tenancy Matters* (Rangoon, 1913), p. 30; *Settlement Reports–Tharrawaddy (1880–81)*, p. 12; *Bassein (1897–98)*, p. 35; *Pegu (1899–1900)*, p. 32; *Hanthawaddy (1897–98)*, p. 16; *Henzada (1899–1900)*, p. 11; *Prome (1903–4)*, p. 9.

63. Government of Burma, Revenue and Agriculture Proceedings, vol. 5107, July 1897, p. 43; *Settlement Reports–Thongwa (1889–90)*, p. 16; *Henzada (1899–1900)*, p. 26; *Prome (1900–1901)*, p. 22; *Myaungmya-Thongwa (1902–3)*, p. 15.

percent of the occupied land in the Delta was owned by nonagriculturists. Of the land alienated to nonagriculturists, 40 percent was held by resident landlords, or those who lived within three miles of their holdings, and 60 percent was held by nonresident owners.[64] The incidence of land alienation to nonagriculturists was the highest in the frontier districts of the tidal Delta and in the districts near Rangoon town where rice production was the most market oriented and where agricultural credit was the most available and agrarian indebtedness the highest. Large estates also tended to be concentrated in circles (*taiks*) near major market centers, along railway lines or major waterways, and in newly occupied areas.[65]

Until the first decade of the twentieth century, most landlords were (or at least began as) agriculturists.[66] Maung Kyaw Din, who was mentioned above, is a superb example of a small landholder who rose to become a large landlord. Kyaw Din migrated to the Maulamyainggyun area of the Myaungmya District from Upper Burma in 1875. When he arrived, the tract was covered with jungle and, with the exception of a few families of fishermen, devoid of inhabitants. He and his family built a hut and after obtaining permission from the nearest subdivisional officer, they cleared and began to cultivate a small holding. In the first years Kyaw Din worked his land without draft animals, plow, or hired laborers in the manner described above. In order to earn extra cash, he sold firewood and bamboo on the side. Kyaw Din's paddy production rose gradually from 150 (forty-six pound) baskets in the first year to 1,000 baskets by the fifth year. At that time he sold 700 baskets for over Rs. 500 profit and bought a pair of bullocks. In the sixth year his holdings were greatly enlarged and produced 2,000 baskets. By the tenth year after his arrival his output reached 4,000 baskets, and he employed ten laborers and three yokes of cattle. During the land boom of the 1890s he lent money on a large scale to new settlers and in many cases added new holdings to his estate through foreclosure of mortgages given as security on loans which were not repaid.

By the first decade of the twentieth century Kyaw Din owned 750 acres, thirty draft animals which he rented out at a profit of Rs. 1000 annually, and a house worth Rs. 5,000. He had also financed the building of a *kyaung* (Buddhist monastery) and pagoda in his village, which cost an estimated Rs.

64. For landownership percentages for the Delta as a whole and by regions, see Adas, "Agrarian Development," Table IV-H, p. 178.

65. Ibid., pp. 178, 558–59; *Settlement Reports–Thongwa (1890–91)*, appendices; *Thaton (1894–95)*, pp. 42–43; *Myaungmya (1897–98)*, app. A; *Pegu (1898–99)*, p. 27; *Prome (1900–1901)*, p. 19; *Maubin (1904–5)*, app. S; *Pyapon (1906–7)*, app. B; Government of Burma, Revenue and Agriculture Proceedings, vol. 6743, July 1903, p. 34.

66. Government of Burma, Revenue and Agriculture Proceedings, vol. 5107, July 1897, p. 44, December 1897, p. 13.

23,000. In the first years of the twentieth century Kyaw Din began to speculate in paddy. At the height of his affluence he handled some 5,000 baskets in a single season. Shortly thereafter he retired, leaving great wealth and extensive holdings to his six sons, who were also agriculturists.[67] Kyaw Din was only one of thousands of diligent cultivators who achieved positions of wealth and local importance on the Delta frontier in the early phase of growth when land was readily available and the demand for and price of paddy rose almost continually.

The great majority of nonagriculturist landlords in Lower Burma were moneylenders, paddy brokers, and village shopkeepers whose activities, as I have noted above, often overlapped. Members of these groups usually acquired large holdings through foreclosures on mortgages which were used by cultivators as security for loans.[68] The alienation of land to moneylenders and traders was particularly severe in tracts which were being brought under cultivation for the first time. The small capital which the new settler possessed, the hazards he confronted, and the small initial output of his holdings often resulted in debts so large that he could not repay them. He was then forced to give up his land to his creditors.[69] Saya Thit, who originally migrated to the Delta from Pakokku in the Dry Zone, began his ascent to landlord status as a trader in the Bogale area of Pyapon. After accumulating about Rs. 1,000, he bought a piece of land which he cultivated himself. In succeeding years he loaned increasing amounts to new settlers and began to build an estate through foreclosures. By the early 1900s Saya Thit owned over four hundred acres, thirty-seven draft animals, and employed forty-two laborers. He also owned several houses and had become the *thugyi* of Bogale. Like Kyaw Din, he began to speculate on the paddy market shortly after the turn of the century, and his holdings and affluence seemed destined to increase manifold.[70] Unlike Saya Thit, few moneylenders or traders personally cultivated land which they acquired. Normally the land was let out to tenants, but occasionally it was resold at a profit.

The third major group of landlords was composed of land "grabbers" who acquired estates by a variety of methods. Since squatter-cultivators could not sell or mortgage their holdings until they had worked them for twelve years, loans were often extended by land grabbers in return for "veiled" mortgages which were not reported to the revenue authorities. There was a clear

67. *Myaungmya-Thongwa Settlement Report, (1902–3),* app. A, p. 118.

68. See citations in footnote 69 and also *Settlement Reports–Bassein (1881–82),* p. 3, *(1882–83)*, p. 11; *Bassein-Henzada (1884–85),* p. 9; *Maungmya-Thongwa (1902–3),* p. 10.

69. Government of Burma, Revenue and Agriculture Proceedings, vol. 8633, November 1911, p. 299; Government of Burma, *Report on the Suspension of Grants in the Hanthawaddy District* (Rangoon, 1910), p. 24; *Thaton Settlement Report (1894–95),* p. 54.

70. *Myaungmya-Thongwa Settlement Report (1902–3),* app. B, p. 118.

understanding between cultivator and creditor that should the former fail to meet his payments, his land would become the property of the lender. If a cultivator defaulted, his land was "sold" to the land grabber at the end of the twelve-year period.[71] Land grabbers also purchased large tracts of land which they registered in the names of their agents and retainers. Their retainers, who were often deeply in debt to them, cultivated the land for the land grabbers in much the same manner as tenants. These two patterns concealed substantial amounts of land held by nonagriculturists and caused their share to be consistently underestimated in government reports.[72] Some land grabbers also acquired their holdings through illegal measures which often involved collusion with indigenous revenue officials. One widely employed technique was vividly described by the settlement officer for the Myaungmya District:

> The Revenue Surveyor for reasons of his own takes his *kwin* map and draws on it a "trapezium" floating in space and enters it in Register I as the property of his friend Maung Pyu, Trader, who sinks a little capital by paying revenue on an imaginary holding for a few years, whilst Maung Me, the *bona-fide* agriculturist is clearing a holding for himself in the jungle. When the clearing has been fully cultivated, Maung Pyu's trapezium is discovered to float on this very spot and Maung Me on being sued for possession of the holding is confronted with Maung Pyu's tax tickets and discovers for the first time that he is merely an agent with no claim on the land whatsoever.[73]

Land grabbers usually let their lands to tenants or placed agents in charge of cropping operations and provided the capital required to hire laborers and bullocks.

In addition to moneylenders, traders, and land grabbers, nonagriculturist landlords were drawn from a wide range of occupational groups including lawyers, government clerks, merchants located in urban centers, retired *thugyis,* schoolteachers, and doctors.[74] Urban firms often owned large amounts of land. The Hon Tein Company of Rangoon, for instance, controlled 2,358 acres of land in the Myaungmya District which was let out to tenants.[75] Another firm acquired large holdings in the Toungoo District

71. Government of Burma, *Report on the Suspension of Grants,* p. 13; *RLAC,* pt. 2, p. 40; Furnivall, *Political Economy,* p. 62.

72. Government of Burma, *Report on the Suspension of Grants,* pp. 16–17; Furnivall, *Political Economy,* p. 61.

73. *Myaungmya Settlement Report (1903–4),* pp. 12–13. See also *Bassein Settlement Report (1912–13),* p. 43.

74. Aye Hlaing, "Trends of Growth," p. 127; *Settlement Reports–Bassein (1884–85),* p. 15; *Thaton (1894–95),* p. 43; *Pegu (1898–99),* appendices, pp. cxxiii–cxxxix; *Pegu (1897–98),* p. 27.

75. *Myaungmya-Thongwa Settlement Report (1902–3),* p. 15.

through an agent named Packeri Sawmy, who was a retired stationmaster. In 1898–99 the firm owned nearly 653 acres outright and held mortgages on an additional 3,300 acres.[76] Throughout the last half of the nineteenth century land was the most secure, profitable, and frequently chosen investment outlet for persons who had accumulated capital through trade, in the professions, or in government service. The steady rise in the price of paddy was paralleled by a similar increase in the value of land. Wealth, status, and local influence were the rewards earned by those individuals who were able to acquire substantial holdings of rich paddy land.

In the early phase of economic growth those members of the second and largest social group in rural Burma, the cultivator-owners, who overcame the difficulties involved in clearing and cultivating new lands in the Delta were well rewarded for their years of assiduous toil. Since most agriculturists owned the land that they worked and their average debt was usually small, a large share of the profits of paddy production went to the cultivators themselves. A comparison of the average annual expenditures and income of landowning families engaged in rice production gives some indication of the standard of living and level of prosperity enjoyed by cultivator-owners in the Delta. In Table 5 I have attempted to draw up a cultivator's balance sheet for selected districts at different times during the 1880–1907 period, which is covered by the settlement report statistics. Since the cultivator ceased to market his own surplus in most areas by the late 1880s, the price he received would have been less than the district market price which was used to determine his gross income. Therefore, the incomes and positive balances for cultivators in the late 1890s and the early 1900s would have been somewhat less than those listed. Marked regional variations in levels of income and expenditure notwithstanding, these figures support the claims of revenue officers that cultivator-owners were for the most part solvent and prosperous during the last decades of the nineteenth century.[77]

The well-being of cultivator-owners and agriculturists generally was also reflected in the substantial dwellings which they built in many areas. Successful agriculturists often lived in houses made of wood rather than the traditional thatch and bamboo. Corrugated iron roofs, which were considered signs of prosperity, were common in the villages of many tracts.[78] Iron roofing was also one of the more visible manifestations of the spread of

76. *Toungoo Settlement Report (1898–99)*, p. 25.

77. Most settlement officers concluded that the agriculturists in the tracts they surveyed were generally well off. Their assertions, however, have little meaning without supporting evidence such as that set forth in Table 5.

78. *Settlement Reports–Bassein (1879–80)*, p. 14; *Thaton (1897–98)*, p. 24; *Henzada (1899–1900)*, p. 11; *Tharrawaddy (1900–1901)*, p. 6; *Maubin (1904–5)*, p. 7; *Maubin, Myaungmya*, and *Pyapon (1905–6)*, p. 9; Nisbet, *British Burma*, 2: 93–94.

Table 5. The Cultivator's Balance Sheet, 1880–1907 (in rupees)

District	Year	Income[a]	Expenditure[b]	Balance
Hanthawaddy	1880–81	1172.5	849.7	322.8
Bassein	1880–81	693	437.4	255.6
Tharrawaddy	1880–81	494	262.8	231.2
Thongwa	1890–91	787.2	519.1	268.1
Hanthawaddy	1897–98	1531.7	1265.3	266.4
Toungoo	1898–99	386.2	309.2	77
Henzada	1899–1900	702.5	451.4	251.1
Pyapon	1906–7	1134.8	737.1	397.7

Sources: Sections and tables on the cost of living, cost of cultivation, average production per acre, and size of holdings from district settlement reports for the dates indicated. Paddy prices taken from Grant, *Rice Crop,* app. 1, p. 48, and Hardiman, *Compilation,* pp. iv–v.

Note: The average cost of living and cost of cultivation estimates listed in the settlement reports vary widely in quality and can at best be viewed as approximations (see appendix, section 5). Paddy grown for home consumption and used for seed was normally included in the costs of living and cultivation, and thus it is deducted from the gross income in determining the cultivator's balance by the above method. Because no income averages are available in the early reports, I have had to calculate these in the manner indicated in the table. My attempts to select reports which seemed to have the most accurate estimates were somewhat hampered by the fact that all the averages required were sometimes not listed in individual reports.

[a] Income equals average paddy production in (forty-six pound) baskets per acre times the value in rupees of a (forty-six pound) basket of paddy times the number of acres in an average holding.

[b] Expenditure equals cost of living plus cost of cultivation plus capitation and land taxes (equal to about 15 percent of the gross income). Payments on the interest and/or principal on loans are not included in the expenditures listed below.

foreign consumer goods among Burmese agriculturists. European and Indian textiles and cheap consumer items like kerosene lamps, canned milk, biscuits or sardines, mosquito nets, soap, and European glassware or crockery were found in all but the poorest villages. In the more fertile tracts cultivator-owners' (as well as landlords') houses commonly contained European furniture, mirrors, artificial flowers, gramophones, English lamps, looking glasses, metal safes or chests, and clocks. Their walls were decorated with portraits of Queen Victoria and Kaiser Wilhelm, Christmas cards, and pictures cut from the illustrated magazines of the day.[79] The alacrity with which Burmese agriculturists developed a taste for a wide range of foreign consumer items was perhaps best epitomized by a Burmese peasant whom a settlement officer spied "smoking a French briar pipe and suckling his motherless babe with an English nursing bottle containing Swiss condensed milk."[80] The widespread diffusion of foreign consumer goods not only reflected the prosperity of the agrarian classes; it also demonstrated that the increased availability of consumer items had played an important role in stimulating surplus paddy production which was the basis of the rice-export economy in Lower Burma.

In most areas of the Delta during the first phase of development tenants enjoyed a standard of living which was roughly comparable to that of cultivator-owners.[81] Settlement officers usually found it difficult to distinguish the two groups and noted that agriculturists who worked their own land often rented additional land in order to increase their income. In some cases, cultivator-owners found it more profitable to let out their own holdings and rent from another landholder.[82] Even those tenants who did not own land were generally in a strong position. Because rental rates were normally fixed and low and tenant holdings were large, it was possible for diligent tenants to clear substantial profits. Tenants could, and often did, use their profits to purchase their own holdings or to clear unoccupied land on the rice frontier. For this reason, tenants usually regarded their position as temporary—as one stage in their progress upward to landholder status.

Until the first decade of the twentieth century the tenants' well-being, mobility, and strong bargaining position vis-à-vis the landlord were insured by the large amounts of unoccupied land available in Lower Burma. They were also supported by the fact that the demand for tenants in most areas far exceeded the supply. A landlord could not afford to oppress his tenants

79. *Settlement Reports–Bassein (1880–81)*, p. 10; *Hanthawaddy-Pegu (1882–83)*, p. 9; *Pegu (1898–99)*, p. 10; *Hanthawaddy (1897–98)*, p. 7; *Bassein (1897–98)*, p. 10; *Myaungmya (1897–98)*, pp. 6–7; *Myaungmya-Thongwa (1902–3)*, p. 10; Government of Burma, Revenue and Agriculture Proceedings, vol. 4043, November 1892, p. 146. In some areas of the upper Delta and the less fertile tracts of other regions the absence of foreign consumer goods was noted. See, for example, *Settlement Reports–Prome (1900–1901)*, p. 9; *Tharrawaddy (1900–1901)*, p. 6; *Myaungmya (1903–4)*, p. 6.

80. *Myaungmya-Bassein Settlement Report (1901–2)*, p. 8.

81. *Settlement Reports–Tharrawaddy (1881–82)*, p. 8; *Bassein-Henzada (1884–85)*, p. 16; *Myaungmya (1897–98)*, p. 16; *Toungoo (1898–99)*, p. 19; *Henzada (1900–1901)*, p. 15; *Tharrawaddy (1900–1901)*, p. 9; *Hanthawaddy (1903–4)*, p. 6; *Myaungmya-Bassein (1901–2)*, p. 12; *Myaungmya-Thongwa (1902–3)*, p. 15. There were areas where tenants were far less well off. See, for instance, *Thongwa (1889–90)*, p. 16, (*1890–91*), p. 24; *Pegu (1898–99)*, p. 28.

82. See above, footnote 65, and also *Settlement Reports–Hanthawaddy (1897–98)*, p. 16; *Tharrawaddy (1900–1901)*, p. 81.

because they would either abandon his lands and move to those of another landlord who offered more favorable terms or migrate to the frontier and take up holdings of their own.[83] The fact that tenants often took advantage of these opportunities is clearly indicated by the highly transitory nature of their tenures. Leases were ordinarily signed for only one year, and tenants seldom remained on the same holding more than two or three years.[84] As late as the first decade of the twentieth century, only about 10 percent of the total tenants had worked the same holding for five years or more. The remaining 90 percent had moved on to other areas, purchased their own holdings, or migrated to the frontier to clear unoccupied land.[85] In this period the high rate of turnover normally reflected the tenants' desire to improve their condition and not the landlords' ability to replace their tenants with others who promised to pay higher rents.[86] In some areas the demand for tenants exceeded the supply to such a degree that landlords were forced to let their lands rent free. The tenant agreed to work the holding and pay the land revenue on it. Although this practice allowed the landlord to retain his holdings, he derived no profit from them.[87]

In addition to cultivator-owners who rented additional land, tenants in Lower Burma were drawn from three main groups: migrants from Upper Burma, young agriculturists starting out on their own, and small landholders who had lost their lands through debt. In-migrants from the Dry Zone often rented land for several seasons after their arrival in the Delta in order to earn capital which they needed to claim their own holdings. There was usually a strong correspondence between an increase in tenancy in a given area and an influx of migrants.[88] Although most in-migrants who rented lands intended to settle in the Delta on a permanent basis, some temporary migrants from the Dry Zone rented lands for one to three years and then returned to Upper Burma with their profits.[89] Young agriculturists also rented lands in the first

83. Government of Burma, Revenue and Agriculture Proceedings, vol. 5107, July 1897, p. 44; *Prome Settlement Report (1903–4)*, pp. 9–10.

84. *Settlement Reports–Bassein-Henzada (1884–85)*, p. 16; *Maubin, Myaungmya, and Pyapon (1905–6)*, p. 15; *Pyapon (1906–7)*, p. 13.

85. These percentages were derived from the tenancy statistics in Hardiman, *Compilation*, and the *Land Revenue Reports, 1901–2, 1905–6.*

86. Government of Burma, Revenue and Agriculture Proceedings, vol. 5107, July 1897, p. 43; *Bassein Settlement Report (1897–98)*, p. 35.

87. Hardiman, *Compilation*, quoting the revenue secretary's File 10A-1, 1895, p. 68; *Settlement Reports–Toungoo (1898–99)*, p. 19; *Myaungmya-Bassein (1901–2)*, p. 11; Government of Burma, Revenue and Agriculture Proceedings, vol. 4886, March 1896, pp. 45, 48.

88. *Land Revenue Report, 1901–2*, p. 30; Hardiman, *Compilation*, p. 40; *Settlement Reports–Bassein-Henzada (1884–85)*, pp. 26–27; *Thongwa (1890–91)*, pp. 24, 26; *Bassein (1898–99)*, p. 22.

89. Hardiman, *Compilation*, p. 64; *Myaungmya-Thongwa Settlement Report (1902–3)*, pp. 5, 15–16.

years after leaving their parental homes. Like most migrants, young men regarded their tenant status as temporary. They viewed tenancy as the best means of acquiring the capital which was required to purchase or clear their own holdings. They often rented from their own parents or relatives and consequently paid lower rates.[90] At times, both migrants and young agriculturists started out as agricultural laborers and after a season or two became tenants, a move which placed them one step closer to their goal of becoming cultivator-owners.[91]

Although tenancy was a means of upward mobility for some agriculturists, for others it represented a loss of status and a failure to retain their own holdings. A large majority of permanent tenants in the Delta were former cultivator-owners who had become so deeply indebted that they were forced to give up their land to their creditors. If an indebted small landholder did not abandon his mortgaged land and migrate to another area of the Delta, he was often allowed to continue cultivating, as a rent-paying tenant, the land which he had formerly owned. This pattern was particularly pronounced in newly settled tracts where debts and loss of land through the foreclosure of mortgages were abnormally high. Since many ex-owners remained deeply indebted to their new landlords, they tended to work the same holding for long periods of time and to be more susceptible to periodic increases in rental rates.[92] Another group which contributed large numbers to the ranks of permanent tenants were cultivators who acted as agents for large landlords and land grabbers.[93]

Since many persons classified as agriculturists let part of their holdings, the area worked by tenants in Lower Burma exceeded that alienated to nonagriculturists. The percentage of the occupied area cultivated by tenants rose steadily from 9 percent in 1885–86 to 25 percent in 1905–6.[94] The amount of land worked by tenants was the highest in the same areas where land alienation was the most pronounced, and for many of the same reasons (see above). The incidence of tenancy was particularly high in frontier tracts where young agriculturists, migrants from Upper Burma, and land grabbers

90. Hardiman, *Compilation,* pp. 39, 44; *Settlement Reports–Thongwa (1889–90),* p. 16, *(1890–91),* p. 26; *RAB, 1883–84,* p. 5, *1885–86,* p. 6.

91. *Settlement Reports–Bassein-Henzada (1883–84),* pp. 11–12; *Thongwa (1889–90),* p. 16.

92. *Settlement Reports–Hanthawaddy (1879–80),* p. 16; *Bassein (1881–82),* p. 9; *Bassein (1897–98),* p. 35; *Maubin (1904–5),* p. 14.

93. Government of Burma, Revenue and Agriculture Proceedings, vol. 8633, November 1911, p. 299; *Settlement Reports–Bassein (1898–99),* p. 21; *Myaungmya-Bassein (1901–2),* p. 11; *Toungoo (1898–99),* p. 25.

94. For a regional breakdown of the amount of occupied area let to tenants at five-year intervals between 1885 and 1906, see Adas, "Agrarian Development," Table IV-K, p. 193.

were the most active. Tenant holdings were also more numerous near large towns, railways, and navigable rivers and in areas protected by government embankments.[95]

Until the late 1880s the normal rate charged on lands let at full rents amounted to about 10 percent of the gross output of the tenant's holding. In most cases the tenant also paid the land revenue.[96] In the last decades of the nineteenth century the customary rent of 10 percent gave way to rents fixed in advance, which varied from 10 percent on poorer soils to as much as 33 percent of the gross output on more fertile holdings.[97] These increases are reflected in an overall rise in the rent per acre on Delta holdings from Rs. 4.1 in 1885–86 to Rs. 10.2 in 1905–6.[98] Despite this rise and the fact that rents were increasingly fixed at the beginning of the cropping season, most landlords granted remissions in bad seasons or when a tenant's paddy crop was diminished by floods or insect pests.[99]

Since most tenants paid their rent in paddy rather than cash, average rates were calculated in terms of local paddy prices. For this reason, many revenue officials attributed rising rent rates primarily to increases in the price of paddy.[100] However, paddy price trends did not always correspond to steadily rising rental rates during the period in question. In most districts rent increases were paralleled by price rises between 1885–86 and 1895–96 and both later rose sharply after 1904. In the decade between 1895–96 and 1903–4, however, paddy prices fell for several years and then leveled off, while the average rent per acre rose from six to nearly ten rupees.[101] It is clear, therefore, that paddy prices alone did not determine the level of rent rates. Equally important factors were growing competition for tenant positions and a general increase in the cost of living. Higher rent rates were also caused in some instances by the movement of large numbers of migrants

95. *Settlement Reports–Toungoo (1899–1900)*, p. 41, and maps; *Hanthawaddy (1899–1900)*, tenancy tables and maps; *Henzada (1900–1901)*, pp. 16, 27, and maps; *Myaungmya (1903–4)*, p. 44, and maps.

96. Anonymous, *Words on Tenure*, p. 5; Hardiman, *Compilation*, pp. 24, 42; *Settlement Reports–Bassein (1881–82)*, p. 9, (*1882–83*), p. 11; *Hanthawaddy (1880–81)*, p. 14; *Hanthawaddy-Pegu (1884–85)*, p. 28; *Tharrawaddy-Prome (1883–84)*, p. 9.

97. *RAB, 1884–85*, p. 6; Baden-Powell, *Land Systems*, 3: 492; *Settlement Reports–Henzada (1899–1900)*, p. 24; *Tharrawaddy (1902–3)*, p. 9; *Myaungmya-Thongwa (1902–3)*, p. 15; *Pyapon (1906–7)*, p. 13.

98. See Adas, "Agrarian Development," Table IV-M, p. 197.

99. *Settlement Reports–Hanthawaddy (1899–1900)*, p. 14; *Henzada (1899–1900)*, p. 25; Hardiman, *Compilation*, p. 42.

100. Hardiman, *Compilation*, "Explanatory Note," secs. 4, 5; Government of Burma, Revenue and Agriculture Proceedings, vol. 4486, December 1894, p. 33, vol. 5107, December 1897, p. 13; Nisbet, *British Burma*, 2: 280.

101. See Adas, "Agrarian Development," p. 197; and the local paddy price statistics in Hardiman, *Compilation*, pp. iv–v.

into a particular region.[102] Despite these increases, the fact that tenants' living and cultivation costs were somewhat lower than those of cultivator-owners allowed most of them to clear profits or at least to break even in good or average seasons.[103] Their ability to do so would last as long as cultivable, unoccupied land was readily available in the Delta.

The low population density and large amounts of unoccupied land that were primarily responsible for the solvency and mobility of tenants in Lower Burma also worked to the advantage of landless agricultural laborers. The demand for laborers, like that for tenants, far exceeded the supply in most areas. The importance of a favorable population-to-land ratio to the well-being of agricultural laborers is indicated by differences in wage rates in various regions. In the districts of the lower Delta where holdings were too large to be worked by familial labor alone, where unoccupied land was readily available, and where the population density was low, laborers' wages exceeded the Lower Burma average. In the upper Delta, on the other hand, where many holdings were small enough to be worked without the assistance of hired laborers, where there was little cultivable open land, and where the supply of laborers was often greater than the demand, the wages of agricultural laborers were well below the Lower Burma average.[104] Interregional differences in wage levels were so pronounced that seasonal laborers from Upper Burma generally bypassed districts in the upper Delta and sought employment primarily in the tidal frontier districts, in the districts around Rangoon town, and in Thaton.[105]

Agricultural laborers were drawn chiefly from three groups: seasonal and permanent migrants from Upper Burma, temporary migrants from India, and local agriculturists who held no land of their own. Most seasonal in-migrants from Upper Burma arrived in the Delta at the beginning of the plowing season in May or June and returned to the Dry Zone in February after the harvest. Some migrated to Lower Burma only in time for the harvest, which began in late November, and remained during the dry season (January–April) to cut and cart firewood. Once a seasonal migrant had found an area where wages were satisfactory, he would return year after year, often to the same

102. *Settlement Reports–Myaungmya (1897–98)*, p. 16; *Bassein (1897–98)*, p. 34; *Henzada (1899–1900)*, pp. 24–25; *Myaungmya-Thongwa (1902–3)*, p. 15.

103. For comparisons on cost of cultivation see *Settlement Reports–Henzada (1900–1901); Hanthawaddy (1897–98), (1899–1900); Myaungmya-Thongwa (1902–3);* and on the cost of living see *Settlement Reports–Myaungmya-Bassein (1901–2); Myaungmya (1903–4); Maubin (1904–5); Maubin, Myaungmya, and Pyapon (1905–6).*

104. Compare *Settlement Reports–Thongwa (1890–92)*, p. 17; *Pegu (1898–99)*, p. 14; *Hanthawaddy (1903–4)*, p. 41; *Pyapon (1906–7)*, pp. 6–7; and *Settlement Reports–Henzada (1899–1900)*, p. 14; *Prome (1903–4)*, p. 7.

105. *Settlement Reports–Toungoo (1899–1900)*, p. 15; *Prome (1900–1901)*, p. 11.

employer.[106] Indian laborers included both migrants who had come to Burma to work as full-time agriculturists and Indian millworkers and dock coolies who reaped paddy on a part-time basis during the slack season for the mills.[107] Local labor was employed mainly in the upper Delta districts, where holdings were often not large enough to support a cultivator's family and substantial numbers of agriculturists were without land. In many of the larger villages in Prome and Henzada, a portion of the population was made up of permanent, landless laborers who supported their families by working on nearby landlords' estates and assisting small landholders in transplanting and reaping their paddy. In some instances, cultivators paid their sons regular laborer's wages to work their fields.[108]

In the first phase of agrarian development laborers were usually hired for the entire cropping season of nine months, or separately for the plowing season from June to October and the reaping season from late November to January. Day laborers, who were often women, were ordinarily hired only for transplanting and in some tracts for reaping.[109] Wages for the entire cropping season and the reaping season were normally paid in paddy at the end of the harvest. Those for the plowing season were also paid in kind, but at the end of the season itself.[110] Although money wages were recorded for day laborers and gang reapers as early as the 1880s, cash payments for seasonal laborers were rare prior to 1907.[111] Whether cash or paddy payments were employed, most landowners provided food for their laborers in addition to their regular wages.

Wage trends for agricultural laborers in the first phase of development can be illustrated by comparing the average rates paid for the plowing season in different decades. In the 1880s the average wages for the Delta as a whole ranged from about Rs. 50–80 plus food. In the 1890s average rates for the plowing season rose slightly to Rs. 55–78 plus food, and they remained fairly stable at Rs. 60–76 plus food in the 1900–1907 period. Wages for the whole cropping season of nine months rose from a Delta average of Rs. 60–110 plus food in the 1880s to an average of Rs. 102–122 in the 1900–1907 period.[112]

106. *RAB, 1884–85,* p. 63; *Settlement Reports–Pegu (1897–98),* p. 9, (*1898–99*), p. 14; *Myaungmya-Thongwa (1902–3),* p. 5.

107. For a detailed discussion of Indian activities and patterns, see Chapter 5 on the plural society.

108. *Settlement Reports–Henzada (1900–1901),* p. 11; *Henzada (Certain Areas–1900–1901),* p. 2; *Toungoo (1899–1900),* p. 15; *Pegu (1899–1900),* p. 17.

109. Government of Burma, Revenue and Agriculture Proceedings, vol. 7513, August 1907, p. 29; *Bassein Settlement Report (1880–81),* pp. 3, 29.

110. Government of Burma, Revenue and Agriculture Proceedings, vol. 7513, August 1907, pp. 22, 29; Hall, "Note," pp. i–iii.

111. *Settlement Reports–Henzada (1900–1901),* p. 11; *Maubin (1904–5),* p. 10.

112. I have calculated these averages from the wages cited in Hall's, "Note," passim; the Revenue and Agriculture Proceedings of the Government of Burma, passim; and the district settlement reports for this period.

Because most of the wage estimates which were used to calculate these averages were stated initially in baskets of paddy, my conversions into monetary equivalents reflect to some extent general increases in the price of goods and services. Therefore, the increases traced represent fairly well the gains in real wages received by agricultural laborers.

The prosperous condition of the cultivating classes of Lower Burma in the last half of the nineteenth century contrasts sharply with their unenviable state in the 1920s and 1930s, which has been emphasized in the writings of historians from Furnivall to Cheng. A high degree of social mobility and general economic well-being characterized rural society in the Delta in this period. Thus, in its early stages the making of a modern, market economy in Lower Burma was impressive not only in terms of paddy exported and the number of rice mills constructed, but also in terms of the benefits derived by agriculturists who constituted the great majority of Burma's population.

4

INDIAN IMMIGRATION TO LOWER BURMA IN THE FIRST PHASE OF DEVELOPMENT

During the first years after the 1852 annexation, British officials felt that migration from the Dry Zone and other areas within Burma would not be sufficient to satisfy the demand for agricultural and industrial labor in the Delta.[1] In retrospect, it seems logical that these officials would come to regard India as the chief source of potential immigrant settlers and laborers for Lower Burma. Burma was part of the Indian Empire, many of the Indian districts which fringed the Bay of Bengal were densely populated and famine-prone, and sea communications between the Indian subcontinent and Lower Burma were rapidly improving. Although some officials did assert that India should be the main source of immigrants,[2] others, including the Chief-Commissioner, Arthur Phayre, initially sought to attract immigrants from China. Chinese immigrants were employed on a number of early public works projects, and proposals were made for schemes to attract Chinese settlers to the Delta. Officials, like Phayre, argued that preference should be given to the Chinese because they were more like the Burmese than the Indians, and because they were far superior to either the Indians or the Burmese in "skill and industry."[3]

1. *RAP, 1855–56,* par. 237.
2. Ibid.
3. *RAP, 1856–57,* par. 177; Government of India, Secret and Political Correspondence, range 201, vol. 15, 20 February 1857, no. 842; Government of India, Political

These early proposals notwithstanding, Chinese immigrants were to play only a secondary role in the development of the Delta. In 1901, after half a century of British rule, the Chinese community in Lower Burma numbered only about 34,400, or less than .8 of 1 percent of the total population.[4] A number of factors accounted for the low level of Chinese immigration to Burma. To begin with, most Chinese immigrants to Lower Burma and the rest of Southeast Asia were from the provinces of Fukien and Kwangtung in South China and they normally traveled by sea.[5] Burma was at the far end of the sea routes from these areas, and there was no regular steamship service between China and Burma on a scale comparable to that between South China and Siam and other Southeast Asian areas.[6] In addition, the Chinese community in Burma was small and uninfluential compared to well-established communities in Siam, Malaya, Indo-China, the Philippines, and the Netherlands Indies. Entrepreneurial and mercantile opportunities were more limited in Burma, where British and Indian merchants and financiers became dominant in the last half of the nineteenth century, than in Siam and Malaya, where the Chinese had strong positions in mining, plantation agriculture, processing industries, trade, and finance. This factor was of vital importance to Chinese agriculturists, who made up the larger portion of immigrants to Southeast Asia, for their ambition was to advance socially and economically in the name of family and lineage. Therefore, they considered mercantile opportunities in Southeast Asia a primary avenue of upward mobility.[7] Finally, the volume of Chinese immigration was limited by the fact that few laborers went to Lower Burma after the first decade of British rule. The immigration of Chinese coolies was strongly opposed by the Chinese Chamber of Commerce in Rangoon, whose success was demonstrated by the fact that most Chinese in the Delta throughout the British period were engaged in mercantile activities.[8]

---

and Foreign Proceedings (General), range 205, vol. 10, June 1862, nos. 58–60, India Office Records, London, Eng.

4. *Burma Census, 1901,* Imperial Tables, vol. 2, population by race. These figures would presumably include those Chinese who spoke Burmese and sons of Chinese and Burmese marriages who were raised as Chinese. It would not include daughters of mixed marriages who were raised as Burmese. See Max and Bertha Ferrars, *Burma* (London, 1900), pp. 156–57.

5. G. William Skinner, *Chinese Society in Thailand* (Ithaca, N.Y., 1957), pp. 28–29, 35–52; G. William Skinner, "The Chinese Minority," in *Indonesia,* ed. Ruth T. McVey (New Haven, Conn., 1963), pp. 101–2; Norton Ginsburg and Chester Roberts, *Malaya* (Seattle, Wash., 1958), pp. 249–52.

6. Skinner, *Chinese in Thailand,* pp. 32, 41–45; Edgar Wickberg, *The Chinese in Philippine Life, 1850–1898* (New Haven, Conn., 1965), p. 61.

7. Skinner, *Chinese in Thailand,* pp. 92–95.

8. Dudley Stamp, "Burma: An Undeveloped Monsoon Country," *Geographical Review* 20, no. 1 (January 1930): 108. Stamp does not indicate and I have not been able

In the centuries prior to the British conquest, Indians in Lower Burma, like those elsewhere in Southeast Asia, were primarily engaged in trade. In Konbaung times and the preceding periods, the small Indian community, which was located almost wholly in Rangoon, dominated overseas commerce in the Delta.[9] After 1852, however, Indians migrated to Lower Burma in increasing numbers to fill a wide range of positions created by the expanding economy and greatly enlarged bureaucracy of the new province of the Indian Empire. The scale of Indian immigration is reflected in the rapid growth of the Indian community in the Delta in the late nineteenth century. In 1872 the 37,500 Indians enumerated in Lower Burma composed only 2 percent of the total population. By 1901 there were over 297,000 Indians, and they made up 7 percent of the population. The importance of migration as the basis of this great increase in the Indian community is clearly demonstrated by the fact that over 86 percent of the Indians enumerated in 1901 had been born outside of Burma.[10]

Both conditions in India and opportunities in Lower Burma influenced the great influx of Indian immigrants into the Delta. Since they were drawn from many areas of the subcontinent, a discussion of the factors which caused Indians to move to Burma must be preceded by an analysis of the composition of the migrant stream during the period under consideration. Given the complexity and great regional diversity of Indian society, writers like K. S. Sandhu, who seek to explain "causes" of emigration through descriptions of *general* social dislocations and economic distress in India as a whole,[11] tell us little about *actual* motivations for migration. Aside from the questionable historical accuracy of the themes set forth by Sandhu and other writers,[12] they are of little analytical value because they are not linked to

---

to ascertain when the Chinese Chamber of Commerce began to put this policy into effect.

9. See Peter Floris, *His Voyage to the East Indies in the Globe, 1611–15*, ed. W. H. Moreland (London, 1934), p. 119; and Symes, *Account of Ava*, 2: 4.

10. See Adas, "Agrarian Development," Table V-A, p. 226, and app. 12, p. 561.

11. *Indians in Malaya: Immigration and Settlement, 1786–1957* (Cambridge, 1969), pp. 32–42. Since Sandu's study as a whole is the finest to date on Indian migration to Southeast Asia, his handling of the factors that stimulated emigration from India is particularly illustrative of the tendency to treat these determinants in general terms.

12. Sandhu, voicing the opinions of earlier writers like William Digby and R. C. Dutt, contends that British economic imperialism was mainly responsible for the social and economic conditions which gave rise to large-scale Indian emigration. As Morris D. Morris has indicated in his article entitled "Towards a Reinterpretation of 19th Century Indian Economic History," the impact of British rule on the society and economy of India has only begun to be examined in an objective and scholarly manner. The evidence which has appeared to date tends to disprove rather than support the general themes which Sandhu employs in his discussion of the "push" factors behind Indian migration. See also Morris, "Trends and Tendencies in Indian Economic History," *Indian Social and Economic History Review* 5 (December 1968): 319–88.

specific groups of migrants from known areas of origin. Migrants are made by conditions and events in a particular area of origin and/or opportunities in an area of destination, not by general historical trends.

Most Indians who emigrated to Lower Burma were from the Madras and Bengal presidencies of the Indian Empire. Over 60 percent of the Indians in Burma in the last decades of the nineteenth century were from Madras, while the number from Bengal ranged from 30 percent in 1881 to 25 percent in 1901. Only small numbers emigrated to Burma from the other major political divisions of the Indian Empire: Bombay, the Northwest Provinces, Oudh, the Central Provinces, and the Punjab. The total number of migrants from princely states like Mysore and Hyderabad and the more distant kingdoms of Rajputana made up less than 1 percent of the Indians enumerated in Lower Burma in the 1881–1901 period.[13] (See Map 3, inset.)

Indian immigrants from Madras were drawn primarily from seven districts on the east coast of the Presidency. In order of their importance between 1891 and 1901, these were Tanjore, Ganjam, Godavari, Vizagapatam, Madras City, South Arcot, and Kistna.[14] (See Map 3.) Districts of origin in Bengal are more difficult to determine because, aside from Chittagong, emigrants tended to be more evenly distributed than those from Madras. Approximately 40 percent of the immigrants from Bengal to the Delta were from Chittagong, north of Arakan on Burma's western littoral.[15] Substantial numbers were also from the Puri District in Orissa, from the districts of Shahabad and Patna in Bihar, and from Calcutta and its environs.[16]

The best indices of the social composition of the Indian community in Lower Burma are the caste[17] statistics first compiled in the census of 1891. There are, however, a number of serious problems involved in the use of these statistics in the Burman context. To begin with, many Indians living in Burma refused to state their caste. In 1911, for example, nearly 100,000 Indians refused to list their caste classification for census officials.[18] This high percentage of unlisted persons greatly impairs the accuracy of the totals listed in the caste tables. In addition to Indians who repudiated caste altogether, many others claimed a higher status than they would have been accorded in India. This practice reflected the struggle of numerous low-caste groups, such as the Shanans and Vanniyans of Tamilnad, to achieve a position in the caste

13. See Table V-B, p. 228, in Adas, "Agrarian Development."

14. *Madras Census, 1901,* Report, p. 33.

15. *Bengal Census, 1891,* Report, p. 52.

16. Government of India, Emigration Proceedings, vol. 932, 1 May 1875, no. 8.

17. Unless otherwise stated, I use the term caste in this study to denote a "caste-cluster," a collection of endogamous *jati* (subcastes) which follow similar occupations in a particular region of India. Most of the groups listed in the Burma census reports fit this definition of caste as it has been set forth in Irawati Karve's *Hindu Society–An Interpretation* (Poona, 1961), esp. pp. 15–49.

18. *Burma Census, 1911,* Report, pp. 242–43.

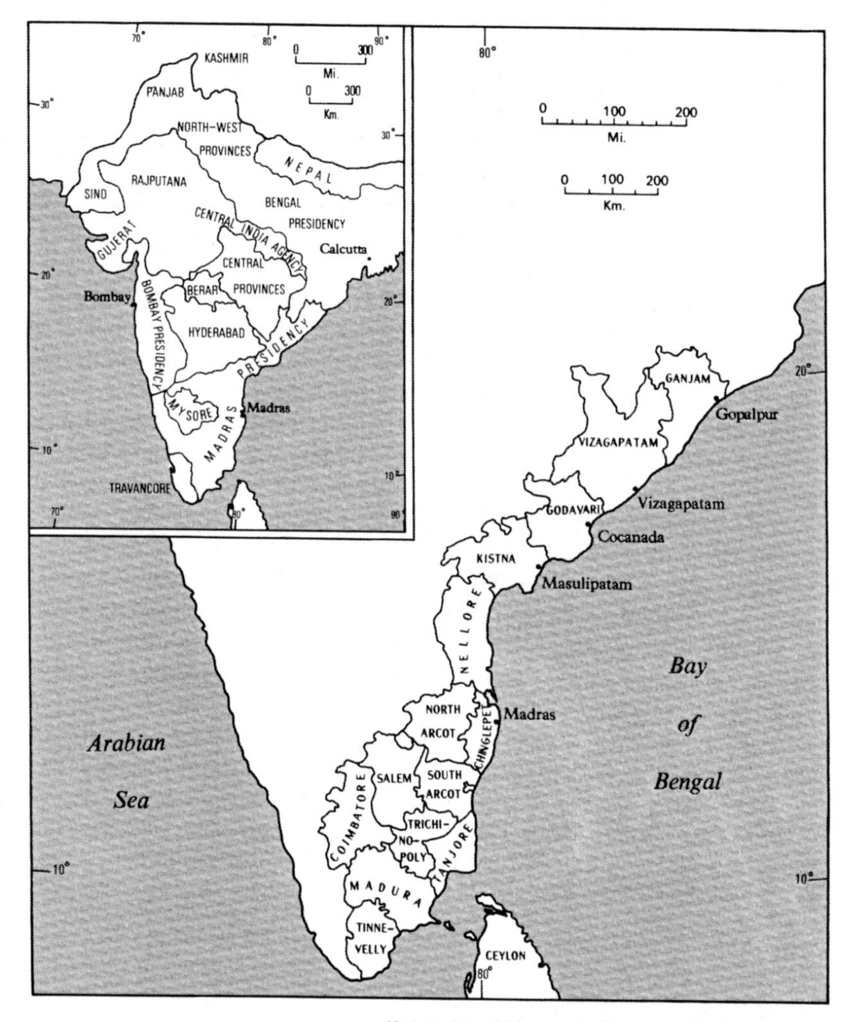

University of Wisconsin Cartographic Laboratory

Map 3. South Indian Districts Supplying Large Numbers of Migrants to Lower Burma. Inset shows the major political divisions of the Indian Empire. Source (for South India map): Dharma Kumar, *Land and Caste in South India* (Cambridge, 1965).

hierarchy commensurate with newly won economic or political power. These groups invariably claimed high-caste status and prerogatives and often changed their caste name.[19] These changes must have resulted in even greater difficulties for Burmese census takers, many of whom were unfamiliar with the Indian caste structure, than they caused for census officials in India.[20] Although caste statistics are virtually useless for determining the actual number of a particular caste found in Lower Burma, they are the best data available relating to the caste composition of the Indian community in Burma. They are especially important for this study because they make it possible to identify the groups which made up the Indian portions of the industrial and agricultural laboring force in Burma.

The largest nonagriculturist castes found in Lower Burma can be divided into five main groups on the basis of the occupations which most members of each caste pursued: government service, the police or military, the professions (law, education, medicine, etc.), banking or trade, and domestic service. Kayasthas from north India and Brahmans[21] held a large share of the posts in the provincial government which were filled by Indians. Rajputs and Sikhs[22] were numerically predominant in Indian regiments of the army and police force. Members of the professional classes were drawn from numerous caste groups, the most important being Brahmans from various regions. Indian involvement in the financial and mercantile sectors of the Delta economy was shared by Nattukottai (Tamil) Chettiars, Telegu Chetties, and Telegu Komatis from South India, and Banias,[23] Chatris, and Marwaris[24] from north India. Dhobis and Kahars were the largest castes who provided domestic services of various kinds.

The great majority of Indians in Lower Burma were from agriculturist castes or castes following occupations related to agriculture. The Indian

19. The best studies of this process may be found in R. L. Hardgrave's *The Nadars of Tamilnad* (Berkeley, Calif., 1969); and Lloyd I. and Suzanne H. Rudolph's *The Modernity of Tradition* (Chicago, 1967), esp. pp. 36–64.

20. *Burma Census, 1921,* Report, p. 126; Rudolph and Rudolph, *Modernity,* pp. 46–47, 51–52; Dharma Kumar, *Land and Caste in South India* (Cambridge, 1965), pp. 55–58.

21. Brahman is not really a caste designation as I use the term. Brahmans in the census reports are not broken down into regional groups and thus the term is used in the sense of a *varna* division, or one of the four-fold divisions of traditional Indian society. *Varna* distinctions are largely hypothetical and thus the functional value of the Brahman category in the Burma censuses is limited.

22. Sikh is a religious rather than a caste term. It refers to the sect founded by Nanak in the sixteenth century in the Punjab region of northwest India.

23. Bania is not a caste name but rather a general term applied throughout most of north India to traders, moneylenders, and shopkeepers.

24. Strictly defined, a Marwari is a person from the region of Marwar in western India. However, the term has come to stand for a bania from that area, and was used in this sense in Burma.

laborers who worked on the wharves and in the rice mills of the Delta's port centers and those who were engaged in paddy production in the rural areas were drawn almost totally from these groups. Unfortunately, most Indian agriculturists in Burma were low-caste and thus the most likely to renounce their ascribed status or claim higher rank. For these reasons, the numbers of each of these castes cannot be accurately determined. However, the main groups can be identified from the available estimates.

The north Indian agricultural castes found most frequently in the Delta were Kurmis from Bihar and the Jats. Two regional branches of the large north Indian cowherding caste also reported substantial numbers in Lower Burma. These were the Ahirs of upper India and the Gwalas of Bihar. Agriculturist castes from South India can be divided into two groups. The first were Sat (or clean)-Śudras[25] and included the Kammas and Reddis (also called Kapus) of the Telegu-speaking areas and the Vellalas of Tamilnad. The largest agriculturist castes were the "depressed" or "scheduled" castes of South India. The dominant groups among these were the Pallis or Vanniyans[26] and the Paraiyans of the Tamil south and the Malas from the Telegu districts on the northeast coast of Madras. Substantial numbers of Kallans, who were traditionally professional thieves but had become important landholders in some Tamil districts, also migrated to the Delta.

The large number of low-caste Tamil and Telegu laborers employed in the Delta explains the preponderance of Hindus in the Indian community of Lower Burma in the last decades of the nineteenth century. In 1872 Hindus and Muslims were nearly equally represented, but by 1901 Hindus made up 67 percent of the Indian population in the Delta while the Muslims totaled only 31 percent.[27] The predominance of transient laborers also accounts for the high ratio of males to females and the high percentage of young persons in the Indian immigrant stream. The sex ratio for the Indian community as a whole was more than 400 males per 100 females. Due primarily to caste restrictions on female travel, the ratio of males to females among various Hindu groups was much higher, reaching a peak of over 3200:100 among Hindu migrants from Orissa.[28] Many of the low-caste Hindu women found in Burma, particularly those from Oriya- and Telegu-speaking areas, were

25. In the tripartite *varna* structure of South India, Sat-Śudras ranked below Brahmans. Śudra caste groups were (and are) extremely large and powerful in South India.

26. Including the *Pandaiyachis.*

27. These percentages are based on the figures given in the population-by-religion tables in the *RAB* for 1872–73 and the 1901 Burma census. The remainder of the Indian community was comprised of Christians, Parsis, and Sikhs.

28. I have calculated the sex ratios listed from the religion and place-of-birth tables for the Burma censuses, 1881–1901. They represent averages of the male-female totals for different categories from two or three census counts. For tables and a more detailed discussion, see Adas, "Agrarian Development," pp. 234–36.

prostitutes who thrived in the slums of Rangoon, where large numbers of single, young males were crowded into squalid tenements with little to divert them after long hours of hard labor.[29] The disproportionate sex ratio and the fact that few Indians settled permanently in Lower Burma were reflected in the preponderance of males between the ages of 15 and 44 and the low numbers of infants and persons over 55.[30]

The high-caste groups which monopolized the bureaucratic, professional, and commercial positions filled by Indians in Lower Burma migrated largely in response to the "pull" of prospective social or economic gains. At the lower levels of the Indian social scale a blend of conditions in India and opportunities in Burma influenced migration. The following analysis of the motivations and responses of immigrant Indian laborers is focused on the agricultural castes of the Telegu- and Tamil-speaking districts identified above. These castes, from whose ranks "emigrants from South India were largely drawn,"[31] were among the most oppressed groups of the Indian subcontinent. The Malas of the Telegu-speaking areas and the Paraiyans of Tamilnad were untouchables. Shunned and degraded by high-caste Hindus, they performed the lowly tasks that other groups regarded as polluting or beneath their stations. The Palli or Vanniyan caste of Tamilnad, which was the only agricultural laboring caste not considered untouchable,[32] was socially slightly better off than the Malas or Paraiyans but economically equally exploited and deprived. Until 1843 those Pallis and Paraiyans who were *pannaiyals* (permanent farm servants) were virtually slaves in many Tamil districts, including Tanjore and South Arcot. They could be sold or mortgaged, and for many their state of bondage was inherited by their children for generations. Although the laboring classes' servitude was less widespread and harsh in Telegu areas, Malas in some districts were held in debt and "hereditary servitude."[33] Act V of 1843 did not immediately free all low-caste laborers who had been reduced to slavery,[34] but it signified the end to Indian government support of servitude based on debt or caste standing. The government's refusal to find and return

29. E. J. L. Andrew, *Indian Labour in Rangoon* (Calcutta, 1933), pp. 182–83, 187–88; Government of India, *Manual of the Administration of the Madras Presidency* . . . , 3 vols. (Madras, 1885), 1: 500.

30. See Adas, "Agrarian Development," Figure V-A, p. 237.

31. Kumar, *Land and Caste,* p. 59; see also Andrew, *Indian Labour,* passim; and the caste-composition tables in the Burma censuses for this period.

32. Kumar, *Land and Caste,* p. 58.

33. Ibid., pp. 41–48. The Telegu areas included Vizagapatam, Ganjam, Godavari, and Kistna districts, from where most emigrants to Burma were drawn.

34. Ibid., pp. 74–75.

pannaiyals or debt slaves who absconded permitted large numbers to leave their debts and servitude behind and emigrate to Burma and other areas.[35]

Those Malas, Pallis, and Paraiyans who were *padiyals* (Tamil) or *palalus* (Telegu), free hired laborers, were in some ways worse off than those held in servitude. Employment for *padiyals* and *palalus* was highly uncertain and irregular. They found "regular employment only at the busy seasons of the year and during the remainder of the year had to depend on such work as [they] could find on the roads and other public works. . . ."[36] The wages of *padiyals* and *palalus,* which were normally paid in kind, were considerably lower than those earned by agricultural laborers of the Śudra castes, and most Śudra laborers lived at subsistence levels.[37] In many areas of South India, such as Tamil-speaking Tanjore, "powerful social sanctions" prevented low-caste laborers from owning land.[38] Because they were landless and possessed no certain source of employment, in years of famine or scarcity (which were frequent in late nineteenth-century Madras) Malas, Pallis, Paraiyans, and other low-caste groups either found employment on government works, emigrated to areas like Burma, or perished.[39]

For the low-caste agricultural laborers of South India emigration to Lower Burma (and Ceylon or Malaya) provided economic opportunities and potential social mobility that were invariably denied them in their districts of origin. In Burma they could earn comparatively high wages in agriculture or industry, and the rates paid were determined according to the amount and type of work done and not on the basis of caste rank.[40] The importance of wage differentials between India and Burma can best be seen in terms of the cost and returns approach set forth by L. A. Sjaastad.[41] The "money costs" of migration for laborers in the late nineteenth century included travel inside India, steamship fare (deck passenger class), the *maistry*'s (Indian recruiter's) commission if the laborer were recruited, and the cost of food for the journey. Assuming that steamship fares, which averaged Rs. 20 round-trip

35. S. S. Raghavaiyanger, *Memorandum on the Progress of the Madras Presidency During the Last Forty Years of British Administration* (Madras, 1892), p. 153; *Tanjore Gazetteer,* vol. A, p. 111.

36. Government of India, *Manual of the Administration of Madras,* 1: 295.

37. Raghavaiyanger, *Memorandum,* p. 143. He estimates that wages for untouchables were as much as 25 percent lower than those paid to Sudra laborers for similar tasks.

38. Kumar, *Land and Caste,* p. 31.

39. Raghavaiyanger, *Memorandum,* p. 147; Holderness, *Narrative of the Famine,* p. 39; Kumar, *Land and Caste,* p. 59. There is some evidence that low-caste laborers were the most affected throughout India. See B. M. Bhatia, *Famines in India, 1860–1965* (London, 1967), pp. 10–13.

40. Some Indian landlords in Burma may have paid lower wages to low-caste Indians, but there is no evidence of this practice in the sources I have consulted.

41. "Costs and Returns," pp. 80–93. The following analysis is based on the wage and fare rates current in the late 1880s when the most complete statistics are available.

between the ports of the northern *circars* (Vizagapatam, Gopalpur, etc.) and Rangoon in the late 1880s, were the major item of expenditure, the maximum cost of transportation both ways was approximately Rs. 30. "Opportunity costs" or "earnings forgone while traveling, searching for, and learning a new job"[42] were minimal. If their positions had not been arranged in advance through *maistries* or friends and relatives, laborers quickly found employment after their arrival in Rangoon. The "psychic costs" of migration were considerable, but these are impossible to quantify.

The Indian immigrant laborer's "money" returns consisted chiefly of the increment to his earnings which resulted from his decision to seek employment in Burma. The magnitude of this return can best be seen through specific comparisons of wage levels in India and Burma. In 1887, of the major districts of origin in the Madras Presidency, agricultural laborers earned the highest wages in Vizagapatam. Their earnings were Rs. 6 per month, or Rs. 72 per year.[43] In Rangoon in the same year the average wage for industrial workers was Rs. 22.5 per month, or Rs. 270 per year. An agricultural laborer in Lower Burma received about Rs. 15 per month in 1887, or Rs. 180 per year.[44] Thus, the annual increment to an industrial laborer's income (minus Rs. 30 for transport) was Rs. 168, while that for an agricultural laborer was Rs. 78. The higher cost of living in Rangoon reduced somewhat the real amount of additional wages received. However, if one takes into consideration the fact that most laborers remained in Burma from three to five years, the increment for both industrial and agricultural laborers would have been far greater. In addition, a sizable percentage of most laborers' earnings was either remitted to their relatives in India or carried home when the laborers themselves returned from Burma. Money earned in Burma would buy far more in India because most prices were lower on the subcontinent. Clearly money returns far offset the costs of migration to Burma.

The higher wages which Indian immigrants to Lower Burma received were supplemented by other monetary and nonmonetary rewards. Laborers' earnings could be used to buy land, to support their families in India, or to purchase cheap consumer goods. Even in areas in South India where low-caste laborers were allowed to buy land, it was extremely difficult for them to raise the money to purchase a holding and even harder for them to cultivate at a level of profit that would allow them to retain it. The low wages paid to an agricultural laborer in Madras coupled with the high price of land, high taxes,

42. Ibid., p. 84.

43. Kumar, *Land and Caste,* p. 163. The yearly total is, of course, high because it is unlikely that a laborer found work for all twelve months at the Rs. 6 rate. It is useful, however, for purposes of comparison.

44. Nolan, *Report,* p. 4. The source for the wage estimate does not specify whether or not it refers to skilled workers, unskilled workers, or both.

fragmentation of holdings, and the depletion of the soil in many areas[45] placed land acquisition and holding beyond most laborers' means. If a laborer were frugal, after several years' work in the mills and paddy fields of Lower Burma he would have saved enough money to purchase land which was readily available in the Delta. Rather than settle in an alien land, however, most laborers preferred to return to India and purchase holdings in their districts of origin.[46] Some Indians speculated in land in Lower Burma and returned home with sizable fortunes. One agriculturist, who sold his holdings during the pre-1907 land boom at a good profit, returned to India with nearly Rs. 10,000.[47]

Most Indian immigrants remitted large sums of money to their relatives in India.[48] The magnitude of the sums which laborers sent to India to support relatives in their districts of origin can be inferred from J. R. Andrus' estimate that in the 1930s remittances by money order alone averaged nearly thirty million rupees annually.[49] In the same period several millowners reported to the Baxter Commission that unskilled Indian laborers normally saved from 40–80 percent of their wages, which were sent to India by post.[50]

But not all of the workers' surplus funds were saved or remitted to India. Many laborers purchased consumer goods that they could not have afforded at the wage rates current in India. These purchases account for the contrast between their appearance on arrival in and departure from Burma. E. J. L. Andrew wrote that most laborers disembarking from the steamships which brought them from Madras had "only a mat and an earthen receptacle which contained their food on the voyage. They are generally very lightly clad. The

45. On declining yields and fragmentation of holdings in the Madras Presidency, see G. S. Iyer, *Some Economic Aspects of British Rule in India* (Madras, 1903), pp. 66–72. For a detailed discussion of revenue policy in the Telegu-speaking areas of Madras in this period, see A. V. Raman Rao, *Economic Development of Andhra Pradesh, 1766–1957* (Bombay, 1958), pp. 201–17, 224–29. Underlying these problems was the high population density in most districts of origin. For instance, the number of persons per square mile in the Vizagapatam, Ganjam, and Godavari districts in 1901 (excluding the agency divisions) was 435, 345, and 443, respectively, and in Tanjore it reached 561 (*Madras Census, 1901*, Report, p. 20). These densities contrast sharply with Lower Burma, where the number per square mile in 1901 was only 150 in the most densely populated district, Henzada, and 41 in Toungoo, the least populated district.

46. *Madras Census, 1911*, Report, p. 26, *1931*, Report, p. 93; *Pyapon Settlement Report (1921–22)*, p. 8.

47. Thomas Couper, *Report on Land Alienation, Indebtedness, and [the] Condition of Tenants in [the] Thaton District* (Moulmein, 1909), pp. 10–11.

48. N. R. Chakravarti, *The Indian Minority in Burma* (London, 1971), pp. 75–76; *Burma Census, 1891*, Report, p. 177.

49. *Burmese Economic Life*, p. 182. There are no statistics on the amount remitted in the late nineteenth century, or even reliable statistics for later decades; see Chakravarti, *Indian Minority*, pp. 75–76.

50. James Baxter, *Report on Indian Immigration* (Rangoon, 1941), p. 91.

men wore a dirty cloth covering their loins and a similar strip wound round their heads; their women are clothed only in an old *sari.*" When they returned to India after a few years' employment in Burma, the laborers were "generally better clad; the men are dressed in shirts, coats, dhotis or loin cloths and turbans, while the women are clothed in clean petticoats and *saris* and wear jackets." In addition, Andrew noted that many workers took bedding, baggage, and small pieces of furniture home to India with them.[51]

Beyond the material advantages derived from emigration to Burma, many low-caste laborers found some release from their degrading social status. Their rejection of their lowly ascribed status is perhaps best epitomized by a Paraiyan laborer's reply to the tongue-lashing which he received from a Brahman after the two had collided on a quay in Rangoon harbor. The laborer informed the irate Brahman that he had left his caste behind in India and that he would not take it up again until he returned to Madras.[52] Like the Paraiyan, many thousands of low-caste Indians attempted to leave their degrading caste attributes behind merely by refusing to state their caste designation or by claiming a higher caste rank than that accorded them in India.

For most low-caste laborers, however, their life without caste or at a higher caste level was short-lived. Upon their return to India their old caste labels and their concomitant restraints would be reimposed. Those laborers who sought to resist the return of caste restrictions probably went through a period of emotional stress before finally acquiesing to the station which had been alloted to them by their *karma.* A few returned with enough money to buy status and respect in an area where their origins were not known, preferably in an urban area like Madras. Some remained in Burma, where they sought to make a new life. Harold Isaacs has recorded the history of one such man,[53] a Mala cowherd, who decided to remain in Rangoon after his laborer's contract had expired. He became a tailor's apprentice and brought his family to Rangoon once he was established. His son told Isaacs: "He [the father] decided to change things and become another kind of man. He wanted me to be like him and not all the others who went just to labor and come back. . . . for some years I learned how to be a tailor." Isaacs relates that the cowherd's son later received a college education and rose to become a minister in Nehru's cabinet. Admittedly the cowherd and his son were exceptions, but the potential for social mobility existed for most laborers, especially in the first phase of economic growth in the Delta.

In many respects low-caste laborers of South India and other areas of the subcontinent were better able to respond to opportunities in Burma than

51. *Indian Labour,* pp. 20–21.
52. *Madras Census, 1911,* Report, p. 26.
53. In his study of *India's Ex-Untouchables* (Bombay, 1965), pp. 69–70.

other groups. Despite the strong prohibitions placed on the movement of even low-caste Telegu and Oriya women with regard to overseas travel, untouchable Malas or Paraiyans and low-caste Pallis were far less constrained than high-caste groups by fears of pollution on crowded steamships or in alien lands. Wage laborers like the *padiyals* and *palalus* and *parakudi* (nonresident) tenants were not normally tied into the *jajmani* structure of a particular community. Members of these groups were not likely to live in joint or extended families, which some writers have viewed as impediments to mobility.[54] Finally, the "limited horizons" and narrow provincialism attributed to Indian agriculturists[55] were often overcome by *maistry* recruiters or laborers returning from Burma. *Maistries* moved about from village to village exhorting laborers to migrate by "representing, in bright colors, prospects of enrichment and advance. The ignorant coolies believe easily and while some volunteer to go to try their fortune, many are persuaded."[56] In addition, many laborers emigrated because friends or relatives who had previously been to Burma told them of the high wages obtainable there and assured them that employment could easily be found.[57]

Although the movement of Indians between the subcontinent and Burma was influenced by a combination of "push" and "pull" factors, specific events in India were largely responsible for fluctuations in the volume of *net* migration. As early as 1865–66 and again in 1889, large-scale emigration from Vizagapatam to Lower Burma averted the spread of famine from neighboring areas into that district.[58] After a severe cyclone in Chittagong in 1897, large numbers of emigrants left the district to settle in Burma.[59] In 1896–97 the number of emigrants from Ganjam to Burma doubled and those from Vizagapatam tripled as a result of widespread famine in these districts.[60]

The connection between adverse conditions in India and increases in the volume of *net* migration is also supported by the transit statistics for Indian migration which were compiled during the last decades of the period under consideration. These statistics, which are set forth in Table 6, show significant increases in the number of *net* migrants between 1885–86 and 1886–87,

54. See Kingsley Davis, *The Population of India and Pakistan* (Princeton, N.J., 1951), p. 108. See also Nolan, *Report,* p. 5.

55. Davis, *Population of India,* p. 108; Sandhu, *Indians in Malaya,* pp. 59, 154.

56. From the Government of Madras, Public Proceedings, as quoted by Sandhu, *Indians in Malaya,* p. 79. See also Andrew, *Indian Labour,* p. 38, and the passages on *maistries* below.

57. H. Bernardelli, "New Zealand and Asiatic Migration," *Population Studies* 6, no. 1 (July 1952): 40.

58. *Vizagapatam Gazetteer,* pp. 148–49.

59. *Chittagong Gazetteer,* p. 51.

60. Government of Madras, *Report on the Famine in Madras Presidency During 1896 and 1897,* 2 vols. (Madras, 1898), 2: 23.

Table 6. *Net* Migrants Recorded at Rangoon between 1882 and 1907 (to the nearest thousand)

Date	Net migrants[a]
1882–83	35,000
1883–84	38,000
1884–85	11,000
1885–86	5,000
1886–87	23,000
1887–88	38,000
1888–89	24,000
1889–90	22,000
1890–91	32,000
1891–92	31,000
1892–93	32,000
1893–94	25,000
1894–95	10,000
1895–96	5,000
1896–97	48,000
1897–98	30,000
1898–99	41,000
1899–1900	63,000
1900–1901	not given
1901–2	47,000
1902–3	23,000
1903–4	50,000[b]
1904–5	58,000[b]
1905–6	62,000[b]
1906–7	40,000[b]

Source: *RAB, 1882–1907.*

Note: The figures listed are only approximate counts of *net* Indian migrants. They list the number of migrants from all ports who landed at or departed from Rangoon in the years listed. An estimated 90–94 percent of these, however, were Indians (Andrew, *Indian Labour,* p. 3). For discussions of the other factors which impaired the accuracy of transit statistics for external migration, see Baxter, *Indian Immigration,* pp. 10–11; and Cheng, *Rice Industry of Burma,* pp. 263–64.

[a]Equals the difference between the number of immigrants arriving at Rangoon and the emigrants departing.

[b]Provincial total, no figures for Rangoon only available in these years.

when there were major floods in Godavari and Tanjore, and again between 1889–90 and 1890–91, when there was a severe famine in Ganjam.[61] From 1890–91 to 1892–93 a level of over 30,000 *net* migrants was sustained by floods in Tanjore, Godavari, and Shahabad, a serious cholera outbreak in Ganjam, local food shortages in Vizagapatam, and general scarcity in the Madras Presidency in 1892. The sharp rise in the volume of *net* migration between 1895–96 and 1896–97, the year of the "Great Famine," clearly demonstrates the impact of events in India on fluctuations in the volume of *net* migration.[62] The jump from 1898–99 to 1899–1900 paralleled floods in South Arcot and Tanjore, plague in Shahabad, and a cholera epidemic in Puri. The final rise after 1902–3 was touched off by floods, plague, and scarcity in Shahabad, floods in Patna and South Arcot, and a cyclone in Godavari.[63]

The mass movement of temporary and seasonal laborers between India and Burma was made possible by the growing availability of cheap transportation in the last decades of the nineteenth century. In the first decade after the British annexation, Indian merchants and laborers traveled to the Delta on small, Indian-owned sailing vessels which moved slowly among the coastal ports that fringed the Bay of Bengal.[64] The British India Steam Navigation Company established the first regular steamship service between Calcutta, Akyab, and Rangoon on a monthly basis in 1861. In subsequent years the company increased its runs from one to two per month and extended its service to Madras city and the ports of the northern *circars* (Cocanada, Vizagapatam, Bimlipatam, Kalingapatam, Burwa, and Gopalpur). By the 1870s the B.I.S.N. Company's steamships had almost completely displaced Indian sailing vessels as passenger carriers and thus had gained a virtual monopoly of the India-Burma run. Its monopoly was broken by the Asiatic Steam Navigation Company in 1880. Both companies provided weekly steamship service between Calcutta, the *circar* ports, Madras city, and the

61. Unless otherwise stated, the following information concerning conditions in India is taken from the sections on famine and natural disasters in the gazetteers for the districts of Tanjore, South Arcot, Vizagapatam, and Godavari in Madras, Patna and Shahabad in Bihar, and Puri in Orissa.

62. The "Great Famine" of 1896–97 affected most of the major districts of origin including Ganjam, Vizagapatam, and Godavari in Madras, Shahabad in Bihar, Sultanpur and Fyzabad in the United Provinces, and Puri in Orissa. See the district gazetteers for these areas and Holderness, *Narrative of the Famine,* p. 66.

63. A number of indicators show that "pull" factors were not strongly related to sharp fluctuations in *net* migration in this period. The number of rice mills (a gauge of the availability of employment), for example, remained fairly constant until after 1895 (Cheng, *Rice Industry of Burma,* app. IV-B, pp. 80, 253). In addition, there is little connection between the number of tons of rice exported from Rangoon and flux in the volume of migration. Compare Grant, *Rice Crop,* app. 1, p. 48, with the figures listed in Table 6.

64. Government of India, Emigration Proceedings, vol. 1862, February 1882, no. 28.

ports of Burma.[65] An Indian-owned line, the Bengal-Burma Steam Navigation Company, began regular service between Chittagong and Burma ports in the 1890s, and additional service between the *circar* ports and the Delta was provided by the Andhra-Burma Steamship Company beginning in the second decade of the twentieth century.[66]

The high percentage of industrial and agricultural laborers in the Indian migrant stream was reflected in the great seasonal fluctuation in the volume of arrivals in and departures from ports in Burma. Most migrants entered Burma between October and December, which were the months of the paddy harvest in the Delta which preceded the peak period for the mills and wharves of Rangoon and Bassein.[67] The majority of migrant laborers remained in Burma from one to four years, though large numbers from the Telegu-speaking areas on the northeast coast of Madras and Chittagong in Bengal migrated annually for the harvest and/or milling seasons in Lower Burma.[68]

The *maistry* recruiting system, which dominated Indian labor movement to and supply in Lower Burma in the twentieth century, was not as developed or as pervasive in the last decades of the nineteenth century.[69] *Maistries* were usually experienced Indian workers who were hired by millowners or shipping agents in Burma to recruit laborers in India. New *maistries'* employers often gave them advances to finance recruiting operations. Established *maistries* could normally pay the costs of recruiting labor from personal funds derived from earlier operations. The *maistry* hierarchy which Andrew describes as it worked in the 1920s[70] had apparently not fully evolved in the 1880s and 1890s. A single *maistry* usually recruited, directed the transportation of, and acted as overseer for a gang of workers. The number of laborers in a gang varied. The average number was twenty to fifty workers, but some gangs had as many as five hundred members. The *maistries* who controlled gangs of the latter size must have had subordinates though there is no mention of them in the sources for this period.

The *maistry* paid the steamship fare and supplied food to the members of

65. Aye Hlaing, "Trends of Growth," p. 108; Pearn, *Rangoon*, p. 234; Government of India, *Report of the Deck Passenger Committee*, 2 vols. (Calcutta, 1921), 1: 4, 10–11.

66. *Chittagong Gazetteer*, p. 132; Andrew, *Indian Labour*, p. 47.

67. *Burma Census, 1891*, Report, p. 177; Hall's "Note," appended to Nolan, *Report*, p. 1; Cheng, *Rice Industry of Burma*, pp. 124–26.

68. *Burma Census, 1872*, p. 8; Government of India, *Manual of the Administration of Madras*, 1: 500; *Madras Census, 1881*, Report, p. 131; *Bengal Census, 1881*, Report, p. 152. The one-to-four-year pattern corresponded to that reported by British officials for the twentieth century. See Andrew, *Indian Labour*, p. 20, and Baxter, *Indian Immigration*, p. 105.

69. The following description of the *maistry* system in the last half of the nineteenth century is taken from the Government of India, Emigration Proceedings, vol. 693, July 1874, no. 31, vol. 1862, February 1882, no. 28.

70. *Indian Labour*, pp. 42–43.

his gang during the trip from India to Burma. On their arrival in Rangoon, he provided food and lodging and placed them in positions which had been arranged with the managers of a rice mill or shipping firm. The *maistry*'s advances to his gang were repaid with interest from the wages which they received in Burma. The interest rates were agreed upon before the *maistry* signed the worker on and were fixed by contract. Interest charges were apparently not high in the first phase of economic development. The *maistry* also received a commission from the mill or firm which he served which varied according to the number of laborers he provided. He also derived profit from his ability to buy steamship tickets at bulk rates. The *maistry* charged the members of his gang the full fare and retained the difference as a charge for his service.

In contrast to Burmese in-migrants, Indian immigrants in Lower Burma were concentrated in Rangoon and other urban areas. Most Indians entered Burma through the port of Rangoon and a large number remained in the city. Because Rangoon was the administrative, mercantile, and industrial center of Burma and its chief port, Indian immigrants from all social classes with diverse occupational skills found ready employment in the growing city. In the early 1870s, 70 percent of the Indians in Lower Burma were living in Rangoon. Due primarily to the increasing participation of Indian laborers in agricultural production in the last decades of the nineteenth century, the percentage of Indians in Rangoon had fallen to 42 percent by 1901.[71] Although Rangoon's share of the total Indian population in Lower Burma declined, the absolute number of Indians in the city increased rapidly between 1852 and 1901. In 1872 Indians made up only 26.5 percent of the population of Rangoon. In the last decades of the nineteenth century, however, the Hindu and Muslim (Indian) communities of the city grew at a far faster rate than the Buddhist (Burmese).[72] By 1901, 51 percent of the inhabitants of the city were Indians.[73] Rangoon had become and would remain for most of the period of British rule an Indian city.[74]

Beyond Rangoon the Indian community was concentrated in the largest towns of each Delta district, and in the rural areas of districts around the port cities of Rangoon, Bassein, and Moulmein. Indian professional groups,

71. For the distribution of the Indian community in this period see Table V-F in Adas, "Agrarian Development," p. 255.

72. *Burma Census, 1901*, Report, p. 26.

73. Imperial table on population by religion in the *Burma Census, 1901*.

74. For the location of various Indian groups within the city and the living conditions of low-caste laborers, see O. H. K. Spate and L. W. Trueblood, "Rangoon: A Study in Urban Geography," *Geographical Review* 32 (1942): 56–73; Andrew, *Indian Labour*, pp. 166–77; Chakravarti, *Indian Minority*, pp. 46–50; Adas, "Agrarian Development," pp. 256–58.

domestic servants, bureaucrats, and military personnel were clustered in towns like Henzada, Toungoo, and Myaungmya because district administrative offices, district courts, and military garrisons were located in these centers. These towns also served as the foci of local and regional market networks and as such attracted Indian financiers and merchants and their retainers.[75] The districts around port centers like Rangoon and Bassein were the most accessible to immigrant Indian laborers, merchants, and moneylenders. Proximity was most important to laborers who could easily move from the mills in Rangoon or Moulmein during the slack season in order to work in the paddy fields in nearby districts. In addition, these districts and the other areas on the lower Delta frontier were favored by Indian workers because they contained large holdings which required the extensive employment of seasonal laborers, and because wages were generally higher there than in the upper Delta. The percentage of Indians in the total population of the districts of Lower Burma in 1901 ranged from 17 percent in the Hanthawaddy-Insein District in the lower Delta to only 1 percent in Prome in the far north.[76]

In the rural areas of Lower Burma, Indians adopted a number of settlement patterns. Both the shop and residence of Indian (and Chinese) moneylenders and merchants were usually located in a single building built of brick and guarded by iron bars on the windows. Indian moneylenders usually lived in the largest or most accessible village in a particular tract or in the small towns which grew up along the railroad lines.[77] As an Indian landlord class evolved in parts of the Delta, an "estate-hamlet" pattern of residence developed. This type of settlement was centered on a large house where the landlord and/or his wife and the landlord's factor (or overseer) lived. The huts of permanent laborers, cattle and implement sheds, granaries, and tanks were situated around the central dwelling. This cluster of buildings was normally surrounded by a hedge.[78] Resident Indian tenants, laborers, and cattle keepers, who did not dwell in "estate-hamlets," lived on the edge of Burmese villages or in groups of two or three houses in the rice fields. Indian dwellings, which were normally built of mud and wattle, contrasted sharply with the more spacious wood and thatch houses of the Burmese.[79] Seasonal Indian

75. See the population-by-religion, civil-condition, and similar tables in the provincial tables of the 1901 Burma census.

76. Calculated from the population-by-religion tables in the 1901 Burma census. See also Map V-A in Adas, "Agrarian Development," p. 260.

77. Spate, "Burmese Village," pp. 531–32; *Banking Enquiry Report,* 2: 132; *Insein Gazetteer,* p. 52.

78. *[Hanthawaddy] Syriam Gazetteer,* p. 47; *Myaungmya Settlement Report (1916–19),* p. 24.

79. *[Hanthawaddy] Syriam Gazetteer,* p. 47; *Insein Gazetteer,* p. 52; Spate, "Burmese Village," p. 532; *Hanthawaddy Settlement Report (1930–33),* p. 8.

laborers built *dhani* thatch and bamboo huts on the fringes of the rice fields where they lived during the cropping season.[80]

Kingsley Davis has estimated that nearly 2,600,000 Indians migrated to Burma between 1852 and 1937. Although these immigrants represented only a small percentage of the population of their districts of origin, their numbers far exceeded those of immigrants to other areas outside the Indian subcontinent. The number of immigrants who chose Burma as their area of destination was 42 percent of Davis' estimate of the total number of Indian immigrants in the British period. It exceeded the number of immigrants to Ceylon, which ranked second as a recipient area, by over one million.[81] The great influx of Indian immigrants into Burma, and primarily into the Delta, was in part due to the proximity of the two areas and the transportation links that were established soon after Lower Burma came under British control. The large volume of Indian immigration was also a function of the fact that Burma was a part of the Indian Empire.

These explanations are not in themselves sufficient, however, for Ceylon was closer than Burma to the densely packed Tamil districts from which most of its immigrants were drawn, and Malaya, Mauritius, and East Africa were not a great deal more distant from India. In addition, communications between India and Ceylon were as good as or better than those between the subcontinent and Burma. Finally, although they were not part of the Indian Empire, Ceylon, Malaya, and East Africa became parts of the British Empire and received far greater attention from the Government of India with regard to the regulation of migrants and labor supply than did Burma.

The fundamental reasons for Burma's pre-eminence as an area of destination lie primarily in responses of Indian laborers who made up a large majority of the migrant stream. For the Indian laborer, Burma offered opportunities which far surpassed those of other potential destinations. To begin with, numerous positions in industry and port labor were available in addition to employment in public works, agriculture, and domestic service, which were the main sectors opened to Indian laborers in other areas.[82] The number of positions in industry and on the wharves increased as the processing and harbor facilities of Lower Burma developed, and wages in

80. *Thaton (Kyaikto) Settlement Report (1928–30),* p. 8; Government of Burma, Agriculture Department, *Notes on "Homesteads" in Burma,* bull. no. 24 (Rangoon, 1928), pp. 7–8.

81. *Population of India,* p. 101. It is important to point out that this total is a very rough approximation and contains a good deal of double counting since many laborers went back and forth between India and Burma several times. Ceylon's count was for a longer period, 1834–1938.

82. Sandhu, *Indians in Malaya,* pp. 245–82; B. H. Farmer, *Ceylon: A Divided Nation* (London, 1963), p. 40, et passim; E. F. C. Ludowyk, *The Story of Ceylon* (London, 1962), p. 206.

these sectors were far higher than those in agriculture. In the agricultural sector of the Delta economy the Indian immigrant functioned as a free, wage laborer whose services were in great demand throughout most of the British period. In Ceylon or Malaya, workers were normally tied to a tea or rubber plantation where they worked under conditions that were quite poor and for wages that were low by Delta standards.[83] For Indian migrant laborers, the range of economic opportunities was broader in Burma, the potential for mobility greater, and the remuneration better. The laborers' awareness of differences in potential returns from migration to different areas is clearly shown by the disproportionate numbers who chose Burma as their destination.

83. Compare, for example, the discussions in Sandhu, *Indians in Malaya,* and Ludowyk, *Story of Ceylon,* on the conditions of employment for laborers in Malaya or Ceylon with those in Lower Burma described above.

5

THE GENESIS OF THE PLURAL SOCIETY IN LOWER BURMA: The Era Of Symbiosis

After the annexation of the Delta to the Indian Empire in 1852 the relatively underdeveloped political and economic systems which had existed in Konbaung times evolved into far more complex structures. Their expansion and elaboration produced many new niches to be filled in administration, trade, industry, and agriculture. These new positions in turn attracted European, Indian, and Chinese immigrants to the Delta area. A far more heterogeneous society than that found in the Konbaung era resulted from the combination of these immigrant groups with the indigenous peoples of Burma. Nearly three decades ago J. F. Furnivall labeled the social system which was produced by this combination the plural society. Furnivall's formulation was basically descriptive. He saw the plural society of Burma as

> . . . a medley of various peoples–European, Chinese, Indian and Native. It is in the strictest sense a medley, a mixture, for they mix but do not combine. Each group holds its own ideas and ways of life. As individuals they meet together; but only in the market place, in buying and selling. Under native rule the social organisation had a plural character; under Western rule it has been transformed into what may be termed a plural society, with different sections of the community living side by side but separately within the same political unit.[1]

1. "The Political Economy of the Tropical Far East," *Journal of the Royal Central Asian Society* 29, nos. 3, 4 (1942): 198. Furnivall's thinking on the plural society was

In recent years a number of sociologists and anthropologists, working mainly with societies in the Caribbean and Africa, have attempted to refine Furnivall's concept and to test its potential for social analysis. Their efforts have produced a sizable literature on plural societies and an ongoing debate concerning the manner in which the concept can most effectively be applied.[2]

My use of the plural-society framework in this study stems from a desire to develop its potential for historical analysis, rather than from an intent to become deeply involved in the controversies which have arisen with regard to terminology and the conceptual assumptions which are implicit in certain scholars' approaches. My concern is to examine changes in social and economic relationships and in the interaction between the divergent groups which made up Delta society over a time span which corresponds roughly to the period of British rule in Lower Burma, 1852–1941. It is this concern that distinguishes the historical or dynamic approach which I employ from the "static" treatment which the plural society has received in the studies of most sociologists and anthropologists.[3] In order for this historical analysis to be effective, however, some refinement of Furnivall's original concept is essential. In this study I apply what Leo Kuper has aptly termed the "conflict model" of the plural society.[4] In developing this framework I make considerable use of the works of M. G. Smith on Caribbean and African variants of the plural society. Smith's formulations, however, require substantial qualification in view of both the realities of the Delta situation

---

expressed in a number of earlier writings, but the concept was first fully developed in this article, which formed the basis for his often cited passages in *Colonial Policy and Practice.*

2. For a discussion of some of the main issues raised thus far, see M. G. Smith, "Some Developments in the Analytic Framework of Pluralism," in *Pluralism in Africa,* ed. Leo Kuper and M. G. Smith (Berkeley, Calif., 1969), pp. 415–58.

3. Recent works have produced a number of important exceptions to this general tendency to neglect the historical dimensions of plural societies. See, for examples, the contributions in *Pluralism in Africa,* ed. Kuper and Smith, and Leo Despres, *Cultural Pluralism and Nationalist Politics in British Guiana* (Chicago, 1967).

4. As opposed to the "equilibrium" model of pluralism popular among social scientists dealing with the United States; see "Plural Societies: Perspectives and Problems," in *Pluralism in Africa,* ed. Kuper and Smith, pp. 7–16. The application of the "conflict" model to the early period of communal accommodation described below may seem inappropriate. However, even though there was little overt hostility between different communal groups in this period, Delta society was characterized by dissensus, cultural incompatibility, sectional domination based ultimately on force (see Kuper, "Plural Societies," p. 10n), and latent communal hostility. More important, no significant noneconomic links were forged between different cultural groups in Lower Burma in this period. When the favorable economic conditions that had permitted accommodation in the late nineteenth century gave way to economic crises after World War I, hostilities became manifest and the intergroup violence quickly severed the frail economic ties that had linked different cultural groups.

and of more general questions raised by a number of other scholars. In addition, my approach, particularly the importance I assign to treating the concept historically, has been influenced by the lectures of John R. W. Smail on the modern history of Southeast Asia.[5]

Differential responses to common economic opportunities brought a number of cultural groups together in Burma and resulted in the formation of a plural society.[6] As Smith has correctly asserted, the distinguishing characteristic of this and other plural societies lies in the institutional[7] differences between the cultural[8] groups which composed it. Each of the four main cultural groups found in Burma—the Europeans, Indians, Chinese, and Burmese—had a different set of what Smith has called "compulsory" or "basic" institutions. These included kinship, education, religion, property, recreation, and "certain sodalities." As a result each of these groups had "distinctive systems of action, ideas and values, and social relations," and each spoke different languages and possessed different material cultures.[9] The four groups were organized into "corporate sections or segments whose boundaries demarcate[d] distinct communities and systems of social action."[10] Since these segments were unequal in status and controlled varying shares of the available resources, an extreme form of pluralism was found in Burma where cultural, social, and structural features were all present.[11]

Contrary to the assertions of Smith,[12] race also played a fundamental role in the structuring of society in Burma. Although feelings of racial

5. These scholars bear no responsibility for my application of their ideas and may in fact disagree with some of the conclusions which I have drawn from their writings and suggestions.

6. After Smith, I define a society as a "self-sufficient, self-perpetuating and internally autonomous system of social relations." See "Institutional and Political Conditions of Pluralism," in *Pluralism in Africa,* ed. Kuper and Smith, p. 29. In this theoretical discussion I speak of Burma as a whole, for the entire province became a plural society in the British period. In analyzing the workings of the plural society I deal only with the Delta.

7. S. F. Nadel has provided perhaps the broadest definition of institutions by regarding them as "standardized modes of co-activity." See *The Foundations of Social Anthropology* (London, 1951), p. 108.

8. After Julian Steward, I define culture as "learned modes of behavior that are socially transmitted from one generation to the next and [may be transmitted] from one society to the next." See "Levels of Socio-Cultural Integration: An Operational Concept," *Southwest Journal of Anthropology* 5, no. 7 (1951): 374.

9. M. G. Smith, *Plural Society in the West Indies* (Berkeley, Calif., 1965), pp. 79–87.

10. M. G. Smith, "Analytic Framework," in *Pluralism in Africa,* ed. Kuper and Smith, p. 444.

11. Ibid., pp. 439–48. On the relationship between the different forms of pluralism, see also Pierre van den Berghe, *Race and Racism: A Comparative Perspective* (New York, 1967), pp. 132–36.

12. *West Indies,* pp. 85, 89.

differentiation may or may not have had a biological basis, they were present in the relations between different cultural segments. As H. Hoetink has indicated, the "underlying myth" of race served as an ideological prop for the culturally based institutional differences which divided the society.[13] Racial factors were also important determinants of both the avenues and degree of vertical social mobility open to individuals in Burma.[14] In practice, individuals were identified as members of different groups on the basis of their physical features, not according to the institutional patterns which they followed. Only by admitting the importance of racial barriers can one justify combining Hindus and Muslims in a single segment as Indians. On the basis of structural criteria or of institutional variation these groups were clearly distinct, yet in actual interaction or conflict with other groups they were normally lumped together as Indians. This pattern represents an extreme example of the tendency on the part of members of different groups in a plural society to view other cultural groups as undifferentiated wholes.[15]

The diverse segments of a plural society are held together by a common political system. Smith has placed increasing emphasis on the importance of political control and regulation to the maintainence of such a society. He has argued that, given the absence of shared "compulsory" institutions which can produce conformity with regard to social norms, regulation by a dominant cultural minority which monopolizes the instruments of force is indispensible to the preservation of a plural society.[16] Although coercion (in the form of military conquest) and the assertion of political control by alien cultural groups (the British and their Indian allies) were prerequisites to the genesis of a plural society in Burma, it is wrong, I think, to conclude that throughout its history that society was held together solely by political domination. This emphasis on political regulation obscures the importance of a second level of "common"[17] institutions which members of the divergent cultural groups in Burma shared. Beyond the government and related political agencies and activities stressed by Leo Despres,[18] common institutions in Burma included

13. *The Two Variants in Caribbean Race Relations* (London, 1967), pp. 96–97.

14. For a discussion of this aspect of racial divisions, see H. Hoetink, "The Concept of Pluralism as Envisaged by M. G. Smith," *Caribbean Studies* 7, no. 1 (April 1967): 37–40.

15. This pattern has been noted by a number of authors, among them H. S. Morris, "The Plural Society," *Man* 57, no. 148 (1957): 124; and Burton Benedict, "Stratification in Plural Societies," *American Anthropologist* 64, no. 4 (1962): 1238.

16. Compare Smith's statements on regulation in *West Indies,* p. 86, with those in his more recent essay on the "Conditions of Pluralism" in *Pluralism in Africa,* ed. Smith and Kuper, pp. 32–33, 36, et passim.

17. This term was suggested in Leo Kuper's essay on "Plural Societies," in *Pluralism in Africa,* ed. Smith and Kuper, p. 15.

18. For a detailed discussion of these factors see "The Implications of Nationalist Politics in British Guiana for the Development of Cultural Theory," *American Anthropologist* 66, no. 5 (1964): 1051–77.

Western education and law and the wide range of economic subsystems which evolved in the British period. In Burma, as in South Africa,[19] economic interdependence played a vital role in the maintainence of the plural society. In fact, in the first phase of development, when there were more than enough positions and ample profits for all, the economic interdependence of the different cultural segments and the mutual advantages derived by the members of each were the primary factors which held the plural society together.[20]

Plural societies are characterized by a lack of concensus and the absence of a sense of community extending beyond each of the cultural groups which compose them. Divisions and the potential for conflict are far stronger than the forces which serve to integrate the various segments.[21] Identification is primarily with one's own segment and its set of compulsory institutions. Interaction between the members of different segments is primarily at the level of common institutions and normally asymmetrical, functionally specific, and predominantly instrumental. A number of writers have suggested that in societies affected by European colonization this interaction served to integrate the members of different cultural segments by involving them in the common process of "Westernization" or modernization.[22] As Pierre Van den Berghe has pointed out, acculturation to European norms may in fact merely increase the cultural heterogeneity of the plural society.[23] More important, in Burma as in all colonial areas intensive Westernization was confined to small minorities. The great majority of the cultural groups which made up the plural society in Burma adhered to their traditional institutions and participated only marginally, if at all, in Western institutions beyond those in the economic sphere. Below the level of the English-educated elite integrative bonds were tenuous and easily broken in times of stress.

Because of the emphasis placed in this study on the interaction between different cultural segments and their involvement in common economic

19. See Pierre van den Berghe, "Pluralism and the Polity: A Theoretical Explanation," in *Pluralism in Africa,* ed. Smith and Kuper, pp. 73–74.

20. Furnivall stressed the importance of common economic institutions (see above), and in his more recent writings Smith has given some attention to the economic implications of pluralism. See "Conditions of Pluralism," in *Pluralism in Africa,* ed. Smith and Kuper, pp. 54–56.

21. As Pierre Van den Berghe has correctly asserted, the consensual, "monistic" model which has dominated functionalist sociology is not adequate for the analysis of plural societies. See "Towards a Sociology of Africa," *Social Forces* 43 (October 1964): 12–13. For an opposing view see Lloyd Braithwaite, "Social Stratification and Cultural Pluralism," *Annals of the New York Academy of Sciences* 83 (January 1957): 816–31.

22. Floyd and Lillian Dotson, *The Indian Minority of Zambia, Rhodesia and Malawai* (New Haven, Conn., 1968), pp. viii, 395, 407; H. S. Morris, *The Indians in Uganda, Caste and Sect in a Plural Society* (London, 1968), pp. 168–69.

23. "Towards a Sociology," p. 15.

institutions related to the Delta rice industry,[24] no attempt is made to describe in detail the nature of the compulsory institutions of the various segments nor to delineate the differences between them. Thus, the questions raised by a number of scholars regarding means of measuring institutional differentiation remain unanswered.[25]

My emphasis on intergroup relations also tends to obscure the important cleavages which existed within each cultural segment.[26] As in all colonial societies there were divisions within the ruling elite. The European community was divided between official and nonofficial, civil servants and military personnel, and stratified in terms of social class. The Indian community was split along religious, sectarian, caste, and class lines.[27] There were also groups, such as the Anglo-Indians, which sprang from combinations of the basic cultural segments but belonged to none. Most important, there were deep vertical cleavages within the indigenous Burmese community which had developed centuries before the British conquest. These cleavages led to violence between the Burmans and Karens and other ethnic groups in the British period, and have produced some of the major problems confronting Burma since independence.

The fact that I do not analyze these intrasegmental cleavages should not be interpreted to mean that I do not consider them important. Since it is impossible to deal adequately with all aspects of the complex society which evolved in Lower Burma in a single study, I have chosen to focus on intersegmental relationships, particularly on the interaction between Indians and Burmese.

In a plural-society situation cultural attributes (social and religious values, family structure, caste or clan ties, etc.) and previous experiences (training, length of contact with particular types of economic institutions, etc.) determine the sectors and occupations in which the members of different cultural segments will tend to be concentrated. Many authors have presented the social structure which results from this tendency towards occupational

24. I have chosen to focus on the rice industry because I believe it to be the core subsystem of Delta society in this period. It is also the best documented nonpolitical aspect of Burma's history under British rule.

25. See, for example, R. T. Smith, "Review of *Social and Cultural Pluralism in the Caribbean*," *American Anthropologist* 63, no. 1 (February 1961): 156; Morris, *Indians in Uganda*, p. 169.

26. Both Burton Benedict and H. S. Morris have suggested that these cleavages may be more important than the differences between cultural segments in, respectively, "Stratification," p. 1237, and "The Plural Society," p. 124.

27. The deep split between the Hindu and Muslim communities in Burma actually led to violence on a number of occasions, most notably in the 1893 riots in Rangoon. See Pearn, *Rangoon*, p. 259; and Julius Smith, *Ten Years in Burma* (Cincinnati, Ohio, 1902), pp. 96–102. For later friction see the *Rangoon Gazette*, 11 January 1932, p. 22.

specialization along cultural lines as a layered pyramid. Europeans normally control the upper layers of the pyramid, while non-European immigrants (Chinese, Indians, Syrians, or Lebanese) control the middle layers as merchants or subordinate administrators. The great majority of the indigenous population is consigned to the base of the pyramid either as the laboring force of the economy or the voiceless subjects of the colonial administration.[28] For Burma at least, this layered view of the plural society is highly inaccurate and misleading. In Burma each of the cultural segments which made up the plural society contained representatives of widely divergent classes. Differences in background, motivation, and capacity existed not only between cultural segments, but also among the classes and groups which composed each of them. As a result, members of different segments were found in varying proportions at most levels of common institutional systems. Rather than a layered pyramid, there was a complex and highly variegated hierarchy in Lower Burma in which the members of each cultural group tended to be concentrated in particular niches in all sectors and at most levels.

In overview, the migration of Europeans, Indians, Chinese, and Burmese into Lower Burma in the last half of the ninteenth century can be viewed as a reallocation of the factors of production within the British Empire. The Delta was rich in land and natural resources, but lacked capital (both money and machine) and entrepreneurs and was labor-poor. Immigrant and in-migrant groups were drawn to the Delta in response to the opportunities which resulted from these deficiencies. For some, such as the Indian Chettiars or European capitalists, their role in the rice-export economy was clear from the outset. However, the positions that other groups, such as the mass of Indian laborers and most of the indigenous population, would come to occupy were not apparent in the beginning. The degree of involvement on the part of these groups varied considerably in particular sectors at different times and their predominance in certain niches evolved haphazardly and often in ways that seemed to deny their past experience and cultural predilections.

When the restrictions which the Konbaung regime had placed on external trade were abrogated in the years after the annexation of 1852, European merchants, shippers, and financiers rapidly became involved in a wide range of activities ranging from teak exports and shipbuilding to the importation of cheap consumer goods. In the rice industry, they dominated the export trade and processing. Europeans, particularly English and German milling firms and merchants, monopolized the Delta's rice trade with European markets, which

28. For examples of this approach see Sandhu, *Indians in Malaya*, esp. pp. 42–59; R. B. Winder, "The Lebanese in West Africa," *Comparative Studies in Society and History* 4 (1961–62): 296–333; and Benedict's criticism of the layered approach in his article on "Stratification," pp. 1240–42.

were the main outlets for Burma rice in the first phase of development.[29] An Australian, Thomas Sutherland, built the first steam mill for processing paddy in Rangoon in 1860.[30] By 1898 there were forty-seven rice mills in Lower Burma, and Europeans owned nearly 64 percent of these, including all of the largest mills, which were concentrated in Rangoon. The remaining mills, which were generally much smaller than those of the Europeans, were owned by Burmese (15 percent), Chinese (13 percent), and Indians (9 percent).[31] In addition to their control of rice exportation and processing, European capitalists also owned the companies which provided rail and steamboat transportation within the Delta and steamship communications with India, the Far East, and Europe.

As Cheng Siok-Hwa has pointed out, because of their great "financial resources, technical know-how and business experience,"[32] European millers, merchants, and shippers were able to take the fullest advantage of the potential which the Delta offered for investment in trade and industry. Some European capitalists were representatives of long-established firms which also had enterprises in India, while others were young businessmen seeking to make their fortunes in the Delta. The movement of Europeans into the economic niches created by the Delta's annexation to the Indian Empire represented a further extension of the modern commercial network which Europeans had been building on a global scale since the fifteenth century.

Although the concentration of Europeans at the apex of the occupational pyramid of the Delta economy conforms to the conventional notion of a layered plural-society structure, the middle positions, contrary to this view, were shared by both immigrant Asians and the indigenous Burmese. The emphasis placed in most works on the role of the Indian Chettiar in providing credit for agricultural production has tended to obscure the extensive participation of the Burmese in moneylending and internal marketing. As I have indicated in Chapter 3, in the early decades of the Delta's development agricultural credit came almost wholly from indigenous sources. Even after the Chettiars, other Indian bankers, and the Chinese became heavily involved in rural moneylending in the last decades of the nineteenth century, Burmese lenders continued to far outnumber their foreign competitors. It is probable that professional Burmese moneylenders alone exceeded the total number of Chinese, Chettiars, and other Indians engaged in credit provision at this time. If part-time Burmese lenders, such as successful agriculturists, local merchants, paddy brokers, and local government officials are included, the

29. Cheng, *Rice Industry of Burma,* pp. 200–206.

30. *RAP, 1860–61,* p. 33.

31. Cheng, *Rice Industry of Burma,* pp. 89–90, 92. I have calculated the percentages cited in the text from the figures provided by Cheng.

32. Ibid., pp. 83, 201.

number of indigenous lenders would exceed that of foreign lenders by many times.[33]

In numerical terms the Burmese also dominated internal, wholesale marketing operations in the Delta rice industry. Throughout the first phase of development, a large majority of the paddy brokers and rice merchants in Lower Burma were Burmese. Burmese control of paddy marketing within the Delta complemented their overall dominance in the wholesale marketing of all agricultural produce and in Burma's substantial timber industry.[34]

The extensive participation of the Burmese in credit provision and wholesale marketing contrasts sharply with the comparatively low level of involvement in these activities on the part of indigenous peoples in other areas in Southeast Asia. In Thailand and on Java, for example, wholesale trade and credit provision were left largely to the Chinese minorities.[35] In Malaya both Chinese and Indian immigrants filled most of the middleman's niches, while in the Philippines the Chinese and Chinese *meztizos* vied for control of internal trade and finance.[36]

The large numbers of Burmese engaged in moneylending and internal marketing, as well as the great mobility and adaptiveness displayed by Burmese agriculturists in response to economic incentives, force one to question the assumptions of many authors that Burmese values are inimical to involvement in a competitive, market-oriented economy. Mya Maung has made perhaps the fullest statement of this position in his study on "The Genesis of Economic Development in Burma: The Plural Society."[37] He contends that the doctrines of Theravada Buddhism, which is the religion of the great majority of the Burmese people, discourage the pursuit of material gain by identifying it as a source of insatiable craving and thus evil. Mya Maung

33. Because there are no quantitative estimates of the cultural composition of the moneylending class for this period, I have based these assertions on the qualitative evidence provided in the settlement reports and inference from later decades when some statistics are available.

34. Government of Burma, *Interim Report of the Riot Inquiry Committee* (Rangoon, 1939), p. 20; Furnivall, *Political Economy*, p. 158.

35. Skinner, *Chinese in Thailand*, pp. 104–9; James Ingram, *Economic Change in Thailand Since 1850* (Stanford, Calif., 1954) pp. 55–56, 71–74; Alice Dewey, "Trade and Social Control in Java," *The Journal of the Royal Anthropological Institute of Great Britain and Ireland* 92, nos. 1, 2 (January–December 1962): 177, et passim. Ingram presents some evidence (pp. 65–66) which suggests that agricultural credit at the local level was supplied mainly by Thais, but this point has not as yet been substantiated by detailed research.

36. Sandhu, *Indians in Malaya*, p. 42, et passim; Wickberg, *Chinese in Philippine Life*, esp. pp. 67–80. Ethnic groups, such as the Minangkabau on Sumatra, provide other important exceptions to these general trends.

37. Ph.D. diss., Catholic University of America, 1962. See also his more recent article on "Cultural Value and Economic Change in Burma," *Asian Survey* 4 (March 1964): 757–64.

also points out that the accumulation of wealth (or capital) runs counter to Buddhist doctrines such as the Four Noble Truths, which stress nonattachment and the concept of *anatta* (the nonexistence of a permanent self).[38] However, the evidence set forth in this study and in recent anthropological works suggests that prohibitions regarding the pursuit of profit were largely doctrinal and not rigidly observed in actual practice. Melford Spiro's fieldwork in Upper Burma provides evidence which supports this supposition. He points out that doctrines such as the Four Noble Truths and *anatta* were neither understood nor accepted by the villagers whom he studied.[39] Furthermore, Manning Nash concludes that "except for a restricted number of life-taking occupations, Buddhism is neutral in its bearing on economic roles and it does not encourage any particular activity positively . . . there is no religious tradition despising work or fixing one to a small number of ways to earn bread."[40] David Pfanner points out that, along with agriculture, trade and commerce are viewed as "harmless employment" because they do not require the taking of life.[41]

Although Burmese moneylenders far outnumbered Indian or Chinese, the scale of Burmese lending operations was generally much smaller than and their organization was far inferior to their foreign competitors, particularly the Chettiars. Despite the fact that there were only a few thousand Chettiar moneylenders in the Delta at the end of the nineteenth century, the size and extent of their operations make it probable that Chettiar lenders accounted for a larger share of agricultural loans than Burmese brokers, merchants, and moneylenders and Chinese shopkeepers combined.[42] The Chettiars' share of the total credit extended was enhanced by the fact that they often provided capital which Burmese moneylenders in turn loaned to agriculturists. These patterns indicate that the proper questions for the historian to ask with regard to the distribution of positions in finance in the Delta rice industry is not why so few Burmese were involved, but why foreign groups, like the Chettiars, were able to operate on a greater scale than the Burmese and how

38. Ibid., pp. 98–99, 100–101, 110. These views are also set forth by E. Sarkisyanz in his study on *Buddhist Backgrounds of the Burmese Revolution* (The Hague, 1965), pp. 141–43, 148, and by numerous other authors.

39. "Buddhism and Economic Action in Burma," *American Anthropologist* 68, no. 3 (October 1966):1163–65. In a number of places Mya Maung admits that religious behavior often does not coincide with religious doctrine, but he concludes that doctrines like nonattachment and nonself actually motivate the large majority of Burmese.

40. Nash, *Golden Road,* pp. 159–60.

41. David E. Pfanner and Jasper Ingersoll, "Theravada Buddhism and Village Economic Behavior: A Burmese and Thai Comparison," *Journal of Asian Studies* 21, no. 3 (May 1962): 345.

42. Again there is no quantitative information on this point for this period. The comments of settlement officers and the strong position of the Chettiar in the 1920s (see Chapter 7) support this assertion.

they came to play such an important role in the economy of an alien land. The answers to these questions can be found through an examination of the differences between the Burmese and their immigrant competitors in terms of their previous experiences, social organization, and cultural values. In the following discussion of these factors, I shall concentrate on a comparison of the Burmese with the Chettiars, who were by far the most important group of foreign middlemen in Lower Burma.

Opportunity explains why the Chettiars migrated to Lower Burma and proximity accounts for the fact that they, rather than some other foreign mercantile group, came to dominate credit provision in the Delta's rice industry. Capital was scarce in the Delta in the decades after 1852. Although British merchants and entrepreneurs provided some of the capital necessary for the region's development, their investments were concentrated in transportation, processing, and external trade. Capital to finance marketing and the expansion of agrarian production was badly needed. The limited sources of rural credit available in Lower Burma in the first decades after the annexation of 1852 would not have been sufficient to support the rapid growth of the rice industry in the last decades of the nineteenth century. However, the Nattukottai Chettiars possessed both the necessary capital and a desire to establish new outlets for investment. They soon acted to fill the niches in the commercial sector of Lower Burma's economy which British or European investors did not control. Because their homeland in the Madura and Ramnad districts of the Madras Presidency was just across the Bay of Bengal, they were in close touch with developments in the Delta and only a rather short journey by steamship away. In moving into Lower Burma, they merely extended the commercial network which they had established throughout much of the Madras Presidency and in Arakan and Tenasserim between 1826 and 1852. In time Lower Burma would become their most important area of operations.

Throughout most of their recorded history the Chettiars have been extensively involved in commerce, and thus they came to Burma well prepared to assume the middleman's role in the Delta economy. The origins of the Chettiar community, like those of most caste groups in India, are obscure and expressed in legends.[43] It is known, however, that Chettiars were engaged in commerce as early as the period of the Chola dynasty's hegemony in Tamilnad (c.900–1250). In Chola times they were engaged primarily in maritime trade, but in the sixteenth and seventeenth centuries they began to concentrate on banking and moneylending.[44] The Chettiar caste was of the Vaiśya *varna,* which means that its members were considered twice-born like Brahmans and Kśatriyas and ranked above Śudras (traditionally agriculturists)

43. See Edgar Thurston, *Tribes and Castes of South India,* 7 vols. (Madras, 1909), 5: 258–61.

44. C. H. Rau, "The Banking Caste of Southern India," *Indian Review* (Madras), 8,

and outcastes. Because of their great wealth and generous contributions to Hindu temples and charities, the Chettiars had long been a powerful and highly respected community in South India.[45]

Despite the fact that they showed little inclination to learn or adopt Western methods until the twentieth century, Chettiars had had much more extensive contacts than the Burmese with European merchants and shippers in the centuries prior to the Delta's annexation. Chettiars and other mercantile castes had, of course, functioned in rather well-developed market and money economies long before the Europeans had begun to trade in India. However, long centuries of dealing with Europeans prepared them for extensive involvement in the Delta economy after 1852.[46] Especially important were Chettiar connections with Western banks and joint-stock companies, such as the Imperial Bank of India and the Indian Overseas Bank, which provided them with sources of working capital which were not readily available to Burmese brokers, merchants, and moneylenders.[47]

In contrast to the experience gained by the Chettiars through centuries of commercial enterprise, the nature of the pre-British economy in Burma proved a serious handicap for Burmese who became involved in marketing or credit provision after 1852. In the largely subsistence economy of Konbaung Burma, merchants played a marginal role. External commerce by sea was largely in the hands of foreigners, and the overland trade to China was controlled by the Chinese. Internal trade was localized and mainly of a peddling nature. In the absence of a developed monetary system, credit facilities were crude and moneylenders' operations were small scale. Because there were few ways in which wealth might profitably be invested, there was little impetus to save. In fact, in a society where dacoity was widespread, warfare periodic, and government officials often rapacious, hoarded wealth was a tempting target. As a result, the level of investment in mercantile or handicraft enterprises was low.

In addition to the limitations imposed by the nature of Konbaung society itself, the isolation of the Burman kingdom placed those Burmese who sought to fill positions in trade or finance after 1852 at a disadvantage vis-à-vis their foreign competitors. The vast majority of Burmese, including members of the small mercantile class, had had only fleeting contacts with foreigners in the

---

no. 8 (August 1907): 593; Philip Siegelman, "Colonial Development and the Chettiar: A Study in the Ecology of Modern Burma, 1850–1941" (Ph.D. diss., University of Minnesota, 1962), pp. 121–22.

45. *Madura Gazetteer,* p. 101; Rau, "Banking Caste," p. 594. A fixed percentage of their profits, termed *magamai,* was set aside for charity.

46. Unfortunately, the nature and extent of these dealings have not yet begun to be explored. It is probable, however, that the Chettiars and other South Indian banking castes played as important a role in the development of European trade and political influence in South India as the Shroffs and other groups did in the North.

47. Tun Wai, *Currency and Credit,* pp. 49–50; *Banking Enquiry Report,* 2: 95, 97.

Konbaung period. They had almost no knowledge of European business techniques and marketing practices. Even more important, no group of Burmese possessed contacts with European banking firms comparable to those of the Chettiars and to a lesser extent the Chinese and other Indian merchants. Consequently, Burmese merchants and moneylenders were normally not able to take advantage of the great capital resources of these establishments.

Centuries of involvement in commercial enterprises had shaped the social patterns and oriented the values of the Chettiar community. The homelife and upbringing of a Chettiar child inculcated values of thrift and self-reliance and prepared him for a position in a Chettiar firm when he came of age. Chettiar parents were expected to set aside a certain amount of money at the birth of each son. The money with accumulated interest was later used to finance the boy's education. Although Chettiar families normally resided in joint households, each married member cooked and ate his meals separately. Fixed allotments of food and other provisions were divided among married members of the family annually, and they were expected to use their supplies judiciously so that they would not be caught short. The wives of even the most wealthy Chettiars dressed simply, performed menial household tasks, and wove baskets or spun thread to help pay household expenses. When a Chettiar visited his relatives, he received only his first meal free. If he stayed longer, he would be "quietly debited" the cost of the rest of his stay.[48]

Until the age of ten or twelve Chettiar boys studied in Tamil schools, where they learned bookkeeping techniques and the caste's special counting system. At the age of twelve they went to work as apprentices for Chettiar firms. During the period of their apprenticeship, which could last as long as nine years, Chettiar youths received little in the way of theoretical training, for the Chettiars considered experience the best teacher. If he were successful, the young Chettiar would begin to work his way up the hierarchy from accountant to cashier after four or five years, and become an assistant or subagent in a *utkade* or outstation after seven or eight years. Between the ages of twenty-two and twenty-five the successful trainee would receive a position as an agent and, if he were talented, eventually become a partner in a firm.[49]

There was no group in Burmese society whose family structure and rearing practices were geared to success in commerce to a degree comparable to that of the Chettiars. Although contemporary studies of Burmese village communities suggest that Burmese Buddhist values are not inimical to commercial pursuits, they indicate that Buddhist practices may place

48. Thurston, *Tribes and Castes*, pp. 250–53, 270; *Banking Enquiry Report*, 1: 192.
49. Rau, "Banking Caste," p. 595; *Banking Enquiry Report*, 1: 208, 2: 133; Thurston, *Tribes and Castes*, pp. 252–53.

considerable limitations on the extent to which an individual can become involved in financial endeavors and on the scale of his operations. These limitations result from the fact that Theravada Buddhist beliefs militate against the economically productive use of wealth. Pfanner has observed that "the accumulation of wealth as an end in itself is not admired in rural Burma, but the accumulation of wealth for the purposes of merit-making is highly valued."[50] Nash states that rich villagers of Nondwin near Sagaing in the Dry Zone are expected to spend lavishly on Buddhist ceremonies, pagoda and monastery building or repair, and the support of local monks. According to popular Buddhist belief, the rich have the greatest opportunity to make merit by using their wealth for these ends. A survey taken by Nash in Nondwin showed that these expectations were fulfilled in actual practice, for religious donations constituted a far higher percentage of the annual expenditure of rich than of poor peasants.[51]

There is a considerable body of nineteenth-century evidence which demonstrates that rich agriculturists and prosperous villages spent great sums on merit-making. Maung Kyaw Din and Saya Thit, whose biographies were sketched in Chapter 3, both spent large amounts on works of merit. Kyaw Din built a monastery and pagoda for his village which cost nearly Rs. 23,000. Over a period of years Saya Thit spent Rs. 10,000 on works of merit which equaled nine times the amount he spent on his own house.[52] Settlement officers noted that rich villages normally devoted large sums to the erection of teak monasteries and gilded pagodas, and that often these buildings were built by a single individual.[53] One officer commented that large debts incurred for expenditures on religious festivals and donations demonstrated the wealth not the poverty of the borrower.[54] The merit-making syndrome would have greatly hindered effective Burmese participation in moneylending and commerce by diverting the resources of those individuals who were best able to engage in these activities to nonproductive (in economic terms) channels.[55]

In competition with Burmese moneylenders, Chettiars also derived great advantage from their superior organization and group solidarity. While most Burmese moneylenders worked as individuals, Chettiars were invariably

50. Pfanner and Ingersoll, "Buddhism and Behavior," p. 345.

51. Nash, *Golden Road,* pp. 160–61. See also Spiro, "Buddhism and Economic Action," pp. 1168–69; Pfanner and Ingersoll, "Buddhism and Behavior," p. 348; C. S. Brant, *Tadagale: A Burmese Village in 1950* (Ithaca, N.Y., 1954), p. 12.

52. *Myaungmya-Thongwa Settlement Report (1902–3),* p. 118.

53. *Settlement Reports–Toungoo (1898–99),* p. 34; *Tharrawaddy (1901–2),* p. 7.

54. *Myaungmya Settlement Report (1897–98),* p. 7.

55. As noted above, Chettiars also gave extensively to charity, but given the scale of their operations and the relatively limited amount of their profits spent on charity, this practice did not constrict their commercial involvement in the same way merit-making limited Burmese economic investment.

members of firms. There are no statistics pertaining to the number of Chettiar firms in Lower Burma at the end of the nineteenth century, but they certainly exceeded one hundred and they were organized in a standard fashion. Chettiar firms were owned on a partnership basis by several persons who were usually related. An agent-supervisor directed the day-to-day operations of the firm from its headquarters, which was located in Rangoon or Moulmein. The firm normally had agencies in the larger towns of the Delta which were run by agents and staffed with cashiers, accountants, and clerks. Beginning in the 1880s outstations which were run singlehandedly by subagents were established in growing numbers of villages in Lower Burma.[56]

Chettiar combinations not only provided superior sources of capital to invest and lend, but they also strengthened community ties, which were vital to Chettiar predominance in Burma. Alice Dewey has shown that Chinese success in trade on Java can to a large degree be attributed to the "informal" or nonlegal sanctions through which members of the community insure that debts are paid, orders delivered on time, and contracts kept on a continuing and long-term basis. She points out that by reducing the element of risk involved in commercial activities, these sanctions have given the Chinese a decisive edge over the Javanese, whose supravillage business ties are "transient" and "intermittent."[57] Through caste and kinship networks and their firm organizations, Chettiars in Burma institutionalized informal sanctions. Prosperous Chettiars were often partners in several firms, and in the late nineteenth century a firm in financial difficulty was invariably given aid by other firms.[58] The main Chettiar temple on Mogul Street in Rangoon, which was called the "Chettiar exchange," served as a focal point for the community's activities in Burma. On the upper floor in a large room before the community shrine to Siva, Chettiars held periodic meetings, determined current interest rates, settled disputes, formed common opinions regarding important political issues (such as proposed tenancy or land alienation legislation), and exchanged gossip.[59]

Although they were less well organized and had more limited access to capital for investment, other Indian mercantile groups, such as the Chatris and Komatis, possessed many of the same advantages as the Chettiars in their commercial activities in Lower Burma. The Chinese, who also filled middleman niches in the Delta rice-export economy, probably minimized the risk involved in their enterprises through the same informal sanctions which

56. Andrus, *Burmese Economic Life*, p. 76; *Banking Enquiry Report*, 1: 204–8.

57. "Trade and Social Control," pp. 179–85. Dewey's "informal sanctions" were paralleled by "personal ties" which Maurice Freedman believed helped the Chinese and Indians to control the commercial sector in Malaya. See "The Growth of a Plural Society in Malaya," *Pacific Affairs* 33, no. 2 (1960): 168.

58. W. R. Winston, *Four Years in Upper Burma* (London, 1892), pp. 38–39.

59. *Banking Enquiry Report*, 1: 193.

immigrant Chinese employed in other areas of overseas activity. The Chinese preference for trade, moneylending, and shopkeeping in Burma was almost certainly determined by the same factors which G. W. Skinner has distinguished as responsible for their concentration in similar occupations in Thailand. The qualities of thrift and industriousness instilled by the grim struggle to survive in South China, the desire to advance family and kin, and the belief that commerce offered the greatest potential for upward mobility all predisposed the Chinese to share the middleman's role in the Delta economy with Indian mercantile groups and the Burmese.[60]

Given their many handicaps, it is remarkable that so many Burmese participated successfully in trade and credit provision in the Delta rice industry. One factor that may explain their ability to survive despite the superior organization and capital resources of their foreign competitors was the informal division of clientele that had developed between Burmese and Chettiar lenders by the 1880s. Chettiars lent mainly to reliable persons who could offer good security. Burmese moneylenders, on the other hand, who had a better knowledge of local conditions and a personal acquaintance with prospective customers,[61] often gave loans to persons whom Chettiars had turned down.[62] This difference in the type of person who borrowed from Chettiars and Burmese moneylenders may explain in part why the former charged a lower rate of interest.

In landowning as in moneylending, the emphasis that most historians have placed on the Depression period of Burma's economic development conveys the impression that the Chettiars were dominant from a very early date. Throughout the late nineteenth century, however, a large majority of landlords in most areas of the Delta were Burmese. The predominance of Burmese as large landholders is illustrated by the figures provided in several settlement reports for districts in the lower Delta at the turn of the century. These show that the percentage of Burmese landlords in various districts ranged from 96 to 75, while the highest percentage owned by Indians in any district was 25.[63] Unfortunately, statistics relating to the composition of the landlord class were not included in reports for other districts. Nonetheless, textual evidence indicates that an equal or greater percentage of landlords in

60. Skinner, *Chinese in Thailand*, pp. 91–96.

61. The Chettiars' disadvantage in this respect was compounded by the fact that firms rotated their agents every three years. This meant that no agent could gain a thorough knowledge of any one area. See *Banking Enquiry Report*, 1: 209–10.

62. Government of Burma, Revenue and Agriculture Proceedings, vol. 8633, November 1911, p. 496; *Bassein Settlement Report (1897–98)*, p. 14.

63. These percentages were calculated from the tables on persons owning more than one hundred acres in *Settlement Reports–Myaungmya (1897–98), Maubin (1904–5), Pyapon (1906–7)*.

other areas was Burmese.[64] The Hanthawaddy and Pegu districts, especially circles near Rangoon where Indian moneylenders were very active, were an exception to this general pattern.[65]

Of the Indian landlords in the Maubin and Pyapon districts, 70 and 60 percent respectively were Chettiars. This meant that they controlled only 17 and 12 percent of the holdings which exceeded one hundred acres in these areas. The low percentage of land held by Chettiars in comparison to that held by Burmese moneylenders, merchants, and agriculturists supports the belief of most revenue officials that Chettiars did not generally want land. British administrators argued that it was in the Chettiars' interest to keep their investments fluid and not to become involved in extensive landholding in an alien land. In most areas, Chettiars took over debtors' lands only as a last resort in order to prevent further monetary losses. They attempted to sell the holdings which they were forced to claim as soon as possible.[66] In contrast with the Chettiars, many British officers concluded that the local Burmese moneylender was often a "dangerous landgrabber" who was "far more anxious" than the Chettiar to acquire land. In some areas, village moneylenders provided agricultural loans primarily in the hope that they would eventually gain control of large estates through foreclosures.[67] Although some Burmese moneylenders may have been "landgrabbers," it is likely that most, like the Chettiars, were forced to take over cultivators' holdings when it became clear that their loans would not be repaid. The fact that Burmese moneylenders generally extended credit to less reliable customers than did the Chettiars may best explain the higher incidence of foreclosures in transactions involving indigenous lenders.

Very few Indians were cultivator-owners in the first phase of development. Most Indian laborers who accumulated substantial savings preferred to return to India to purchase land, renew their former way of life, or take up new occupations in urban areas. Some laborers, however, rose to become tenants and landowners and, if they were fortunate, large landlords in the Delta.[68] Aside from this small minority who were found on isolated holdings

64. *Settlement Reports–Bassein (1881–82)*, p. 3; *Tharrawaddy (1900–1901)*, p. 8; *Prome (1900–1901)*, app.; *Maubin, Myaungmya, and Pyapon (1905–6)*, p. 14.

65. Government of Burma, Revenue and Agriculture Proceedings, vol. 7237, May 1906, p. 105; *Pegu Settlement Report (1898–99)*, app., pp. cxxiii–cxxix.

66. *Settlement Reports–Myaungmya-Thongwa (1902–3)*, p. 17; *Maubin, Myaungmya and Pyapon (1905–6)*, p. 14; Government of Burma, Revenue and Agriculture Proceedings, vol. 4886, March 1896, pp. 36–37, vol. 7238, August 1906, p. 63, vol. 7237, May 1906, pp. 25–26.

67. Government of Burma, Revenue and Agriculture Proceedings, vol. 7237, May 1906, pp. 25–26, 89–92, vol. 7238, August 1906, p. 63; *Myaungmya-Thongwa Settlement Report (1903–4)*, p. 17.

68. Government of Burma, Revenue and Agriculture Proceedings, vol. 8633, November 1911, p. 3; *Land Revenue Report, 1903–4*, p. 28; *Hanthawaddy Settlement Report (1898–99)*, p. 18.

throughout Lower Burma and a few settlements of Indian agriculturists,[69] the cultivator-owners of the Delta were Burmese.

By the last decades of the nineteenth century there was a fairly clear division of labor at the lower levels of the Delta's economy between the urban sphere, which was dominated by Indian immigrants, and agricultural production, which was largely the preserve of the indigenous Burmese. The available sources indicate that this division resulted largely from preference on the part of the Burmese rather than from Indo-Burmese competition for the control of various sectors. Burmese laborers generally favored village over urban life. A number of nineteenth-century observers remarked that the average Burmese would rather "scratch out a living on poor land" than be a "coolie earning good wages."[70] In addition, the Burmese usually avoided positions in construction or industry which required them to live in coolie barracks or laborers' tenements, where it was often impossible for their families to live with them.[71] The Burmese also avoided positions which might be classified as "industrial manual labor" because they disliked the regimentation and low prestige normally associated with them.[72] As agriculturists, once they had obtained their own holdings, the Burmese were their own masters. In industrial positions or as heavy laborers they would be ordered about by others. Therefore, although they accepted employment as supervisors or skilled laborers, the Burmese preferred to leave the "dull, monotonous" tasks of "coolies" and the menial tasks of servants to Indians.[73]

Indian laborers were rarely able to pick and choose the positions they would occupy in Burma. In many cases *maistries* had arranged the laborers' place of employment in advance of their migration to Burma. In addition, immigrant laborers were often driven to Burma by famine or hard times in India and their major concern was merely to begin earning wages and remitting money to their relatives in India as soon as possible. Whether or not they were driven by famine, Indian laborers were invariably from over-populated districts where wages were extremely low compared to those obtainable in Lower Burma. Consequently, they saw immigration to Burma as one solution to the Malthusian dilemma that faced them in Madras or the United Provinces. Their great need for employment may account for their seeming lack of aversion to the regimented life of the dreary company barracks which many authors attributed to the Indians' more "docile" nature

69. *Settlement Reports–Bassein (1880–81)*, p. 2; *Hanthawaddy-Pegu (1883–84)*, pp. 3–4.

70. Government of Burma, *Report on the Famine in Burma*, p. 26.

71. Baxter, *Indian Immigration*, pp. 84–86; N. Gangulee, *Indians in the Empire Overseas* (London, 1947), p. 135.

72. Maung, "Economic Genesis," pp. 127–30.

73. Baxter, *Indian Immigration*, pp. 85– 87; Maung, "Economic Genesis," p. 130.

or the fact that they had become "accustomed" to deprivations.[74] European millowners and shippers preferred to hire Indian laborers because they made fewer demands and generally accepted lower wages.[75] Thus, Indian immigrants came to fill niches in transportation, industry, and construction which the Burmese were willing to relinquish because there was plenty of land and opportunities in other sectors.

Immigrant Indian laborers gained control of the processing and transport sectors of the Delta rice industry gradually during the last half of the nineteenth century. Substantial numbers of Burmese laborers worked in the Bassein rice mills until the 1880s. It is probable, however, that Indian workers were dominant in the processing plants in the city of Rangoon by the mid-1870s and perhaps earlier.[76] Wharf labor in Rangoon, on the other hand, was largely in the hands of the Burmese until the 1880s.[77] Over the next two decades it became a near monopoly of Indians who worked in gangs under *maistries.* Although the stages in the transformation of Lower Burma's urban labor force from Burmese to Indian control cannot be traced precisely, it is clear that by the early 1890s the working classes of Rangoon, Bassein, and most Delta towns were predominantly Indian.[78]

Beyond the urban sphere, Indian laborers were often associated with Indian employers and concentrated in the districts around Rangoon. Normally Indian tenants rented their holdings from Indian landlords. In the 1890s and early 1900s Chettiar landholders in a number of areas imported Indian laborers to work the estates which they had acquired through the foreclosure of mortgages. Chettiars in some areas of the Delta were forced to let to Indians because Burmese seasonal migrants from the Dry Zone who had once worked their lands had ceased coming for the cropping season.[79] Other Chettiar landlords let to Indian tenants because they offered higher rents than the Burmese would agree to pay.[80] Government officials reported that some Chettiars rack-rented Indian tenants, who seemed less willing than the Burmese to move about in search of better conditions.[81] Indian tenants were the most numerous in the lower Delta districts and especially in circles near Rangoon and other large towns. However, Burmese agriculturists made up the

74. Gangulee, *Indians in the Empire,* p. 135; Baxter, *Indian Immigration,* p. 87.

75. Furnivall, "Safety First," p. 31.

76. Ibid.

77. Furnivall, *Colonial Policy and Practice,* p. 53.

78. Government of Burma, Revenue and Agriculture Proceedings, vol. 4043, November 1892, nos. 1, 6, pp. 158–59.

79. *Land Revenue Report, 1905–6,* pp. 28–29.

80. *Pyapon Settlement Report (1906–7),* p. 13.

81. *Land Revenue Reports, 1905–6,* p. 29, *1907–8,* p. 29; *RAB, 1907–8,* p. 17; Government of Burma, Revenue and Agriculture Proceedings, vol. 6279, January 1902, p. 11; *Pegu (Bawni) Settlement Report (1900–1901),* p. 32.

greater share of the tenants in these regions and almost all of the tenants in other areas of the Delta.

Two types of Indian immigrant workers were involved in agricultural production at the level of landless laborers in the pre-1907 period. The first were industrial workers who migrated to the rural areas during the reaping season. The second consisted of permanent agricultural laborers who found employment on public works, repairing bunds, or running paddy barges during the dry season. The first type of laborer was far less important in this period than it became in later decades. Apparently the yearround demand for labor in excess of that which the Burmese could supply was so great that many Indian immigrants worked only in agricultural production. B. R. Pearn wrote of large numbers of Indian laborers who remained in Rangoon only overnight or for a few days after their arrival in Burma. They had come to the Delta to find agricultural employment and thus moved quickly into the rural areas.[82]

Burmese agricultural laborers were drawn mainly from the Dry Zone and other Burma divisions outside the Delta, although increasing numbers came from local villages in the last decades of the period. Both Indian and Burmese laborers were found in all areas of Lower Burma, but Indians concentrated their operations in the Hanthawaddy, Bassein, and Thaton districts and in the frontier districts of the lower, central Delta. Burmese laborers were predominant in the upper Delta and in the Pegu district east of Rangoon town. They were also numerous in circles away from large towns in Thaton and in the lower Delta.[83] Burmese laborers were usually hired for the plowing season, while Indians were normally employed as reapers. Indians almost invariably worked in gangs under *maistries,* while the Burmese hired out individually. In some areas by the 1890s, Burmese laborers had organized into gangs after the Indian practice. Most Indian gangs insisted on cash payments, but the majority of Burmese laborers were paid in kind.[84] Several sources mention that Indians were cheaper to hire and there were conflicting opinions regarding the quality of the work done by laborers of each group. These issues will be considered at some length in the discussion on occupations by cultural groups in the post-1907 period for which more data is available.

The interaction of different cultural groups in the Delta economy in this period was strikingly noncompetitive and highly fluid. At most levels, there

82. *Rangoon,* pp. 234–35, 257, 287.

83. *Settlement Reports–Hanthawaddy (1897–98),* p. 9; *Pegu (1897–98),* p. 9, *(1899–1900),* p. 17; *Thaton (1897–98),* p. 6; *Bassein (1897–98),* p. 16, *(1898–99),* p. 14; *Myaungmya-Bassein (1901–2),* p. 5; *Myaungmya-Thongwa (1902–3),* p. 5; Hall, "Note," in Nolan, *Report,* pp. i–iii.

84. *Settlement Reports–Pegu (1897–98),* p. 9; *Thaton (1897–98),* p. 6; *Myaungmya-Bassein (1901–2),* p. 5; *Myaungmya (1903–4),* p. 9; *RAB, 1884–85,* p. 63.

were more than enough positions to be filled and, depending on his training or capital resources, an individual could choose between a number of options. Outside of the political sphere, no niches were the total monopoly of any one group, and control of positions at different levels was continually changing. Symbiosis rather than competition best characterizes the relationship between different cultural groups in the first phase of agrarian development. Indian laborers eagerly sought positions which the Burmese did not have the numbers or the desire to fill. Indian moneylenders provided a major source of credit for Burmese agriculturists, and for many Burmese moneylenders, merchants, and rice brokers as well. Indians rarely competed with Burmese for positions as tenants or agricultural laborers. Since the demand for both far exceeded the supply, Indians complemented rather than competed with Burmese. Each group needed the other, and both were vital to the growth and well-being of the Delta economy. At the end of the nineteenth century few persons in Lower Burma would have disagreed with the settlement officer who claimed that Indians generally "get on well" with the Burmese and were "useful members" of Delta society.[85]

85. *Bassein Settlement Report (1897–98)*, p. 7.

Part III

THE DECADES OF TRANSITION, 1908–30

6

THE CLOSING RICE FRONTIER AND NEW PATTERNS OF AGRARIAN DEVELOPMENT

In terms of rice exported, acres brought under cultivation, and the amount of revenue collected, the economic development of Lower Burma in the first decades of the twentieth century appears to have been a continuation of the rapid and generally healthy growth which began after 1852. Rice acreage rose from six million acres in 1905–6 to over eight million acres in 1930–31, while the amount of rice and paddy exported from Burma increased from two to almost three million tons in the same period. The price of one hundred baskets of paddy at Rangoon rose from Rs. 120 in 1906 to as high as Rs. 195 in the early 1920s. The number of rice mills in Lower Burma nearly quadrupled from 124 in 1908 to 486 in 1930.[1]

These often cited indices of provincial prosperity concealed from most observers the gravity of growing problems in the agrarian sector. Government officials and Burmese nationalists alike failed to recognize or act to prevent the gradual deterioration of the condition of the agrarian classes in the Delta until the very last years of the decades of transition.[2] Their failure has been reflected in the works of many historians of modern Burma who have emphasized the impact of the Great Depression on the economy and society

1. *Season and Crop, 1905–6, 1930–31,* acreage use tables; Grant, *Rice Crop,* pp. 48, 56; Cheng, *Rice Industry of Burma,* pp. 253–55.

2. There were important exceptions, including Sir H. T. White and numerous settlement officers, but their efforts at the turn of the century to introduce legislation to protect the agriculturists were defeated by powerful and vocal opposition.

of Burma and neglected the changes in the early 1900s which made the crisis of the 1930s inevitable. This emphasis has obscured the root causes of that crisis, which lay in the very nature of the economic system which evolved in the Delta. Although they became more intense in the late 1920s and 1930s, there were serious agrarian problems long before the Great Depression.

One of the most important determinants of the rapid economic development which had occurred and the general prosperity which had been achieved in Lower Burma in the late nineteenth century was the presence of a frontier. Because there were no major changes in agricultural technology, increased rice production was largely a function of the extension of paddy cultivation into new areas. Consequently, the rapid growth of the Delta rice industry as a whole was largely dependent on the continuing availability of cultivable land. The presence of large amounts of fertile, unoccupied land was also essential to the well-being of the cultivating classes, particularly tenants and landless laborers. In the first decades of the twentieth century, however, the limits to the extension of rice cultivation were reached in most areas of the Delta.[3] Local shortages of cultivable, unoccupied land were reported as early as 1897,[4] and by the time of the First World War available land suitable for rice cultivation was confined mainly to circles in the lower, central Delta and the Toungoo District.[5] By the mid-1920s government officials observed that most of the land in Lower Burma which cultivators could profitably bring into paddy production had been occupied.[6]

The Delta rice frontier closed gradually and unevenly. No government proclamations marked its end; in fact few government officials noted its demise and only a handful understood its importance. As the frontier closed, however, the potential and protection that it had provided for the cultivating classes also came to an end. With the open land buffer gone, problems

3. It is important to point out that some government reports continued to list substantial amounts of arable, unoccupied land in areas where settlement officers reported that the limits of paddy cultivation had been reached. As Thomas Couper pointed out in 1924 (*Report of Inquiry into the Condition of Agricultural Tenants and Labourers* [Rangoon, 1924], pp. 28, 67), this discrepancy arose from the fact that administrative reports listed all arable land, while settlement officers estimated only the amount of unoccupied land which could be brought into profitable production by the average Delta agriculturist.

4. *Thaton Settlement Report (1897–98)*, p. 29.

5. *Settlement Reports–Thaton (1907–8)*, p. 3; *Hanthawaddy (1907–10)*, p. 2; *Tharrawaddy (1913–15)*, p. 2; *Prome (1914–16)*, p. 22; *Bassein (1912–14)*, p. 2; *Pegu (1913–14)*, p. 1.

6. A. McKerral, "Climatic Tracts, Distribution of Crops, etc.," in Government of Burma, *Agriculture in Burma*, . . . (Rangoon, 1927), p. 5; C. W. Dunn, "Some General Characteristics . . . ," in Government of Burma, *Agriculture in Burma*, p. 23; *Maubin Settlement Report (1925–28)*, pp. 15, 33. This trend for the whole Delta was reported as early as 1911. See Harold Clayton, *Rural Development in Burma* (Rangoon, 1911), pp. 6–7.

inherent in the nature of economic development in Lower Burma grew more intense and an era of apparent prosperity and content gave way to decades of conflict and unrest.

The decline in the amount of unoccupied land was a major factor behind the great increase in the sale price of Delta land. The average price of an acre of land in the Prome District, for example, rose from Rs. 29 to Rs. 103 between 1900 and 1915. In the Hanthawaddy District in the lower Delta, the price of land rose from about Rs. 20 per acre around 1900 to Rs. 70 in 1910, and to Rs. 105 in the early 1930s.[7] The rising cost of land greatly impaired the average cultivator-owner's ability to extend his holdings, and the high cost of bringing marginal unoccupied areas under cultivation greatly restricted his capacity to settle on the rapidly vanishing rice frontier. Consequently, the extension of rice cultivation after 1900 was due primarily to the efforts of large landlords and land grabbers to increase their production for the market. The rate of expansion slowed considerably and fluctuated in response to market conditions. Between 1910 and 1920 there was less than a 12 percent increase in the area under paddy cultivation in the Delta, compared to a 76 percent increase during the last decade of the nineteenth century. Due to a sharp rise in prices in the early 1920s, the rate of extension accelerated somewhat until 1925, but the post-1925 market slump and a concomitant drop in the rate of expansion left the area increase for the 1920–30 period at only 15 percent.[8]

Increases in paddy acreage were due primarily to the extension of the area under the *kaukkyi* and *kauklat* cropping patterns which had dominated Delta production in the nineteenth century. However, population growth and the greatly diminished availability of unoccupied land led to the introduction of a number of new cultivation patterns. These were designed to make use of marginal land that had previously been left uncultivated and to permit the cultivator to remain productive during the slack season after the main harvest. In parts of the upper Delta and of the west-central districts of the lower Delta, the *mayin* pattern of paddy cultivation which was widely practiced in Upper Burma was introduced in the decades of transition. *Mayin* paddy was planted in late October or November in low-lying marshes or on small islands that were flooded during the rainy season. It required irrigation during the dry months and was harvested in the slack season in late February or March.[9]

7. These averages are taken from the sale price statistics quoted in the settlement reports for Prome and Hanthawaddy. No regular sale price statistics for Lower Burma generally or individual districts at regular intervals were recorded. The averages are considerably understated because sale prices were often underreported to keep down registration costs.

8. For regional and general trends in cultivation extension in this period, see Adas, "Agrarian Development," pp. 363–65.

9. *Maubin Settlement Report (1925–28)*, p. 26; Dunn, "Some General Characteristics," in Government of Burma, *Agriculture in Burma*, p. 23; Cheng, *Rice Industry of*

There was also a substantial increase throughout the Delta in the amount of land cropped by the *tadaungbo* or deep-water technique, which had been introduced in the late nineteenth century. *Tadaungbo* planting began before the rainy season and involved the use of rice strains that made it possible to bring heavily flooded tracts previously left unused into production.[10]

Although the area planted in *mayin* and *tadaungbo* made up only a small percentage of the total land under paddy cultivation in the Delta,[11] the introduction of new rice strains was among the major innovations in agricultural technology during the entire period covered by this study. The decreasing availability of open land did not lead, as one might expect, to more intensive cultivation, to major changes in production techniques, or to the use of more modern implements. In the first decades of the twentieth century, as in the nineteenth, most cultivators who wished to increase their output acquired more land rather than changing their cropping patterns. Consequently, as the amount of unoccupied land diminished, output stagnated and then declined on holdings that were worked for year after year without being fertilized, fallowed, or cultivated by more productive methods.[12]

Agriculturists in most areas of the Delta continued to eschew the use of either artificial or natural fertilizers. Nurseries were usually manured as they had been in the nineteenth century, but cultivators normally could not afford or did not see the need to fertilize their entire holdings.[13] Government efforts to develop artificial fertilizers had little impact because until the very end of the transition period they were too expensive. By the time cheap fertilizers became available, the Depression had deprived most agriculturists of the means to make any improvements whatsoever.[14] Some large

---

Burma, p. 37; acreage use tables in *Season and Crop* for 1915–16, 1920–21, 1925–26, 1930–31.

10. *Settlement Reports–Maubin (1904–5)*, p. 3; *Maubin, Myaungmya and Pyapon (1905–6)*, p. 11; *Tharrawaddy (1903–4)*, p. 2; *Prome (1903–4)*, p. 5; *Maubin (1925–28)*, pp. 7–8, 28, 33; *Thaton (Pa-an) (1928–30)*, p. 22.

11. Land under *mayin* paddy accounted for 0.3 percent of the total rice land in Lower Burma in 1930–31. See area use tables, *Season and Crop, 1930–31.* No figures are available for the acreage under *tadaungbo,* but it is probable that it did not greatly exceed the area under *mayin.*

12. The lack of substantial innovation, despite growing population density, illustrates the importance of focusing on other factors, particularly those related to the market, in addition to the demographic variables stressed by Ester Boserup (in *The Conditions of Agricultural Development* [Chicago, 1965]) in attempting to determine the stimuli for changes in land use or cropping techniques.

13. David Hendry, *Fertilizers for Paddy: Results Obtained at the Hmawbi Agricultural Station* (Rangoon, 1928), p. 1. In some tracts of the tidal Delta cultivators deliberately avoided the use of fertilizers because they lengthened the paddy stalks, causing them to fall over into the water in the fields and rot. See *Hanthawaddy Settlement Report (1907–10)*, p. 5.

14. Hendry, *Fertilizers*, pp. 3, 11–13; Furnivall, *Political Economy*, p. 19.

landholders could afford to use the artificial fertilizers developed by the Department of Agriculture,[15] but the vast majority of cultivators did little more to replenish the soil than to burn off stubble and plow under stalks and chaff.

The adverse effects of the failure of Delta agriculturists to fertilize their holdings were compounded by the fact that large tracts of land were deprived of enrichment from natural sources. Embankments built to protect paddy fields from flooding during the monsoon season also prevented silt and nutrients carried by the Delta's rivers from being deposited. As a result the original fertility of the soil was soon lost. After an initial decline in fertility, however, the quality of the soil remained fairly constant.[16] Nonetheless, the output per acre in most regions dropped gradually in the first decades of the twentieth century.[17] The overall decline in per acre yield was also due to the extension of cultivation into lands of marginal fertility and those prone to flooding. The yield per acre of *tadaungbo* paddy, for example, was considerably below that of other varieties. By the end of the transition period, the average productivity of an acre of paddy land in the Delta was below that recorded in most other rice-growing countries.[18]

The fact that cultivators did not fertilize holdings declining in productivity was only one manifestation of a general paucity of significant advances in agricultural technology in the 1907–30 period. In most tracts seed selection remained at the same rudimentary level observed in the late nineteenth century.[19] Toward the end of the decades of transition the Department of Agriculture attempted to introduce a number of improved seed varieties, including foreign and high-quality hybrids. The cultivators in the areas where these improved seeds were available apparently sought them eagerly once their superiority had been demonstrated, but the available supply never caught up with the demand. As a result, less than 2 percent of the total area under rice cultivation in Burma in 1929–30 was planted with improved varieties.[20]

In the face of declining yields and the closing of the frontier, the substitution of transplanting for broadcast sowing techniques was surprisingly limited in this period. The increasing availability of cheap hired labor required for the more productive transplanting mode prompted some cultivators to

15. *Hanthawaddy Settlement Report (1930–33)*, pp. 24–25.

16. Hendry, *Fertilizers*, pp. 1–2, 11–12; Government of Burma, Revenue and Agriculture Proceedings, vol. 8633, November 1911, p. 501.

17. This decline can be traced in *Season and Crop* for this period or in Adas, "Agrarian Development," Table VIII-B, p. 368.

18. Hendry, *Fertilizers*, p. 2; Cheng, *Rice Industry of Burma*, p. 28.

19. *Settlement Reports–Bassein (1912–13)*, p. 14; *Myaungmya (1916–19)*, p. 60.

20. Hendry, "Rice in Burma," p. 53. I have calculated the percentage from the acreage total given in the Government of India, *Moral and Material Progress Report (1929–30)*, p. 131.

change, while soil depletion provided the major stimulus for others. With the exception of tracts in north Insein and Toungoo and west Pegu, however, broadcast sowing remained the dominant form of planting in those areas where it was found in the late nineteenth century.[21]

The implements used by the average cultivator were virtually the same as those used in the first phase of development. The area plowed with the traditional Burman plow (*hte*) increased considerably, and rotary harrows (*settuns*) were more widely used.[22] In addition, attempts by officials from the Department of Agriculture to introduce more advanced plows were somewhat more successful than they had been in the nineteenth century. *Theikpan,* or soil-inverting, plows were said to be "gradually gaining popularity" by the end of the 1920s.[23] As late as 1936, however, J. R. Andrus noted that the *hte* was still favored by most agriculturists.[24] Some new implements proved impractical for conditions in the Delta. Western-style plows sometimes cut too deeply into the soil, exposing it to the tropical sun and turning up the less fertile undersoil that lay beneath the thin layer of rich alluvium.[25] American disc harrows, which cultivators near Bassein town in the west Delta used for a brief period, proved too heavy for Burmese bullocks to pull.[26]

In the late 1920s attempts were made to mechanize paddy production. Landlords and cultivator-owners in the lower Delta purchased approximately sixty tractors, which they often rented to their neighbors at high rates. They soon discovered, however, that the tractors were useless on flooded soil. Because low-lying fields which were to be planted under *tadaungbo* paddy were plowed before the rains, the tractors came to be used almost solely for this purpose. The dry, clay-like soil was hard on the tractors, and thus operating costs and rental fees were high.[27] An additional impediment to the mechanization of paddy production was the fact that even the largest holdings in Lower Burma were divided by field bunds or *kazins,* which were essential to water control during the growing season. Tractors were never widely adopted, and the ones which had been imported fell into disuse during the Depression. In many ways their introduction was superfluous, for as Furnivall has pointed out,[28] the presence of a large pool of cheap labor, both

21. See the sections on cropping techniques in the settlement reports for this period.

22. *Settlement Reports–Toungoo (1910–13),* p. 21; *Tharrawaddy (1913–15),* p. 17; *Prome (1914–16),* p. 31; *Pegu Gazetteer,* p. 63.

23. Grant, *Rice Crop,* p. 13; Bruen, "Agricultural Geography," p. 103.

24. *Rural Reconstruction in Burma* (Oxford, 1936), p. 12.

25. *Thaton Settlement Report (1908–10),* pp. 6–7.

26. *Bassein Settlement Report (1912–14),* p. 22.

27. Bruen, "Agricultural Geography," pp. 103–4; *Settlement Reports–Maubin (1925–28),* pp. 41–42; *Hanthawaddy (1930–33),* p. 23.

28. *Political Economy,* p. 70.

Indian and Burmese, made the mechanization of agriculture seem unnecessary.

Perhaps the most substantial change in agricultural technology during the entire period of British rule was in terms of the organization of cultivating operations. On the large "estates" of the lower Delta, particularly those in the vicinity of Rangoon and in the frontier areas of the central Delta, a new pattern of production evolved which Furnivall has labeled "industrial agriculture."[29] As Furnivall stressed, the term industrial did not refer to mechanization, but rather to the extreme specialization and large scale which characterized this pattern of production. He observed that the division of labor, which was usually associated with industry, had been applied to agriculture in Lower Burma and been carried "as far as possible."[30]

The large pool of semi-skilled, agrarian wage laborers which had developed in the late nineteenth century was essential for this elaborate division of labor. Both Indian and Burmese workers were normally familiar with cropping techniques in Lower Burma and increasingly organized in gangs. These trends made it possible to employ them in seasonal or operational shifts and at lower wages because gang rates averaged less per person than wages paid on an individual basis. The fact that the slack season for the Rangoon mills coincided to some extent with the busy season in agricultural production meant that more than sufficient labor was available when required. The noncontiguous "estates" which were built up by the accumulation and amalgamation of numerous individual holdings allowed many landlords to operate on a very large scale. Some large landholders employed hundreds of workers during a single cropping season. The constant and rising demand for paddy for export through most of the transition period and regular and dependable rainfall and climatic patterns in Lower Burma made large-scale rice production both profitable and secure.[31]

On "estates" where production was organized along industrial lines, the whole rice-cropping operation was broken down into a series of separate activities and different laborers were employed for each. This elaborate division is outlined in Table 7. Each operation was contracted separately. Individual laborers were normally paid on a piece-work basis, while gangs were paid for an entire operation. It was rare for one man to perform more than one operation, and if he did so, it was usually for different employers. At times landlords personally directed cropping operations, but more often

29. This pattern of production was first observed in the Pegu District in the late 1890s. R. E. V. Arbuthnot, the settlement officer of the Hanthawaddy District between 1907 and 1910, was the first writer to describe it in detail. Presumably, Furnivall drew heavily on the superb material provided by Arbuthnot. See *Settlement Reports–Pegu (1898–99)*, p. 14; and *Hanthawaddy (1907–10)*, pp. 6–7.

30. *Political Economy*, p. 90.

31. Government of Burma, *Report on the Suspension of Grants*, p. 21; Furnivall, *Political Economy*, p. 74.

Table 7. Cropping Operations and Industrial Agriculture in Burma

Month	Operation	Labor
February-May	*kazin* (bund) repair	Indians, hired individually
May to mid-July	plowing and nursery planting	Burmese, occasionally Indians, hired in teams
Mid-July to August	transplanting or sowing	Burmese, employed in two sets, one which pulled up and transported the paddy plants and another which planted them out
August to November or December	herding	Indians, hired individually
	weeding and grass cutting	Burmese or Indians, hired individually
November to February	harvesting	Indian or Burmese reapers, hired in gangs
	threshing	Burmese teams
	winnowing	Burmese teams or individuals
	carting	Indians and Burmese in teams

Sources: *Hanthawaddy Settlement Report (1907–10)*, pp. 6–7; Furnivall, *Political Economy*, p. 74, "Industrial Agriculture," *Journal of the Burma Research Society* 48, no. 1 (June 1965): 95–97.

they hired agents or divided their holdings among tenants who agreed to work their shares in an "industrial" manner.

In terms of the level of agricultural technology maintained in Lower Burma, the rise of industrial agriculture represented a setback rather than an advance. The system embodied all of the characteristics of land alienation and tenancy with regard to lack of improvements in technique and poor land care. Although some large landholders made improvements on the "estates" they acquired,[32] most landlords invested little in their holdings. Since their major concern was to maximize profits and minimize costs, landlords rented to cultivators who promised to pay the highest rent rather than to those who would cultivate the most carefully. Aside from making sure that their tenants paid their full rents on time, nonresident landlords normally had little to do with cropping operations on their estates.[33]

For their part, tenants had neither the capital nor the incentive to innovate. Because leases were normally for only one year, they did not have

32. *Settlement Reports–Insein (1913–14)*, p. 7; *Hanthawaddy (1930–33)*, pp. 24–25.

33. *Hanthawaddy Settlement Report (1907–10)*, p. 20; Furnivall, *Political Economy*, p. 62; Government of Burma, Revenue and Agricultural Proceedings, vol. 8633, November 1911, p. 178.

the time to become familiar with the land they rented or to introduce fertilizers or new paddy varieties. Tenants had little inclination to spend time or their limited capital on improvements because the profits from these would go either to the landlord in the form of enhanced rents or to the tenants who succeeded them. Since tenants, like landlords, were primarily concerned to earn the greatest profit with minimal inputs, they usually cultivated in an extremely negligent fashion. They did not manure, repair field bunds or drainage canals, cut down weeds before seeding, transplant, or make other changes which might have sustained or increased the productivity of the land.[34]

The concern displayed by both landlords and tenants for short-term gains to the detriment of the long-term productivity of their holdings was carried to extremes on estates where industrial agriculture was practiced. The agents who were employed to run the estates showed even less concern for improvements than had the landlords. The laborers which the agents employed to work the estates were even more transient, negligent, and capital-poor than tenants. Consequently, landlords who resorted to industrial agriculture were able to run their estates with lower inputs of capital and concern, but the productivity per acre of their land declined and its long-term potential was seriously impaired.[35]

In the first decades of the twentieth century a number of authors expressed the belief that advances in agricultural technology had been limited primarily by the fact that most cultivators did not have sufficient capital to purchase fertilizers or improved seeds and implements, or to experiment with new cropping techniques.[36] Abundant evidence of the great proliferation of agrarian credit sources, reduced interest rates, and the ready availability of large loans to the average cultivator-owner in the transition period forces one to question this causal relationship between lack of capital and the low level of technological change. One index of the spread of credit facilities in this period is the increase in the number of persons enumerated in Lower Burma who were engaged in credit provision, banking, or finance, which rose from 3200 to over 7400 between 1901 and 1931.[37] Although these figures included some bankers and financiers who did not extend money to

34. Couper, *Report into Agricultural Condition,* pp. 5, 42; Furnivall, *Political Economy,* p. 66; Couper, *Report on Thaton District,* p. 19.

35. Government of Burma, *Report on the Suspension of Grants,* pp. 21–22.

36. The most detailed exposition of this line of reasoning was set forth by Lawrence Dawson in his article on "Agricultural Banking in the Delta of Burma," in Harold Clayton, ed., *Proposals for the Extension of Agricultural Banking in the Delta of Burma . . .* (Rangoon, 1918), pp. 13–14. See also Hendry, *Fertilizers,* pp. 12–13.

37. I have calculated these figures from the Imperial Tables listing population by occupation in the Burma censuses of the dates cited.

agriculturists, they greatly understated the number of sources of agrarian credit because they listed only persons primarily engaged in moneylending or banking. In the transition phase of development, as in the early period, a large portion of money advanced to agriculturists was provided by paddy brokers, merchants, large landlords, and other persons who were not included in the census count.

During the first decades of the twentieth century Chettiar moneylenders gradually established themselves as the main source of agricultural credit in the Delta. By the late 1920s Chettiar firms directly provided well over half of the crop loans and a large share of the long-term loans recorded in Lower Burma.[38] They also greatly increased the amount of capital which they lent indirectly to the cultivator through advances to paddy brokers and large landholders.[39] The magnitude of the Chettiars' investment in agricultural production is indicated by the fact that by the late 1920s there were over 1,650 Chettiar firms in the main rice-growing districts of Burma. These firms advanced an estimated 450 to 500 million rupees per year in both crop and long-term loans to cultivators or middlemen who lent to cultivators. This amount was from 30 to 80 million rupees greater than the market value of the current rice crop in Lower Burma.[40]

Although indigenous moneylenders far outnumbered Chettiars, they provided a considerably smaller share of the capital loaned to agriculturists. The Banking Enquiry Committee estimated that there were well over fifteen thousand indigenous moneylenders in all of Burma by the late 1920s.[41] Although some indigenous moneylenders were engaged solely in credit provision, most loans at the local level were provided by persons for whom moneylending was only a subsidiary occupation. Numerous village shopkeepers, prosperous cultivators, and wealthy widows supplied small amounts of capital to their neighbors.[42] In some areas friends and relatives remained a source of credit, but their role was far less important, even in remote tracts, than it had been in the early phase of economic development.[43] Full-time Burmese moneylenders usually resided in large towns and trade centers. Some, like U Thet Shwe, whose operations were centered in the area around Pyapon town in the central Delta, lent very large sums of money to large

38. *Banking Enquiry Report,* 1: 67, 2: 1–33, 80–92; Government of Burma, *The Marketing of Crops in Burma* (Rangoon, 1928), p. 67.

39. *Banking Enquiry Report,* 3: 14–31; Government of Burma, Revenue and Agriculture Proceedings, vol. 8633, November 1911, pp. 496, 504, 508, et passim; *Settlement Reports–Insein (1910–12),* p. 24; *Pyapon (1921–22),* p. 11.

40. *Banking Enquiry Report,* 1: 204, 210–13.

41. Ibid., pp. 67–68.

42. Ibid. pp. 68, 294, 2: 93; *Settlement Reports–Insein (1910–12),* p. 24; *Toungoo (1910–13),* p. 14; *Pegu (1911–13),* p. 12; *Pegu (1924–25),* p. 3.

43. *Settlement Reports–Pegu (1911–13),* p. 12; *Tharrawaddy (1914–15),* p. 11.

clienteles. U Thet stated that he had two million rupees in loans outstanding in 1929, compared to an estimated 5,500,000 rupees then loaned by all of the Chettiars in Pyapon town.[44] Most Burmese moneylenders, large- and small-scale or full- and part-time, also owned land or engaged in the paddy trade. As in the nineteenth century, the distinction between indigenous moneylender, merchant, paddy broker, and landlord remained vague in most cases.[45]

Changes in marketing patterns and land tenure caused paddy brokers and large landholders to provide credit on a growing scale in the last decades of the nineteenth century. Both of these groups became major sources of loans for agriculturists in the transition phase. As the number of cultivators who sold their surplus directly to the agents at the mills declined sharply, the role of the paddy broker in credit extension increased. In the face of rising competition from other brokers, one way a jungle (or local) broker could secure the paddy which he had promised the agents of various milling firms was to advance funds to cultivators in the monsoon season. In return, the cultivators would agree to repay the amount advanced by the broker in paddy on the threshing floor. No interest was paid on the money given by the broker. His return came in the form of a lien on the cultivators' produce, which insured him of a supply for which his competitors could not outbid him. Local millers, speculators, moneylenders, or the agents of the large urban milling firms readily supplied jungle brokers with the capital which they in turn loaned to cultivators.[46]

The spread of tenancy beginning in the last decades of the nineteenth century gave rise to a new class of agriculturists who required loans for cultivation and living expenses. Since tenants who had little or no security could not normally obtain loans from moneylenders, they came to rely on the owners of the lands they worked for credit. The landlord normally borrowed from a Chettiar at regular rates of interest and then advanced funds to his tenants at higher rates. In most regions of Lower Burma, 70–80 percent of tenants took short-term loans from their landlords.[47] If a tenant had jewelry or cattle which he could offer as security, he preferred to borrow from a Chettiar, who would give him more money at lower rates. Tenants

44. *Banking Enquiry Report,* 2: 96. See also *Settlement Reports–Hanthawaddy (1907–10),* p. 25; *Pyapon (1912–13),* p. 4; *Tharrawaddy (1914–15),* p. 11.

45. *Banking Enquiry Report,* 2: 116; E. G. Pattle, "Some Factors . . . ," in Government of Burma, *Agriculture in Burma,* p. 118.

46. Government of Burma, *Marketing of Crops,* p. 6; Government of Burma, Revenue and Agriculture Proceedings, vol. 8633, November 1911, p. 407; Cheng, *Rice Industry of Burma,* pp. 50, 53.

47. The one exception was the Insein District, where the percentage was estimated at 35. However, the compiler of the *Banking Enquiry Report* questioned the accuracy of this estimate. See 2: 11–33.

repaid loans extended by their landlords with interest in paddy at harvest time.[48]

Despite a number of new programs designed to provide the cultivator with loans at low rates of interest and aimed at the eventual elimination of the need for moneylenders, the government's role in credit provision remained marginal.[49] The amount of money extended through the loan acts of the early 1880s was very small when compared to that advanced by private moneylenders. For example, the 1,300,000 rupees loaned in 1925–26 under the provisions of the Agriculturists Loans Act was only a small fraction of the 450 to 500 million rupees per year loaned by the Chettiars alone in the same period. The amount issued under the Land Improvement Loans Act was even smaller, totaling less than 20,000 rupees.[50] The bureaucratic delays, red tape, and restrictions involved in obtaining government loans continued to outweigh the lower rates which were offered.[51]

Through the introduction of cooperative societies in 1905–6, the government sought to involve the cultivators themselves in credit provision. The movement was begun with considerable fanfare and optimism, but within a decade numerous settlement officers expressed disappointment over the fact that few Burmese agriculturists in the Delta had joined local cooperatives. By the mid-1920s the movement was clearly recognized as a failure. Less than 5 percent of the eligible agrarian householders belonged to about 4,500 cooperatives in all of Burma. In the districts of the upper Delta where the movement enjoyed the greatest success, less than 10 percent of all agrarian loans were obtained from cooperatives. Although some officials were inclined to blame the agriculturists for the movement's failure, the Calvert Commission, which was appointed in 1927 by the Government of Burma to examine the cause of its decline, attached much of the responsibility to official mismanagement, poor staff training, and other administrative problems.[52]

In addition to the sources described above, Dawson's Bank, Chinese shopkeepers, and non-Chettiar Indian moneylenders and merchants

48. Ibid., 3: 11–33, 2: 101–2; H. Clayton's *Report on Indebtedness,* as quoted in Hardiman, *Compilation,* pp. 47, 64, 68; *Maubin Settlement Report (1925–28),* p. 64.

49. More detailed descriptions of government efforts in the field of credit provision may be found in Cheng, *Rice Industry of Burma,* pp. 190–97; and Tun Wai, *Currency and Credit,* pp. 68–78, 83–85.

50. Dunn, "Some General Characteristics," in Government of Burma, *Agriculture in Burma,* p. 24.

51. Government of Burma, Revenue and Agriculture Proceedings, vol. 8633, November 1911, p. 497; *Thaton (Pa-an) Settlement Report (1928–30),* pp. 15–16; *Banking Enquiry Report,* 1: 71–72.

52. Pattle, "Some Factors," in Government of Burma, *Agriculture in Burma,* pp. 120–23, 128–29; *Banking Enquiry Report,* 3: 11–33; Government of Burma, *Report of Committee on Co-operation, 1928–29,* pp. 8–9.

(Marwaris, Multanis, Chatris, etc.) also extended credit to agriculturists in Lower Burma in the 1907–30 period. Dawson's Bank was originally established in 1905 to assist cultivators in redeeming mortgages which had been offered as security for loans from Chettiar moneylenders. In the early 1920s the bank also began to make advances for cultivating expenses. Although it lent at low rates and grew fairly rapidly in the 1920s, Dawson's loans to cultivators totaled only seven million rupees per year as late as 1929.[53] Unlike Dawson's Bank, Chinese shopkeepers did not provide a favorable alternative to Chettiar or indigenous moneylenders. They normally lent food, implements, or other goods in the monsoon season and collected their loans with high *sabape* interest charges at harvest time. Like Burmese merchants and landlords, Chinese shopkeepers often used the grain they collected to speculate on the paddy market.[54]

The interest rates charged in the transition period varied by location, the lender, the type of loan, and the security offered, but they were generally lower than those charged through most of the nineteenth century. *Ngwedo* loans could be obtained in most areas at 1.25 to 3 percent interest per month if land security were offered. Lower rates were offered on gold or jewelry, while *sabape* rates, which were the highest, ranged from 10–12 percent per month.[55] Small-scale moneylenders, landlords, and local shopkeepers generally charged the highest interest, while Chettiars and large-scale Burmese moneylenders demanded lower and roughly equal rates.[56] Competition among the many agents providing agrarian credit in the transition period was the major cause of lower interest rates in most areas of the Delta.

Although the percentage of cultivators in debt and the amount per capita which they owed rose steadily in the pre-1907 period, a credit squeeze in 1907 and the slump that followed accelerated the growth of indebtedness, particularly in the districts of the lower Delta. Many cultivators borrowed heavily from Chettiars and other moneylenders to speculate in land during the late nineteenth- and early twentieth-century boom. When the Chettiars suddenly called in their loans in 1907 and the following years, these cultivators were faced with large repayments which they could not meet because the land they had purchased at highly inflated rates had fallen sharply in value.[57] The increase in indebtedness in the years immediately

53. Tun Wai, *Currency and Credit,* pp. 78–82.

54. *Banking Enquiry Report,* 1: 81, 294; *Settlement Reports–Pyapon (1921–22),* p. 8; *Maubin (1925–28),* pp. 15, 21–22.

55. *Banking Enquiry Report,* 1: 80, 2: 73, 3: 11–33; Clayton, *Rural Development,* pp. 59–60.

56. *Banking Enquiry Report,* 1: 79–81, 2: 94, 97; *Settlement Reports–Insein (1913–14),* p. 6; *Pegu (1914–15),* p. 9; *Maubin (1925–28),* p. 23.

57. Couper, *Report on Thaton District,* pp. 10–11; Couper (citing Clayton), *Report into Agricultural Condition,* p. 2.

after 1907 was abnormally high. The rate of debt increases leveled off somewhat in the following decade, but it remained considerably higher throughout the decades of transition than it had been prior to 1907. By the end of the transition period the number of indebted cultivators who were able to repay their loans at the end of a single cropping season had fallen to less than 30 percent. Of the remaining debtors, 55 percent had debts ranging from one-half to the total value of their holdings, while 15 percent had debts which exceeded the total value of their holdings.[58] Although there are no reliable estimates of per capita indebtedness in monetary terms, the great burden of agrarian debt is indicated by the Banking Enquiry Committee's estimate that the amount owed to the Chettiars (whose operations were centered in Lower Burma) alone by the late 1920s was from five to six hundred million rupees.[59]

The disputes among government officials regarding the reasons for agrarian debt intensified as more and more cultivators became hopelessly involved. Few observers cited the same causes or agreed on the relative importance of each.[60] Most officials acknowledged that landlords, cultivator-owners, and tenants alike needed to borrow annually to meet cultivation expenses. The Banking Enquiry Committee went so far as to suggest that crop loans which were repaid in full at the harvest of the same cropping season in which they were taken could not be considered debts in the strictest sense.[61] The dispute then was not over the agriculturists' need to borrow to cover cultivation costs, but over the causes of chronic indebtedness, which eventually ended in the alienation of the debtor's land.

Some officials argued that this second form of debt, like the crop-loan, could not be avoided given economic conditions in the Delta. They asserted that the rising costs of living and cultivation and the high rates demanded by those who extended credit combined with declining productivity and profits made it impossible for the average cultivator to break even. If he borrowed to buy more land, build a new house, or make improvements on his holdings, the cultivator often incurred debts which he could not repay. In addition, he might be caught in the debt spiral if his cattle fell ill or died, if his crop were flooded, or if some other calamity struck. Officials who held this view claimed that cultivators normally took loans for "productive" purposes, though they conceded that some expenditure by agriculturists was "extravagant" or "nonproductive." They implied that the fault lay primarily with problems of the whole economy, not with the individual agriculturist.

58. *Banking Enquiry Report,* 3: 264–68.

59. Ibid., 1: 53.

60. This summary of the views on the causes of indebtedness is based on the various reports on indebtedness found in the Government of Burma's Revenue and Agriculture Proceedings, vol. 8633, November 1911, and the sections on indebtedness in the settlement reports for this period.

61. *Banking Enquiry Report,* 1: 52.

The opposing view, which was held by most officials in this period, stressed the "improvidence" of the Burmese "peasant" and his failure to understand the workings of a modern, market-oriented economic system. Those who held this view felt that agriculturists not only borrowed too much, but that they spent a high proportion of their earnings and the money they borrowed on religious ceremonies, festivals, jewelry, gambling, and other "nonproductive" pursuits. A much higher proportion of officials listed the cost of *ahlus, shinbyus*, or other ceremonies as a major, or *the* main, cause of debt in the early twentieth century than they had in the first phase of development. They asserted that agriculturists squandered money that should have been saved for the next season's cultivating expenses or for times of illness or bad harvests. They concluded that the attitudes and actions of the cultivators themselves were primarily responsible for chronic debt and not the economic system in which they operated.

As I shall attempt to show in the conclusion, these two seemingly contradictory viewpoints were in fact complementary. Both contained elements of truth, but neither explored the more fundamental issues which each suggested. The causes of agrarian debt were rooted in the values and attitudes of the Burmese cultivator, in his inability to fully comprehend the workings of a modern market economy, as well as in the nature of that economy itself.

The closing of the rice frontier in the first decades of the twentieth century was one of the major causes of a sharp decrease in social mobility in the rural Delta. Not only did it become more difficult for an agriculturist to move upward on the social scale after 1900, but distinctions between groups at different levels also became more pronounced. The social and economic position of a small segment of Delta society, the large landholders, improved substantially, while the solvency and well-being of the great majority of persons engaged in agricultural production was gradually undermined.

The groups who made up the landlord class in Lower Burma possessed great advantages in the struggle for land which intensified in the first decades of the twentieth century. They had accumulated or could borrow the large sums of capital which were required to purchase land at the high prices demanded. Since a sizable portion of large landholders were moneylenders or other persons who extended loans to agriculturists, the increasing indebtedness of cultivator-owners also led to a concentration of paddy land in the hands of the landlord class. Government officials generally agreed that most land was alienated through the foreclosure of mortgages which cultivators had used as security for loans.[62] In addition to heavy capital expenditure and moneylending activities, landowners in the districts of the lower Delta

62. Government of Burma, *Report on the Suspension of Grants*, p. 22; Furnivall, *Colonial Policy and Practice*, pp. 86–87.

resorted to bribes and force to amass great estates. The collusion between large landowners or land "grabbers" and subordinate employees in the Burma Land Records Department continued in this period.[63] In the absence of effective police control in many frontier tracts in the lower Delta, however, local land magnates often bypassed time-consuming and costly attempts to win over local officials. They merely directed their retainers to forcibly eject cultivator-owners on lands which the landlords wished to add to their estates. In some cases threats were sufficient to frighten squatters off their lands, but often it was necessary for the landlord's hired ruffians to harvest the cultivator's crop and cart it away to their master's granaries and then burn the squatter's field hut. If the small landholder persisted, beatings and possibly murder soon put an end to his resistance.[64]

The great increase in the percentage of land alienated to nonagriculturists in the transition phase indicates that large landlords were highly successful in their attempts to amass estates by the means outlined above. The amount of occupied area in Lower Burma controlled by nonagriculturists rose from 18 percent in 1906–7 to 31 percent in 1929–30. Most of this increase was due to additions to the estates held by absentee landlords, whose holdings rose from 12 to 23 percent of the Delta total in this period, while the percentage owned by resident landlords increased only slightly from 6 to 8 percent.[65]

The highest percentage of alienated land continued to be found in the districts around Rangoon (Hanthawaddy, Pegu, and Insein) and those in the central, lower Delta (Myaungmya, Pyapon, and Maubin). The great estates, which were largely a twentieth-century development, were also found in these areas. In the upper Delta districts and Bassein, for example, large holdings averaged one to two hundred acres and rarely exceeded five hundred acres, though the Tharrawaddy District was somewhat exceptional in this respect.[66] In the districts around Rangoon and in the central Delta, large estates often exceeded five hundred acres and some were over three thousand acres.[67] Industrial agriculture was centered on the estates in these areas, especially in the circles around Rangoon and other major urban centers where whole tracts were devoted almost solely to the production of rice for the export market. In almost all cases both large and small estates were collections of noncon-

63. See, for example, the *Myaungmya Settlement Report (1924–25)*, p. 12; Pattle, "Some Factors," in Government of Burma, *Agriculture in Burma*, p. 113; and Government of Burma, *Collection of Reports on the Yandoon Island Colonisation Scheme . . .* (Rangoon, 1923), p. 55.

64. *Myaungmya Settlement Report (1924–25)*, pp. 10–11, 112–13.

65. For a regional breakdown of increases in land alienation by five-year intervals in this period, see Adas, "Agrarian Development," p. 395.

66. *Settlement Reports–Bassein (1912–13)*, pp. 18, 20, (*1912–14*), p. 36; *Tharrawaddy (1913–15)*, p. 22; *Prome (1914–16)*, pp. 45–46.

67. *Settlement Reports–Hanthawaddy (1907–10)*, pp. 14–15; *Pyapon (1921–22)*, p. 27; *Maubin (1925–28)*, p. 60.

tiguous holdings scattered over several *kwins.* Although large holdings tended to be more widely spread within the districts of Lower Burma than in the late nineteenth century, they continued to be concentrated in tracts near important towns, along the railway lines, and near trade centers on the rivers of the Delta.[68]

Most large landlords, particularly those who had obtained their estates as moneylenders, preferred to live in market or railway towns because credit and consumer facilities were greater there and because the danger of dacoit raids was considerably less. The owners of the larger estates in the lower Delta lived in fine houses of teak or brick with iron or tile roofs. These dwellings were often embellished with carved-wood posts, beams, and doors. Many estate holders possessed motor launches, and they normally owned large quantities of jewelry, clothes, and Western furniture. Some were affluent enough to electrify their homes and install telephones. Landlords whose estates ranged from one to three hundred acres also lived in wood houses with iron roofs and purchased prestige items like pianos, bicycles, and watches. Both large- and small-scale landlords usually sent their children to Western schools and encouraged them to become civil servants and barristers or groomed them to take over the family holdings.[69]

The strong and solvent position of cultivator-owners in the first phase of agrarian development was gradually eroded by a number of factors in the transition period. The declining yield per acre of paddy land in the Delta meant that cultivators had less surplus to market and thus that their annual income was reduced. Because of the high price of land, they were less able than in earlier decades to extend their holdings to compensate for lower yields. As the productivity of cultivators' lands declined and the size of their holdings stabilized or diminished, the cost of goods and services rose steadily. The combination of these trends made it increasingly difficult for cultivator-owners to break even. Balance sheets for the 1910s and 1920s which are set forth in Table 8 illustrate their growing dilemma.

Until World War I cultivator-owners continued to clear substantial profits as they had in the last half of the nineteenth century. During and after the war, however, their earnings were substantially reduced, with the exception of the large balance left to cultivators in Pyapon in 1921–22. This incongruously large margin of profit was greatly due to the high output for Pyapon in that year, the extremely high prices paid for paddy on the Delta market, and the fact that the per acre cost of cultivation estimate was probably too low.

68. See, for example, *Settlement Reports–Thaton (1907–8)*, pp. 10–11; *Insein (1910–12)*, pp. 37, 183; *Myaungmya (1910–12)*, p. 21; *Bassein (1912–14)*, p. 36; Hardiman, *Compilation*, p. 132.

69. *Settlement Reports–Tharrawaddy (1913–15)*, p. 24; *Pyapon (1921–22)*, p. 9; *Maubin (1925–28)*, p. 64.

Table 8. The Cultivator's Balance Sheet, 1907–30 (in rupees)

District	Year	Income	Expenditure[a]	Balance[b]
Thaton	1907–8	1559.3	1031.4	527.9
Hanthawaddy	1907–10	1953.6	1451.9	501.7
Myaungmya	1910–12	1072.0	763.0	309.0
Bassein	1912–14	557.7	508.4	49.3
Tharrawaddy	1913–15	853.1	625.2	227.9
Myaungmya	1916–19	1078.7	1040.5	38.2
Pyapon	1920–21	1437.8	816.3	621.5
Maubin	1925–28	1669.2	1613.6	55.6
Thaton-Kyaikto	1928–30	748.8	965.3	-216.5

Sources: The manner of calculating the figures cited and the sources used are the same as those for Table 5. For local prices after 1911, *Season and Crop Reports* rather than Hardiman, *Compilation*, were used.

[a] Plus interest and/or principal on loans.
[b] Minus interest and/or principal on loans.

In addition to declining yields per acre and the stagnation of holding sizes, inflation, adverse market conditions, and increased indebtedness were the major factors behind the great reduction in cultivators' profits after the First World War. Increases in both the cost of living and cultivation (which were reflected in higher totals for expenditures) canceled out whatever gains the cultivator may have received from higher paddy prices. The magnitude of consumer price increases in the transition period can be gauged from the index numbers of average wholesale prices which were published annually by the Director of Statistics for the Government of India. These indices show that the wholesale prices of thirty-nine kinds of standard goods rose from a base of 100 in 1913 to 158 in 1925.[70] In the early twentieth century cultivator-owners were much more affected by price increases than they would have been in the early phase of development. Because of their greater involvement in paddy production for the market, cultivators had become

70. Dunn, "Some General Characteristics," in Government of Burma, *Agriculture in Burma,* p. 20. The index went as high as 196 in the years right after the war. The rising cost of food, clothing, and other necessities for the cultivator was somewhat offset by lower wages for hired laborers.

dependent upon others for goods and services which had once been supplied by members of the self-sufficient family. They had to purchase firewood, bamboo, and thatch as neighboring forests were depleted or claimed by the government or private owners. They came to prefer cheap manufactured cloth, and domestic production declined sharply in Lower Burma. Cultivators also developed a taste for imported consumer goods which they found difficult to curb despite rising prices.[71]

In the first decades of the twentieth century the cultivator's income was reduced by both the proliferation of middlemen in domestic marketing and after World War I by several brief, but severe, pre-Depression market slumps. As noted in Chapter 3, the incomes listed on the cultivator's balance sheet are somewhat overstated because the paddy values used in calculating them were determined by the rates current in district market centers. By the late 1880s, however, it was rare for a cultivator to carry his surplus produce to market. In the early decades of agrarian development, cultivators near large towns often marketed their own paddy. Since they were less dependent at that time on the sale of surplus rice for their livelihood, they could store the paddy and hold it off the market unless high prices were offered.[72] This pattern disappeared in most areas as cultivators became increasingly involved in production for the market and rice millers became more dependent on brokers and rice merchants for their supply of paddy. By the 1890s most cultivators had a number of payments to make soon after the end of the harvest season, including land and capitation taxes, the interest and/or principal on crop and long-term loans, and their laborers' wages. They did not have the means or the time required to carry their surplus to the nearest market or mill. They could also not afford the time and risks involved in market speculation or the losses which resulted from the forays of rats and insect pests into the thatch granaries used to store rice in the Delta.[73]

As the position of the cultivator vis-à-vis the market grew weaker, that of the millers and brokers improved. The large-scale millers of Rangoon and other urban centers supported fairly successful combinations or price agreements by the 1890s. These combinations were aimed at controlling domestic paddy prices by eliminating competition among millers. In doing so they undermined the bargaining position of the cultivator and upcountry rice

71. Government of Burma, Revenue and Agriculture Proceedings, vol. 8633, November 1911, pp. 315, 501; Couper, *Report into Agricultural Condition,* p. 3; *Henzada Gazetteer,* p. 37; *Tharrawaddy Gazetteer,* pp. 41–44.

72. *RAP, 1859–60,* p. 16, *1860–61,* p. 13; *Rangoon Gazetteer,* p. 3; J. G. Scott, *The Burman: His Life and Notions* (New York, 1963), p. 246; Furnivall, *Colonial Policy and Practice,* p. 95.

73. *Banking Enquiry Report,* 3: 150; *Maubin Gazetteer,* p. 46; E. Thompstone, *Granary Pests* (Rangoon, 1909), pp. 1–2; Cheng, *Rice Industry of Burma,* pp. 48–49; Hendry, "Rice in Burma," p. 34.

merchant.[74] At the same time, speculators and paddy brokers came to control the cultivator's surplus from the time it left the threshing floor until it arrived at the mill. An elaborate hierarchy developed which extended from the powerful agents employed directly by the European millers to the "jungle" brokers who worked at the local level to secure adequate supplies for the mills at the apex of their particular network.[75] Thus, although cultivators in most areas were thoroughly acquainted with prices current in Rangoon and other market towns,[76] they had to accept considerably lower prices for their surplus because it was usually sold on the threshing floor and at harvest time, when the price was low.

In addition to profits lost to middlemen and millers, cultivators shared the reverses which these groups suffered as a result of unfavorable fluctuations in the international market. The very low balance for Myaungmya in 1916–19, for example, was in part due to the brief but serious slump which hit the Burma rice market in the years after World War I. Paddy prices fell well below pre-war levels, but the cost of goods and services continued to rise. Consequently, the value of the surplus which cultivators marketed was even less than the low market prices for the 1915–19 period indicate.[77] Government controls were applied beginning in 1918–19, but they proved unnecessary as the market soon recovered and soared to new highs in the early 1920s (which were reflected in the large positive balance for Pyapon). The market declined again, however, in the late 1920s. Increasing competition from rice producers elsewhere in Asia, Europe, and the United States cut into Burma's traditional market outlets and resulted in lower prices.[78] The severe impact of the second slump can be seen in the large deficits for cultivators in the Thaton District in the 1928–30 period.

The balance left to cultivators in the twentieth century was also diminished by the great increase in per capita agrarian debt. Even if one assumes that only a portion of the average cultivator's debts were for crop loans or interest due on long-term loans, the amount owed would in most cases exceed the margin of profits listed in Table 8. For example, at least 43 percent of the cultivators in the Pyapon district in 1921–22, which showed

74. For discussions of various combinations and their impact on domestic prices, see Cheng, *Rice Industry of Burma,* pp. 64–68; Furnivall, *Colonial Policy and Practice,* pp. 97–98; Spate, "Beginnings of Industrialization," pp. 81–82.

75. Cheng, *Rice Industry of Burma,* pp. 50–54; Government of Burma, *Marketing of Crops,* pp. 14–15.

76. Government of Burma, *Marketing of Crops,* p. 6; D. F. Chalmers, "Marketing," in Government of Burma, *Agriculture in Burma,* p. 100.

77. Dunn, "Some General Characteristics," in Government of Burma, *Agriculture in Burma,* pp. 19–21.

78. F. D. Odell, *Note on Burma Rice Prices . . .* (Rangoon, 1932), pp. 1, 15, 18, 26–28; *Banking Enquiry Report,* 1: 22; Cheng, *Rice Industry of Burma,* pp. 204–10, 213.

the highest balance in the post-war period, would not have cleared a profit if their debts were subtracted.[79] In other districts with much smaller balances, deficits would have been far greater. Thus, well before the Great Depression had begun to affect the Delta rice industry, the average cultivator-owner was fortunate to break even or at least to earn enough money to pay off his crop loans and meet payments on long-term debts and thus to prevent foreclosure.

Most of the factors which adversely affected the position of cultivator-owners in the transition period also worked against the interests of the rapidly expanding tenant class. Declining yields and unfavorable market conditions combined with rising costs gradually deprived tenants of the margin of profit which had allowed many to move up the social and economic scale to the status of landholders. In the early decades of the twentieth century the movement of tenants was increasingly downward to the level of landless, agricultural laborers. Tenancy became a dead end for most agriculturists or a temporary respite in their fall from cultivator-owners to landless laborers, rather than the avenue of upward mobility it had been in the nineteenth century. By the 1920s the laborer-tenant-landowner progression that was such a dominant feature of rural Delta society in the first phase of agrarian development was a thing of the past in most areas.[80]

The decreasing availability of unoccupied, cultivable area and its concomitant, higher land prices, greatly reduced the tenant's geographical mobility and hence his bargaining power vis-à-vis the landlord. Tenants who were dissatisfied with their landlords' terms could rarely afford to migrate to tracts where land was still available and clear their own holdings. Because moneylenders rarely lent money to tenants or strangers without security in this period, it was virtually impossible for an ex-tenant arriving in a frontier area to obtain the capital he needed to survive as a small landholder.[81] In addition, continued population growth coupled with the closing of the rice frontier in many areas altered the population-to-land ratio in the landlords' favor. The supply of tenants came to exceed the demand in most tracts, and

79. This estimate is based on the fact that 43 percent of the indebted cultivators in Pyapon in 1929–30 held loans that totaled over one-half the value of their holdings, or over Rs. 831. Hence, the deficit would stand even if one allows for the time differential. See Adas, "Agrarian Development," Table VIII-E, p. 388.

80. *Settlement Reports–Tharrawaddy (1913–15)*, p. 24; *Pyapon (1921–22)*, pp. 10, 28; *Maubin (1925–28)*, pp. 67–69; *Land Revenue Report, 1923–24*, p. 19. Robert Sansom has also seen the closing of the frontier as the key factor in the declining position of the much larger tenant and laboring classes of the Mekong Delta in the 1930s. See *The Economics of Insurgency in the Mekong Delta of Vietnam* (Cambridge, Mass., 1970), pp. 18–52.

81. Government of Burma, Revenue and Agriculture Proceedings, vol. 5804, November 1900, p. 1, vol. 7238, August 1906, p. 86; Couper, *Report into Agricultural Condition*, pp. 28–29.

large landholders could normally choose among an increasing number of competitors for each of the tenant positions they sought to fill. The growing strength of the landlord at the tenants' expense was reflected in higher rent rates, new practices devised by landowners to maximize their profits, and increasing friction between the two groups.

The rise in the average rent per acre paid by tenants in each of the Delta regions was fairly gradual until after the First World War. Rent enhancements between 1905–6 and 1915–16 were continuous but low in most regions and corresponded roughly to increases in the costs of cultivation and living and the price of rice. In this decade the average rent per acre for the Delta as a whole rose only from Rs. 10.2 to Rs. 12.4. After 1915–16, however, rent rates rose sharply in all regions despite the fact that the price of rice fell through the 1915–20 period. By 1920–21 the average rent per acre stood at Rs. 19.1.[82] No annual district-by-district figures are available for the 1920s, but references to rents in official reports for this decade indicate that enhancements continued to be made at a higher rate than that recorded for increases in general prices or wages.[83]

As the competition among prospective tenants intensified, the percentage of the total output on rented lands demanded by Delta landlords rose sharply. By the time of the First World War, the customary 10 percent plus revenue rate charged through most of the first phase of development had virtually disappeared from use. The amount tenants agreed to pay in the decades of transition varied according to the location, size, and fertility of the holdings they rented. Rates on all but the poorest land exceeded 20 percent of the gross output in the 1910–20 period. In fertile areas landlords charged from 30 to 45 percent of the total output, while tenants who rented good land near railway lines or in coastal or riverine tracts normally paid as high as 40 or 50 percent.[84] By the mid-1920s rents for inland tracts also averaged as high as 45 or 50 percent of the gross output. Rents less than 20 percent were extremely rare and confined mainly to circles with very poor soil. In some circles of districts in the upper Delta landlords demanded over 50 percent of their tenants' total output.[85] In some cases, the higher rates charged by landlords may have been somewhat offset by the fact that the owner paid the land revenue rather than the tenant as in the pre-1907 period.[86]

82. Averages calculated from the figures given in *Season and Crop* for the 1905–6 to 1920–21 period. See also Adas, "Agrarian Development," Table VIII-K, p. 408.

83. Couper, *Report into Agricultural Condition*, pp. 29–33; *Banking Enquiry Report*, 3: 79.

84. *Settlement Reports–Toungoo (1910–13)*, p. 27; *Pegu (1911–13)*, p. 24, (*1913–14*), p. 9; *Myaungmya (1916–19)*, p. 98; Government of Burma, Revenue and Agriculture Proceedings, vol. 8633, November 1911, pp. 512, 517.

85. Couper, *Report into Agricultural Condition*, pp. 29–33.

86. *Settlement Reports–Insein (1910–12)*, p. 41; *Bassein (1912–13)*, p. 19.

Rent rates once determined by custom were normally fixed by contract prior to the plowing season. Tenants paid for the printing and the cost of the stamps affixed to written contracts, which had become fairly common by the 1920s. Whether written or verbal, contracts were almost always for only one year. Most tenants agreed to pay their rent in paddy on the threshing floor, though in some areas cash was used as early as the 1890s.[87] As their position grew more favorable, many landlords began to insist that their tenants cart paddy for rental payments to the landlords' residences or to their granaries, which were often located at a considerable distance from the tenants' fields. The tenants, of course, paid the cost of carting.[88]

The refusal of many landlords to grant rent remissions when flooding or insect pests reduced their tenants' output was another expression of the growing strength of the landlord class. Remissions had been a widely accepted feature of landlord-tenant relations in the first phase of development, but in the decades of transition many landlords would not allow them no matter how desperate their tenants' situation.[89] In more heavily populated tracts, unscrupulous landlords devised even more oppressive measures to extract the highest possible profit from their tenants. Some demanded bonuses in addition to the rent, while others subdivided their holdings into small plots in order to accommodate a greater number of tenants. In certain cases landlords were known to attach the whole of their tenants' produce for rent arrears and debts, and in many areas large landholders used baskets which exceeded the standard government size in measuring out their tenants' rents.[90]

Some tenants turned to theft and deception to counteract the measures taken by landholders to maximize profits. They took crop loans without security from their landlords and then disappeared suddenly after working their holdings for a week or two. Other tenants completed the cropping cycle, but then surreptitiously harvested part or all of the paddy they had grown, sold it, and absconded before the landlord could claim his due. In cases where tenants paid the revenue, they sometimes used the tax ticket, which because of the widespread acceptance of the squatter system was often used as a title,

87. *Settlement Reports–Henzada (1899–1900)*, p. 25; *Hanthawaddy (1907–10)*, p. 18; *Insein (1910–12)*, p. 41; *Toungoo (1910–13)*, p. 27; *Bassein (1912–14)*, p. 37; *Pyapon (1921–22)*, p. 29; Hardiman, *Compilation*, p. 34.

88. *Settlement Reports–Hanthawaddy (1907–10)*, p. 19; *Insein (1910–12)*, p. 41; *Myaungmya (1910–12)*, p. 24; *Pegu (1913–14)*, p. 9; *Pyapon (1921–22)*, p. 30.

89. *Settlement Reports–Hanthawaddy (1907–10)*, p. 20; *Bassein (1912–13)*, p. 20; *Maubin (1925–28)*, p. 66; Binns, *Agricultural Economy*, p. 18. In some areas landlords continued to give remissions. See, for example, *Settlement Reports–Toungoo (1910–13)*, p. 29; *Myaungmya (1916–19)*, p. 93.

90. Couper, *Report into Agricultural Condition*, pp. 15–16, 30–33; Couper, *Report on Thaton District*, p. 21; *Settlement Reports–Hanthawaddy (1907–10)*, pp. 19–20; *Myaungmya (1916–19)*, p. 93; Government of Burma, Revenue and Agriculture Proceedings, vol. 5804, November 1900, p. 1, vol. 7328, August 1906, p. 86.

to claim the land they rented as their own.[91] Indian and indigenous landlords responded by hiring *durwans* or watchmen to oversee the tenants who worked their fields. In the harvest season landlords often personally supervised operations.[92] Despite repeated assertions in official reports that relations between landlords and tenants were "cordial" or "on the whole satisfactory,"[93] these practices clearly demonstrate that in the transition phase an increasingly bitter contest developed between landlord and tenant. In the late 1920s and 1930s this contest would erupt into violence.

The detrimental effects of the growing tension between landlord and tenant were multiplied by the fact that the area occupied by tenants increased steadily in the transition period. Between 1906–7 and 1929–30 the area let to tenants at full rents rose from 30 percent to almost 46 percent of the total occupied land in the Delta. The amount of land let to tenants was the highest in the lower Delta, where land alienation was the most pronounced and holdings generally larger.[94]

New demographic patterns and the deteriorating conditions of agriculturists in Lower Burma were the primary determinants of changes in the composition of the tenant class in the period of transition. The percentage of tenants who were former cultivator-owners who had lost their lands because of debts increased substantially.[95] The number of Indian immigrants who rented land in the Delta also rose sharply.[96] In addition, older agricultural laborers and permanent tenants, or cultivators who had been tenants throughout their productive life, made up a large portion of the tenant class.[97]

Because the volume of in-migration from divisions within Burma fell, the percentage of tenants who were newly arrived settlers from the Dry Zone and other areas in the province declined.[98] The percentage of landholders who rented extra land also decreased greatly. This decrease is indicated by the fact that there are no references to cultivator-owners who were part-time tenants

91. Government of Burma, Revenue and Agriculture Proceedings, vol. 8633, November 1911, p. 178; Couper, *Report into Agricultural Condition,* p. 21; *Myaungmya Settlement Report (1924–25),* pp. 11–12.

92. Couper, *Report on Thaton District,* p. 19; *Settlement Reports–Maubin (1904–5),* p. 16; *Hanthawaddy (1907–10),* p. 20.

93. *Land Revenue Reports, 1920–21,* p. 20, *1923–24,* p. 19, *1925–26,* p. 21.

94. Percentages calculated from the tables on rented area in the *Land Revenue Reports* for this period. For a regional breakdown, see Table VIII-L, p. 412, in Adas, "Agrarian Development."

95. See citations in footnote 89 and *Settlement Reports–Myaungmya (1916–19),* p. 87; *Pyapon (1921–22),* p. 31.

96. Heightened Indian penetration into the agrarian sector at all levels will be treated in detail in Chapter 7 on the mature plural society.

97. *Settlement Reports–Toungoo (1910–13),* p. 29; *Myaungmya (1916–19),* p. 29; *Pyapon (1921–22),* p. 31.

98. For changes in Burmese migration patterns see below, Chapter 7.

in the sources for the post-World War I period. Since landholders rented extra land in order to increase their earnings, it is probable that far fewer did so when it became difficult for tenants to clear profits in the decades after 1907. The number of tenants who were allowed to work holdings rent-free while they cleared unoccupied land for large landholders and land "grabbers" also fell steadily. As the extension of cultivated acreage slowed and landlords increasingly employed agents who hired landless laborers rather than renting their lands, the need for "clearing" tenants was reduced.[99]

The degree to which the tenant's position deteriorated in the decades of transition can be gauged from the fact that in the 1920s his condition was usually compared to that of the landless agricultural laborer,[100] rather than to that of the cultivator-owner as it had been in the late nineteenth century. Although the tenant's standard of living was generally higher, in many respects he was little better off than the landless laborer. In fact, in some tracts, laborers were able to remain solvent and clear fair profits in good seasons, while tenants fell deeper and deeper into debt.[101] In most areas of the Delta, the social and economic distinctions between tenants and laborers became increasingly blurred, while those between tenants and landholders rigidified.[102]

Due to the spread of industrial agriculture and the large size of holdings, the demand for agrarian labor rose considerably in the first decades of the twentieth century. Although there were a few tracts where only familial labor or village labor employed on a mutual-assistance basis were used,[103] in most areas hired laborers were essential to agricultural production. However, the supply of labor rose at a faster rate than the demand, and by the time of the First World War laborers in most tracts of the Delta were faced with stiff competition for positions as plowmen, planters, or reapers. The gradual decline in the number of seasonal laborers who in-migrated from Upper Burma and other divisions within the province was more than offset by the greatly accelerated movement of Indian industrial laborers into the agrarian sector during the off season for the rice mills and port centers. In addition, the ranks of landless laborers were swelled by cultivator-owners who lost their land and tenants who were outbid for the holdings they rented. The sharp decrease in vertical mobility in this period also meant that many persons who would have achieved higher social and economic status as landholders or tenants in the nineteenth century remained landless laborers in the decades of

99. *Land Revenue Report, 1929–30,* statement 11, p. 55.

100. Couper, *Report into Agricultural Condition,* p. 50; *Settlement Reports–Pyapon (1921–22),* pp. 10–11; *Maubin (1925–28),* p. 54.

101. *Banking Enquiry Report,* 2: 80.

102. Couper, *Report into Agricultural Condition,* p. 49.

103. *Settlement Reports–Insein (1910–12),* p. 26; *Thaton (Pa-an) (1928–30),* p. 62.

transition. As a result, there developed a large class of persons who were landless laborers throughout the most productive years of their lives. Only when they had grown too old and weak to perform the concentrated, arduous tasks demanded of an agricultural laborer did they seek positions as tenants, domestic servants, or cowherds. Landless laborers became the dominant element in the population of many villages in Lower Burma.[104]

Both the increased availability of laborers in the Delta and the closing of the rice frontier in many areas contributed to intensified competition for employment. Greater competition had the same adverse effects on the living standard and working conditions of landless laborers as it had had on those of tenants. Just as rent rates were the best gauge of the worsening position of tenants, wages were the best index for laborers. The available data show a moderate decline in laborers' wages between the 1880s and the 1910–20 period.[105] The continuing decline in laborers' wages in the 1920s is indicated by the fact that *gaungsaungs* (expert plowmen) could make as much as 145 rupees plus food in the Pyapon District in 1912–13, but they could earn no more than 120 rupees plus food in 1921–22.[106]

Figures cited in the settlement reports do not show, of course, the decrease in *real* wages paid to agricultural laborers because they do not take into account rising living costs. If the price of rice, which rose 25 percent between 1880 and 1915,[107] is used as an index of fluctuations in the costs of goods and services, it becomes clear that the *real* wage rates or agricultural laborers fell even more in this period than the 20 percent estimated by Furnivall.[108] Although wage rates for casual laborers rose slightly in the upper Delta, workers hired on a daily basis generally earned about the same wages as they had in the late nineteenth century.[109] Although cash wages for both seasonal and day laborers were far more widespread in the post-1907 period than they had been before, wages were still paid in paddy in many areas of the Delta. Cash wages seem to have been more common near large towns or in areas where land alienation and large estates were concentrated than in remote tracts or areas where agriculturists held most of the land.[110]

104. *Banking Enquiry Report,* 1: 20; Dunn, "Some General Characteristics," in Government of Burma, *Agriculture in Burma,* p. 16; *Maubin Settlement Report (1925–28),* p. 53.

105. See W. T. Hall's "Note," in Nolan's *Report,* and the settlement reports for the 1880s and 1910s. Comparisons are also set forth in Adas, "Agrarian Development," Table VIII-M, p. 418.

106. *Settlement Reports–Pyapon (1912–13),* p. 8; *Pyapon (1921–22),* p. 21.

107. I have calculated this percentage from the paddy price averages in Grant, *Rice Crop,* p. 48.

108. *Political Economy,* p. 77.

109. *Settlement Reports–Insein (1913–14),* p. 8; *Pegu (1914–15),* p. 10; *Prome (1914–16),* p. 33; *Thaton (Kyaikto) (1928–30),* p. 34.

110. Couper, *Report into Agricultural Condition,* p. 45; Dunn, "Some General Characteristics," in Government of Burma, *Agriculture in Burma,* p. 25; *Maubin Settlement Report (1925–28),* p. 54.

Despite the fact that laborers usually received food, and often betel and tobacco, in addition to their regular pay, their conditions of employment grew worse in a number of ways beyond decreases in the wages paid for their work. Laborers often had to borrow in the monsoon season to support their families until harvest. Because most laborers had no security to offer, persons who gave them advances, whether they were shopkeepers, landlords' agents, or tenants, normally demanded *sabape* rates of interest. Consequently, a large portion or all of many laborers' wages went to pay the principal and interest on loans.[111] Until the time of the First World War, however, a laborer could break even as long as he remained healthy and could find employment. If the other adult members of his household also worked, the family might even earn enough to buy a pair of bullocks and move up to tenant status. On the other hand, laborers who were ill for any length of time might lose their position and fall deeply into debt. By the 1920s the combined efforts and salaries of all the adult members of a laborer's household were often not sufficient to meet rising living costs. Consequently, many agricultural laborers were forced to work part-time as carters or coolies. Some migrated to urban areas to find employment, while others turned to crime in their struggle to survive in an economy that was increasingly unfavorable for persons engaged in agrarian production.[112]

111. *Banking Enquiry Report,* 2: 80; Couper, *Report into Agricultural Condition,* p. 45; *Maubin Settlement Report (1925–28),* p. 23.

112. *Banking Enquiry Report,* 2: 80; Couper, *Report into Agricultural Condition,* p. 10; *Settlement Reports–Myaungmya (1916–19),* p. 26; *Pyapon (1921–22),* p. 21; *Maubin (1925–28),* pp. 53–54.

7 CHANGING MIGRATION PATTERNS AND THE RISE OF COMPETITION IN THE MATURE PLURAL SOCIETY

The closing of the rice frontier and the mounting agrarian crisis in Lower Burma were major determinants of changes in both internal and foreign migration patterns in the decades of transition. The decrease in available, cultivable land and the worsening condition of the rural population in Lower Burma greatly reduced the "pull" that the Delta had exerted on Dry Zone agriculturists in the late nineteenth century. While the influx of migrants from Upper Burma declined, the volume of Indian immigration increased dramatically in response to continuing hardships in India and increasing opportunities in Lower Burma that ironically were generated by the same dislocations that so adversely affected the Burmese. These contrasting migration trends led to fears that Burma would be swamped by a swelling tide of Indian immigrants,[1] and, in the face of a slower rate of economic growth, resulted in greatly intensified competition and at times led to violent conflict between Indians and Burmese.

Between 1901 and 1931 the number of persons enumerated in Lower Burma who were born in Burma divisions outside the Delta fell from 411,000

1. For evidence of these fears as early as the first decade of the twentieth century, see Guy Rutledge's comments in "Some Notes on the Burma Census," *Journal of the Burma Research Society* 2, no. 2 (1912): 153–60; and for an Indian reply to official and popular criticisms of the role of migrants from India, see R. G. Sambandam, "Indians in Burma," *Indian Emigrant* 1, no. 8 (March 1915): 228–32.

to 179,000, or from 10 to 3 percent of the total population of Lower Burma. The fact that this sharp decrease occurred despite increases in migration from Arakan and Tenasserim in this period clearly demonstrates the importance of the Dry Zone as a source of migrants for the Delta. In 1931, after three decades of decline, the Dry Zone's share of migrant settlers in Lower Burma was still 76 percent, while the proportions from Arakan and Tenasserim were only 6 and 12 percent, respectively.[2] Hence, the bulk of the decrease between 1901 and 1931 was due to the fact that the volume of out-migration from the Dry Zone was not sufficient to replace earlier settlers who died in the Delta. The decrease also resulted in part from the return of migrants who had settled in Lower Burma to their original homes in the Dry Zone.[3] In addition, because the censuses for this period were compiled later in the cropping season than those for the first phase of development,[4] the proportion of seasonal in-migrants still found in the Delta was even less than in the late nineteenth century.

The sharp decrease in migration southward from the Dry Zone after 1900 was not only due to diminishing opportunities in the Delta, but it was also strongly influenced by improved conditions in Upper Burma. Cheng Siok-Hwa has stressed the importance of agricultural changes in the Dry Zone as determinants of the decline in migration to Lower Burma,[5] but she has not established direct causal links between these improvements and decreased out-migration. She makes no attempt to determine if new cropping patterns were introduced in those Dry Zone districts which supplied the largest number of migrants to the Delta, or if there was actually a correspondence between these measures and significant decreases in out-migration from specific areas. The uneven impact of these factors was reflected in differences between nineteenth- and twentieth-century migration patterns displayed by the districts of the Dry Zone. Both the volume of out-migration from individual districts and the percentage of the total in-migrants which each district supplied to the Delta varied substantially from former patterns. Table 9 illustrates these changes and provides the basis for an analysis of the differential impact of new crops and public works on out-migration from the Dry Zone.

The spread of irrigation facilities and new patterns of agricultural production were the main factors responsible for changes in the volume of

2. These trends and percentages were derived from the place-of-birth tables in the Burma censuses for the 1901–31 period.

3. For discussions concerning return emigration see *Settlement Reports–Toungoo (1910–13)*, p. 8; *Shwebo (1918–23)*, p. 13; the *Insein Gazetteer*, p. 25; and the *Henzada Gazetteer*, p. 33.

4. The census dates for this period were 10 March 1911, 18 March 1921, and 24 February 1931.

5. *Rice Industry of Burma*, pp. 116–17.

Table 9. In-Migrants from the Dry Zone in Lower Burma

	1901		1911		1921		1931	
	1	2	1	2	1	2	1	2
Mandalay	55,000	15	33,000	12	20,000	10	13,000	9
Myingyan	44,000	12	33,000	12	21,000	11	16,000	12
Minbu	44,000	12	28,000	10	15,000	7	8,000	6
Pakokku	34,000	10	26,000	9	18,000	8+	12,000	9
Thayetmyo	34,000	10	28,000	10	23,000	11	14,000	10
Shwebo	34,000	10	25,000	9	17,000	8	11,000	8
Lower Chindwin	28,000	8	20,000	7	12,000	6	9,000	6
Magwe	29,000	8	21,000	7	22,000	10	13,000	9
Meiktila	23,000	6	28,000	10	25,000	12	19,000	14
Sagaing	22,000	6	18,000	6	13,000	6+	8,000	6
Yamethin	5,000	2	22,000	8	19,000	9	14,000	10
Kyaukse	3,000	1	1,000	0–1	1,000	0–1	800	0–1
		100		100		100		100

Source: Place-of-birth tables from the Burma censuses for the dates listed.
Note: Column 1 indicates the number of persons in Lower Burma whose birthplace was in the Dry Zone, and column 2 the percentage of the total out-migrants from the Dry Zone from each district therein, 1901–31.

out-migration after 1901. Irrigation projects not only made crop output in Upper Burma more secure; they also provided employment for Burman agriculturists in the off-season and in times of scarcity.[6] The construction of new irrigation works was extensive in Mandalay, Shwebo, Minbu, Kyaukse, and Yamethin, while comparatively small additional areas in Sagaing and Lower Chindwin were irrigated for the first time.[7] In most cases there was a strong correspondence between changes in the amount of irrigated area and fluctuations in the volume of out-migration from Dry Zone districts. There were significant decreases both in the number of persons from Mandalay, Shwebo, and Minbu who were found in the Delta and in the percentage of

6. Pattle, "Some Factors," in Government of Burma, *Agriculture in Burma*, p. 114.
7. *Season and Crop*, tables on areas irrigated, 1901/2–1930/31.

in-migrants supplied by each of these districts between 1901 and 1931. The volume of out-migration from Sagaing and Lower Chindwin fell more slowly and the percentage of out-migrants from these districts remained about the same. Kyaukse had always been a marginal area of origin for migrants to the Delta and it became almost negligible in this period. Sharp decreases in the amount of irrigated area in Meiktila and Magwe resulted in increases in the percentage of out-migrants from these districts and, in the case of Meiktila, a rise in the absolute number of in-migrants supplied to the Delta. The parallel between increased irrigation and lower out-migration displayed by the above districts was not supported by patterns in the Yamethin district. Both the volume and percentage of out-migrants from Yamethin rose sharply in this period, despite substantial construction of irrigation works at least until 1915–16.

The second major change in agricultural technology in the Dry Zone which was related to the decline in out-migration was the introduction of cash crops. The two most important of these in terms of their impact on population movement were peanuts and sesame (or groundnuts and *til* as they were called in most government reports). Beginning in the late nineteenth century both peanuts and sesame were important market crops within Burma, and peanuts were exported on a sizable scale beginning in the first decade of the twentieth century.[8] Cultivation of these crops not only gave agriculturists in the Dry Zone an additional crop buffer against the uncertainty of rainfall in the region,[9] but they also provided a means by which Upper Burmans could obtain cash to purchase the consumer goods which had attracted migrants to the Delta in the last half of the nineteenth century. Peanut picking, which required the employment of hired laborers, also provided a source of local employment for laborers who had formerly migrated to Lower Burma on a seasonal basis.[10]

Peanuts were first introduced into the Dry Zone from the Shan States in the 1880s, but government officials did not actively encourage their cultivation on a large scale until 1907.[11] Since the areas where the crop was grown on a large scale were concentrated in the districts of Myingyan, Pakkoku, and Magwe,[12] it was only in these areas where its introduction had a significant impact on the decline in the volume of out-migration. In the case of Myingyan and Pakokku, this impact was particularly significant because both districts had been major areas of origin in the late nineteenth century. The cultivation of peanuts on a smaller scale in Shwebo, Lower Chindwin,

8. Maung Shein, *Burma's Transport*, p. 121.

9. Peanuts thrive in sandy soil and are "to some extent" drought resistant. *Pakokku Settlement Report (1905–10)*, p. 8.

10. *Magwe Settlement Report (1915–19)*, p. 12.

11. F. D. Odell, *Groundnuts in Burma* (Rangoon, 1932), p. 2.

12. *Season and Crop*, acreage use tables, 1915/16–1930/31.

Sagaing, and Meiktila may have contributed to the decline in out-migration from these areas. The rise in the acreage under peanuts in Meiktila after 1920 corresponds to a fall in out-migration from that district beginning in the 1911–21 period. In terms of change in the percentage of migrants from individual districts, it is interesting to note that the proportionate decline from peanut areas was less dramatic than that of Mandalay and Minbu, where irrigation was the major innovation.

The large-scale production of sesame was more widespread than that of groundnuts. Increased sesame cultivation provided an alternative to migration in Meiktila, Yamethin, Thayetmyo, Pakokku, Magwe, Shwebo, and Lower Chindwin.[13] The drop in Myingyan's share of the total in-migrants to the Delta between 1911 and 1921 may also have been influenced by an increase in the previously extensive production of sesame in that district. This inference is supported by the rise in the district's share of migrants in the 1921–31 period following a decline in the area under sesame after 1915–16.

Although Meiktila showed a large increase in the area under sesame and Yamethin in both the area under sesame and the area irrigated, the percentage of total migrants from these districts rose considerably in the 1901–31 period. They were also the only districts which displayed gains in absolute numbers of out-migrants after 1901. These trends seem to contradict the assertions that public works and new crops strongly affected the volume of out-migration from the Dry Zone. This contradiction is partially explained, however, by the fact that the rise in acreage under sesame cultivation in Meiktila was more than offset by a sharp decline in the area under irrigation in the same period. In addition, the available evidence indicates that there was a belated, but large-scale, movement of migrants from Yamethin, which was rather densely populated in relation to the amount of arable land, to the fertile plains of the neighboring Toungoo District.[14] Toungoo was one of the few areas in Lower Burma where the extension of cultivation continued on a sizable scale after 1900.

Innovations comparable to the new crops and irrigation networks that had reduced the volume of out-migration from the Dry Zone were not introduced on a large scale in either Arakan or Tenasserim. Consequently, the conditions in these divisions that had stimulated migration in the nineteenth century were not ameliorated. In fact, population increases in Kyaukpyu and Sandoway in Arakan and the Amherst District in Tenasserim intensified the factors that had formerly "pushed" migrants from these areas. The limited land that was available along the coast line of the mountainous districts of Kyaukpyu and Sandoway in south Arakan was all but exhausted by the first decade of the twentieth century. Although seasonal migration to Akyab

13. Ibid.
14. *Yamethin Settlement Report (1925–26)*, p. 12.

relieved some of the population pressure in these districts,[15] growing numbers of agriculturists crossed the Arakan Yomas to seek work or land in Bassein and Myaungmya.[16] Surprisingly, Akyab, the most populous district in the Province of Burma and an area where holdings were extremely fragmented in many tracts, supplied very few in-migrants to Lower Burma or any other area.[17]

Along with the districts of the Delta, Amherst District was one of the thirteen principal rice-growing areas in Burma. In the period of transition most of the agrarian problems which afflicted Lower Burma were also present in Amherst. However, Amherst ran out of available, cultivable land before neighboring Thaton, and large numbers of agriculturists from Amherst crossed the Sittang in search of land. This movement was sufficient to sustain the volume of out-migration from Amherst at its late nineteenth-century level.[18]

There were a number of important changes in the composition of the internal migrant stream in the decades of transition. The proportion of seasonal to permanent migrants increased steadily until, by the 1920s, permanent migration into most areas of the Delta was negligible.[19] The volume of seasonal migration fluctuated much more widely from year to year than it had in the nineteenth century,[20] and the area worked by laborers from the Dry Zone was gradually reduced. By the 1920s substantial seasonal migration of Burmese laborers was confined to the districts of the upper Delta.[21] Since most seasonal laborers were males, the proportion of males to females in the migrant stream during this period rose. This shift was not reflected in the census totals, which indicated that there were 140–150 males per 100 females between 1911 and 1931, because most seasonal migrants had returned to their homes by the time of the census counts. As in the nineteenth century, most internal migrants to Lower Burma in the first decades of the twentieth century were agriculturists, though some traders from Upper Burma still peddled their goods annually along the rivers of the lower Delta.[22]

It is somewhat paradoxical that the worsening economic conditions in the rural Delta that led in part to the decline in Burmese in-migration provided

15. *Akyab Gazetteer*, p. 10.

16. *Sandoway Gazetteer*, pp. 1–2, 16–17, 20–21.

17. *Akyab Gazetteer*, p. 104.

18. *Amherst Gazetteer* (1913), pp. 23, 30–33; *Amherst Gazetteer* (1935), pp. 29–43.

19. As noted above there was a substantial influx of permanent migrants from Yamethin into Toungoo as late as the mid-1920s.

20. *Burma Censuses–1911*, p. 69, *1921*, p. 93.

21. *Settlement Reports–Myaungmya (1916–19)*, p. 24; *Yamethin (1925–26)*, p. 12.

22. *Burma Census, 1921*, p. 94; *Bassein Settlement Report (1912–14)*, p. 12.

additional attractions for Indian immigrant laborers. The sharp increase in the amount of land alienated after 1900, for example, led to growth in the size of the Indian landlord class in Lower Burma. Since Indian landlords continued to prefer Indian tenants and laborers, Indian immigrants found greater opportunities for employment in agricultural production. In addition, Burmese landowners who had once depended on seasonal laborers from the Dry Zone for assistance in cultivation increasingly hired Indians to plant and/or harvest their crop. Decreases in the level of Burmese in-migration also meant that Indian immigrants came to be relied upon to meet the growing demand for labor which resulted from the extension of rice cultivation.

The growth of the rice-processing industry and rice-export trade was also a major contributor to increased employment opportunities for Indian laborers in Lower Burma. Due to the proliferation of small-scale "upcountry" mills and increases in the size of the mills in Rangoon and other urban centers, the number of rice-mill employees grew from less than 6,000 in 1898 to nearly 39,000 in 1929.[23] The increase in rice exports, as well as growth in the export of other products such as teak and peanuts, and rising imports meant that more and more labor was needed on the wharves and in the harbors of the Delta's ports. In most cases, Indians filled the positions created by the expansion of these sectors of the economy. Although the *real* wages which laborers in industry and shipping received dropped somewhat due to rising prices,[24] wage levels in Lower Burma remained far above those in India. The monetary returns derived by immigrant Indian laborers continued to far exceed the costs of their journey to Burma.

Expanded opportunities in Lower Burma were paralleled by the continuation and in some areas the intensification of agrarian problems which had "pushed" migrants from India in the first phase of development. Long-term declines in agricultural productivity and income in the major regions of origin caused the volume of emigration to Burma to rise well above pre-1907 levels. In Madras, Bengal, and the United Provinces the rate of foodgrain production fell considerably behind the rate of population growth. The availability of foodgrains in this period also decreased at a rate only "slightly less unfavorable" than the rate of per capita output.[25] Although the output of nonfoodgrain crops increased in the three major regions of origin, the rate of all-crop output lagged beyind population growth in each.[26] The effect of these trends on per capita income was severe. George Blyn estimates

23. Cheng, *Rice Industry of Burma,* app. IV-B, and pp. 253–55, 85.

24. E. J. L. Andrew, as quoted in Government of India, *Report of the Deck Passenger Committee,* 2: 80; Aye Hlaing, "Trends of Growth," pp. 120–26.

25. George Blyn, *Agricultural Trends in India, 1891–1947: Output, Availability, and Productivity* (Philadelphia, 1966), pp. 98–107. See also Leach, "Rice Industry of Burma," pp. 61–73.

26. Blyn, *Agricultural Trends,* pp. 111–14, 118–23.

that after 1911–12, per capita agricultural output for India as a whole declined by 0.72 percent a year, while the population of the subcontinent increased by 1 percent per year. At this rate, he concludes, nonagricultural output would have had to increase at about 2 percent per year for per capita income to have remained constant.[27] These downturns in production and income had the greatest impact on the poorer classes of agricultural earners[28] who made up the bulk of immigrants to Lower Burma.

Since few detailed studies of regional economic conditions in India have as yet been attempted for this period, it is difficult to discuss changes in local factors which "pushed" emigrants from districts which have been determined major areas of origin. The trends set forth by Blyn, however, and the local evidence that is available[29] indicate that the condition of agriculturists in these areas grew considerably worse. This is particularly true of the United Provinces, which doubled the percentage of the total volume of immigrants which it supplied to the Delta after 1900. To a large degree this increase was probably due to the consequences of the ecological devastation which Elizabeth Whitcombe has traced to the poorly planned and supervised irrigation projects introduced into the United Provinces in the last half of the nineteenth century.[30] In most of the densely populated districts of the Indo-Gangetic plain the limits of cultivation were reached, the area cropped stagnated, and the yields of a number of major crops declined. The efforts of *taluqdari* landlords to enhance rents paid by their tenants compounded serious agrarian problems which were rooted in market malfunctions, extreme fragmentations of holdings, and inefficient methods of production.[31] These problems were particularly pronounced in Fyzabad and Sultanpur, which were two of the most densely populated districts in the provinces,[32] and led to the agrarian riots which erupted in the United Provinces in 1920 and subsequently to the Eka (unity) movement among the tenants of that area. These dilemmas also stimulated large-scale emigration, which was increasingly directed to Bombay and Burma after 1901, because the demand for labor in these regions was greater than in Bengal and Assam, where the majority of emigrants had formerly gone.[33]

27. Ibid., pp. 124–25.

28. See S. G. Tiwari, *Economic Prosperity of the United Provinces . . . , 1921–1939* (Bombay, 1951), pp. 358–59.

29. For Godavari and Kistna in Madras, for example, see Rao, *Economic Development*, pp. 292–95.

30. *Agrarian Conditions in Northern India: The United Provinces under British Rule, 1860–1900* (Berkeley, Calif., 1972), especially pp. 7–13, 75–96.

31. Walter C. Neale, *Economic Change in Rural India* (New Haven, Conn., 1962), pp. 99–102, 148–55, 179–208.

32. *Census of the United Provinces of Agra and Oudh, 1931,* Report, pp. 22–23, 88–89.

33. Ibid., *1911,* Report, p. 45.

As in the first phase of development, there was a strong correspondence between natural calamities and food shortages in India and sharp fluctuations in the volume of *net* migration between India and Burma. The jump in the number of *net* migrants in 1910 and 1911, which is shown in Table 10, came after a series of severe food shortages and epidemics in Sultanpur, Fyzabad, and other areas of the United Provinces between 1907 and 1910. In addition, a cyclone struck Ganjam, and floods caused local shortages in Shahabad in these same years.[34] The great increase between 1913 and 1914 was paralleled by drought and serious food shortages in Fyzabad and cyclones in Ganjam and Vizagapatam. The sharp drop in the volume of *net* migrants in the 1916–18 period was due to shipping shortages caused by the First World War.[35] The resurgence of migration in the years following the end of the war resulted from both the resumption of regular steamship services and a general famine in 1918–19 in India which affected most of the major districts of origin of migrants to Burma.[36] The brief rise after 1922 followed seasons of cyclones in Ganjam and Vizagapatam and severe flooding in Shahabad. Finally, the last peak between 1926 and 1928 came after a series of poor crops in the United Provinces.

The elaboration and extension of *maistry* operations in this period also contributed to the rising volume of immigration to Burma.[37] *Maistries* provided propaganda which made migration attractive to poor Indian laborers and funds which made it possible. Their operations gave some semblance of organization and coordination to labor recruiting and deployment among Indians. Consequently, Indian workers had considerable advantages when competing with Burmese workers for jobs. Indians, not Burmese, usually profited from new employment opportunities, particularly those in urban areas.

Expanding opportunities in Lower Burma and continuing distress in India resulted in the growth of the Indian community in the Delta from 297,000 in 1901 to 583,000 in 1931.[38] This growth represented an increase in the proportion of Indians to the total population of Lower Burma from 7 to 10 percent. The largest increase in this period occurred between 1901 and 1911, when the number of Indians rose to 415,000, or 9 percent of the Delta total.

34. Ibid., *1931*, Report, p. 24, and district gazetteers. Unless otherwise noted, the following discussion is based on information derived from the district gazetteers for the areas mentioned.

35. *Indian Emigrant* 2, no. 1 (August 1915): 26.

36. *Madras Census, 1921*, Report, p. 11; *Census of the United Provinces of Agra and Oudh, 1931*, Report, p. 26.

37. For detailed discussions of the *maistry* system in the transition period, see Andrew, *Indian Labour*, pp. 37–45, 83, et passim, or Adas, "Agrarian Development," pp. 345–48.

38. As in Chapter 5, all estimates of the Indian population are based on the composition-by-religion tables in the Burma censuses.

Table 10. *Net* Migrants Recorded at Rangoon between 1908 and 1930 (to the nearest thousand)

Date	Net migrants
1908	25,000
1909	3,000
1910	51,000
1911	67,000
1912	16,000
1913	41,000
1914	143,000
1915	93,000
1916	29,000
1917	−10,000
1918	32,000
1919	71,000
1920	100,000
1921	40,000
1922	54,000
1923	98,000
1924	82,000
1925	28,000
1926	78,000
1927	75,000
1928	94,000
1929	45,000
1930	−11,000[a]

Source: Andrew, *Indian Labour,* app. 1, Table A, p. 221. Both Baxter and Andrew have separate statistics for migration from Indian ports only. However, these were not compiled until 1913. I have also used the statistics relating to *net* migration from all foreign ports to retain consistency with the figures used in Chapter 4.

[a] From Baxter, *Indian Immigration,* app. 6 (b), p. 122.

In the next two decades the rate of growth slowed and the percentage of Indians remained around 10 in both 1921 and 1931. As in the pre-1901 period, most Indians in Lower Burma were born outside of the province. In 1931, 427,000 or 73 percent of the 583,000 Indians in the Delta listed districts in India as their birthplaces. This figure represents a decrease in the number of immigrants in the Indian community from 84 percent in 1901. This drop was probably due to the fact that more Indians were engaged in agricultural production as landowners and tenants after 1901, and therefore were more likely to settle on a permanent basis and raise their families in Lower Burma. The composition of the Indian migrant stream varied remarkably little from that of the late nineteenth century.[39]

The high degree of social harmony which existed among different cultural groups in the first phase of agrarian development was dependent upon rapid and sustained economic growth. Although some of the newly created niches which migrants were drawn in to fill after 1852 were political or military, the plural society which developed in the Delta was largely a product of the great expansion of the area's economy. Throughout most of the late nineteenth century, the number of positions available in different sectors of the rice industry increased as fast as or faster than the number of indigenous and in-migrant Burmese, or immigrant Indians, Chinese, and Europeans who sought to fill them. In agrarian production, credit provision, transportation, processing, and trade, the demand for new investors, managers, and workers exceeded the supply in most instances until the first decade of the twentieth century.

This abundance of positions was essential to the continuance of the cooperation and interdependence which characterized relations between the different cultural groups who made up the plural society in Lower Burma. The Burmese, for example, could afford to relinquish control of processing and wharf labor to Indian immigrants because there were more than enough openings for them in internal transportation, trade, and, most important, agricultural production. Likewise, the expansion of Chettiar moneylending operations into the rural Delta did not mean a corresponding decline in the role played by indigenous moneylenders. Despite the fact that the Chettiars soon predominated in terms of the quantity of the capital they supplied, Burmese moneylenders continued to far outnumber their Indian counterparts. In addition, the overall extension of credit facilities in Lower Burma meant that even though the indigenous moneylenders fell behind their Indian competitors in relative terms, the total lending activities of the Burmese increased. Because Chettiars often supplied the capital which Burmese

39. Changes in internal migration within the Delta and population distribution will be treated below in the discussion on the mature plural society.

moneylenders loaned to agriculturists, it can be argued that the spread of Chettiar activities contributed substantially to, rather than impeded, the growth of an indigenous moneylending class. These examples indicate that in the last decades of the nineteenth century there were numerous alternatives and an overabundance of positions open to the members of different cultural groups in the Delta.

In the first decades of the twentieth century the rate of economic expansion in Lower Burma slowed. The leveling off of rice exports in the early 1900s[40] and the much lower rate of increase in acreage under paddy cultivation after 1905 were major manifestations of a general deceleration of economic growth in the decades of transition. The positions created by the great increase in the number of rice mills, which were mainly small upcountry mills,[41] were not sufficient to offset the loss of potential positions which resulted from a slower rate of growth in other sectors of the rice industry.[42]

Despite this slowdown, the population of the Delta continued to grow at a rate comparable to that recorded in the boom decades of the nineteenth century. Between 1911 and 1931, for example, the population of Lower Burma increased by 1,333,000, which was nearly equal to the 1,481,000 added in the boom decades between 1881 and 1901.[43] In terms of the plural balance achieved in the nineteenth century, the 1911–31 increase is particularly significant because it was fed largely by the rising volume of Indian immigration in this period. Thus, increasing numbers of Indian migrants, and Burmese males who had been born in the decades of prosperity with their concomitant high rates of natural increase in the late nineteenth century, were entering the working force of an economy that was increasingly unable to accommodate them. This trend is vividly illustrated by the decline in rice exports from Burma on a per capita basis. In 1901, 0.5 tons of paddy per person of the Delta population were exported from Burma. By 1921 tonnage per capita had dropped to 0.4.[44] Economic growth was clearly falling behind population increase.

40. Grant, *Rice Crop,* p. 56.

41. Cheng, *Rice Industry of Burma,* pp. 82–95.

42. The expansion of other industries which were important to the Delta economy, such as saw-milling, was of marginal significance in terms of new employment opportunities provided. The steady growth of the administration, military, police department, and professional classes was also of minor importance in terms of new positions created. The fact that small minorities of Europeans and English-educated Indians or Burmese largely monopolized political and professional niches in Lower Burma further reduced the impact of the expansion of employment opportunities at these levels.

43. Population variation table, 1881–1931, in the *Burma Census, 1931,* pt. 2, p. 6. The average annual rate of increase in Lower Burma in the 1901–31 period fell to just over 1 percent.

44. Since most of the rice exported from Burma was grown in the Delta districts and the economy of Lower Burma was dominated by the rice industry to a very high degree, rice exports are the best gauge of increases or decreases in *per capita* output.

As the supply of persons seeking employment came to exceed the demand in many sectors, competition intensified greatly. Because of the plural social arrangement this competition developed in most instances along cultural or, in terms of the participants' perception, racial lines. As alternatives for employment decreased, the Burmese came to resent the fact that Indians dominanted many niches of the Delta economy. They felt increasingly threatened by the growing influx of Indian laborers into the urban and rural Delta. Their resentment and concern were expressed initially in demands for a larger share of positions in niches controlled by Indians and later by attempts to wrest control of these niches from Indians and other immigrant groups. For their part, the Indians sought to strengthen their hold over the niches which they had come to dominate in the late nineteenth century. At the same time they were forced by the great increase in their numbers to expand their activities into sectors which had largely been left to the Burmese in the first phase of development.

As competition for control of the common institutions of Delta society became more pronounced, the members of each of the cultural segments which composed it grew more and more conscious of the differences which distinguished their group from the others. The cleavages between cultural groups hardened, and their interaction was increasingly hostile. The divisions which separated them were further emphasized by the growth of nationalism in India, China, and Burma. Even as it matured, the plural society in Burma began to break down. The fluidity and accommodation of intercultural relations in the early period gave way to rigidity and confrontation in the decades of transition. This confrontation was centered in both the agrarian and industrial spheres of the rice industry. Competition between Indians and Burmese in the rural Delta was most intense among tenants and agricultural laborers. Due to the gradual closing of the rice frontier and the oversupply of both tenants and laborers which resulted, Burmese agriculturists became increasingly resentful of Indian competition for these positions. Their discontent was exacerbated by the fact that more and more Indian immigrants became involved in agrarian production in the decades of transition.

Increased Indian involvement at the tenant level in the first decades of the twentieth century was reflected in the rise in the proportion of the tenant class that was Indian from 1 or 2 percent in the 1890s to over 8 percent in 1931.[45] Although competition from Indian tenants remained the most

45. I have calculated these percentages from the tables on occupations by race by provincial divisions in the Burma censuses for 1921 and 1931. They were taken from the statistics for the "Delta" division, which in both enumerations includes only and all of the districts used for this study except the Prome District in the upper Delta. Since the number of Indians in Prome was lower than in most other areas, these percentages are probably a bit high. On the other hand, the number of tenants, laborers, and cultivator-

pronounced near Rangoon and in the districts of the central, lower Delta where it had been confined prior to 1900, by the end of the decades of transition their presence was felt in all but the most remote circles.[46] Burmese tenants found Indian competition particularly injurious because Indians could normally pay higher rents than indigenous tenants. Consequently, the movement of Indians into an area was generally followed by rent increases.[47] Most government officials believed that Indians could pay higher rents because they had a lower standard of living and thus could afford to give up a larger share of their produce to the landlord. Although this view was presumably also held by Burmese agriculturists and has been popularized by Furnivall and other writers,[48] some of the available statistics relating to the cost of living of Delta tenants by "race" seem to contradict it. These figures show that although in most cases the cost of living of the Burmese family was far more than that of the Indian, the Indian family was in many cases smaller. This meant that on a cost per capita basis the amount required to support an Indian was often actually higher than that for a Burmese.[49]

The apparent contradiction between some cost of living averages and the belief that Indian tenants had a lower standard of living can perhaps be resolved if one takes into account the composition of the Indian tenant "family" in Lower Burma. Most Indian tenants were temporary migrants who left their wives or children behind in Tamilnad or Telengana. Therefore, the Indian tenant "family" listed in these surveys often consisted of two or three brothers, or cousins, a husband and wife, or several friends from the same village in India. The government officials who conducted the cost of living surveys counted only those Indians present in Burma. It is probable, however, that a sizable portion of the amount which Indian tenants estimated to be their cost of living went in the form of remittances to support parents, children, and other relatives in India. Thus, these dependents *in absentia* would have to be added to the Indian family size when calculating per capita expenditure. It is not possible to determine how much of an Indian tenant's

---

owners was considerably smaller in Prome than in other districts, and thus its exclusion is less significant than it might have been if a larger district in the lower Delta had been excluded.

46. *Settlement Reports–Myaungmya (1916–19)*, p. 183; *Pyapon (1921–22)*, p. 7; *Thaton Gazetteer*, p. 39; *Bassein Gazetteer*, p. 31.

47. Couper, *Report into Agricultural Condition*, p. 7; Government of Burma, Revenue and Agriculture Proceedings, vol. 8633, November 1911, p. 149.

48. *RAB, 1908–9*, p. 19; Government of Burma, Revenue and Agriculture Proceedings, vol. 8633, November 1911, pp. 315, 652; *Pyapon Settlement Report (1921–22)*, p. 8; Furnivall, *Colonial Policy and Practice*, p. 88, *Political Economy*, p. 67.

49. See *Settlement Reports–Hanthawaddy (1907–10)*, p. 21; *Insein (1910–12)*, pp. 142–51; *Pegu (1911–13)*, pp. 100–107; *Pegu (1914–15)*, p. 61; and *Thaton (Kyaikto) (1928–30)*, p. 14. For tables summarizing this data see Adas, "Agrarian Development," app. XIII, pp. 562–64.

income was used for remittances, but it is likely that he had more dependents than the average head of a Burmese tenant household. Therefore, Indian tenants may have had even lower living standards, in comparison with Burmese agriculturists than has generally been believed.

Another reason why Indian tenants could afford to pay higher rents was related to the fact that most of their "families" consisted of productive adults, which meant that they could cut their costs of cultivation by hiring fewer laborers. Burmese tenant families, on the other hand, normally consisted of several dependents, and thus more outside labor was required to assist in paddy production. Because greater profits could be made from letting their lands to Indian tenants, many Burmese and most Indian landlords preferred them to indigenous agriculturists. This was especially true of nonagriculturist landlords.[50] Chettiar landlords continued to import Madrasi tenants to work their holdings as they had in the late nineteenth century. These tenants in turn sometimes hired laborers from their home villages in India to help them work the Chettiars' holdings.[51] Landlords who owned land in flood-prone or infertile tracts usually let to Indians because Burmese tenants could not normally earn a living on holdings in these areas.[52]

Despite the fact that he could not afford to pay the high rents of his Indian competitors, the Burmese tenant appealed to those agriculturist landlords who were as concerned for the care of their holdings as they were to realize profits. According to Thomas Couper and other contemporary observers, Burmese tenants were generally better cultivators than Indians. They plowed and transplanted more carefully than Indians and spilled less rice while reaping. Indians, on the other hand, spent more time repairing field bunds and often agreed to cart paddy used to pay their rent to the landlords' houses or granaries.[53] In areas where landlords could choose between Indians and Burmese tenants, they usually opted for higher profits and let their lands to Indians. Throughout much of the Delta, however, not enough Indian tenants were available, and thus Burmese made up the bulk of the tenant class. As Indian competition became more widespread, tension between Indian and indigenous tenants mounted and this friction became more ominous as the tenant class of Lower Burma grew.

50. Government of Burma, Revenue and Agriculture Proceedings, vol. 8633, November 1911, pp. 177–78; *Settlement Reports–Hanthawaddy (1907–10)*, p. 20; *Hanthawaddy (1930–33)*, p. 39.

51. Government of Burma, Revenue and Agriculture Proceedings, vol. 8633, November 1911, p. 149; *Pyapon Settlement Report (1921–22)*, p. 8.

52. Government of Burma, Revenue and Agriculture Proceedings, vol. 8633, November 1911, p. 203; *Pyapon Settlement Report (1921–22)*, p. 32.

53. Couper, *Report into Agricultural Condition*, p. 51; Government of Burma, Revenue and Agriculture Proceedings, vol. 8633, November 1911, p. 203; *Hanthawaddy Settlement Report (1930–33)*, p. 36; *Banking Enquiry Report*, 2: 81.

Because the main increase in Indian agricultural laborers in the decades of transition came from the ranks of mill-workers, competition between Indian and Burmese agricultural laborers was the most intense in areas near urban-industrial centers. The migration of Indian mill-hands into the rural Delta became a dominant feature of paddy production in the districts of the lower Delta, especially in the vicinity of Rangoon, Bassein, and Moulmein. Until the late 1920s few Indians were found in the upper Delta, where local laborers and seasonal migrants from Upper Burma predominated. The main alternative to Indian workers throughout the Delta as a whole were indigenous landless laborers who lived in villages in the circles where they worked. It was these local laborers whom Indian competition affected the most directly and who most resented the growing influx of foreign urban workers into agricultural production.[54]

The fact that most Indian agricultural laborers were also mill-hands meant that their competition was confined mainly to the reaping season from late August to January, which coincided with the slack season for the large Rangoon mills. Although some Indian immigrants continued to be engaged solely in agricultural production and thus employed as plowmen, planters, and threshers, these stages of the production cycle were left in most areas to indigenous agriculturists.[55] Aside from reaping, the one aspect of agricultural production in which Indians were dominant was *kazin* or field bund repair, which was monopolized by full-time Indian agricultural laborers as a means of support in the dry season.[56] The seasonal concentration of Indian laborers made their role in terms of the total supply of agricultural labor appear less important than it actually was. In both 1921 and 1931 only 6 percent of the persons listed as agricultural laborers in Lower Burma were Indians.[57] It is probable, however, that because the censuses for these years were taken in mid-March and late February respectively, most part-time Indian laborers had returned to the mills and docks and were enumerated as urban workers. It is also likely that many immigrant Indians who were engaged primarily in agricultural labor had returned to India for the dry season or were engaged in subsidiary occupations such as carting, loading rice, river transport, and railway or warehouse labor.[58]

54. *Settlement Reports–Hanthawaddy (1907–10)*, p. 7; *Insein (1910–12)*, p. 17; *Myaungmya (1912–13)*, pp. 8, 13; *Pyapon (1912–13)*, p. 8; *Bassein (1912–13)*, p. 30, (*1912–14*), p. 11; *Prome (1914–16)*, p. 33; *Myaungmya (1916–19)*, p. 25; *Pyapon (1921–22)*, pp. 20–21; *Maubin (1925–28)*, pp. 15, 54; *Thaton (Kyaikto), (1928–30)*, p. 33; *Bassein Gazetteer*, p. 51; *Insein Gazetteer*, p. 48; *Toungoo Gazetteer*, p. 38.

55. See, for examples, *Settlement Reports–Hanthawaddy (1907–10)*, pp. 6–7; *Pegu (1911–13)*, p. 14; *Pyapon (1921–22)*, p. 21; *Banking Enquiry Report*, 2: 80.

56. *Settlement Reports–Hanthawaddy (1907–10)*, p. 6; *Bassein (1912–14)*, p. 11; *Myaungmya (1912–13)*, p. 8.

57. See footnote 45.

58. Despite efforts on the part of census officials to insure that the respondent's primary occupation was recorded (see *Burma Census, 1921*, pt. 1, Report, pp. 235–36),

In competition for positions as agricultural laborers, Indians possessed the advantages of better organization and lower costs, while Burmese workers generally performed their tasks more skillfully. Two main forms of organization were found among Indian agricultural workers in the decades of transition, voluntary associations and *maistry* gangs. Voluntary associations consisted of from ten to twenty men from the same village in India who migrated to Lower Burma as a group and then traveled about the Delta offering their services for different cropping operations. Two or three laborers who had previously been to Burma formed the nucleus of the voluntary associations, but all the members of a group received an equal share of its earnings.[59] Even though the voluntary association had become quite popular among Tamil laborers by the 1920s, the *maistry*-gang arrangement remained the standard form of organization for Indian workers as a whole. The *maistry* who organized and headed a particular gang normally knew Burmese and acted as a spokesman for the laborers in his charge, thereby facilitating bargaining, bookkeeping, and remuneration. The *maistry,* who was often a Brahman, supervised the work of his gang, disciplined its members, and distributed their food and wages.[60] Both the *maistry* gang and the voluntary association were well suited to agricultural conditions in the Delta. As many as fifty to sixty men could be organized under the *maistry* system and from ten to thirty under the voluntary arrangement. Large groups of reapers, such as these, were essential on the estates of the Lower Delta districts where the rice crop was planted to ripen at the same time.[61]

The best indication of the superiority of Indian organization was the fact that it was adopted by Burmese laborers as early as the 1880s and 1890s. Burmese gangs, however, were generally smaller and less well-disciplined than Indians. They also tended to be less permanent because despite the demonstrated advantages of gang organization, Burmese laborers continued to prefer to work as individuals on a seasonal basis.[62]

The superior organization of Indian laborers made them considerably cheaper to hire than Burmese workers. To begin with, it cost less for a landlord to hire on a piecework or operational basis than on a seasonal or annual one because he was spared the cost of supporting his laborers during slack periods. In addition, the *maistry* of an Indian gang had firm control over its members and could unilaterally determine the level of their wages. Thus,

---

it is highly probable that many Indian agricultural laborers were listed for one of the subsidiary occupations they were performing at the time of their enumeration.

59. Special inquiry regarding Indians employed as agricultural laborers, as quoted in Baxter, *Indian Immigration,* p. 47.

60. Ibid., p. 47; Furnivall, "Industrial Agriculture," p. 95.

61. *Banking Enquiry Report,* 1: 18–19; *Pyapon Settlement Report (1921–22),* p. 21; Government of Burma, *Report on the Suspension of Grants,* p. 22.

62. *Banking Enquiry Report,* 2: 80; Dunn, "Some General Characteristics," in Government of Burma, *Agriculture in Burma,* p. 22; *Burma Census, 1911,* Report, p. 70.

he could outbid Burmese gangs, whose rates normally had to be agreed upon by all the laborers involved. The *maistry* could also ask for lower rates because the standard of living of his workers was lower than that of Burmese laborers.[63]

Burmese laborers, like Burmese tenants, compensated for their somewhat higher costs by performing their tasks more carefully. Indian reapers generally cut the paddy stalks too high, and their sheaves were often too small and badly formed. They also spilled more grain while harvesting than Burmese reapers. Indigenous workers were also better than Indians at reaping in areas where the paddy had been flattened or twisted by the wind or waves.[64] In all stages of paddy production from plowing to threshing, settlement officers reported that Burmese laborers were more efficient, but Indian workers were cheaper. Thus, in hiring laborers Delta landholders had to weigh the advantages of lower wages against those of higher output and profits.

The competition and friction which became dominant features of relations between Indian and Burmese tenants and laborers in the 1907–30 period were practically unknown among landholders in the Delta. At the level of the small landholder or cultivator-owner, there was little rivalry because there were very few Indian owners. In 1931 less than 2 percent of the cultivator-owners in the Delta were Indian.[65] Unlike tenants and laborers, these owners were not spread over whole districts, but scattered in small pockets in the districts near Rangoon and the circles around Bassein town.[66] Most Indians with small landholdings had originally been industrial or agricultural laborers who had worked their way up to ownership status in the boom decades at the end of the nineteenth or the first decade of the twentieth century.[67] In the transition period significant increases in their numbers were limited by the same factors that prevented most Burmese laborers or tenants from becoming landholders and by the fact that most Indians in Burma were there on a temporary basis.

As in the late nineteenth century, Indian landlords controlled only a small

63. Settlement officers and other revenue officials were in complete agreement on this point. For specific comparisons see *Settlement Reports–Pegu (1897–98)*, p. 9; *Bassein (1912–14)*, p. 24; and *Insein (1913–14)*, p. 8.

64. *Settlement Reports–Hanthawaddy (1879–80)*, p. 5; *Pyapon (1906–7)*, p. 11; *Pyapon (1912–13)*, p. 8; *Bassein (1912–13)*, p. 30.

65. See footnote 45.

66. *Settlement Reports–Insein (1910–12)*, pp. 25, 39; *Pyapon (1921–22)*, p. 8; *Maubin (1925–28)*, pp. 15–16; *Bassein Gazetteer*, p. 31. The Hanthawaddy District was something of an exception to this general rule. In 1907–10, 20 percent of the area in the district was listed as worked by Indian owners. See *Hanthawaddy Settlement Report (1907–10)*, p. 140.

67. See Chapter 5; the *Hanthawaddy Settlement Report (1907–10)*, pp. 6, 14; and the *Pegu Gazetteer*, p. 50.

percentage of the land in most areas of the Delta in the decades of transition. In 1930, for example, only 6 percent of the total occupied area in the twelve Delta districts and Amherst belonged to Chettiars. Their holdings amounted to just 19 percent of all the land alienated to nonagriculturists.[68] Although other Indians, such as Muslim traders and non-Chettiar moneylenders, also owned large holdings in some districts,[69] the total area controlled by Indian landlords was probably not more than 8 to 9 percent. The remaining landlords were mainly Burmese merchants, moneylenders, agriculturists, paddy brokers, barristers, and retired civil servants. In some districts, Chinese shopkeepers and rice merchants had accumulated sizable estates by the 1920s.

The holdings of Chettiar, Chinese, and other foreign landlords were concentrated in the districts near Rangoon and those of the lower, central Delta. Indian landlords also held extensive holdings on the rice plain east of the Salween River in the Thaton District and in the central circles of the Tharrawaddy District.[70] With the exception of the Tharrawaddy District, there were few Indian or Chinese estate owners in the upper Delta (including Toungoo) or in the Maubin and Bassein districts. Burmese landlords, both Burman and Karen, monopolized estate ownership in these areas, and also formed a majority of the estate owners in the districts of the lower Delta right up to the end of the transition period.[71]

Except for reports of clashes between the retainers of Burmese and Indian landlords in certain tracts of the remaining frontier areas, there is little evidence of friction between different cultural groups at the level of the large landholder. In 1921 a struggle between several land "speculators" in the Myaungmya District for the control of a tract which had just recently been brought under cultivation led to the largest recorded clash between Indian and Burmese estate owners. One of the "speculators" was an Indian; the others were Burmese. Unable to divide the spoils between them, each landlord sent his band of followers to drive his competitors from the area. The Indian landlord's Chittagonian retainers, who were armed with sticks and *dahs* (long Burmese knives), met the band of one of the Burmese "specu-

68. *RLAC*, pt. 2, p. 39.

69. *Settlement Reports–Hanthawaddy (1907–10)*, p. 14; *Toungoo (1910–13)*, p. 29; *Prome (1914–16)*, p. 46.

70. *Settlement Reports–Hanthawaddy (1907–10)*, p. 15; *Tharrawaddy (1913–15)*, p. 22; *Myaungmya (1916–19)*, p. 183; *Pyapon (1921–22)*, pp. 8, 29; *Myaungmya (1924–25)*, pp. 10, 53; *Pegu (1924–25)*, p. 2; *Thaton (Pa-an) (1928–30)*, p. 32; *Hanthawaddy Gazetteer*, p. 44.

71. See, for example, *Settlement Reports–Toungoo (1910–13)*, pp. 26, 29; *Bassein (1912–14)*, p. 36; *Tharrawaddy (1913–15)*, p. 22; *Prome (1914–16)*, p. 46; *Maubin (1925–28)*, p. 60; *Thaton (Kyaikto) (1928–30)*, p. 39.

lators" and "defeated" them in a pitched battle in which several men were badly injured.[72]

Clashes such as this were exceptional because most Indians did not want to acquire large estates in Burma. In addition, given the large debts of many cultivator-owners there was ample opportunity for those Burmese and Indians who wanted to accumulate large holdings to do so. As in the first phase of development, revenue officials reported that Chettiars, who made up a large portion of the Indian landlord class, usually eschewed becoming heavily involved in landownership. In instances where they were forced to take over paddy lands for unpaid debts, they normally tried to resell them as soon as possible. Only if they were unable to dispose of them without too great a loss would Chettiars normally assume the role of part- or full-time landlords.[73]

Although some of the Chettiars who became landholders earned bad reputations because of the high rents they charged and their refusal to grant remissions,[74] most of them compared favorably with Burmese estate owners. Chettiars often demanded lower rents than their Burmese counterparts, and they generally allowed their tenants and agents more freedom of action. In addition, Chettiars seem to have had a greater concern for the holdings they acquired than Burmese landlords demonstrated. There are several references to considerable sums spent by Chettiars to improve their estates, but none in the sources which I have examined refer to similar expenditures by Burmese owners.[75] Likewise, according to R. E. V. Arbuthnot, the "industrial" pattern of paddy production, which represented a decline in agricultural technology, was first introduced by Burmese landholders. Only when Indian landlords found that the "industrial" pattern was far cheaper than hiring labor on a seasonal basis did they change over to the new method of organization.[76]

In the decades of transition the main threat which Chettiars posed for indigenous agriculturists in Lower Burma was connected to their role as moneylenders, and not to their secondary and relatively minor involvement in

72. *Myaungmya Settlement Report (1924–25)*, p. 11.

73. Hardiman, *Compilation*, p. 23, and quoting Harold Clayton, *Report*, pp. 64, 68; *Banking Enquiry Report*, 3: 85; *Settlement Reports–Thaton (1908–10)*, p. 9; *Hanthawaddy (1907–10)*, p. 25; *Tharrawaddy (1913–15)*, p. 24. There were cases of Chettiars who gave up moneylending to become full-time landowners, but these were apparently rare (*Myaungmya Settlement Report [1916–19]*, p. 25).

74. See, for example, Hardiman, *Compilation*, p. 17; Couper, *Report into Agricultural Condition*, p. 41.

75. Government of Burma, Revenue and Agriculture Proceedings, vol. 8633, November 1911, pp. 501–2, 522; *Settlement Reports–Thaton (1908–10)*, p. 8; *Tharrawaddy (1914–15)*, p. 27; *Pegu (1924–25)*, p. 15.

76. *Hanthawaddy Settlement Report (1907–10)*, p. 8.

landowning. Because Chettiars provided a large portion of the capital loaned to persons engaged in agricultural production, their hold over Burmese landowners, both large- and small-scale, became more and more evident as rural indebtedness rose sharply. The estimates provided by the Banking Enquiry Committee show that by the end of the transition period Chettiars provided nearly 60 percent of the crop loans extended to agriculturists in Lower Burma, compared to 17 percent for Burmese moneylenders, 9 percent for Chinese shopkeepers, and 7 percent each for government agencies and non-Chettiar Indian moneylenders. The share of long-term loans provided by Chettiars fell to 45 percent, compared to 15 percent given by Burmese moneylenders, 11 percent by Chinese shopkeepers, 3 percent by non-Chettiar Indian lenders, and 26 percent by government agencies. With the exceptions of the Prome and Maubin districts, where indigenous lenders and government cooperatives played unusually large roles, Chettiars had become the chief source of both long- and short-term credit throughout the Delta by 1930.[77]

The dominance of Chettiars in credit provision did not mean that Indian agriculturists could obtain loans more easily than Burmese, for the Banking Enquiry Committee found that moneylenders generally lent to all "races" on equal terms.[78] In addition, Chettiars continued to provide loans at rates as low as or lower than those of indigenous moneylenders for the same reasons they had been able to do so in the late nineteenth century.[79] The Banking Enquiry Committee and numerous government officials concluded that Chettiars, both in their capacity as moneylenders and as landlords, dealt with their clients and employees in a manner no worse, and often quite better, than their indigenous counterparts. Despite this fact, the combination of their singular appearance and alien customs, their social exclusiveness, and their extensive involvement in credit provision made the Chettiars a likely scapegoat. Burmese agriculturists, often at the suggestion of Burmese nationalists, increasingly singled out the Chettiars as the main source of Burma's economic woes. They proved a lucrative and vulnerable target for the attacks of Burmese dacoits and petty thieves, whose numbers increased as the agrarian crisis grew more severe. In the mid-1920s a number of anti-Chettiar organizations, which were called *Sibwaye* (development) *athins* were formed.

77. Percentages calculated from the district estimates in the *Banking Enquiry Report,* 3: 11–33 (crop loans), 80–92 (long-term loans). The smaller share of long-term loans given by the Chettiars was due mainly to the higher risk involved in such loans and the agent rotation system, which made them harder to manage.

78. Ibid., p. 23. The Chinese in Myaungmya were apparently an exception to this general rule. They preferred to lend to other Chinese. There is also some evidence that Tamil cultivators received better terms from Chettiar lenders in some areas. See the *Pyapon Settlement Report (1921–22),* p. 8.

79. See Chapter 5; Government of Burma, Revenue and Agriculture Proceedings, vol. 8633, November 1911, pp. 499–500; and *Banking Enquiry Report,* 1: 78, 2: 106.

The members of these *athins* sought to force Chettiars to reduce debts owed by Burmese cultivators and ultimately to bring about an end to Chettiar involvement in the economy of Burma. They applied force, including arson and murder, to compel villagers to cooperate with their anti-Chettiar campaign.[80]

A number of sources indicate that the cooperation and mutual acceptance which existed between Chettiars and indigenous lenders in the pre-1907 period had given way to rivalry in many areas by the late 1920s. One of the major signs of this change was the decline in the Chettiars' practice of extending loans to Burmese moneylenders. This pattern was noted in several districts early in the transition phase, but in 1929 the Banking Enquiry Committee reported that with the exception of the Prome and Myaungmya districts most Burmese moneylenders no longer borrowed from Chettiars.[81] This general observation was confirmed by reports of surveys in local areas. The Chettiars of Bogale in the Pyapon District, for example, stated that they lent to each other, but that they did not lend to non-Chettiars because "these [were] not trusted."[82] It is probable that the cessation of this practice greatly restricted the capacity of many indigenous moneylenders, since Chettiars had provided their main link with the capital supplies of banks owned by Europeans or Indians. When Chettiar funds were no longer available to Burmese lenders, the latter may have come to resent the Chettiars' connections with banking firms which were active in the Delta, just as indigenous shopkeepers resented the ties between Indian or Chinese merchants and wholesalers in Rangoon.[83]

Despite signs of growing competition, the informal division of clientele between Chettiar and Burmese moneylenders was retained in most instances. Chettiars continued to lend primarily to landowners who could offer security and at low rates, while Burmese moneylenders often lent at higher rates to persons who had no security and in many cases had been turned down by Chettiars.[84] Even this long-standing division of clientele, however, did not apparently prevent Chettiars from gaining customers at the expense of Burmese lenders in some areas. The Banking Enquiry Committee reported, for example, that the amount of money lent by indigenous moneylenders in the Dedaye area of Pyapon was halved in the decade between 1918 and 1928. A gradual increase in the number of Chettiar shops, which outnumbered the

80. Cady, *Modern Burma*, p. 252; A. D. Moscotti, "British Policy in Burma, 1917–1937" (Ph.D. diss., Yale University, 1950), pp. 36–38.

81. *Banking Enquiry Report*, 3: 22.

82. Ibid., 2: 110. One case was cited of lending in the reverse direction. U Thet She (sic.?), one of the leading moneylenders in Pyapon town, lent money to Chettiars stationed in the area when they ran short (p. 95).

83. Ibid., pp. 74, 78, 89–91.

84. *Settlement Reports–Bassein (1912–13)*, p. 10, (*1912–14*), p. 18; *Banking Enquiry Report*, 1: 78.

Burmese two to one in 1928, was largely responsible for the decrease in Burmese transactions.[85]

As the position of persons engaged in agricultural production weakened and as Indian competition intensified, more and more Burmese agriculturists sought employment in other sectors of the Burma rice industry. Burmese small landholders who lost their land because of debts, tenants who were outbid by Indians or other Burmese, and landless laborers who could no longer earn enough to support their families vied for positions as coolies, paddy barge operators, and unskilled rice mill or wharf laborers. Until the 1920s most Burmese had considered these occupations, particularly those involving unskilled labor, too monotonous, arduous, and low-paying to warrant serious consideration. By the late 1920s, however, Burmese competition posed a serious challenge to the Indian laborers who had long been entrenched in the urban sectors of the Delta rice-export industry.[86]

Although the following discussion of Indo-Burmese competition in the non-agrarian niches of the Delta economy concentrates on the rice-processing industry and dock labor in Rangoon harbor where their rivalry was the most marked, some mention should first be made of the situation in other sectors. The possibility of Burmese agriculturists becoming paddy brokers or grain merchants in the decades of transition was greatly restricted by the limited number of positions available in this area of the economy. Opportunities for employment in internal marketing were further reduced in the last decade of the transition period by the attempts on the part of large milling and export firms to do without the services of paddy brokers and to buy their rice directly from the cultivator.[87] The partial success of their efforts is reflected in the decline in the number of persons listed as grain or pulse brokers and dealers from over 39,000 in the Delta districts alone in 1921 to less than 30,000 in all of Burma by 1931.[88] In view of these cutbacks in the number of persons engaged as marketing middlemen, it is unlikely that newcomers were able to find employment as brokers or rice merchants. Established dealers who had accumulated both working capital and experience were far

85. *Banking Enquiry Report,* 2: 105.

86. Baxter, *Indian Immigration,* pp. 84, 90–91, 107; J. J. Bennison, *Report on an Enquiry into the Standard and Cost of Living of the Working Classes in Rangoon* (Rangoon, 1928), pp. 91–92; Aye Hlaing, "Trends of Growth," p. 135.

87. The information on the campaign to eliminate the broker-middleman is extremely scanty. There is no mention of this trend, for example, in the more detailed reports on marketing published in the 1920s and 1930s or in Cheng Siok Hwa's fine chapter on internal marketing. The trend is noted, however, in the Government of Burma, *Interim Riot Report,* p. 20, and further discussed by Maung Shein in *Burma's Transport,* pp. 159–60.

88. See footnote 45.

more able to survive the millers' attempts to eliminate them than were newcomers who had neither the capital nor the skills required.

Another trend that would have discouraged the entry of frustrated Burmese agriculturists into internal marketing was the increasing involvement of immigrant Asians in this sector. Throughout the British period, the marketing niches in the Delta economy had been dominated by the Burmese. Although no statistics relating to the ethnic composition of rice brokers or merchants at various levels are available, Burmese control of these professions is demonstrated by the fact that nearly 82 percent of the paddy brokers or grain dealers in the Delta in 1921 were indigenous. Indians made up less than 12 percent of the persons engaged in these activities and the Chinese 6 percent. By 1931, however, the number of Burmese paddy brokers had declined to 77 percent while the Indians' share had risen to 15 percent and the Chinese to 7 percent.[89] Detailed local information regarding the displacement of Burmese traders by Chinese and/or Indians is unfortunately lacking, but the settlement officer of the Pegu District reported that in the years prior to World War I paddy marketing in that area was rapidly falling into Chinese hands. He noted that the Chinese were better organized than the Burmese, that they had more capital at their disposal, and that they used better business methods.[90] Presumably, these factors lay behind the success which Indian and Chinese merchants enjoyed in their attempts to infiltrate the marketing network in other areas of Lower Burma. It is highly unlikely that many Burmese agriculturists, who were leaving occupations where opportunities were decreasing and foreign competition increasing, would become involved in internal marketing where the same conditions existed.

It is even less likely that Burmese agriculturists attempted to become involved in external trade, which was almost totally monopolized by immigrant groups. European merchants controlled the rice-export trade between Burma and Europe and the main markets in Africa and the Americas, while Indian merchants dominated the trade with India, Ceylon, and Indonesia. Chinese merchants, on the other hand, confined their operations mainly to exports to China, Japan, and Malaya.[91] Successful participation in the export trade required large amounts of capital, considerable organization, and business connections both in Burma and overseas. Burmese agriculturists had none of these, and thus it was virtually impossible

89. See footnote 45. Since the 1931 breakdown was for all of Burma, the percentage of Burmese brokers had declined even more than these figures show. In Upper Burma, which is included in the 1931 breakdown, Burmese merchants were even more dominant than in the Delta. Thus the Burmese percentage should have risen when combined. Instead it fell.

90. *Pegu Settlement Report (1911–13)*, p. 9.

91. Cheng, *Rice Industry of Burma*, pp. 198–219.

for them to survive as merchants in the rice-export sector of the Delta economy.

No capital and little previous experience were necessary for a former tenant or laborer who wished to become a crewman on one of the multitude of paddy barges that plied the creeks and rivers of Lower Burma. Burmese agriculturists could also take up positions as coolies who loaded paddy onto barges, steamboats, and railway cars at upcountry stations which fed port centers like Rangoon and Bassein. Although there were large numbers of positions in both of these related niches of the Delta economy, not many were available because of the strong hold which Indian laborers had gained in internal transportation throughout much of Lower Burma. Indian, especially Chittagonian, crews were predominant in the districts of the lower Delta,[92] and most of the cargo boatmen in Rangoon harbor and surrounding areas were either Chittagonian or Telegu immigrants.[93] There is some evidence that Burmese laborers began to compete for jobs in this sector in the early 1920s,[94] but there are no statistics relating to the ethnic composition of the persons involved in internal paddy transportation at different times. There is also little mention of Indo-Burmese competition in this sector at later dates. It is probable that the struggle for control of internal marketing and transportation was overshadowed by the rivalry which developed in the 1920s in the rice-processing industry and among the dock laborers in Rangoon harbor.

In terms of the size of its labor force, the rice-processing industry seemed to offer the greatest opportunities for young Burmese who were forced to seek employment in sectors other than agricultural production. Burmese laborers soon found, however, that Indian immigrants held most of the positions in the rice mills, particularly those in Rangoon, which had by far the most employees. Prior to the 1930s no statistics regarding the ethnic composition of the rice-mill labor force were compiled. In 1921 a special industrial census was carried out under the supervision of S. Grantham, but there were no separate listings for the rice-processing industry. This survey showed, however, that in all industrial establishments in Burma employing more than ten persons, Indians made up 55 percent of the skilled and 73 percent of the unskilled working force, while Burmese laborers constituted only 37 and 23 percent, respectively.[95] The figures from the 1930s, which deal specifically with rice-milling, show that the earlier overall statistics

92. Andrew, *Indian Labour*, pp. 35–36; *Settlement Reports–Insein (1910–12)*, p. 18; *Hanthawaddy (1930–33)*, p. 8; *Insein Gazetteer*, p. 48; *Maubin Gazetteer*, p. 17; *Thaton Gazetteer*, p. 39.

93. Bennison, *Report on Rangoon Working Classes*, pp. 86–89.

94. *Burma Census, 1921*, Report, p. 225.

95. Bennison, *Report on Rangoon Working Classes*, p. 91; C. Kondapi, *Indians Overseas, 1839–1949* (New Delhi, 1951), p. 363.

underestimated the degree of Indian control in Burma's leading industry. According to a survey taken in 1934, 74.4 percent of the skilled and 80.9 percent of the unskilled rice-mill workers in Burma were Indians. By 1939 the Indian share of mill-hands had fallen to 62.5 percent among skilled laborers and 79 percent among unskilled. At both dates, the remaining percentages of workers were Burmese.[96] The 1939 survey also showed that Indian control was the most pronounced in the large mills of Rangoon and its environs. In the city of Rangoon, Indians constituted 86 and 96 percent respectively of the skilled and unskilled working force. In the small upcountry mills of the upper Delta, the Indian percentage of workers fell as low as 18 percent of the skilled and 35.4 percent of the unskilled labor.[97]

Because no unemployment statistics for either Indians or Burmese were compiled in the British period,[98] it is difficult to gauge the degree to which one group displaced the other in the processing industry during the transition period. In 1928 J. J. Bennison noted that unskilled Burmese labor was practically nonexistent in Rangoon, but he warned that Burmese competition for industrial jobs would surely increase given the great slowdown of growth in the rural sphere. He also pointed out that there was already an excess supply of Indian laborers in Burma and argued that as Burmese competition for occupations traditionally held by Indians grew, this oversupply of Indians would come to be strongly resented by the Burmese.[99] Several years after Bennison's report, the Royal Commission on Labour in India observed that because of economic conditions, the Burmese wanted to obtain a larger share of jobs in industry which they had once left to Indians.[100] The fairly substantial decline in the percentage of mill-hands who were Indian between 1934 and 1939 indicates that Burmese were replacing Indians at least at the unskilled level. The changeover, however, was slow and the tensions which it produced fed the communal friction and violence which erupted in Rangoon and other areas in the 1930s.

The seedbeds of the communal disturbances which broke out in the decade of crisis, 1930–41, proved to be the wharves of Rangoon harbor rather than the rice mills along the Pazundaung Creek as one might expect. The number of jobs available on the docks of the Delta's port centers were far fewer than those in its rice-processing sector, but Indians were even more firmly in control of wharf labor than they were of the working force in rice-milling. Prior to 1930 virtually all of the four to six thousand (depending on the season) dock laborers in the Rangoon area, which handled most of

96. Baxter, *Indian Immigration*, pp. 64–66. The surveys were taken in early May when the milling season was at its peak.

97. Ibid., pp. 67–68; Cheng, *Rice Industry of Burma*, pp. 132–34.

98. Government of Burma, *Interim Riot Report*, pp. 26–27.

99. *Report on Rangoon Working Classes*, p. 92.

100. *Report of the Royal Commission on Labour in India* (London, 1931), p. 440.

Burma's imports and exports, were immigrant Indians.[101] Both the laborers who loaded and unloaded cargo vessels on the wharves and in midstream under the direction of the stevedores and the foreshoremen who transferred the cargos from the wharves to the port *godowns* were organized in small *maistry* gangs. These gangs were often composed of members of the same family or caste, or young men from the same village in India. Normally a worker who left for India was replaced by a relative or acquaintance, and thus it was very difficult for outsiders, even Indians, to break into the gangs. If a replacement was not immediately forthcoming, the stevedores or *maistries*, who recruited for the Port Commissioner who was in charge of foreshore labor, hired only immigrant Indians who were readily available.[102] In the decades of transition, Indian laborers in Rangoon were in oversupply and those who worked regularly on the wharves were underemployed. In the busy season, for example, a cargo coolie averaged only from fourteen to seventeen days of work in a month, and in the slack season he worked far less.[103]

The first attempt on the part of Burmese laborers to gain employment in Rangoon harbor came in 1924 during a strike of Indian dockyard workers. Several European stevedores or foremen sought to break the strike by bringing in other Indian and Burmese workers. The Burmese proved inefficient at tasks to which they were not accustomed, and after the strike was settled Indian laborers again claimed the wharves as their exclusive preserve.[104] But a new precedent had been set. Despite the failure of Burmese leaders to establish programs to train Burmese workers so that they could compete effectively with the Indians, Burmese laborers began to regard positions on the wharves as "new, possible avenues of employment."[105] Their demands for employment in Rangoon harbor added to the tensions which increasingly marked the relations between the Indian and Burmese communities in Burma. An attempt on the part of Burmese laborers to force their way into this sector in 1930 would touch off the first round of communal violence which ushered in the last decade of British rule and Burma's time of troubles.

An economic crisis, such as that which slowly took hold of the Delta's rice industry in the first decades of the twentieth century, would have led in most nonplural societies to social tensions and divisions along class lines or between the members of different social strata. In a relatively homogenous, agrarian-based society worsening economic conditions have historically resulted in

101. Andrew, *Indian Labour*, app. 12, p. 294.

102. Ibid., pp. 56–64; Baxter, *Indian Immigration*, pp. 52–55.

103. Baxter, *Indian Immigration*, p. 107.

104. Usha Mahajani, *The Role of the Indian Minorities in Burma and Malaya* (Bombay, 1960), p. 12; Andrew, *Indian Labour*, app. 12, p. 297.

105. Mahajani, *Role of Indian Minorities*, p. 12.

struggles between the classes which are actually engaged in production (small landholders, tenants, landless laborers) and the classes which control the factors of production (large landholders, moneylenders, and urban speculators). In a plural society, such as that which evolved in the Delta, divisions were primarily along cultural or ethnic lines, and confrontations in most instances were between different communal groups. The friction that was produced by economic competition was expressed mainly in the relations between the members of different cultural segments at the same social and economic level. But even animosity that cut across class lines was expressed in communal terms. Displaced Burmese landowners, tenants, and laborers, for example, directed their hostility mainly toward the Chettiar landlord and the Chettiar moneylender even though the members of this caste made up only a small minority of these classes in Lower Burma.

Because members of different cultural segments had become established at all social and economic strata, economic competition was found at all levels of Delta society. As I have attempted to show in this chapter, rivalry was more pronounced among certain groups—tenants, landless laborers, and dock workers—and in certain sectors—agricultural production, internal marketing, and external transport—than in others. However, there is evidence of competition in varying degrees among other groups and in all sectors of the rice industry. Large-scale traders and moneylenders, millowners and shippers, small landholders and lowly wharf coolies all felt the impact of the slowdown in the rate of growth of the Delta rice economy to some degree. In most cases, economic competition undermined the tolerance or indifference with which members of different cultural segments had regarded each other in the first phase of development. Burmese tenants, landless laborers, and rice brokers came increasingly to regard Indians or Chinese as the main threat to their well-being. They believed that competition from immigrant groups, not from their fellow Burmese, was responsible for their worsening lot. For their part, Indian laborers became more and more conscious of the vulnerability of their position in the Delta in the face of the Burmese awakening and new Burmese demands. They clung tenaciously to positions they had won because they had only their former lives of poverty and low-caste degradation in India to fall back upon and dependents who waited anxiously for their remittances. Europeans, Chinese and Indian merchants, and above all, the Indian Chettiars perched precariously on the upper levels of a social and economic pyramid that threatened to collapse. The struggle for control of the various sectors of the rice industry became increasingly mingled with a wider contest for the control of Burma as a whole. The confrontations of the 1930s and international events decided the outcome of this contest; though even for the nominal winners the returns were mixed.

Part IV

THE YEARS OF SOCIAL AND ECONOMIC CRISES, 1931–41

8

THE DEPRESSION AND BURMA'S TIME OF TROUBLES: Communal Violence and Agrarian Rebellion

The Great Depression, which struck the economy of Burma with its full force in 1930, brutally revealed the extent and gravity of the agrarian crisis that had been building in Lower Burma for decades. The sharp drop in the value of rice on the world market in 1929-30 touched off a series of chain reactions in the various sectors of the rice industry that greatly accelerated economic problems which had already become serious by the early 1920s. Endemic economic ills suddenly became epidemic.

In the years after World War I the export market upon which the Delta economy had grown dependent began to deteriorate. New competitors, including the United States, Spain, and Italy, and a demand in Europe for a higher quality of rice than that produced in Burma caused its share of the European market to decline sharply. Initially, Burma's losses in Europe were more than compensated for by increased exports to India, which replaced Europe as the main outlet for Burma's rice products. A mild postwar slump gave way to what appeared to be a new boom in the early 1920s. The price of one hundred baskets of paddy soared from Rs. 100 in 1918 to Rs. 195 in 1924 on the Rangoon market, and the volume of exports continued to grow. In the late 1920s, however, the market declined somewhat due to the growing capacity of areas like Japan and the Philippines to produce their own supply of rice and to greater competition for Asian outlets from Siam and French Indo-China. Between 1925 and 1929 the volume of Burma's annual rice exports decreased from 3,100,000 tons to 2,800,000 tons, and the wholesale price of one hundred baskets of paddy at Rangoon fell from Rs. 195 to Rs. 160.[1]

The market slump of the late 1920s was a harbinger of the Great Depression; but cultivators, millowners, and merchants in Lower Burma viewed it as merely another temporary setback. Consequently, prior to the arrival of the monsoon in 1930, large landlords, small landholders, and tenants alike took crop loans and calculated production costs and profits on a scale that was based on the assumption that the price of paddy would exceed Rs. 150 per one hundred baskets as it had for the past decade. Sharp price drops in the last months of 1930, however, lowered the average for that year to Rs. 130 per one hundred baskets. In the following year the price of paddy plummeted to an annual average of Rs. 75.[2] Although cultivators produced as much as or more surplus paddy than they had in the previous season, its market value was nearly halved. As a result landholders were hard-pressed to pay their laborers wages set at pre-Depression levels, and landlords and small landholders found it extremely difficult to pay even the interest on loans taken prior to the market collapse. Tenants were unable to meet their rent payments, much less to pay back crop loans extended by the owners of the land they worked.[3] These trends gave added impetus to the spread of indebtedness and land alienation. They also engendered a number of new problems, such as landlord insolvency, which further undermined the viability of the Delta economy.

The market slump also led to a great contraction in the volume of credit extended to agriculturists by both private and government agencies. In most areas Chettiar moneylenders pressed for repayment of loans which they had merely collected the interest on for years. In many cases they refused to grant new loans even when land security was offered by large landowners.[4] A number of Chettiar firms declared bankruptcy because their debtors could not repay their loans, and thus these companies were unable to pay back the money which they had originally borrowed from European-owned banks. This pattern, which was first observed in 1928 just prior to the onset of the Depression, caused other Chettiar firms to be reluctant to borrow from

1. Odell, *Note on Prices,* 1: 15, 26–28; Cheng, *Rice Industry of Burma,* pp. 73, 201–19; Grant. *Rice Crop,* app. 5, p. 56.

2. Cheng, *Rice Industry of Burma,* p. 73.

3. *Season and Crop,* 1930–31, p. 11.

4. *Banking Enquiry Report,* 1: 85; *Land Revenue Report, 1931–32,* pp. 20–21; *Bassein Settlement Report (1935–39),* p. 53; *Burma Situation Report,* 29 May 1931, no. 2693, in Government of India, Political and Judicial Correspondence, file 7347, India Office Records, London, Eng.

European banks. This reluctance led to a reduction in the supply of capital which they could make available to cultivators.[5]

Although there is little mention of indigenous moneylenders in the sources for this period, it is probable that they too sought to collect the principal owed on their loans whenever possible, and that their more limited supplies of lending capital were also reduced by the effects of the market collapse. Landlords, who had become the prime source of credit for the large tenant class of the Delta, also greatly restricted their lending activities. Often a landlord's refusal to extend crop loans to his tenants resulted from his inability to obtain loans from Chettiar lenders who had provided his capital in the decades of transition. Only the largest and richest landlords, who could draw on their own reserves, could afford to advance money to their tenants.[6]

Government credit agencies, whose role had been relatively marginal prior to the Depression, did little to make up for the contraction in credit from private lenders. Although fairly substantial amounts of money for agrarian relief were provided under the auspices of the Agriculturists Loans Act, little use was made of the Land Improvements Act.[7] At the same time, the cooperative credit movement floundered and all but died out. The number of cooperative societies fell from over five thousand in 1927 to less than 1,500 in 1935, and the total membership was nearly halved in the same period. By 1937 the number of societies which were being liquidated exceeded the number which were solvent.[8] Paralleling the cooperative movement's decline was the demise of Dawson's Bank, which went into voluntary liquidation in 1932. Attempts were made to reconstruct the firm, but they do not appear to have been successful.[9]

Given the general contraction of the money supply and the volume of loans extended by professional moneylenders, it is not surprising that *sabape* loans became more common in this period. In many tracts *sabape* transactions largely replaced *ngwedo* loans, which had been the standard prior to 1930. The damage done to the cultivator by this shift, however, was somewhat reduced by the fact that Chinese shopkeepers, who provided most *sabape* loans, charged lower rates of interest than they had in earlier decades. Shopkeepers, who had once demanded from 10-12 percent interest per

5. *Banking Enquiry Report,* 2: 89; *Rangoon Gazette,* 8 August 1929, p. 12; Chakravarti, *Indian Minority,* p. 57.

6. *Hanthawaddy Settlement Report (1930–33),* p. 14; *Banking Enquiry Report,* 1: 85.

7. *RLAC,* pt. 2, pp. 79–81.

8. Ibid., p. 85; Government of Burma, *Annual Report on the Working of the Co-operative Credit Societies in Burma, 1929–30* (Rangoon, 1930), p. 1, *1930–31* (Rangoon, 1931), pp. 1–4; Malcolm Darling, *Note on the Co-operative Movement in Burma* (Rangoon, 1937), p. 1.

9. Darling, *Note,* p. 21.

month on cash advanced during the monsoon season, only asked 5–6 percent during the 1930s.[10] Interest rates on *ngwedo* loans, on the other hand, tended to be somewhat higher than they had been in the decades of transition.[11]

The inability of landowners to repay debts which were suddenly called in by indigenous and Chettiar moneylenders was the chief cause of the great acceleration of land alienation which occurred in the early 1930s. The amount of the total occupied area in Lower Burma held by nonagriculturists rose from 31 percent in 1929–30 to nearly 50 percent by 1934–35. The fact that the percentage owned by resident, nonagriculturists increased only slightly from 8 to 9 percent, while that held by nonresident landlords rose from 23 to nearly 41 percent clearly demonstrates the importance of foreclosure as a cause of accelerated alienation.[12] The role of debt in the continued spread of land alienation is also evidenced by the great increase in the proportion of land held by Chettiar moneylenders. In 1930, for example, Chettiars were listed as the owners of only 6 percent of the total land occupied in the Delta and 19 percent of the area held by nonagriculturists. By 1937 they controlled 25 percent of the cropped area in Lower Burma and 50 percent of that held by nonagriculturists.[13]

The identity of the nonagriculturists who owned the other 50 percent of the land alienated in Lower Burma is not mentioned in the reports of the late 1930s. It is safe to assume, however, that they were mainly indigenous moneylenders, rice merchants, successful Burmese cultivators, urban investors, and Indian merchants other than Chettiars just as they had been in preceding periods. The percentage of land held by Burmese moneylenders and rice merchants probably rose, while that held by former cultivator-owners declined. This trend is suggested by the fact that many large landlords, like small landholders, lost their lands through foreclosures. These landlords had acquired very large debts prior to 1930, and they were no longer able to meet payments on these after the severe price slump of that year. Both Burmese and Indian creditors took over the holdings of these large-scale owners and attempted to recoup some of their losses by letting them out to tenants.[14] Paddy brokers and landlords who invested heavily in the rice trade also lost their holdings when the value of rice and land fell sharply. At the same time,

10. *Settlement Reports–Bassein (1935–39)*, pp. 21–22, 53; *Hanthawaddy (1930–33)*, p. 15.

11. *Hanthawaddy Settlement Report (1930–33)*, p. 15.

12. Percentages calculated from the tables on land ownership in the *Land Revenue Reports, 1929–30, 1934–35.* For a regional breakdown see Adas, "Agrarian Development," Table X-A, p. 479.

13. *RLAC*, pt. 2, pp. 37–38.

14. *Settlement Reports–Hanthawaddy (1930–33)*, p. 40; *Bassein (1935–39)*, p. 40.

a small group of indigenous capitalists took advantage of the insolvency of the landholding classes by buying up large amounts of land at low prices.[15]

A rise in the amount of the occupied area let to tenants from 46 to 59 percent paralleled the sharp increase in land alienation in the 1929 to 1935 period.[16] This substantial increase in rented area came despite a further deterioration in the already unenviable pre-Depression condition of the tenant class. Tenants were perhaps the most affected by the sudden price slump in 1930. Because they were forced to sell their surplus paddy for half its expected value, few tenants were able to pay their laborers' wages, their landlord's rent, and still have money left to repay the crop loans extended by their landlords during the monsoon season. As a result, in 1930–31 an unusually high number of tenants were turned off the holdings which they rented.[17] Many of those evicted competed anew for positions as tenants despite the fact that rental rates remained higher than conditions warranted, that landlords continued to refuse to grant remissions, that most landlords no longer provided crop loans, and that it was normally impossible for a tenant's family to make ends meet.[18]

The "deplorable"[19] condition of the tenant class and the increase in the proportion of nonresident landlords led to even worse relations between these two groups than had existed in the transition period. Landlords hired watchmen to make sure they received their full share of their tenants' produce and formed associations to defend their positions with regard to such volatile issues as their refusal to scale down their rents. For their part, tenants joined countermovements aimed at gaining rent reductions and other concessions from their landlords. Many tenants also cheated their landlords whenever an opportunity arose.[20]

Initially, agricultural laborers fared better than the other classes involved in paddy production because during the first year of the Depression they had agreed to wages set at pre-Depression levels.[21] In the following years, however, laborers faced a growing shortage of jobs. During the Depression period, cultivator-owners and tenants used more family labor and less hired

15. *Hanthawaddy Settlement Report (1930–33)*, pp. 34, 39–40.

16. See footnote 12 and Table X-B, p. 481, in Adas, "Agrarian Development."

17. *Season and Crop, 1930–31*, pp. 11–12; *Hanthawaddy Settlement Report (1930–33)*, pp. 38, 41.

18. *Season and Crop, 1929–30*, p. 14; *RLAC*, pt. 1, pp. 10–12; *Hanthawaddy Settlement Report (1930–33)*, pp. 14, 32, 35–36, 38–39.

19. *Bassein Settlement Report (1935–39)*, p. 54.

20. *Hanthawaddy Settlement Report (1930–33)*, pp. 36, 41; *Rangoon Gazette*, 21 January 1929, p. 8; Government of India, Political and Judicial Correspondence, file 7347, no. 2693.

21. *Season and Crop, 1930–31*, pp. 11–12.

labor than in previous decades in order to cut cultivation costs.[22] Consequently, competition for available positons became even more intense than it had been in the 1920s. Despite increased competition, the real wages received by agricultural laborers do not appear to have fallen significantly in the post-1930 period. The available evidence suggests that there was some decline in cash wages, but that wages paid in kind remained near pre-Depression levels.[23] The fact that laborers' wages in most areas had already been reduced to subsistence levels prior to 1930 may be the major factor accounting for their stability in this period.

In addition to its adverse effects on the condition of the agrarian classes, the onset of the Depression had an unfavorable impact on the level of agricultural technology in the Delta. Land alienation and increased tenancy meant a rise in the proportion of Lower Burma's paddy acreage that was worked by inferior, cost-saving methods without substantial improvements. Many cultivator-owners reduced the amount of outside labor they employed by sowing paddy broadcast rather than having it transplanted.[24] Embryonic attempts to mechanize certain cropping operations, introduce new seed strains, and develop new techniques that had made some headway in the 1920s were all frustrated in the 1930s by the general shortage of capital and by budget cuts in government departments which were promoting these innovations.[25]

These economic dislocations were all the more keenly felt by the Burmese in the Delta because of the weakness of social ties and cultural outlets that might have buffered their growing economic distress. Neither the social nor the cultural institutions characteristic of Burman, Buddhist society had been fully established in Lower Burma during the Konbaung period. Consequently, the political, economic, and social changes introduced by the British had a far greater impact in the Delta than in other areas of Burma, and the decline of Buddhist civilization which was felt in Burma as a whole was more pronounced in Lower Burma.

Protection and patronage of Buddhist institutions were considered major responsibilities of a Burmese monarch. Burmese rulers were expected to build and maintain pagodas and *kyaungs* (monasteries), endow Buddhist scholars

22. *Season and Crop, 1933–34,* p. 11.

23. *Settlement Reports–Hanthawaddy (1930–33),* pp. 24–26; *Bassein (1935–39),* pp. 32, 89. Though the amount of paddy given remained stable, the cash value, of course, dropped sharply.

24. *Season and Crop, 1930–31,* p. 2.

25. Unfortunately, there are no accurate estimates of the yield per acre on paddy land in this period. Without such estimates it is impossible to determine whether per capita rice consumption in Lower Burma fell in the early 1930s in the face of a rise in the volume of rice exports. See Government of Burma, *Report of the Rice-Export Trade Enquiry Committee,* pp. 4–5.

and educational centers, and appoint *thathanabaings* to settle disputes and maintain discipline within the *Sangha* (monastic community).[26] During the period of British rule in Burma, government support for Buddhist institutions was greatly reduced. British efforts to combine Buddhist monastic and modern Western education at the primary level were largely a failure. At the same time the spread of Western education and the potential for advancement it offered diminished the demand for monastic training, especially among Burmese elite groups.[27] Although the office of the *thathanabaing* was retained by the British, his influence was limited because he no longer had the executive means of the government behind his decrees. In addition, his judgments could be disputed in civil courts, where his decisions were sometimes reversed. The weakened position of the *thathanabaing* led to serious divisions within and a general decline in the discipline of the *Sangha.* It also made possible the emergence of large numbers of unruly and violence-prone "political" *pongyis.*[28]

The general disruption of the monastic system was paralleled at the local level in Lower Burma by the neglect of village pagodas and *kyaungs* which were essential parts of the traditional Burman village. According to British revenue officers, this neglect was due to a shortage of *pongyis* and the unsettled conditions on the Delta rice frontier.[29] The decline of Buddhism was reflected in many aspects of the peasant's social and cultural life. His village, traditionally a tightly knit unit integrated and enlivened by an annual cycle of Buddhist festivals and ceremonies, was in many areas of Lower Burma little more than an administrative unit. The Burmese *pwe* (theatrical entertainment) and bullock races, which were extremely popular among agriculturists, were banned in many areas because they had become occasions for brawls and criminal assaults.[30] Buddhist folk customs could not give identity or unity to Delta villages where the population was often ethnically diverse, multi-religious, and highly mobile.[31]

With agrarian outlets closing and the quality of rural life declining, many cultivator-owners and tenants who had been turned off their lands and many laborers who could not find work sought employment in Rangoon and other urban areas where there was already an oversupply of labor in the 1920s.

26. D. E. Smith, *Religion and Politics in Burma* (Princeton, N.J., 1965), pp. 12–19, 23–31, 43–44; Cady, *Modern Burma*, pp. 8–9, 53–56; Sarkisyanz, *Buddhist Backgrounds*, pp. 6, 56, 60, 136.

27. Smith, *Religion and Politics*, pp. 57–66; Cady, *Modern Burma*, pp. 170–73; Furnivall, *Colonial Policy and Practice*, pp. 123–30.

28. Smith, *Religion and Politics*, pp. 43–57; Cady, *Modern Burma*, pp. 168–70.

29. *Settlement Reports–Myaungmya-Bassein (1901–2)*, p. 7; *Maubin (1925–28)*, p. 8; Cady, *Modern Burma*, p. 171.

30. Government of Burma, *Report of the Village Administration Committee* (Rangoon, 1941), pp. 23–24.

31. *Settlement Reports–Pyapon (1906–7)*, pp. 10–11; *Bassein (1912–14)*, p. 19.

Other dispossessed or unemployed agriculturists wandered about the Delta in search of part-time employment or abandoned holdings to cultivate. Nearly a decade before the onset of the Depression, government officials had drawn attention to the fact that this growing class of landless, homeless cultivators was one of the main sources of increases in robbery and other crimes in Lower Burma.[32] In the 1930s it was to provide a fertile recruiting ground for persons who sought to foment rebellion and communal violence.

The form of plural society which evolved in Burma and other areas of Southeast Asia was (and is) an extremely vulnerable and unstable form of social organization. Its existence depends primarily upon the maintenance of a delicate social and economic balance among the different cultural groups which compose it. This balance can be sustained only as long as each group acquiesces in the roles or social, economic, and political niches which it came to occupy during the period of the plural society's formation. When one of the groups begins to covet and compete for a larger share or control of niches held by others, the whole plural hierarchy is threatened. This threat is particularly serious if the dissident group represents the indigenous peoples who make up a large majority of the population. This group must either be repressed or accommodated if the plural society is to survive. The former option is feasible only when the group which controls the administration and military forces of the plural society is sure of itself, and as long as its means of coercion are effective. In many instances, British officials, who headed these branches of Burma's government in the 1930s, were unable to quickly or effectively suppress the violence which erupted sporadically during Burma's time of troubles. Their efforts to check the communal riots which broke out several times in this period were desultory and often belated.[33] It took the government, whose forces were equipped with airplanes, machine guns, and other weapons of modern warfare, nearly two years to end a rebellion of several thousand Burmese agriculturists who were armed mainly with *dahs,* obsolete firearms, and spears. Their inability to curb violence reflected a general impotence on the part of government officials to take meaningful measures to meet the many crises of the last decade of British rule.

The intransigence of Burmese leaders and the economic distress of the Burmese laboring classes made the second course of action, accommodation, all but impossible. Burmese nationalism, which provided an ideological basis for the intransigence of Burmese leaders, peaked in the 1930s, at the same time as the effects of the Depression were swelling the ranks of Burmese

32. Government of Burma, *Report of the Crime Enquiry Committee* (Maymyo, 1923), p. 2. See also Cady, *Modern Burma,* pp. 175–76.

33. On this point see the Government of Burma, *Final Report of the Riot Inquiry Committee* (Rangoon, 1939), pp. 37–39, 225–63; Andrew, *Indian Labour,* app. 11, pp. 279–80.

unemployed. The competition that had developed between the Burmese and Indians in the decades of transition intensified greatly. Unemployed Burmese laborers became more and more resentful of the Indian immigrants who had preempted most of the positions available in Rangoon and other urban centers. The Burmese were also frustrated by the fact that the supply of Indian laborers in Burma considerably exceeded the demand for them. Thus, every time a position opened up in processing or shipping there was "an Indian around the corner waiting to step into it."[34] Many Burmese nationalist leaders used these resentments and frustrations to build up mass support for their political objectives. They rightly perceived that if it were properly exploited, the discontent of the agrarian and urban working classes could be used against the British and Indians with whom they were struggling for control of the plural society.

Those Burmese nationalist leaders who used anti-Indian sentiment to gain support stressed a number of issues. They wrote and spoke against intermarriage between Burmese and Indian, the growth of the *zerabadi* (Indo-Burmese) segment of the population, and insults which Indians had leveled against the Buddhist religion. Their main rallying cries, however, and the ones which are germane to the themes explored in this study, centered on the perils of uncontrolled Indian immigration, Indian competition, and Indian economic exploitation. As I have noted in earlier chapters, both British officials and Burmese notables had shown concern for these problems long before the outbreak of the Depression. In the late 1920s and the 1930s these fears were expounded in Burmese vernacular newspapers and pamphlets and at political rallies. In this way they reached a far larger audience and increased communal tensions at all levels of the plural society.

In leading nationalist newspapers like the *Sun,* the *New Light of Burma,* and *Saithan,* Burmese writers made frequent demands for government restrictions on Indian immigration. To justify these demands they made allusions to the great "mischief" done by Indians in Burma and to the "Indian peril" which seemed to become greater with each editorial.[35] Thein Maung, the prominent nationalist leader and follower of Ba Maw, summarized the nationalist view of the harmful effects of the unregulated Indian influx in a pamphlet published in 1939. He asserted that "the unrestricted Indian immigration has caused a glut in (*sic*) labor market and increased unemployment, in the country."[36] He also listed Burmese demands regarding Indian immigration, which included prohibiting unskilled laborers from entering Burma and the imposition of a tax on all skilled laborers who worked in the Province.[37] Maung Tha Gi, a Burmese journalist, used more provocative

34. A repeatedly expressed belief of the 1930s cited by Baxter, *Indian Immigration,* p. 96.

35. Government of Burma, *Interim Riot Report,* p. 35.

36. *Immigration Problem,* p. 6. Thein Maung's pamphlet was also printed in Burmese.

37. Ibid., p. 34.

language than Thein Maung when he charged that "cheap and docile Indian dock laborers who are no more skilled than the Burmese . . . are taking away their food."[38]

Burmese writers singled out the Chettiars in their polemical assaults against the Indian minority. Chettiar moneylenders and landlords became the "butt of the Burmese cartoonist" and "Public Enemy No. 1."[39] Nationalist editorials demanded that the government stop them from oppressing Burmese landowners. One writer suggested that all cultivators whose lands had been taken from them by Chettiars should form an association aimed at winning back their holdings. In another article, a Burmese journalist insisted that the government pass legislation prohibiting Chettiars from owning land in Burma.[40]

Other nationalist leaders, such as U Saw, accused the Indians of "exploitation" and other misdeeds usually associated with European "imperialists" in nationalist writings. In a pamphlet issued in 1931 in connection with the Saya San rebellion, Saw claimed that the Indians were "birds of passage who have come to this land to exploit by fair means or foul in the fields of labour, industry and commerce."[41] He reasoned that since the British refused to protect the Burmese from Indian exploitation and competition, they were forced to take matters into their own hands, hence the Saya San rebellion which had broken out in 1930.[42] In 1937 an article in *Saithan* claimed that the Indians were in collusion with the British in their oppression of the Burmese people. The author charged that "since the dawn of history, Indians have been the leaders of [the] attack against the Burmans on behalf of the white faces." He concluded ominously, "It would be better if they were not here, I do not want to see them in this country."[43]

Because of the high literacy rate of the Burmese Buddhist population, these inflammatory attacks on the Indian community reached a far larger audience than the small circle of nationalist leaders and activists. Even the illiterate Burmese, however, were made aware of the "Indian problem" by word of mouth and by cartoons which were the specialties of the vernacular papers. The two shown here were reprinted on the frontispiece of Thein Maung's *The Indian Immigration Problem.* The first depicts Burma's exploitation, not only by Indians, but also by the Chinese and British.

The second graphically expresses the fear which obsessed a large number

38. From his column "In the Limelight," as quoted ibid.

39. G. E. Harvey, *British Rule in Burma 1824–1942* (London, 1946), p. 55. See also Mahajani, *Role of Indian Minorities,* p. 19.

40. From excerpts printed in *Saithan* in 1936 and 1938 and cited in Government of Burma, *Interim Riot Report,* p. 36.

41. *The Burmese Situation (1930–31)* . . . (Rangoon, 1931), p. 6.

42. Ibid.

43. Reprinted in Government of Burma, *Interim Riot Report,* p. 36.

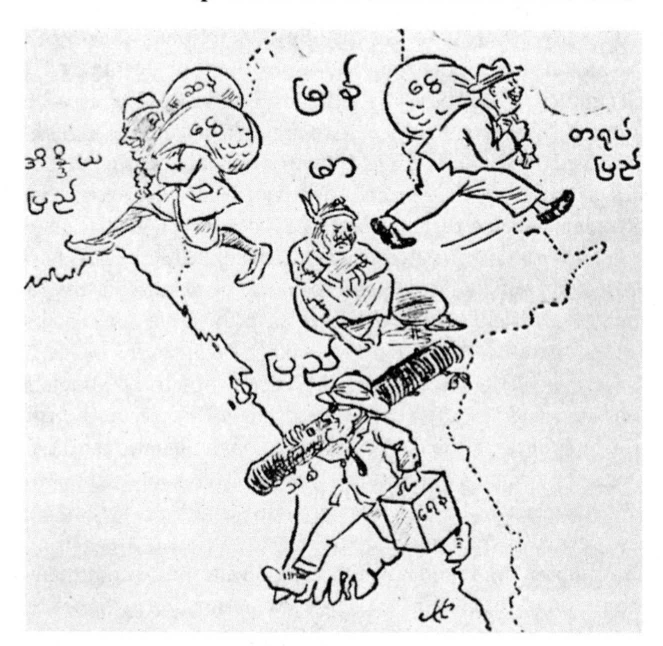

Cartoon 1. "Frightened from the south and taken away from the north, the man in the middle is left with an empty stomach." Courtesy of the British Museum.

of Burmese leaders that the relatively small Burmese population would be swamped by a continued influx of Indians and Chinese.[44]

In addition to direct appeals to anti-Indian sentiment, Burmese nationalists exacerbated communal tensions and economic discontent through speeches, conferences, and campaigns aimed primarily at the British colonial

Cartoon 2. "Crowded out by the guests, such is the lot of the Burmese." Courtesy of the British Museum.

44. See ibid., p. 21; Thein Maung, *Immigration Problem*, pp. 22–23 (on the Indians), p. 25 (on the Chinese).

regime. In the early 1920s some groups of urban nationalists sought to broaden the base of their movement by organizing the "peasantry." In 1921 the General Council of Burmese Associations, in uneasy alliance with the General Council of *Sangha Sametggi* Associations, began to establish village associations called *Wunthanu Athins* ("own race" organizations). Throughout the 1920s these associations provided the major bridge between urban-based, nationalist leaders and the rural masses. They also served as the spearheads for nationalist-led boycotts, campaigns against the capitation tax, and other political protest movements which spread to the rural areas in this period.[45] The *Wunthanu Athins* played important roles in the Saya San rebellion of 1930–32 and in the anti-Separationist campaign of the early 1930s.[46] "Political" *pongyis* like U Ottama and U Wisara, who moved about Burma preaching sedition and boycott, exerted a strong influence on the *athin* movement, which became the major source of ongoing nationalist agitation in the rural Delta. The spread of political agitation to the agrarian classes was paralleled by attempts on the part of nationalist leaders to organize Indian and Burmese urban laborers in Rangoon and other port centers.[47]

In both rural and urban areas economic grievances and communal competition supplied the major issues used by nationalist agitators to attract mass support. Even those groups who led the campaign to prevent Burma's separation from India did so only because they feared that once it was separated, Burma would fall behind in the march to independence. Like the Separatists, they voiced concern over the continued influx of Indian immigrants and heightened Indian involvement in the economy and administration of Lower Burma.[48] As John Cady has pointed out, by the 1930s the "minimal objectives" of most politically active Burmese were to "recover control over their own land and throw out the immigrant (*kalá*) invaders."[49] These sentiments lay at the roots of the violence that erupted in Burma in the 1930s. As economic conditions grew worse, the frail structure of the plural society tottered on the verge of collapse. The communal riots of 1930 signaled the beginning of its painful dissolution.

Isolated incidents of communal violence had occurred in Lower Burma prior to the Depression period,[50] but the riots which broke out in Rangoon in May

45. For a more detailed discussion of the spread of nationalism to the rural Delta in the 1920s, see Cady, *Modern Burma,* pp. 231–38, 250–54, 270–74, 297, et passim.

46. For *athin* involvement in the Saya San see Government of Burma, *The Origin and Causes of the Burma Rebellion (1930–32)* (Rangoon, 1934), pp. 40–42; and on the anti-separationist campaign see Cady, *Modern Burma,* pp. 298–302, 336–47.

47. For the best discussion of agitation among the urban working classes see Mahajani, *Role of Indian Minorities,* pp. 10–15.

48. Cady, *Modern Burma,* p. 302.

49. Ibid., p. 277.

50. See Chapter 7, and the *Rangoon Gazette,* 14 January 1929, p. 1.

of 1930 were the first in a series of bloody encounters that completely upset the delicate balance of the plural society. Their origins were clearly economic.[51] On the sixth of May the Telegu laborers who normally monopolized the working force in Rangoon harbor went on strike to protest the arrest of Mahatma Gandhi in India. After starting to return to work on the following day, they struck again, demanding higher wages. For almost a week the shipping in Rangoon harbor came to a virtual standstill. On May fourteenth, however, several shipping firms decided to recruit Burmese laborers. The Burmese response to the firms' offers was immediate and enthusiastic, but they proved inefficient and slow at work to which they were not accustomed. On the twenty-fourth of May the owners of the shipping firms decided to grant the Telegus a pay raise and on the next day the Telegus voted to return to work. The foremen of the various firms took no measures to retain some of the Burmese laborers or to phase them out gradually. With the exception of the British India Steam Navigation Company, the shipping firms ceased to hire Burmese workers. The Telegu workers were quickly reinstated just as they had been after their strike in 1924.

The Burmese laborers, however, refused to relinquish their newly won positions without contest as they had done six years before. Employment was difficult to find; nationalist sentiment was aroused; and the laborers had come to view these newly won wharf jobs as initial victories in a wide struggle to wrest control of urban employment from Indian immigrants. Early in the morning of May 26, a gang of Burmese laborers gathered near the Lewis Street Jetty where they hoped to find work. They were soon confronted by a crowd of Telegu workers who taunted them and a quarrel began. A scuffle ensued, rocks were thrown, and the badly outnumbered Burmese were forced to retreat into the city. Shortly after the first incident, a crowd of Telegus attacked a second group of Burmese who were waiting for work outside the B.I.S.N. Company's office on Sparks Street. Again the Burmese fled from the much larger group of Indians. The Telegu laborers, armed with iron rods, brickbats, and bottles, then went on a rampage attacking buses, the offices of the Burmese newspaper, *Sun,* and Burmese bystanders in the Lanmadaw quarter and other areas. By midmorning, the Burmese had regrouped and added numerous recruits from Kemmendine, Tamwe, and other suburbs. They armed themselves with *dahs,* pikes, rickshaw shafts, and *lathis* and marched to the center of the city to avenge their humiliation earlier in the day.

For nearly a week thereafter, Rangoon was transformed into a battle-

51. The following account of the 1930 riots is based on the "Report of the Rangoon Riots Committee," which has been reprinted in Andrew, *Indian Labour,* app. 11, pp. 279–92; and on the accounts of the riots in the *Rangoon Gazette,* 2 June 1930, pp. 7–10, 20, 22–24. Only information taken from sources other than these will be documented.

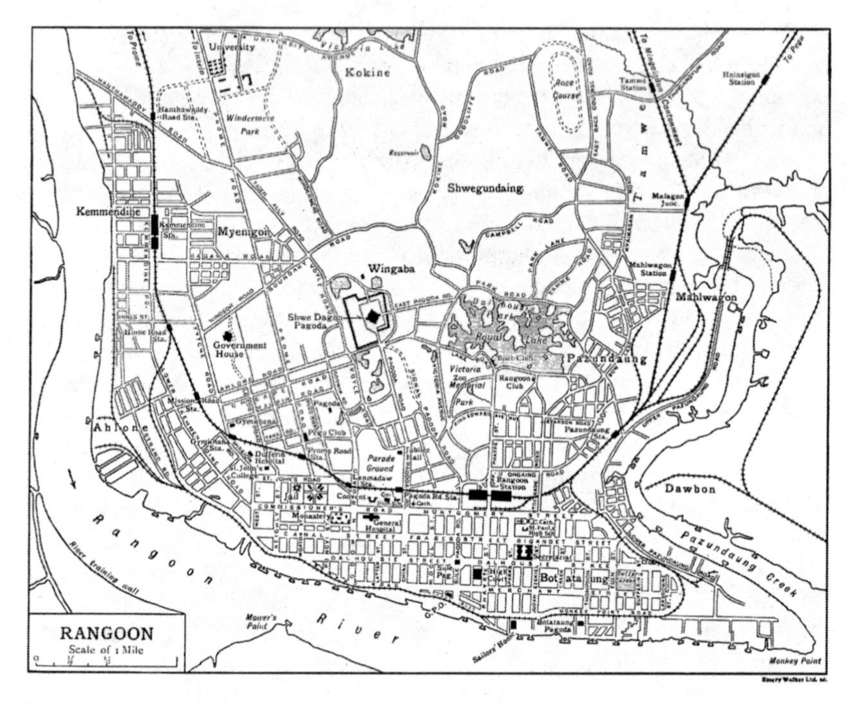

Map 4. Rangoon, circa 1930. Source: John Murray, *A Handbook for Travellers in India, Burma and Ceylon* (Rangoon, 1930).

ground. Burmese and Indian mobs, numbering as many as five hundred on each side, clashed again and again along the main streets in the center of the city. Small gangs on both sides assaulted individual pedestrians, who were sometimes women or children. Burmese laborers, often led by "political" *pongyis,* made numerous forays into the Indian quarters, where they burnt homes, looted shops, and killed Indians whenever they could find them. The Indians, for their part, mounted several counterassaults which grew feebler as the week progressed. Finally, they merely sought refuge and police protection or fled from the city. The worst slaughters occured in the tenements which housed Indian workers in the central city and west of the rice mills along the Pazundaung Creek. The aftermath of a Burmese raid on some of these tenements was described by Maurice Collis in a passage that captures the atmosphere that gripped Rangoon for nearly a week: "The condition of the tenements proved there had been savage play. The corpses had been removed, but everything reeked of blood; boxes had been broken open, their contents looted or slashed; the very walls dripped blood; little pictures of the gods had not escaped destruction."[52]

52. *Trials in Burma* (London, 1953), pp. 159–60.

The police, who were hard pressed to break up or to prevent mob clashes and to protect the main streets, were seldom attacked by either Indians or Burmese. Except for a few incidents when their automobiles were stoned, European civilians were also left alone. Collis tells of several incidents in which he or other Englishmen dissuaded Burmese gangs from intended assaults. He also describes occasions when he walked down streets where Burmese and Indian mobs were locked in combat and he was virtually ignored.[53] The riots were almost wholly expressions of communal hostility produced by economic competition. Before they had been brought under control, over 120 persons had been killed and another 900 wounded.[54]

In the months following the May riots, shipping foremen in Rangoon harbor, acting on the recommendations of a special committee which was appointed by the Government of Burma to determine the causes of the outbreaks, began to hire Burmese laborers on a permanent basis.[55] This policy resulted in an uneasy truce in the dockyards, but little else was done to solve problems in other sectors of the economy or to ameliorate the grievances of other classes, particularly the rapidly increasing number of persons who had been displaced in the agricultural sphere. Fed by rising unemployment and general economic distress, communal tensions continued to grow. Rumors of impending outbreaks were rampant. Government officials, unable to head off impending disturbances, nervously prepared to suppress them if they should break out again.[56]

On June 24 an abortive jailbreak at the main Rangoon prison threatened the frail peace which the government had imposed on the city through the vigorous, if somewhat belated, use of military force. Angered by the recent appointment of an Indian warden at the prison and resentful of their Indian and Eurasian guards, a group of Burmese inmates attempted to take over the jail and kill the warden and his Indian subordinates. They timed their jailbreak to coincide with new riots which were supposed to erupt in Rangoon on the twenty-fourth. However, there were no disturbances in Rangoon and the government was able to concentrate on thwarting the convicts' attempted escape. Several Indian guards and Burmese inmates were killed, but the disturbances were quelled before they could spread to Rangoon or elsewhere in the Delta.[57]

53. Ibid., pp. 144–48, 152–54.

54. These are official estimates. As a number of authors have stated, the real casualties were probably considerably higher.

55. The committee's recommendations are included in Appendix 9 in Andrew, *Indian Labour*, pp. 274–77. The problems involved in putting them into practice are discussed by W. S. Desai in *India and Burma: A Study* (Bombay, 1954), pp. 33–34.

56. The atmosphere during the post-riot period is brilliantly described by Collis, *Trials*, pp. 163–68.

57. *Rangoon Gazette*, 30 June 1930, pp. 6–8; Desai, *India and Burma*, p. 39; Collis, *Trials*, pp. 169–83.

Other, more effective, agents were spreading disaffection and agitating for violence even as the struggle for the prison was in progress. The second main round during Burma's time of crisis was fought out in rural Burma rather than in Rangoon. Its origins were more complex than those of the first disturbances; it proved harder to contain and suppress; and at one point it threatened to bring a premature end to British rule and the plural society in Burma.

On the night of December 22, 1930, after years of preparation, bands of Burmese insurgents raided villages in the southeastern portions of the Tharrawaddy District. The rebels sought firearms and killed those headmen and villagers who dared to oppose them. During the next night their operations were extended into the northern portions of the Insein District, and a successful assault was made on the railway station at Inywa north of Tharrawaddy town.[58] These incidents began a series of risings which have come to be known collectively as the Saya San rebellion, after the ex-*pongyi,* folk doctor, and sometime nationalist who led the first insurrections and was the prime mover behind many of those which followed. These risings and a number of related disturbances affected most of the districts of the Delta and spread to several districts in Upper Burma. They were not completely brought under control until 1932 and resulted in the loss of nearly 1,700 lives and millions of rupees in property damage.[59]

Although the causes of the major risings varied somewhat from one area to the next, the Saya San rebellion as a whole was an expression of nativistic or revitalistic beliefs and hopes held by Burman *pongyis* and agriculturists. The rebellion was the most serious of a series of revolts aimed at the expulsion of the British and the termination of the "modernization" process which their rule had extended to Burma, particularly to the Delta area.[60] The rebel leaders presented themselves as defenders of the Buddhist faith which they claimed was jeopardized by the social and economic changes which had occurred since the advent of British rule. Saya San claimed descent from the Konbaung monarchs, the last and greatest Burman dynasty. He promised to restore Burman rule, revive Buddhism, and re-establish the traditional order of things in Burma. These goals were shaped by the profound political, social, economic, and religious dislocations which had been produced by the rapid growth of a modern bureaucracy and an export-oriented economy in the Delta after the British annexation of 1852. They expressed both a desire to solve Burma's many problems by abandoning or destroying the system which had seemingly produced them, and age-old messianic and millennial expectations held by the Burmans. These beliefs focused on the coming of the

58. Government of Burma, *Report on the Rebellion in Burma up to 3rd May, 1931* (Rangoon, 1931), pp. 2–3, in the *Parliamentary Papers,* vol. 12, 1930–31, cmd. 3900.

59. Letter from R. A. Butler to George Hall, Esq., M.P., 29 May 1934, in the Government of India, Political and Judicial Correspondence, file 7347, no. 2160.

60. See Sarkisyanz, *Buddhist Backgrounds,* pp. 149–59; and below, footnote 62.

Mettaya Buddha and a golden age when Gautama Buddha's *dhamma* (law) would regulate the lives of all mankind.

Although the Saya San rebellion displayed both mesianic and millenarian content, it is wrong, I think, to conclude that it need not necessarily have been caused by perceived grievances related to political, social, or economic dislocations. To argue that revolts of this nature are "self-justifying" or "happen just-so"[61] is to confuse causation with the factors that determine the form of expression adopted by a particular group of dissidents. In the case of the Saya San rebellion social and economic grievances clearly played a major causal role.

The Government of Burma repeatedly denied suggestions that the primary causes of the rebellion were economic. While admitting that economic distress may have contributed to the spread of the disturbances, British officials argued that it could not have caused the initial rising. They pointed out that this outbreak occurred before the sharp drop in the price of rice had begun to affect Burma. They added that in areas where the early risings took place bumper crops were being harvested, taxes had not yet been collected, and the peasants were "all in comfortable circumstances."[62] These arguments ignore the serious agrarian problems, such as tenancy, land alienation, and indebtedness, which had been developing for decades prior to the Depression. The causal significance of these factors is indicated by the distribution of the individual risings which made up the Saya San rebellion as a whole. They were centered mainly in the Tharrawaddy, Pyapon, Insein, Henzada, Prome, and Pegu districts of Lower Burma. The guerrilla resistance, which either followed the failure of these main outbreaks or arose independently of them, was also concentrated in these areas, along with the Toungoo and Myaungmya districts. In addition, communal violence related to the rebellion broke out in Hanthawaddy, Pyapon, Myaungmya, Pegu, and Toungoo. These districts were not those of the historic Burman heartland in the Dry Zone of Upper Burma where one would expect a Burman traditionalist revival to be centered. They composed instead most of the Delta region which had been the most exposed to economic "modernization" and its attendant social changes. In Upper Burma there were major outbreaks only in the Thayetmyo and Yamethin districts which bordered on the Delta. Both of these insurrections were led by persons connected to previous disturbances in Lower Burma.[63]

61. As has Kenhelm Burridge in his stimulating lectures published under the title *New Heaven, New Earth* (New York, 1969), pp. 36, 47, 56, 62, 74, et passim.

62. Government of Burma, *Report to 3rd May, 1931,* pp. 11–12; R. C. Morris, *Cause of the Tharrawaddy Rebellion* (Rangoon, 1931), p. 17; Government of Burma, *Origin and Causes of the Burma Rebellion (1930–32),* pp. 1, 43.

63. Government of Burma, *Report to 3rd May, 1931,* p. 6; Government of Burma, *(Confidential) Report on the Rebellion in Burma, April 1931–March 1932* (Rangoon, 1932), p. 2. Saya San also led a major rising in the Shan States.

The available information relating to conditions and to the leaders of revolts in specific areas supports the assertion that the rebellion's origins were partly economic. Thomas Couper's 1924 inquiry into the conditions of laborers and tenants in the Delta revealed that tenants in Tharrawaddy, where the first rising occurred, were among the most oppressed in Burma. He found that rent rates in the townships where Saya San centered his operations were higher than those recorded in most other areas despite the fact that paddy prices and rental rates were generally lower in the district as a whole. Couper also reported that Tharrawaddy landlords seldom gave remissions in bad years and that they manipulated collections in order to extract the maximum rent from their tenants.[64] In the Dedaye township of Pyapon, where the second major outbreak of the rebellion took place, a high percentage of the cultivated land had been lost to Indian moneylenders. Many of the villagers who supported this rising were deeply in debt to those moneylenders, and two of the principal leaders were former tenants who had been evicted by Indian landlords.[65] In the case of one of these leaders, Aung Hla, eviction was particularly harmful, for he was an old man and the only option left for him was landless agricultural labor. Since this work was generally considered too strenuous for men over forty, it would have been difficult for him to find employment.

Rebel leaders often cited economic grievances to win supporters or to justify their rebellion. In a speech which reportedly inspired the Dedaye disturbances, Saya San protested high taxes which were levied in spite of the "general depression of the paddy market."[66] During the actual conflict in Pyapon, the rebel leaders ordered their followers to resist by force all attempts on the part of government officials to collect capitation taxes.[67] On other occasions Saya San spoke of the coming struggle as one for "the prosperity of the nation" and as a means by which poor people might escape the "trouble and misery" which had resulted from the price slump and high taxes.[68] The leader of the Prome rebellion sought to recruit followers with promises that there would be lower taxes and that debts owed to Indian moneylenders would not have to be paid if the revolt succeeded.[69] The economic grievances cited by these and other rebel leaders and the response these evoked from Burmese agriculturists who made up most of the rank and file of the rebel forces demonstrate the importance of the agrarian crisis as one of the major factors leading to the rebellion.

Insofar as it was economically inspired, the Saya San rebellion was a

64. *Report into Agricultural Condition,* pp. 29–31.

65. *RLAC,* pt. 2, pp. 52–53.

66. Special Tribunal Judgement, 19 June 1931, no. 1869, p. 158, in Government of India, Political and Judicial Proceedings, file 7350.

67. Special Tribunal Judgement, 9 May 1931, no. 3555, p. 3, ibid., file 7349.

68. Special Tribunal Judgement, 19 June 1931, no. 1869, p. 158, ibid., file 7350.

69. Special Tribunal Judgement, 11 March 1932, no. 2901, p. 1, ibid.

product of frustrated hopes rather than hopeless oppression. Although the problems of Burma's economy were very serious by the 1920s, few, if any, persons in the province starved even when the slump was at its worst in the early 1930s. A tenant's or laborer's family might have less rice to consume and little money to spend on *pwes* or other amusements, but normally food and shelter could be found. In the boom decades of the late nineteenth century and the early 1900s, however, the classes engaged in agrarian production had come to expect rather high standards of living and levels of consumption and considerable upward mobility. In the decades of transition, social and economic realities increasingly fell short of these expectations. By the time of the Depression, the social and economic arrangements that had once brought the Burmese cultivator prosperity no longer seemed to work in his favor. Consequently, thousands of agriculturists allied themselves with visionaries and *pongyis* who promised to destroy the institutions that had evolved under alien rule and to bring about a return to an idealized golden age of the past.

The communal disturbances which accompanied the Saya San rebellion were the most serious in the lower Delta districts, where Indian moneylenders, landlords, tenants, and laborers were the most active. In the Hanthawaddy, Insein, Pegu, Pyapon, and Myaungmya districts, government officials reported widespread assaults on Indians. Large bands of Burmese villagers attacked clusters of Indian field huts and raided Indian settlements. They beat, and sometimes killed, the unarmed Indians whom they found. Those Indians who were lucky enough to avoid the Burmese raiders fled to Rangoon, where many sought passage back to India. Burmese rebels and agrarian mobs also robbed Indian moneylenders and looted Indian village shops.[70] Burmese tenants in some areas refused to work the holdings of Indian landlords and forcibly prevented Indians or other Burmese from breaking their boycott.[71] With the exception of the Toungoo District, where communal clashes were as widespread as in the lower Delta,[72] attacks on Indians in other areas of the Delta were isolated and sporadic. In Prome, Maubin, and several districts in Upper Burma, Burmese rebels or local villagers raided Indian homesteads, at times killing whole families.[73]

70. Government of Burma, *Report of 3rd May, 1931,* pp. 13–14; *RAB, 1931–32,* p. 72; Goverment of Burma to the Government of India, Home Dept., 2 April 1931, 165C31, in Government of India, Political and Judicial Correspondence, no. 2351, file 7349; Burma Situation Report, 27 June 1931, no. 3163, ibid., file 7347; *Rangoon Gazette,* 6 July 1931, pp. 8, 10, 26–27.

71. *Season and Crop, 1930–31,* p. 12; Burma Situation Report, 27 June 1931, no. 3663, in Government of India, Political and Judicial Correspondence, file 7347.

72. Government of Burma to Government of India, Home Dept., no. 165C31, in Government of India, Political and Judicial Correspondence, file 7347, pp. 1–2.

73. See, for example, *RAB, 1932–33,* p. 25; *Rangoon Gazette,* 31 July 1931, p. 10; Special Tribunal Judgement, 11 June 1932, no. 4491, pp. 79–80, in Government of India, Political and Judicial Correspondence, file 7350.

Although Burmese cultivators who were not directly involved in the Saya San Rebellion mounted most of the assaults on Indians living in rural Burma, there is considerable evidence that in a number of outbreaks Indians were specified as targets by rebel leaders. Rebel bands killed Indian shopkeepers and looted or burned their stores during the opening nights of the rebellion in Tharrawaddy District.[74] A peasant named San Pwa, who was involved in the Insein disturbances, admitted that he had participated in the murders of several Indians. He stated that he had been ordered to commit these acts in order to frighten all Indians away from Burma and to enable Burmese cultivators to regain their lands.[75] Anti-Indian statements contained in the proclamations and promises of rebel leaders in Pyapon and Prome have been cited above. Finally, one rebel named Po Thu Daw testified that he had been ordered by one of Saya San's officers to loot an Indian's house in Tharrawaddy. The leader promised that "on the last day all Indians would be dealt with."[76]

Although the relatively small Chinese community in Burma had managed to avoid involvement in the May riots in Rangoon, they became targets of communal violence for the first time during the period of the Saya San rebellion. The Tharrawaddy rebels robbed and murdered a Chinese storekeeper on the first night of the revolt.[77] Less than a fortnight later on January 2, 1931, bloody rioting broke out in Rangoon between Burmese and Chinese. Chinese merchants and shops located in the Taroktan quarter were the primary targets of roving bands of Burmese looters who were not brought under control until January 5. By that date, twelve persons had been killed and eighty-eight injured in two days of communal violence.[78] During the remaining months of the rebellion, Burmese rebels occasionally raided Chinese shops or homes in the rural Delta, but they did not make the Chinese a major target of their depredations as Indians had been.

These and numerous other instances of rebel attacks on Indians and Chinese who were not involved in administration or military service demonstrate that the Saya San was more than an anti-British rebellion. The rebels' ultimate target was the destruction of the plural society which had developed under the aegis of British rule. Even before their onslaught began, the demographic basis of that society was breaking down. Immediately after the May riots in Rangoon, large numbers of Indian workers who feared further violence returned to India. In 1929, 294,000 Indians left Rangoon; in

74. Government of Burma, *Report of 3rd May, 1931,* p. 3.

75. Special Tribunal Judgement, 31 December 1931, no. 1622, p. 191, in Government of India, Political and Judicial Correspondence, file 7349.

76. Special Tribunal Judgement, 19 June 1931, no. 1869, pp. 158–59, ibid., file 7350.

77. Government of Burma, *Report of 3rd May, 1931,* p. 3.

78. Pearn, *Rangoon,* p. 291.

1930 the number of emigrants jumped to 314,000.[79] The contraction of the labor market in Burma and the fact that some employers were hiring Burmese for posts once monopolized by Indians were partly responsible for this increase, but government officials stressed the impact of the riots on the level of emigration.[80] At the same time, the numbers of Indians entering Burma declined even more sharply. In 1929, 346,000 Indian immigrants arrived at the port of Rangoon. In 1930 this total fell to 301,000. Many potential immigrants in Madras or the United Provinces postponed trips to Burma because employment opportunities had largely disappeared and wages fallen, or because they were waiting to see if further communal violence would occur. They must have reasoned that it was better to live at subsistence levels in India than to be beaten or killed in search of uncertain employment in Burma.

The Saya San rebellion gave rise to a new wave of departures from Burma and led to a large-scale exodus of Indian tenants, laborers, and moneylenders from the rural Delta into Rangoon and other urban centers. In May of 1931 port officials in India estimated that the number of emigrants returning from Burma was 40 percent higher than it had been in the previous year.[81] For 1931 as a whole, the number of emigrants exceeded the number of Indians entering Burma by over 22,000. Disruptions caused by rebel outbreaks and the flight of Indians from the rural Delta led to lower production and substantial decreases in the area under paddy cultivation in all Lower Burma districts between the 1930–31 and 1931–32 seasons. These decreases were generally highest in districts where the rebellion or the communal disturbances associated with it were the most severe.[82]

After the Saya San rebellion had been suppressed an uneasy calm again settled over the Delta. The number of Indians entering Burma fell less sharply in the mid-1930s, while Indian emigration leveled off somewhat. A positive total for *net* migration was recorded from 1932 to 1938. Paddy production and export recovered to some extent and British officials began to believe, or at least to hope, that the worst was over. However, evidence of periodic clashes between Indians and Burmese throughout the 1930s indicates that their hopes were ill-founded. In 1935, for example, a quarrel between Indian and Burmese villagers in the Hanthawaddy District led to violence. Two Indians were killed and four seriously injured. The Burmese apparently

79. All statistics relating to Indian migration in the late 1930s were taken from Baxter, *Indian Immigration*, app. 6(b), p. 122.

80. *Madras Census, 1931*, Report, p. 75; Baxter, *Indian Immigration*, p. 48; Andrew, *Indian Labour*, p. 286.

81. *Madras Census, 1931*, Report, p. 82.

82. See the tables on land use in *Season and Crop, 1930–31, 1931–32;* and Darling, *Note*, p. 22.

suffered no casualties.[83] In July of the same year, a Muslim schoolteacher attempted to demonstrate Islam's superiority to Buddhism in a lecture to a crowd of villagers in the Toungoo District. His disparaging references to Buddhism greatly angered local Burmese nationalists, and a communal riot was narrowly averted.[84]

Exactly three years later, similar insults touched off another major round of communal riots in Burma's decade of crisis. On July 26, 1938, Burmese political and religious leaders held a meeting on the platform of the Shwe Dagon pagoda in Rangoon. They called the meeting to protest verbal attacks which had been leveled against the Gautama Buddha and the Buddhist faith in a pamphlet entitled *The Abode of the Nats,* written by a Burmese Muslim. The author of the tract, who used the pseudonym of Maung Shwe Hpi, wrote it in reply to his Buddhist opponents in a local religious dispute. It was first published in 1931 and again in 1936, but was known only to a small group of Muslims until 1938. In that year, a minor Burmese author, Maung Htin Baw, published excerpts from Maung Shwe Hpi's tract as appendices to his otherwise uninteresting novel. The Burmese vernacular newspapers, *Sun* and *New Light of Burma,* printed part of the appendices of Maung Htin Baw's novel and embellished them with editorial comments on the threat these attacks posed for the Buddhist faith and inflammatory statements as to what might be done. The reaction of the Burmese press led to the meeting at the Shwe Dagon on the twenty-sixth of July.[85]

Shortly after the meeting had ended and most of the crowd had dispersed, a group of over one thousand Burmese rushed south from the precincts of the pagoda down the road toward the center of Rangoon. The highly emotional speeches given at the meeting by nationalist leaders and *pongyis* denouncing Indian involvement in Burma and Indo-Burmese intermarriage had greatly agitated the young nationalists, laborers, and "political" *pongyis* in the crowd. These groups made up most of the mob that marched towards the Sortee Bara Bazaar and the Indian quarters. As they progressed, their mood grew more hostile. Some of the marchers began to chant slogans, such as "Assault Indians," "Boycott, Boycott," and "Flaming Torch—Burn, Burn," and armed themselves with sticks, green bamboo stalks, and rails taken from the Pagoda Road tram line. When they came upon Indians, the crowd attacked them or chased them into nearby buildings. Groups of Burmese smashed Indian street stalls, pulled Indians off tram cars and beat them, and drove an Indian policeman from his post. After passing

83. Government of India, Political and Judicial Correspondence, Index 1935, Burma General, no. 1033 (destroyed).

84. Government of Burma, *Final Riot Report,* p. 208.

85. These details regarding the precipitant of the 1938 riots were taken from Government of Burma, *Interim Riot Report,* p. 8, and Government of Burma, *Final Riot Report,* pp. 1–11.

unchallenged through a police cordon at the corner of China and Canal streets, the Burmese, by then transformed into a raging mob, pressed into the Sortee Baara Bazaar, where they began to stone and loot Indian shops and homes. The police finally drove the mob from the bazaar area, but a new round of rioting had begun.

For the next week the streets of Rangoon again became a communal battleground, with the Burmese almost entirely on the offensive. After brief and ill-fated counter-attacks by gangs of Indians on the morning of July 28, Hindus and Muslims fled to protected areas or sought to hide until the riots subsided. The military and police managed to control main thoroughfares, but they were not numerous enough to patrol back streets. In the latter, Burmese mobs and small gangs looted and burned Indian mosques, shops, and homes and beat and murdered Indians of all ages and both sexes.[86]

Unlike the 1930 riots, the 1938 communal disturbances spread far beyond the city of Rangoon. Between the twenty-ninth of July and the middle of August, major communal clashes erupted in several towns in the Myaungmya, Maubin, Pyapon, Henzada, Prome, Toungoo, and Pegu districts. There were also serious incidents in the villages in these areas. In addition, there were minor outbreaks of violence in each of the remaining districts of the Delta and a number of more serious disturbances occurred in Upper Burma.[87] Before the orgy of looting, arson, and murder could be brought under control, 204 persons had been killed and over 1,000 injured. Government officials estimated that the loss of property during the riots exceeded two million rupees.[88]

Although Maung Shwe Hpi's polemical tract was the precipitant of the 1938 riots, their underlying causes were the social and economic dislocations whose origins have been traced in this study. The 1938 Riot Inquiry Commission stated:

> . . . whatever may have been the effect in particular places and upon the minds of particular people of the resentment caused by Maung Shwe Hpi's book . . . there had been in operation in Burma for some time a number of underlying influences far older than the publication of the extracts from the book and wholly unconnected with it and the meeting in Rangoon on the 26th July 1938.[89]

The commission went on to discuss the factors which they believed to be responsible for the riots. They stressed the economic crisis brought on by the Depression, particularly as it had affected persons engaged in agrarian

86. This brief account of the rioting in Rangoon is taken from Government of Burma, *Final Riot Report,* pp. 12–41.

87. Ibid., pp. 45–225.

88. Ibid., pp. 281, 284.

89. Government of Burma, *Interim Riot Report,* p. 9.

production. They also cited communal tensions as a chief cause. The latter, they concluded, resulted largely from intensified economic competition and from widespread fears on the part of Burmese that Indians would eventually overrun their homeland.[90] The riots of 1938, like the riots of 1930, were primarily a product of conflicts generated by the plural society arrangement in Burma and were symptoms of the demise of that system.

In the years before the 1938 riots Burmese nationalist leaders had called for government regulation and limitation of Indian labor migration into Burma. The faction led by U Saw had also attempted to break the strong hold of the Chettiars and other Indian groups on the Burmese economy through the introduction of legislation such as the Distribution of Lands and Paddy Rents Control Bills of 1937.[91] Prior to 1938, none of these proposals had been enacted. After the communal riots of that year, however, numerous special enquiry committees were established by the government and a series of bills was introduced into the Burma legislature which was aimed at ameliorating economic distress and communal friction. Acts relating to tenant conditions, land alienation, and labor immigration regulation were passed in the last years before the Japanese invasion in 1941–42, but these measures came too late to shore up the crumbling plural society that had grown up in colonial Burma.[92] Despite some improvement in Burma's economic situation in the late 1930s, in the years after the 1938 riots Indian emigration from Burma again rose while immigration fell off sharply. In 1939 the number of Indians leaving Burma exceeded those arriving by over 16,000.

The slow dissolution of the plural society ended abruptly two years later when the Japanese invasion precipitated its collapse. At one stroke, the imposition of Japanese rule removed the British political and military elite and a large portion of the Indian community. As many as 400,000 Indians are believed to have fled from Burma during the months of the Japanese invasion.[93] The removal of the British colonial administration and military forces was decisive, however, because they had provided the element of coercion which made it possible for the plural society to withstand the shocks of the 1930s. The British reclaimed Burma briefly after World War II, but only the feeblest of efforts were made to restore the plural hierarchy or to see that justice was done to the victims of its downfall. Once the British turned Burma over to its nationalist elite, little remained but a dreary process of disenfranchisement and the often cruel displacement of the Indian community that still remained.

90. Ibid., pp. 11–12, 21–28.

91. Mahajani, *Role of Indian Minorities,* pp. 67–68, 76–79.

92. Cady, *Modern Burma,* pp. 390–91, 404–9; Mahajani, *Role of Indian Minorities,* pp. 88–90.

93. B. R. Pearn, *The Indian in Burma* (Ledbury, Eng., 1946), p. 32.

CONCLUSION

The history of agrarian development and social change on the Lower Burma rice frontier during the period of British rule provides important exceptions to many widely held assumptions regarding the economic impact of European imperialism, the nature of economic policy under European colonial regimes, and the responses of non-Western peoples to the changes generated by the spread of the European commercial-industrial revolution. The case of Lower Burma clearly contradicts the persistent notion that "the central desire of *all* imperialist enterprises [was] the wish to bring a people's products into the world economy but not the people themselves; to have one's economic cake and eat it too by producing capitalist goods with precapitalist workers on precapitalist land."[1] The policies pursued by the British colonial regime after the annexation of the Delta in 1852 were designed to draw the indigenous Burmese, and later Indian immigrants as well, into an expanding capitalist economy. The measures taken by the British to stimulate economic growth, particularly the land tenure system oriented to the "peasant" proprietor which they introduced, were influenced by a sincere desire to insure that the mass of the Burmese obtained real

1. Italics mine, quoting Clifford Geertz, *The Social History of an Indonesian Town* (Cambridge, Mass., 1965), p. 45. For a discussion of this theme in the literature on imperialism more generally see Richard Pares, "The Economic Factors in the History of Empire," *Economic History Review* 7, no. 2 (1937): esp. 137–44.

benefits from participation in Lower Burma's development. The fact that the British were also motivated by concerns to increase the taxable income, export production, and market potential of the fertile Delta region complemented rather than contravened their desire to raise the living standard of the area's inhabitants.

The response of the Burmese to the introduction of a market economy and new patterns of agrarian production was far more dynamic and positive than most writers have assumed. The role of the Burmese went far beyond the provision of "raw" labor "required to pry resources from their natural setting and make them or their immediate product available abroad."[2] Throughout the 1852–1941 period, Burmese not only made up most of the laboring force engaged in agricultural production, but Burmese small landholders and large landlords also controlled most of the land on which surplus paddy was produced. Substantial numbers of Burmese also derived profit from their participation in the Delta rice industry as moneylenders, paddy brokers, rice mill owners or managers, and merchant-speculators. Contrary to the widely accepted assumption that Europeans and Indian immigrants monopolized entrepreneurial roles in the Lower Burma,[3] the Burmese displayed considerable entrepreneurship in J. A. Schumpeter's sense that they put into effect new combinations in the means of production and credit.[4]

Burmese agriculturists displayed little reluctance to participate in the making of an export economy in Lower Burma. Neither coercion nor indebtedness-cum-foreclosure were required to stimulate the Burmese to produce surplus rice for sale.[5] The factors which determined the active and voluntary participation of the Burmese in the development of the Delta are complex and interrelated. They consist of the absence of formidable political or social barriers, of a low level of economic risk, and of positive incentives which were also found in other societies which came under European colonial rule in the late nineteenth century.[6]

2. Hans O. Schmitt, "Decolonization and Development in Burma," *Journal of Development Studies* 4, no. 1 (October 1967): 102, 99–101. See also Jonathan Levin, *The Export Economies* (Cambridge, Mass., 1960), pp. 214–15.

3. See, for examples, Levin, *Export Economies,* pp. 154–60; and L. J. Walinsky, *Economic Development of Burma, 1951–1960* (New York, 1962), p. 22.

4. J. A. Schumpeter, *The Theory of Economic Development* (Cambridge, Mass., 1961), pp. 74–75.

5. Schmitt, after J. H. Boeke, argues that the indebtedness-foreclosure cycle forced the Burmese cultivator to participate in the rice-export economy ("Decolonization," pp. 102–3). Since large number of Burmese agriculturists were producing surplus rice for the market decades before indebtedness or land alienation became significant problems, this causal sequence does not work for Lower Burma.

6. For a fine discussion of risk factors and economic incentives in British colonial areas in Africa, see C. M. Elliot, "Agriculture and economic development in Africa:

Since the Delta was a sparsely populated frontier region in the pre-British period, the elaborate political and social hierarchies and interrelationships normally found in traditional societies were poorly developed and much diluted in the area. Hence, the traditional or precapitalist institutions and ties that have often proved barriers to social and economic change were not major obstacles in Lower Burma. In addition, the imposition of colonial rule brought an end to the sumptuary laws and market restrictions that had impeded economic growth in the Konbaung period. The new British rulers also undertook a broad restructuring of the political and economic institutions of Delta society and introduced public works that improved communications and transport and rendered cultivable vast areas that had once been flooded waste. These measures and the later introduction of government-sponsored technical schools, credit institutions, and agricultural experiment stations created a favorable environment for the growth of an expanding market-oriented economy.

One of the major determinants of the high degree of Burmese participation in the export economy which evolved after 1852 was the very low level of the risks involved. Some changes in cropping and irrigation techniques notwithstanding, the major innovations made by Delta agriculturists were the expansion of their rice production beyond the subsistence level and the sale of the surplus on the Burma market. Since most Burmese agriculturists were familiar with wet-rice cultivation techniques and the output potential of the crop, none of the problems associated with the introduction of unfamiliar crops were present in the Delta. In addition, because rice was the main staple food of the Delta's inhabitants and because the ecology of Lower Burma was ideal for rice production, there was little risk of crop failure, and virtually none of famine. Although the cultivator gradually gave up most of the activities connected with the maintainence of the pre-British, self-sufficient household, opportunity costs involved in agricultural change in the Delta were low due to the fact that the same crop was grown for the market and for subsistence.

Sufficient market outlets and the spread of rural retail networks were key variables in the complex of factors that stimulated Burmese production for export. The Burmese rapidly acquired a strong taste for the variety of cheap consumer goods (most of them Western imports) which they could purchase with the income derived from their surplus production. They also spent their earnings on a wide range of traditional pastimes, such as *pwes,* pagoda festivals, *shinbyu* ceremonies, gambling, and *ahlus.* The responses of the Burmese agriculturists to consumer incentives and opportunities to improve their economic and social status clearly contradict J. H. Boeke's assertion that

theory and experience 1880–1914," in *Agrarian Change and Economic Development,* ed. E. L. Jones and S. J. Woolf (London, 1969), pp. 123–50.

the members of "Eastern" or "Oriental" societies have limited needs or wants.[7] The strong correspondence between rising prices and increased paddy production for the market on the part of both Burmese small landholders and estate owners also forces one to question the validity of Boeke's insistence that there is necessarily a backward-bending supply curve in "Eastern" societies.[8] Although the relationship between production and price flux is more difficult to trace after the 1880s due to the increased activity of middlemen in the Delta economy, the Burmese case clearly supports P. T. Bauer and B. S. Yamey's assumption that "the supply of effort and saleable output offered in the exchange sector tends to vary positively with the rates of reward obtainable in that sector."[9]

The activities of agriculturists in Lower Burma also bring into question the claim that there is almost a complete absence of profit-seeking on a regular and prolonged basis in "Eastern" societies.[10] Each year the cultivator carefully weighed the cost of cultivation against the yield he would receive and the profits he would earn. He would not employ a technique that increased his costs of production unless he were convinced that it would result in a fairly substantial increment to his income.[11] His concern to earn a profit is also illustrated by his desire to keep abreast of price changes on the Burma market. Burmese producers were highly informed regarding price trends and market fluctuations via newspapers, special price sheets, telegraph communications, and word of mouth. Insofar as they were able, they altered their production and sale patterns to take advantage of market fluctuations.[12] The desire of the Burmese cultivator-owner in the Delta to produce regularly at a profit became so pronounced that he completely lost the sentimental attachment to his land that was characteristic of agriculturists in traditional Burman society. By the mid-1890s a British revenue official could write of the cultivator in Lower Burma:

7. *Economics and Economic Policy of Dual Societies* (New York, 1953), pp. 39–40.

8. Ibid., p. 40. Examples of "inverse elasticity" of supply can, of course, be found, but they are neither unique to non-Western societies nor products of an "Eastern" as opposed to a "Western" mentality. For examples of this phenomenon in European economic history, see David S. Landes, *The Unbound Promentheus* . . . (Cambridge, 1969), pp. 59–61. For a discussion of some of the factors which may elicit this response, see M. Sadli, "Reflections on Boeke's Theory of Dualistic Economies" in *The Economy of Indonesia*, ed. Bruce Glassburner (Ithaca, N.Y., 1971), pp. 106–9.

9. *The Economics of Under-developed Countries* (Chicago, 1957), p. 85.

10. See, for example, Boeke, *Economics*, pp. 40–41.

11. J. S. Furnivall, *An Introduction to the Political Economy of Burma*, 3d ed. (Rangoon, 1957), p. 20.

12. Ibid., p. 158; D. F. Chalmers, "Marketing," in Government of Burma, *Agriculture in Burma* (Rangoon, 1927), p. 100; Government of Burma, *The Marketing of Crops in Burma* (Rangoon, 1928), p. 6.

> . . . there seems good reason to believe . . . that money and the luxuries which money brings are the sole or almost the sole object which the landholder has in view in acquiring and keeping land. The Burman cultivator . . . finds that a substantial store of grain is a sure passport to credit and ready cash. It is not to be wondered at then that he is fast being changed from a peasant to a professional grower or paddy purveyor, and that in his eyes one farm or field differs from another solely or chiefly in the quantity of paddy which it is estimated to produce. . . . If it [paddy] could be produced without land, he would drop the land.[13]

The appetite for regular profits was, of course, even more evident among those agriculturists who lent money or speculated on the paddy market on the side and the many Burmese ex-cultivators who were engaged in full-time moneylending, brokerage, or trading activities.

The trends discussed above indicate that traits such as "limited needs" or the absence of profit-seeking motives can be no more accurately applied to the Burmese agriculturist than to large-scale corn producers in Iowa or wheat farmers in Kansas. Maung Kyaw Din and hundreds of thousands of Burmese like him moved from a traditional, largely subsistence, and natural economy to large-scale, surplus production for the market with no special training or introduction to capitalistic or "Western" economic ways. Kyaw Din and his counterparts accumulated capital which was in part invested in more land, more plows and buffalos, additional hired labor, and, in many cases, subsidiary trading or moneylending activities. Without model farms, government information agencies, or the prodding of community development officials, they voluntarily and with remarkable speed passed through the stages which many theorists have seen as prerequisite to the adoption of innovations: awareness, interest, evolution, trial, and acceptance.[14] Their response clearly demonstrates that there is nothing peculiarly "Western" about profit incentives and consumer wants.

The active participation of Burmese agriculturists in the Delta rice-export industry also suggests that generalizations regarding the immobility of labor in "developing" nations may be ill-founded. The migration of hundreds of thousands of Burmese on a seasonal or permanent basis from the Dry Zone and other provincial divisions, as well as from one region in the Delta to another, provides a dramatic demonstration of both geographic and occupational mobility. This great movement, which occurred without government supervision and such coercive measures as hut taxes, indenture contracts, or the indebtedness-foreclosure syndrome, forces one to question

13. Government of Burma, Revenue and Agriculture Proceedings, vol. 4886, March 1896, no. 5, p. 9.

14. See E. M. Rogers and F. F. Shoemaker, *Communication of Innovations* (New York, 1971), pp. 100–101.

the assumptions of Boeke and others that labor in non-Western societies is ipso facto immobile.[15]

The high degree of mobility displayed by the Burmese was equaled by the Indians who migrated to Burma to work in both the urban and rural areas. Throughout most of the period covered by this study their movement was neither regulated nor supported by the government. As in the case of Burmese migration, Indian immigration was stimulated and sustained by individual responses to economic incentives. Government subsidies and special schemes proved unnecessary.

The geographical mobility of the Burmese and Indians was paralleled by considerable occupational mobility on the part of both groups. Burmese ex-agriculturists participated extensively in agricultural credit provision, rice marketing and transport, and rice-mill ownership and management. Their relatively low level of involvement in other sectors, such as port or rice-mill labor, was, at least until the last decade of the transition phase, largely a matter of choice. Immigrant Indian laborers, most of whom were agriculturists in their areas of origin, were active in all sectors of the Delta rice industry. They sought positions as dock laborers, paddy gig pilots, and mill-hands, as well as those related to agriculture with which they were more familiar.

The great importance of the frontier context, of favorable government policies, and a healthy market situation as determinants of the vigorous response of Burmese and Indian agriculturists to new economic incentives in the late nineteenth century underlines the necessity for caution in attempts to generalize from the Delta case. The fact that Boeke and other early writers based their generalizations regarding peasant responses mainly upon their experience among peasant communities in densely populated "core" areas such as Central Java further warrants this caution. These qualifications notwithstanding, cases of agrarian development in other frontier areas, such as Ghana and the Minangkabau region of Sumatra,[16] indicate that in similar circumstances "peasant" responses have strongly paralleled those set forth in this study. These cases also demonstrate that widely held notions, such as the

15. Boeke, *Economics*, pp. 143–44. As Benjamin Higgins has pointed out in his study of *Economic Development* (New York, 1959), p. 283, Boeke himself provides evidence which contradicts his assertions concerning mobility. This same tendency is displayed by Levin, who fails to note that his Burma example clearly does not fit his general statements regarding the immobility of domestic labor in an export economy (see *Export Economies*, pp. 125–28, 207).

16. For detailed studies of "peasant" responses in these areas, see Polly Hill, *Migrant Cocoa Farmers of Southern Ghana* (Cambridge, 1963); and B. Schrieke, "The Causes and Effects of Communism on the West Coast of Sumatra," in *Indonesian Sociological Studies*, vol. 1 (The Hague, 1966), pp. 83–166.

"image of the limited good" in peasant societies,[17] must be qualified to take into account variations in social structure, demography, ecology, and historical circumstances. In future studies of peasant responses to change, attention must be focused on the impact of such factors as government policies, market conditions, the availability of rural credit and cheap consumer rewards, the availability of cultivable land, and the risks involved in new patterns of production. These variables need to be stressed, rather than the generalized assumptions regarding the nature of peasant societies and attitudes, or the stereotyped "characteristics" which have been applied to the peasants of particular societies that have so dominated the literature on peasant communities in the past.

The extensive participation of the Burmese in sectors of the rice industry other than agricultural production and the fact that Burmese controlled most of the rice-producing land in the Delta, even in the 1930s, suggest that the theoretical arguments of a number of contemporary scholars may be based on a misunderstanding of the Burmese colonial experience. In this study I have not dealt directly with many of the issues raised by Jonathan Levin, Hans Schmitt, Cheng Siok-Hwa, and others, but the evidence I have set forth indicates that there is a need for detailed research to determine the historical accuracy of many of the economic theses which these writers propound. Some of the questions raised include: How dual was the colonial economy of Lower Burma? To what degree was that economy monetarized, both at the urban-industrial level and at the level of the "peasant" producer? What share of the earnings of that economy went to the indigenous Burmese and what share to "foreign factors," the Europeans or immigrant Asians?[18] What percentage of the earnings derived by alien groups were remitted or reinvested in Burma? How much of the income available for reinvestment was actually controlled by aliens? How developed was the domestic market in Burma?[19] How extensive was domestic production?[20] Was there in fact an alien

17. This concept has been the most effectively developed by G. M. Foster in his article on "Peasant Society and the Image of the Limited Good," *American Anthropologist* 67, no. 2 (April 1965): 293–315.

18. Although very little statistical evidence has yet been produced on this very important point, the verdict has been heavily in favor of the Indians and Europeans. See Cheng Siok Hwa, *The Rice Industry of Burma, 1852–1940* (Kuala Lumpur-Singapore, 1968), pp. 232–35; W. S. Desai, *India and Burma: A Study* (Bombay, 1954), p. 25; and Levin, *Export Economies,* pp. 6–7, et passim.

19. The strong incentive of imported consumer goods stressed in this study conflicts with Levin's claim that in "export economies" a domestic market scarcely exists (*Export Economies,* p. 8).

20. Aye Hlaing's initial findings ("Trends of Economic Growth and Income Distribution in Burma, 1870–1940," *Journal of the Burma Research Society* 47, no. 1 [June 1964], pp. 103–7) regarding this problem force one to question Levin's view that "few goods above the subsistence level were produced domestically" (*Export Economies,* p. 7).

"luxury-importing" group, as Levin presumes (the Chettiars?), or were the major importers (luxury or otherwise) the Burmese themselves? Because of the relatively high quality of the statistics which were compiled during the period of British rule, it is possible to examine in depth the validity of the assumptions which lie behind these questions.

The history of social and economic change in Lower Burma also has important implications for the study of intergroup relations, particularly those associated with pluralistic societies. The Burmese case underlines the importance of economic factors, which are often neglected, as determinants of stability in such societies. It suggests that in a situation where there is steady economic growth which exceeds or keeps pace with the rate of population increase, diverse cultural/racial groups may develop interdependent economic relations. These ties may be sufficient to maintain a high degree of social harmony with a minimum of overt coercion for long periods of time. However, when population growth begins to outstrip economic expansion and competition for the occupational niches in the society intensifies, there is a strong propensity for it to fragment along cultural/racial lines. Political forces, such as nationalism, may greatly exacerbate intergroup rivalries and animosities and in conjunction with economic distress can result in intergroup violence such as that which ravaged Burma periodically in the 1930s.

Although this study has focused on the Burmese-Indian confrontation in the context of the Delta rice industry, the plural-society framework can be applied to other groups and extended to other aspects of Burma's history. The rivalries between the Burmans and the other ethnic groups which make up the modern nation of Burma (the Karens, Shans, Chins, and so on) or the political struggles between Burmese nationalist and British colonialist elite groups could fruitfully be analyzed through the application of the plural framework. The struggle of the different factions of Burmese nationalists can, for example, be viewed as one aspect of a broader campaign on the part of the Burmese at all levels to destroy the plural society that had evolved in the British period.

A number of interrelated factors led to the agrarian crisis that undermined the healthy economic development which had occurred and the plural society which had evolved in Lower Burma in the late nineteenth century. No single event, group, or policy was responsible for the crisis, and it is futile to attempt to assess the amount of blame that should be apportioned to each group which made up Delta society. The complex causes of the agrarian problems which underlay the political and social turmoil that characterized Burma in the late 1920s and 1930s defy simplistic condemnations of imperialist exploitation, Chettiar ruthlessness, or Burmese ineptitude.

The shortcomings of the Burmese agriculturist in terms of his adaptation to a capitalist economy were important ingredients in the crisis which developed in the early twentieth century. With regard to these shortcomings, it is important to point out that despite their deep and often successful involvement in the modern economy evolving in Lower Burma, most Burmese cultivators had only an imperfect understanding of capitalistic techniques and Western legal forms. Throughout the period covered in this study, settlement officers continually complained of Burmese misconceptions and carelessness concerning borrowing procedures and repayment records, the purchase and sale of land, and the meaning of mortgages. Mistakes in dealing with matters of this nature were understandable in view of the fact that "the Burman and Talaing [Mon] [had] suddenly been taken out of their former environment and placed under a foreign Government, and their whole social fabric brought into contact with an outer and stronger civilization."[21] However, the links which bound the Burmese cultivator to traditional values and patterns extended beyond his inability to fully comprehend the workings of a capitalist economy. They affected the manner in which he invested his earnings and prevented him from fully transforming his mode of agricultural production.

Statements that Burmese agriculturists did not reinvest their earnings in economically "productive" ways abound in the settlement reports and revenue department literature. Numerous British officials deplored the heavy expenditure by Burmese cultivators for *pwes, shinbyus,* and other village feasts and for donations to *pongyis,* monasteries, and pagodas. Even enterprising individuals like Maung Kyaw Din and Saya Thit devoted large sums to these ends. Government observers reasoned that the money spent on these "nonproductive" endeavors could have reduced the agriculturists' need to borrow to meet cultivating costs or provided insurance for bad years or the loss of crops through floods or crop diseases. Many officials saw this "careless expenditure" as the root cause of indebtedness and land alienation. They attributed the Burmese cultivator's bad spending habits to his innate "improvidence" and "care-free nature."

Although some Burmese agriculturists were in fact spendthrifts who squandered their hard-earned profits in gambling and drinking bouts, the vast majority of cultivators devoted their earnings to ends that were in their view both rational and productive. To begin with, one could hardly expect that after months of very hard labor in the tropical heat of the Delta, Burmese agriculturists and their families would not seek to rest and enjoy themselves during the dry season. Pagoda festivals, ox-cart races, *pwes,* and village feasts all provided important social outlets for the Burmese, whose fondness for

21. Quoting H. L. Eales, Commissioner of the Pegu Division, in Government of Burma, Revenue and Agriculture Proceedings, vol. 8633, November 1911, p. 402.

village celebrations and pagoda fairs should rightly be regarded as virtues, not vices as they were often viewed by colonial officials. These activities also served as important means of sharing wealth, cementing social relationships, and promoting a sense of community which was often seriously lacking in rural society in the Delta.[22]

The attraction of village gatherings and donations to *pongyis* and pagodas, however, extended beyond a desire for social prestige or conviviality, though these returns were certainly important. These activities were, in the eyes of the Burmese agriculturists, the most profitable way they could invest their earnings. By giving a *shinbyu,* supplying the village *pongyi* with food and clothing, or gilding the local pagoda, the Burmese could earn merit. Their store of merit not only determined the position into which they would be born in the next life and their good or ill fortune in the future, but a great accumulation of merit was also essential in order for them to achieve *nirvana* and thus the end of the cycle of rebirths and suffering.[23]

Investment in merit was far more advantageous from the average cultivator's viewpoint than investment in increased production or new enterprises. The charge of British officials or economic theorists that the Burmese sacrificed long-term gains for short-term pleasures would be incomprehensible to the Burmese cultivator. He believed that his "present existence [was] but a brief moment in a total life of inconceivably long duration, extending from a remote past to an equally remote future."[24] In this context, the cultivator regarded merit-making, which determined the level of his future existences, as his best long-term investment. He also saw it as the most secure outlet for his earnings. Investment in agricultural production or speculation on the paddy market could and often did lead to financial setbacks and unhappiness during seasons when the market slumped or calamities, such as insect pests or illnesses, struck. Market fluctuations, floods, and other forces beyond the cultivator's control had no effect on his *karma,* or the balance of his merits and demerits. This balance and thus his position in life depended solely upon his own actions. In addition, as Melford Spiro has pointed out,[25] investment in charity (*dana*) which included giving *shinbyu* feasts and the building of pagodas not only produces merit, but it produces merit in direct proportion to the amount spent or donated. Thus agriculturists were encouraged to spend as much as possible and wealthy

22. The importance of leisure activities, particularly their productive implications in social terms, has also been stressed by Elliot in "Agriculture in Africa," pp. 124–26; and Raymond Firth in *Capital Saving and Credit in Peasant Societies,* ed. Firth and B. S. Yamey (London, 1964), pp. 29–30.

23. For a succinct summary of these beliefs, see Melford Spiro, "Buddhism and Economic Action in Burma," *American Anthropologist* 68, no. 3 (October 1966): 1166–67.

24. Ibid., p. 1167.

25. Ibid., pp. 1166–68.

agriculturists were expected to give lavish sums. In this sense, the participation of the Burmese agriculturist in the modern, capitalist economy that evolved in Lower Burma was somewhat contradictory. It reinforced the traditional values and customs that most theorists believe it should have eroded.[26]

In terms of the workings of a capitalist economy in the Delta, these spending patterns were detrimental to the cultivator's material interest. In the first place, he spent large sums of money which he might have saved for a bad season or in case illness or natural calamity should strike. Because the Burmese agriculturist rarely had savings to fall back upon, any of these crises could throw him into debt. Unless he were fortunate enough to have several good seasons in succession thereafter, the cultivator would become more and more deeply indebted. In many cases he was eventually forced to give up his holdings for debts which he could not repay. Even more injurious than this pattern, however, was the tendency on the part of many cultivators to overborrow, either because they needed extra money for a *shinbyu* or *ahlu* or because they wanted to give an especially great feast or large donation. Cultivators who borrowed well beyond their means were, of course, often unable to repay their loans and thus ended up deeply in debt and finally lost their lands. Therefore, large-scale expenditure on merit-making and overborrowing were clearly major causes of the agrarian crisis that developed in the first decades of the twentieth century.

Despite the adverse economic effects of expenditure on merit-making in the context of Delta society in the colonial period, there was an economic rationale for the Burmese agriculturist's tendency to spend heavily for religious purposes. This rationale is connected to the fact that despite considerable innovations in the first decades after 1852, agricultural production in Lower Burma remained traditional in Theodore Schultz's sense that "the state of the arts"[27] remained constant. Prior to the British annexation of 1852, the techniques and tools of Burmese agriculturists had been in "equilibrium" for centuries. A cultivator worked his fields in the same manner and with the same implements that had been employed for centuries. The coming of British rule and the growth of a market economy partially upset this equilibrium, but change came primarily in attitudes rather than in technology. Burmese agriculturists began to produce for the market, rather than just for subsistence. They traded self-sufficiency for dependence on the sale of their surplus produce for their livelihood. In Schultz's terms, new market opportunities caused "the state of preference and motives for

26. This pattern gives added meaning to Susanne and Lloyd Rudolphs' caution that the traditional and the modern should not be seen in a dichotomous, but rather in a dialectical relationship. See *The Modernity of Tradition* (Chicago, 1967), especially the introduction.

27. *Transforming Traditional Agriculture* (New Haven, Conn., 1964), pp. 30–32, 37.

holding and acquiring sources of income" to change.[28] New sources of credit emerged and the scale of production increased dramatically.

These changes were not accompanied by widespread and significant innovations in agricultural technology. Those Burmese who had practiced shifting cultivation settled down. Migrants from the Dry Zone concentrated on flood control rather than irrigation. Many cultivators came to use plows in areas where only harrows had been used previously, and a small percentage of agriculturists introduced new seeds and employed more advanced methods of production. Except for this small minority of producers, however, agriculture in the Delta soon stagnated at a new level of technological equilibrium. The Burmese continued "year after year to cultivate the same type of land, sow the same crops, use the same techniques of production, and bring the same skills to bear in agricultural production."[29] To increase his output, the cultivator almost invariably invested in traditional factors, more land, and labor, rather than in fertilizers or new seeds. Agrarian expansion was almost wholly "horizontal"; there was no in-depth transformation of Burmese agricultural technology.

As long as large amounts of cultivable, unoccupied land remained, most observers did not realize the detrimental effects of this new technological equilibrium. When the rice frontier began to close, however, the price of paddy acreage rose sharply, and few cultivator-owners could afford to enlarge their holdings. Even if they were able to purchase additional land, the rate of return on their rather substantial investments was low. In the transition period the groups who accumulated large amounts of land were mainly moneylenders who acquired estates through foreclosures and speculators who had few other investment outlets for their capital. By the second decade of the twentieth century, land was a costly and not particularly profitable investment. Given this condition, it was logical for the average agriculturist to invest his surplus capital in merit-making, which was religiously sanctioned and socially rewarding.[30]

The investment preferences of Burmese cultivators and the fact that they did not transform their customary mode of agricultural production were, of course, not the only factors which lay behind the agrarian crisis in Burma. One can also trace the origins of that crisis to the frustration of the Government of Burma's policies and its inability to act decisively, as well as

28. Ibid., p. 30.

29. Ibid., p. 31.

30. As E. J. Hobsbawm has noted, even such highly skilled commercial groups as the northern Italian bankers of the Renaissance and the Dutch in the seventeenth century devoted large amounts of surplus capital to art and other economically "nonproductive" ends due in part to the paucity of highly profitable outlets for reinvestment. See "The General Crisis of the European Economy in the 17th Century," *Past and Present* 5 (May 1954): 42–43.

to some of the lending practices followed by the Indian Chettiars and other moneylenders.

The efforts of the government to determine the course and influence the nature of Burma's economic development were largely unsuccessful. Its early attempts to introduce crops other than paddy and thus avert dependence on a single crop failed. After the 1890s, agricultural indebtedness, mortgage foreclosures, and land alienation increasingly frustrated its ideal of a land of small peasant proprietors producing for export. The government's attempts to regulate or stimulate Indian immigration resulted in costly and unnecessary failures. Government schemes to control the rice-milling interests were short-lived and ineffective. The agencies which it established to provide agricultural credit and agrarian relief were badly administered, poorly financed, and far too small-scale to meet the needs of the province. Although the agriculture department and the other agencies charged with the task of introducing new tools and techniques realized some successes in the first decades of the twentieth century, the scope of their operations was too limited and their experiments came too late.[31]

Many critics of the colonial regime in Burma have singled out the government's failure to pass legislation for agrarian regulation and relief as its greatest fault. These critics, however, ignore the fact that in the first phase of the struggle to pass agrarian legislation, it was British officials, like S. M. Smeaton and H. T. White, who led the way. Their major, at times their only supporters, were settlement officers and other revenue officials. Many Burmese and Indian elite groups, on the other hand, and the European milling interests vigorously opposed the proposals set forth by the government. The opposition of these groups plus the problems which resulted from similar legislation which was passed in India caused the matter to be shelved by Sir Harvey Adamson in 1914. By the time legislation was passed in the 1930s, it was far too late.[32]

Much of the criticism of the Government of Burma's handling of the agrarian crisis has been based on hindsight[33] and standards that are products of an age when governments are expected to take active roles in economic development and to provide for the social welfare of their citizens. It is inappropriate to judge the actions of British officials in the late nineteenth and early twentieth century, when laissez faire doctrines were in vogue, by

31. In fairness to the government, it should be noted that chemical fertilizers, new rice strains, and better implements were in most cases only beginning to be developed prior to World War II. In addition, technological advances developed in Japan or elsewhere were often not suitable to the ecological givens in other regions, or were initially too expensive to be disseminated widely.

32. For a fuller discussion of the struggle to pass land alienation and tenancy legislation, see Cheng, *Rice Industry of Burma,* pp. 147–56, 166–70.

33. Furnivall is something of an exception in this respect.

contemporary standards. It is equally unfair to expect British administrators to have run Burma like a welfare state when in fact it was part of an empire. It is fair to point out, however, that the history of Lower Burma's development under what must be judged as one of the most beneficent of European colonial regimes clearly demonstrates the shortcomings inherent in imperialistic enterprises and laissez faire postures set in the context of unstable, export-oriented, capitalistic economies. Ongoing government adjustments and regulation were essential to the continued well-being of agriculturists and urban laborers who were struggling to adapt to a new and alien social and economic order. Effective government intervention may have greatly alleviated the disorders which came to dominate the last decades of Burma's colonial history. In the absence of that intervention, market forces, avaricious speculators, and political opportunists took a heavy toll. The casualties in most cases were small landholders, tenants, and rural or urban laborers who were least able to fend for themselves.

Both the defenders and opponents of the Chettiars have tended to overstate their case. Neither as moneylenders nor as landlords were the majority of Chettiars the "hard-hearted lot" who were guilty of "swindling, cheating, deception and oppression,"[34] as many of their detractors have charged. Chettiar moneylenders provided a large number of agriculturists in Burma with ready capital on easier terms and at rates lower than their Burmese competitors. Their role in lowering the interest rates in most areas of the Delta and the reasons they were able to do so have been discussed in earlier chapters. Throughout much of the period covered by this study, the Chettiars also provided a substantial portion of the capital lent by Burmese moneylenders. The Chettiars were far more accessible and required far less red tape than government agencies which were set up to provide alternative sources of credit. The available evidence also indicates that most Chettiars wished to be moneylenders, not landlords. As noted above, until the 1930s, Chettiars held only a small percentage of the land alienated in Burma and most of the land they acquired during the Depression came to them against their wishes.

Writers who stress the importance of Chettiar capital in the Delta's development have overstated their positive contribution almost as much as detractors have inflated their negative impact. Contrary to statements made by many writers,[35] there were other sources of agricultural credit and considerable economic growth did take place in the rural Delta before the

34. These epithets were propounded by a Karen witness before the Banking Enquiry Committee. See Government of Burma, *Report of the Burma Provincial Banking Enquiry Committee, 1929–30,* 3 vols. (Rangoon, 1930), 1:189.

35. Levin, *Export Economies,* p. 207; Usha Mahajani, *The Role of the Indian Minorities in Burma and Malaya* (Bombay, 1960), p. 19; N. R. Chakravarti, *The Indian Minority in Burma* (London, 1971), pp. 64, 67–68.

Chettiars arrived on the scene in the late 1870s. The Chettiars' additional inputs of capital accounted to a large extent for the great acceleration of Lower Burma's economic growth in the last decades of the nineteenth century, but that growth would have taken place, albeit more slowly and on a smaller scale, without them. By the early 1900s Chettiar capital was clearly essential to continued expansion and to sustain the level and pace of the development that had been achieved. This fact and the Chettiars' predominance in the 1920s and 1930s, however, should not obscure the importance of indigenous sources of credit and that provided by Chinese shopkeepers, rice-mill agents, other Indian groups, and in some areas government agencies.

Perhaps the most detrimental aspect of the Chettiars' operations in Lower Burma was their tendency to overlend. If a prospective client could offer adequate security, Chettiars would grant large loans without any attempt to determine the borrower's actual needs or the reasons why he took the loan. Consequently, the agriculturist who was frequently unfamiliar with the workings of a money economy often borrowed beyond his means or needs. As a result, many cultivators found themselves unable to repay the full amount of the loan. Gradually they would build up a backlog of interest charges and debts and eventually be forced to turn their land over to the Chettiar lender. Thus, the Chettiars' lending practices contributed to chronic indebtedness and land alienation which were central to the agrarian crisis.

Underlying the shortcomings and problems associated with the major groups involved in the Lower Burma's development was the Delta's dependence on the production of a single primary product for export. The economy of Lower Burma, and to a large degree of Burma as a whole, was overwhelmingly dominated by rice production in the period of British rule. Almost 92 percent of the total area cultivated in Lower Burma in the 1930-31 season was planted or sown with paddy.[36] In the Province of Burma as a whole, twelve of sixteen million acres cultivated were under paddy and over 75 percent of the population was engaged in growing, marketing, transporting, or milling rice.[37] In the mid-1930s Burma provided 38 percent of the total world exports of rice, and most of this surplus came from the twelve districts of the Delta.[38]

The extreme monocrop dependence of Lower Burma meant that market fluctuations in the price of a single product determined to a large degree the state of the Delta and the provincial economy. Dependence on rice sales made the economy particularly vulnerable because the prices of primary products tend to fluctuate more widely than those of manufactured goods. International market slumps, especially that which occurred during the Great Depression, resulted in serious financial losses at all levels of the Delta

36. Calculated from the statistics on land use in *Season and Crop, 1930–31.*

37. F. D. Odell, *Note on Burma Rice Prices . . .* (Rangoon, 1932), p. 1.

38. B. O. Binns, *Agricultural Economy in Burma* (Rangoon, 1948), pp. 50–51.

economy and greatly exacerbated domestic social and economic problems. Thus, the history of agrarian development in Lower Burma not only provides an excellent case study of economic growth in a colonial society, it also vividly illustrates the liabilities and dangers which have come to be associated with economies based on the production of one or two primary products.

GLOSSARY

APPENDIX

BIBLIOGRAPHY

INDEX

GLOSSARY

ahlu	a religious work or donation
athin	association; local unit of a Burmese political organization
*Bania	general term applied throughout north India to traders, moneylenders, and shopkeepers
*Chatri (Khatri)	trading caste of north India
chaung	small stream
*Chettiar (Chettie)	member of a moneylending subcaste from South India
dah	chopper; knife of any sort
dhani	palm for thatching roofs
**dhobi*	a washerman, one who washes clothes
hte (te)	Burmese plow
htun	Burmese harrow
*Kahar	caste term applied to a number of types of domestic servant in north India

*Denotes an Indian term.

kaing	tough, thick grass that grows in uncultivated areas up to ten feet high
*Kallan	agriculturist and bandit caste residing in Tamilnad in South India
*Kamma	high Telegu caste, composed mainly of agriculturists
kanazo	type of tree found in the fresh water areas of Lower Burma which grows to a height of fifty feet
kaukkyi	"winter" rice, longest crop, grown between July and January (life, 170-200 days)
kauklat	"autumn" rice, grown between July and November (life, 150-170 days)
kaukti, kaukyin	rice grown under canal irrigation, March to August (life, 140-150 days)
kazin	small bund around a rice field
kondan	a stretch of high ground or low hills
kwin	compact block of land demarcated separately for survey, usually from one to two square miles in area or from 600 to 1,000 acres; basic survey block
kyaung	Buddhist monastery
**maistry*	headman; applied to Indian immigrant recruiting system
*Mala	Telegu outcaste
mangrove	tree found in the swampy thickets which fringe the islands of the Irrawaddy delta area
*Marwari	merchant or moneylender from the Marwar region in western India
mayin	hot-weather rice, grown under irrigation between December and June (life, 170-200 days)
myo	designation for a township in the Konbaung and early British period
my-ok, myothugyi	township officer
ngapi	pounded fish preserved in brine
ngwedo	type of loan which is given in cash, with repayment of both principal and interest in cash
paddy	unhusked rice

*Palli (Vanniyan)	member of low-caste Tamil group mainly engaged in agricultural production
*Paraiyan	Tamil agricultural laboring group; outcaste; menial servant
**patta*	land granted by the government before the cultivator had cleared it
pongyi	Burmese Buddhist monk
pwe	traditional Burmese theatrical entertainment
*Reddi (Kapu)	a high Telegu caste of cultivators
**ryot*	a cultivator
**ryotwari* system	a form of land tenure by which assessments were made directly on individual landholdings
sabape	advances of goods or money repayable (both principal and interest) in paddy at harvest
shinbyu (simbyu)	Buddhist initiation ceremony
settun	a disc harrow
sittan	Burman revenue roll made during the Konbaung period
*Śudra	member of the fourth or agriculturist *varna*
tadaungbo	deep-water paddy
taik	a "circle," the lowest unit of administration in Konbaung and early British times
thugyi	local Burmese administrative and revenue official
**varna*	traditional four-fold divisions of the Hindu caste system
*Vellala	powerful agriculturist caste from Tamilnad
wunsa	paddy set aside for seed and home consumption
yoma	mountain range (literally "backbone")

APPENDIX: Discussion of Major Statistical Sources

1: EARLY BRITISH STATISTICS

Local indigenous officials gathered almost all of the statistics which are available in various reports for the early decades of British rule in Lower Burma. Hamlet or village headmen passed head counts or revenue information to *taikthugyis* (circle headmen), who in turn reported to *myothugyis* or *myo-oks* (township officers). The first check on the accuracy of these compilations came when the *myothugyi* or *myo-ok* reported to the Deputy Commissioner, who was a European and firmly attached to the British administration. At all of the lower levels of the administration there were possibilities for "errors." Indigenous officials felt little loyalty toward the new and alien British regime. In addition, they seldom understood the measurement systems or techniques employed by the British. Since there were not enough Europeans or trained Indian or Burmese officers to closely supervise the revenue and census work of local officials, many of the latter used their positions to their own advantage. This practice was institutionalized in pre-British times, when officials depended on gifts, bribes, and embezzlement to supplement their meager formal remuneration. They derived a large portion of their income from the practice of underreporting. The *taikthugyi*, for example, would report and pay taxes for only part of the households in his circle. He would, however, collect from all the households and pocket the difference.[1] This practice was widely followed in the first decades of British rule and seriously affected the accuracy of both demo-

1. Mya Sein, *Administration of Burma*, pp. 71–72.

graphic and revenue statistics in that period.[2] Arthur Phayre, the first Chief Commissioner, believed that the population of the Rangoon and Bassein districts in 1853–54 was *three times* more than that reported.[3] As late as 1899 a comparison of the cropped-area totals compiled by regular settlement officers and local *thugyis* in the Thongwa district revealed that the latter had underreported by as much as 75 percent.[4] The British did not supervise the census work of local officials or begin regular revenue settlements until the 1880s. Therefore, the first reliable census is that compiled in 1881, and the regular settlement reports (which began in 1879) provide the first reasonably accurate agricultural statistics.

2: THE 1856–57 RAP FIGURES FOR POPULATION COMPOSITION

These figures represent one of the few attempts by British officials to distinguish between Mons and Burmans on a district-by-district basis. Since many Mons spoke Burmese by the end of the Konbaung period, it was very difficult to distinguish between the two groups. Thus the "Talaings" (or Mons) and "Burmans" columns in the report may be highly inaccurate. This problem is compounded by the fact that the Burman population in Henzada is not given and it was known to have been sizable. The Mon population there, on the other hand, seems to have been overestimated. The numbers of Burmans in the Delta would probably have been lower than normal at this date, since many fled or were conscripted during the 1852 war. Karens would have been far less accessible than other groups and very difficult to count. There are clearly too few (5,841) Talaings listed for Bassein. Finally, the categories listed are often imprecise. For instance, the distinction between "Natives of India" and "Hindus," "Patans," "Muslims (Moguls)," and "Coringees" is not clear.

3: PLACE-OF-BIRTH STATISTICS

Migration statistics throughout the Indian Empire were recorded in this form. Therefore, social scientists dealing with Indian migration in the period of British rule are faced with the problems involved in the use of place-of-birth statistics. The best discussion of their shortcomings may be found in K. C. Zachariah, *A Historical Study of Internal Migration in the Indian Sub-Continent, 1901–1931* (London, 1964), pp. 46–50. In addition to the problems discussed in Chapter 2, Zachariah points out that migration statistics in this form are prone to errors resulting from boundary changes. A

2. See, for examples, Government of India, Political and Foreign Proceedings, range 201, vol. 63, 8 August 1856, no. 160; and Mya Sein, *Administration of Burma,* p. 111.

3. Government of India, Foreign Department to the Court of Directors, in Political Letters Received from India, Secret and Political Correspondence, vol. 30, no. 83, 22 August 1856, par. 179.

4. *Bassein-Thongwa Settlement Report (1888–89),* p. 23.

person born in a village in the Rangoon district in the 1860s, for instance, who moves to another area may continue to give his birthplace as Rangoon in the 1880s and 1890s, after the district has been divided into Hanthawaddy and Pegu. The enumerator could record his birthplace as Rangoon, and thus he would be counted as born in the city rather than in Hanthawaddy or Pegu. Errors due to boundary changes are more likely to occur in estimates of internal migration *within* the Delta, where district changes were frequent and often major. Since the district boundaries in the other divisions of the province were more stable, the chance of this type of error in estimates of movement *into* the Delta is less likely. Place-of-birth statistics are also problematical because they tell one very little about the composition of the migrant stream. They make no distinction between permanent and seasonal, young and old, or urban and rural migrants. Therefore, these aspects of migration analysis must be dealt with on the basis of qualitative information insofar as it is possible.

4: GENERAL OBSERVATIONS ON SETTLEMENT REPORT STATISTICS

There are a number of major problems involved in the use of statistics from district settlement reports. To begin with, the reports for different areas were made in series over several years rather than simultaneously. Even though the series can be grouped by decade (i.e., 1880s, 1890s, 1900s), comparisons from region to region in any decade are somewhat inaccurate. The settlements for Bassein and Hanthawaddy in the 1880s, for instance, were carried out in the first half of the decade, while those for Maungmya and Thongwa were conducted in the last years of the decade. In regional comparisons, therefore, one must allow for differences due to price inflation between the figures quoted for regions within a decade, as well as those quoted from one decade to the next. Some statistics, such as crop output or the number of tenants, were not affected by price inflation and thus can be more accurately compared within decade groups and over several decades. The great variation in the quality of the statistics found in different settlement reports is also a major source of difficulty. Some settlement officers were careful in their calculations and based their estimates on adequate samples. Other officers were less accurate and used only very small samples from limited areas. Some officers explain in detail the manner in which they derived their estimates and averages, while others merely list the figures, with little discussion of the sample or calculations which were used to arrive at them. The averages derived from tables in the settlement reports are problematical because they are arithmetic means, and thus conceal abnormal values within the district or regional grouping. The large average size of holdings in Hanthawaddy, for instance, is mainly due to the large estates in the vicinity of Rangoon. The average size of the majority of holdings in Hanthawaddy would be somewhat below the average cited if the large estates were considered in a different category. Unfortunately, no attempt is made to categorize holdings in the settlement reports, and thus the average derived from the arithmetic mean is the best available. For comparative purposes, the distortion is compensated for by the fact that the averages for all districts are based on similar calculations. Despite their shortcomings, the settlement figures are the best or only ones available for most aspects of agrarian development in the last half of the nineteenth century. If they are viewed as indices of general trends rather than precise statements of specific facts, they are extremely useful for discussions of patterns of agrarian development.

5: COST OF LIVING AND COST OF CULTIVATION STATISTICS

The samples from which most settlement officers derived their estimates of the average costs of living and cultivation were generally very limited. There was little uniformity in the items which were included by different settlement officers, and the proportionate importance of different items often varied widely. Most officials felt that cost estimates were unreliable because the majority of cultivators did not itemize their expenditures and did not fully understand the government's questionnaires. Because many cultivators were suspicious of the government's reasons for questioning them about their spending habits, they often deliberately overstated expenditure on certain items and concealed other purchases. The quality of cost-of-living and cultivation estimates improved in the later settlement reports. The size of samples increased, price calculations were more carefully worked out, and the items listed varied less from one report to the next. A list of the items usually included in estimates of each form of expenditure is given below.

Cost of Cultivation

1. Depreciation of implements
2. Labor
   a. hire
   b. food
3. Cattle
   a. hire
   b. grazing
   c. death
4. Seed paddy

Cost of Living

1. Rice for average family size
2. Food other than rice
3. Clothing
4. House repair and items for same
5. Charity (to *pongyis*, village religious buildings, etc.)
6. Luxuries (betel, tobacco, *pwes*, etc.)
7. Capitation tax (included only in the later settlement reports)

BIBLIOGRAPHY

MANUSCRIPT SOURCES
(Located in the India Office Records, London, Eng.)

Government of Burma

Revenue and Agriculture Proceedings.

Government of India

Emigration Proceedings of the Department of Revenue, Agriculture and Commerce.

Extracts and Observations Respecting the Dominions of Ava Chiefly from a Journal Kept by Dr. Francis Buchanan (now Hamilton) Accompanying Colonel Symes in His Embassy to the Court of Amarapura in 1795. India Office Archives, MSS. European, D. 106.

Foreign Proceedings (General).

Foreign Proceedings (Revenue).

Instructions from the Governor-General to the Bengal Deputation to Ava, 1787–1795. India Office Archives, MSS. European, E. 63.

Land Revenue and Settlement Proceedings of the Department of Agriculture, Revenue and Commerce.

Political and Foreign Proceedings.

Political and Foreign Proceedings (General).

Political and Judicial Correspondence. Files 7347–7351 (1930).

Secret and Political Correspondence, 1855–1858.
Statistical Proceedings of the Department of Agriculture, Revenue and Commerce.

GOVERNMENT PUBLICATIONS, BURMA
(Published by the Superintendent of Government Printing and Stationary, Rangoon, unless otherwise noted.)

Special Reports

Agricultural Leaflets. 2 vols., 1927.
Agriculture in Burma: A Collection of Papers Written by Government Officials for the Royal Commission on Agriculture 1926–28. 1928.
Chalmers, D. F. "Marketing." Pp. 100–110.
Couper, Thomas. "Area Farmed, Crops Grown, Tenure of Land, Assessment of Revenue." Pp. 6–12.
Dunn, C. W. "Some General Characteristics of Agricultural Economics in Burma." Pp. 15–27.
McKerral, A. "Climatic Tracts, Distribution of Crops, etc." Pp. 1–5.
Pattle, E. G. "Some Factors Affecting the Economic Position of Agriculturists." Pp. 111–29.
Atlas of the Province of Burma. 1923.
Baxter, James. *Report on Indian Immigration.* 1941.
Bennison, J. J. *Report on an Enquiry into the Standard and Cost of Living of the Working Classes in Rangoon.* 1928.
Binns, B. O. *Agricultural Economy in Burma.* 1948.
Burma Village Manual and Village Act. 1907.
Circulars of the Director of the Department of Land Records and Agriculture in Burma, 1888–1899. 1899.
Collection of Reports on the Yandoon Island Colonisation Scheme in the Ma-ubin District, 1912–22. 1923.
Couper, Thomas. *Report of Inquiry into the Condition of Agricultural Tenants and Labourers.* 1924.
———. *Report on Land Alienation, Indebtedness, and Condition of Tenants in Thaton District.* Moulmein, 1909.
Darling, Malcolm. *Note on the Co-operative Movement in Burma.* 1937.
Dawson, Lawrence. "Agricultural Banking in the Delta of Burma." In *Proposals for the Extension of Agricultural Banking in the Delta of Burma . . .* , edited by Harold Clayton. 1918.
English, A. E. *A Handbook of Co-operative Credit for Burma.* 1911.
Final Report of the Riot Inquiry Committee. 1939.
Ghosh, C. C. *Insect Pests of Burma.* 1940.
Grant, J. W. *The Rice Crop in Burma, Its History, Cultivation, Marketing, and Improvement.* Agriculture Department, Survey no. 17. 1932.
A Handbook of Agriculture for Burma. 1898.
Hardiman, J. P. *Compilation on Tenancy Matters.* 1913.
Hendry, David. *Fertilizers for Paddy: Results Obtained at the Hmawbi*

Agricultural Station. Agriculture Department, bull. no. 25 of 1928. 1929.
Interim Report of the Riot Inquiry Committee. 1939.
McKerral, A. *The Supply of Plough Cattle in Burma.* 1929.
The Marketing of Crops in Burma. Agriculture Department, Survey no. 5 of 1928. 1928.
Morris, R. C. *Causes of the Tharrawaddy Rebellion.* 1931.
Notes on "Homesteads" in Burma. Agriculture Department, bull. no. 24. 1928.
Odell, F. D. *Groundnuts in Burma.* Agriculture Department, Survey no. 11. 1932.
———. *Note on Burma Rice Prices: An Enquiry into the Reasons for the Present Market Depression.* 1932.
The Origin and Causes of the Burma Rebellion (1930–32). 1934.
Report of the Burma Provincial Banking Enquiry Committee, 1929–30. 3 vols. 1930.
Report of the Committee on Co-operation in Burma, 1928–9. 1929.
Report of the Crime Enquiry Committee. Maymyo, 1923.
Report of the Floods Enquiry Committee, 1924–5. 2 vols. 1927.
Report of the Land and Agriculture Committee. 1938.
Report of the Rice-Export Trade Enquiry Committee. 1937.
Report of the Village Administration Committee. 1941.
Report on the Famine in Burma in 1896–7. 1898.
(Confidential) Report on the Rebellion in Burma, April 1931–March 1932. 1932.
Report on the Rebellion in Burma up to 3rd May, 1931. 1931.
Report on the Suspension of Grants in the Hanthawaddy District. 1910.
Thompstone, E. *Granary Pests.* Agriculture Department, bull. no. 1. 1909.

Series Reports

Annual Reports on the Administration of the Province of Burma.
Annual Reports on the Working of the Co-operative Credit Societies in Burma.
Reports on the Administration of the Province of Pegu, 1853/54–1860/61.
Reports on the Department of Land Records and Agriculture.
Reports on the Land Revenue Administration of Burma.
Reports on the Operations of the Department of Agriculture in Burma.
Season and Crop Reports.

Settlement Reports, Lower Burma
(Author of report follows in parentheses.)

Report on Settlement Operations in the Syriam Township, Hanthawaddy District, 1879–80. 1880 (B. A. Parrott).
Report on Settlement Operations in the Bassein District, 1879–80. 1880 (J. E. Bridges).
Report on Settlement Operations in the Tharrawaddy District, 1880–81. 1882 (H. Adamson).

Report on Settlement Operations in the Syriam Township, Hanthawaddy District, 1880–81. 1881 (B. A. Parrott).

Report on Settlement Operations in the Bassein District, 1880–81. 1881 (J. E. Bridges).

Report on Settlement Operations in the Tharrawaddy District, 1881–82. 1884 (H. Adamson).

Report on Settlement Operations in the Hanthawaddy District, 1881–2. 1883 (B. A. Parrott).

Report on Settlement Operations in the Bassein District, 1881–2. 1883 (J. E. Bridges).

Report on Settlement Operations in the Tharrawaddy District, 1882–83. 1884 (H. Adamson).

Report on Settlement Operations in the Hanthawaddy and Pegu Districts, 1882–3. 1884 (B. A. Parrott).

Report on Settlement Operations in the Bassein District, 1882–3. 1884 (J. E. Bridges).

Report on Settlement Operations in the Tharrawaddy and Prome Districts, 1883–4. 1885 (H. Adamson).

Report on Settlement Operations in the Bassein and Henzada Districts, 1883–4. 1885 (J. E. Bridges).

Report on Settlement Operations in the Hanthawaddy and Pegu Districts, 1883–4. 1885 (B. A. Parrott).

Report on Settlement Operations in the Prome District, 1884–5. 1886 (H. Adamson).

Report on Settlement Operations in the Bassein and Henzada Districts, 1884–5. 1886 (W. T. Hall).

Report on Settlement Operations in the Henzada District, 1885–6. 1886 (W. T. Hall).

Report on Settlement Operations in the Bassein and Thongwa Districts, 1889–9. 1890 (H. M. S. Mathews).

Report on the Settlement Operations in the Thongwa District, 1889–90. 1891 (H. M. S. Mathews).

Report on the Settlement Operations in the Thongwa District, 1890–91. 1892 (H. M. S. Mathews).

Report on Settlement Operations in the Amherst and Thaton Districts, 1894–5. 1896 (A. Gaitskill).

Report on Settlement Operations in the Amherst and Thaton Districts, 1895–6. 1897 (A. Gaitskill).

Report on the Settlement Operations in the Kyaikto Sub-Division, 1896–7. Thaton District) 1898 (H. Des Voeux).

Report on Revision Settlement Operations in the Hanthawaddy District, 1897–8. 1900 (R. G. McKerron).

Report on Revision Settlement Operations in the Maungmya District, 1897–98. 1899 (James MacKenna).

Report on the Revision Settlement Operations in Pegu, 1897–8. 1899 (H. Des Voeux).

Report on the Revision Settlement Operations in the Bassein District, 1897–98. 1899 (James MacKenna).
Report on the Revision Settlement Operations in the Hanthawaddy District, 1898–9. 1901 (R. G. McKerron).
Report on the Settlement Operations in the Toungoo District, 1898–99. 1900 (H. Des Voeux).
Report on the Revision Settlement Operations in the Pegu District, 1898–9. 1900 (W. E. Lowry).
Report on Revision Settlement Operations in the Bassein District, 1898–9. 1900 (James MacKenna).
Report on the Revision Settlement Operations in the Hanthawaddy District, 1899–1900. 1902 (R. G. McKerron).
Report on the Revision Settlement Operations in the Henzada District, 1899–1900. 1901 (James MacKenna).
Report on the Settlement Operations in the Toungoo District, 1899–1900. 1901 (W. V. Wallace).
Report on the Revision Settlement Operations in the Pegu District, 1899–1900. 1901 (W. E. Lowry).
Report on the Revision Settlement Operations in Prome, 1900–01. 1902 (W. E. Lowry).
Report on the Revision Settlement Operations in the Tharrawaddy District, 1900–01. 1902 (E. A. Moore).
Report on the Settlement of Certain Areas in the Henzada District, 1900–01. 1902 (James MacKenna).
Report on the Settlement Operations in the Bawni Circle of the Pegu District, 1900–01. 1902 (W. V. Wallace).
Report on the Revision Settlement Operations in the Henzada District, 1900–01. 1902 (James MacKenna).
Report on the Revision Settlement Operations in the Tharrawaddy District, 1901–2. 1903 (E. A. Moore).
Report on the Settlement Operations in the Myaungmya and Bassein Districts, 1901–2. 1903 (James MacKenna).
Report on Settlement Operations in Myaungmya and Thongwa, 1902–3. 1903 (James MacKenna).
Report on the Settlement Operations in the Tharrawaddy District, 1903–4. 1905 (C. M. Webb).
Report on the Settlement Operations in the Prome District, 1903–4. 1905 (C. M. Webb).
Report on the Revision Settlement Operations in the Myaungmya District, 1903–4. 1905 (W. E. Lowry).
Report on the Settlement Operations in the Hanthawaddy District, 1903–4. 1905 (C. M. Webb).
Report on the Revision Settlement Operations in the Ma-ubin District, 1904–5. 1906 (W. E. Lowry).
Report on the Revision Settlement Operations in the Ma-ubin, Myaungmya, and Pyapon Districts, 1905–6. 1907 (T. L. Ormiston).

Report on the Revision Settlement Operations in the Pyapon District, 1906–7. 1908 (D. F. Chalmers).

Report on the Revision Settlement of the Thaton District, 1907–8. 1909 (G. P. Andrew).

Report on the Third Settlement of the Twante, Kungyangon, Kyauktan, Thongwa and Kayan Townships of the Hanthawaddy District, 1907–10. 1911 (R. E. V. Arbuthnot).

Report on the Second Settlement of the Paung, Pa-an and Hlaingbwe Townships, Together with the First Settlement of Newly Surveyed Areas in the Above Townships of the Thaton District, 1908–10. 1911 (T. Couper).

Report on the Settlement Operations in the Insein District, 1910–12. 1913 (W. S. Morrison).

Report on the Revision Settlement Operations in the Einme and Myaungmya Township, 1910–12. 1913 (C. H. Duffin).

Report on the Second Settlement of the Toungoo District, 1910–13. 1915 (S. A. Smyth).

Report on the Settlement of the Rangoon Town District, 1911–12. 1913 (W. S. Morrison).

Report on the Second Settlement of Nyaunglebin Subdivision and Original Settlement of a Part of Thanatpin Township in the Pegu District, 1911–13. 1914 (C. F. Grant).

Report of the Second Settlement of the Main Portion of the Ngaputaw Township and Third Settlement of the Southern Portion of the Bassein Township of the Bassein District, 1912–13. 1914 (C. H. Duffin).

Report on the Original Settlement of the Thakan and Kalateik Tracts of the Pyapon District, 1912–13. 1914 (C. F. Grant).

Report on the Third Settlement in the Thabaung, Kyaunggon, Kyonpyaw and Ngathainggyaung Townships and in Part of Bassein Township Together with the First Settlement of the Newly Surveyed Areas in the Thabaung and Ngaputaw Townships of the Bassein District, 1912–14. 1915 (P. E. Jamieson).

Report on the Third Settlement of the Kawa Township of the Pegu District, 1913–14. 1915 (C. F. Grant).

Report on the Third Settlement of Hlegu Township, Insein District, 1913–14. 1915 (C. F. Grant).

Report on the Third Settlement of the Tharrawaddy District, 1913–15. 1916 (J. L. McCallum).

Report on the Third Settlement of the Pegu Township and Part of the Thanatpin Township, 1914–15. 1916 (A. J. Page).

Report on the Revision Settlement of Prome, 1914–16. 1917 (S. G. Grantham).

Report of the Summary Settlement of the Kadonbaw Colony, Hanthawaddy District, 1916–17. 1917 (J. C. Saunders).

Report on Settlement Operations in the Myaungmya District, 1916–19. 1920 (S. G. Grantham).

Initial Report on Revision Settlement of the Pyapon District, 1921–2. 1912 (O. M. Rees).
Final Report on the Revision Settlement of the Pyapon District, 1921–25. 1927 (U Tin Gyi).
Report on the Original Settlement Operations in the Labutta Townships of the Myaungmya District, 1924–5. 1926 (U Tin Gyi).
Report on the Original Settlement of the Mamauk Tract in the Kawa Township of the Pegu District, 1924–5. 1926 (R. C. Barber).
Report on the Second Revision Settlement of the Ma-ubin District, 1925–8. 1929 (U Tin Gyi).
Report on the Second Revision Settlement of the Kyaikto and Thaton Subdivisions of the Thaton District of Lower Burma, 1928–30. 1931 (U Tin Gyi).
Report on the Third Settlement of the Pa-an and Hlaingbwe Townships of the Thaton District Together with the First Settlement of Newly Surveyed Areas in the Above Townships, 1928–30. 1931 (R. B. Abigail).
Report on the Third Revision Settlement of the Hanthawaddy District, 1930–33. 1934 (U Tin Gyi).
Report on the Revision Settlement of the Bassein District, Together with the Original Settlement of Certain Areas in the Yegyi, Thabaung, Bassein West and Ngaputaw Townships, 1935–39. 1941 (U Maung Maung Gyi).

Settlement Reports, Upper Burma

Report on the Settlement Operations in the Minbu District, 1893–97. 1900 (O. S. Parsons).
Report on the Settlement Operations in the Magwe District, 1897–1903. 1905 (W. A. Hertz).
Report on the Settlement Operations in the Pakokku District, 1905–10. 1910 (F. C. Owens).
Report on the Settlement Operations in the Sagaing District, 1915–18. 1921 (B. W. Swithinbank).
Report on Revision Settlement Operations in the Magwe District, 1915–19. 1921 (H. O. Reynolds).
Report on the First Revision Settlement of the Yamethin Subdivision of the Yamethin District, 1925–7. 1928 (C. J. Richards).
Report on Revision Settlement Operations in the Shwebo District, 1918–23. 1924 (A. Williamson).

GOVERNMENT PUBLICATIONS, INDIA
(Published by the Superintendent of Government Printing, Calcutta, unless otherwise noted.)

Reports

Holderness, T. W. *Narrative of the Famine in India in 1896–7.* London: HMSO, 1897.

Manual of the Administration of the Madras Presidency in Illustration of the Records of Government and Yearly Administrative Reports. 3 vols. Madras, 1885.

Moral and Material Progress Report (1929–30). 1930.

Noel-Paton, F. *Burma Rice.* 1912.

Nolan, Philip. *Report on Emigration from Bengal to Burma and How To Promote It.* Calcutta: Bengal Secretariat Press, 1888.

Raghavaiyanger, S. S. *Memorandum on the Progress of the Madras Presidency During the Last Forty Years of British Administration.* Madras, 1892.

Report of the Deck Passenger Committee. 2 vols. 1921.

Report of the Royal Commission on Agriculture in India (Great Britain). *Parliamentary Papers,* Reports, vol. 8, cmd. 3132, 1928.

Report of the Royal Commission on Labour in India. London: HMSO, 1931.

Report on the Famine in Madras Presidency During 1896 and 1897. 2 vols. 1898.

Census Reports and Tables

(In chronological order with the name of the report volume's author in parentheses.)

Report on the Census of British Burma. Rangoon, 1872.

Bengal Presidency, 1881. Calcutta, 1883 (J. A. Bourdillon).

British Burma, 1881. Rangoon, 1881 (F. S. Copelston).

Madras Presidency, 1881. Madras, 1883 (Lewis McIver).

Bengal Presidency, 1891. Vol. 3. Calcutta, 1893 (C. J. O'Donnell).

Burma, 1891. Vol. 9. Rangoon, 1892 (H. L. Eales).

Madras Presidency, 1891. Vol. 13. Madras, 1893 (H. A. Stuart).

Burma, 1901. Vol. 12. Rangoon, 1902 (C. C. Lowis).

Madras Presidency, 1901. Vol. 15. Madras, 1902 (W. Francis).

Bengal, Bihar, Orissa and Sikkim, 1911. Vol. 5. Calcutta, 1913 (L. S. S. O'Malley).

Burma, 1911. Vol. 9. Rangoon, 1912 (Morgan Webb).

Madras Presidency, 1911. Vol. 12. Madras, 1912 (J. C. Molony).

United Provinces of Agra and Oudh, 1911. Vol. 11. Allahabad, 1912 (E. A. H. Blunt).

Bihar and Orissa, 1921. Vol. 7. Patna, 1921 (P. C. Talents).

Burma, 1921. Vol. 10. Rangoon, 1923 (S. G. Grantham).

Madras Presidency, 1921. Vol. 13. Rangoon, 1922 (G. T. Boag).

Bihar and Orissa, 1931. Vol. 7. Patna, 1933 (W. C. Lacey).

Burma, 1931. Vol. 11. Rangoon, 1933 (J. J. Bennison).

Madras Presidency, 1931. Vol. 14. Madras, 1932.

United Provinces of Agra and Oudh, 1931. Vol. 13. Allahabad, 1933 (A. C. Turner).

Gazetteers

Akyab District. Rangoon, 1917 (R. B. Smart).

Amherst District. Rangoon, 1913 (P. E. Jamieson).

Amherst District. Rangoon, 1935 (B. O. Binns).
Bassein District. Rangoon, 1916 (H. P. Hewett and J. Clague).
The British Burma Gazetteer. Rangoon, 1880 (H. R. Spearman).
Chittagong District. Calcutta, 1908 (L. S. S. O'Malley).
Fyzabad District. Allahabad, 1905 (H. R. Nevill).
Godavari District. Madras, 1907 (F. R. Hemingway).
Henzada District. Rangoon, 1915 (W. S. Morrison).
Imperial Gazetteer. Vol. 3. London, 1885 (W. W. Hunter).
The Imperial Gazetteer of India. Vol. 9. Oxford, 1908.
Insein District. Rangoon, 1914 (J. S. Furnivall and W. S. Morrison).
Madura District. Madras, 1914 (W. Francis).
Maubin District. Rangoon, 1931 (U Tin Gyi).
Patna District. Calcutta, 1907 (L. S. S. O'Malley).
Pegu District. Rangoon, 1917 (A. J. Page).
Puri District. Calcutta, 1908 (L. S. S. O'Malley).
The District of Rangoon. Rangoon, 1868 (Malcolm Lloyd).
Sandoway District. Rangoon, 1912 (W. B. Tydd).
Shahabad District. Calcutta, 1906 (L. S. S. O'Malley).
Shwebo District. Rangoon, 1929 (A. Williamson).
South Arcot District. Madras, 1906 (William Francis).
Sultanpur District. Allahabad, 1903 (H. R. Nevill).
[Hanthawaddy] Syriam District. Rangoon, 1914 (J. S. Furnivall and W. S. Morrison).
Tanjore District. Madras, 1906 (F. R. Hemingway).
Tharrawaddy District. Rangoon, 1920 (S. G. Grantham, R. G. McDowall, and B. W. Swithinbank).
Thaton District. Rangoon, 1931 (U Tin Gyi).
Thayetmyo District. Rangoon, 1911.
Toungoo District. Rangoon, 1914 (B. W. Swithinbank).
Vizagapatam District. Madras, 1907 (William Francis).

CONTEMPORARY TRAVEL ACCOUNTS AND DESCRIPTIONS

Balbi, Gasparo. "His Voyage to Pegu, and Observations There, Gathered out of His Own Italian Relation." In *Hakluytus Posthumus or Purchas His Pilgrims,* compiled by Samuel Purchas. Vol. 10. Glasgow, 1905.
Bell, Henry G. *An Account of the Burman Empire.* Calcutta, 1852.
———. *A Narrative of the Late Military and Political Operations in the Burmese Empire with Some Account of the Present Condition of the Country, Its Members, Customs and Inhabitants.* Calcutta, 1852.
Bird, George W. *Wanderings in Burma.* London, 1897.
Cox, Hiram. *Journal of a Resident in the Burmhan Empire, and More Particularly at the Court of Amarapoorah.* London, 1821.
Crawfurd, John. *Journal of an Embassy from the Governor-General of India to the Court of Ava in the Year 1827.* London, 1829.

Floris, Peter. *His Voyage to the East Indies in the Globe, 1611–15,* edited by W. H. Moreland. London, 1934.
Frederick, Cesar. "Voyages and Travels in India." In *A General History and Collection of Voyages and Travels,* compiled by Robert Keer. Edinburgh, 1812.
Gouger, H. *A Personal Narrative of Two Years Imprisonment in Burma.* London, 1864.
Griffith, William. *Journals of Travels in Assam, Burma, Bootan, Afghanistan and the Neighboring Countries.* Calcutta, 1847.
Hall, D. G. E. *The Dalhousie-Phayre Correspondence.* London, 1932.
Malcolm, Howard. *Travels in South-Eastern Asia Embracing Hindustan, Malaya, Siam, and China; with Full Notices of Numerous Missionary Stations and a Full Account of the Burman Empire.* 2 vols. Boston, 1840.
Maw, H. L. *Memoir of the Early Operations of the Burmese War.* London, 1832.
Sangermano, V. *The Burmese Empire.* Westminster, 1893.
Saw, U. *The Burmese Situation (1930–31): A Letter to the Right Hon'ble William Wedgewood Benn, M.P., Secretary of State for India.* Rangoon, 1931.
Smith, Julius. *Ten Years in Burma.* Cincinnati, 1902.
Snodgrass, J. J. *A Narrative of the Burmese War.* London, 1827.
Symes, Michael. *An Account of an Embassy to the Kingdom of Ava Sent by the Governor-General in 1795.* 3 vols. London, 1800.
Trant, T. A. *Two Years in Ava.* London, 1827.
Winston, W. R. *Four Years in Upper Burma.* London, 1892.
Yule, Henry. *A Narrative of the Mission Sent by the Governor-General to the Court of Ava in 1855 With Notices of the Country, Government and People.* London, 1858.

SECONDARY SOURCES, BURMA

Adas, Michael. "Agrarian Development and the Plural Society in Lower Burma, 1852–1941." Ph.D. diss. University of Wisconsin, 1971.
———. "Imperialist Rhetoric and Modern Historiography: The Case of Lower Burma before and after Conquest." *Journal of Southeast Asian Studies* 3 no. 2 (September 1972): 175–92.
Andrew, E. J. L. *Indian Labour in Rangoon.* Calcutta, 1933.
Andrus, J. R. *Burmese Economic Life.* Stanford, 1948.
———. *Rural Reconstruction in Burma.* Oxford, 1936.
——. "Three Economic Systems Clash in Burma." *Review of Economic Studies* 3 (1935–36): 140–46.
Anonymous. *A Few Words on the Tenure and Distribution of Landed Property in Burma.* Rangoon, 1865.
Aye Hlaing, U. "Trends of Economic Growth and Income Distribution in Burma, 1870–1940." *Journal of the Burma Research Society* 47, no. 1 (June 1964): 89–148.
Brant, C. S. *Tadagale: A Burmese Village in 1950.* Ithaca, N.Y., 1954.

Bruen, K. E. "The Agricultural Geography of the Irrawaddy Delta with Special Reference to Rice." Ph.D. diss., University of London, 1939.
Burney, Henry. "On the Population of the Burmah Empire." *Journal of the Royal Statistical Society of London* 4, no. 4 (1842): 335–47.
Cady, John. *A History of Modern Burma*. Ithaca, N.Y., 1958.
Chakravarti, N. R. *The Indian Minority in Burma*. London, 1971.
Cheng Siok-Hwa. *The Rice Industry of Burma, 1852–1940*. Kuala Lumpur-Singapore, 1968.
Christian, J. L. *Modern Burma: A Survey of Political and Economic Development*. Berkeley, Calif., 1942.
Clayton, Harold, ed. *Proposals for the Extension of Agricultural Banking in the Delta of Burma: With a Criticism by the Author*. Rangoon, 1918.
———. *Rural Development in Burma*. Rangoon, 1911.
Collis, Maurice. *Trials in Burma*. London, 1953.
Donnison, F. S. V. *Public Administration in Burma*. London, 1953.
Dunn, C. W. *Studies in the History of Tharrawaddy*. Cambridge, Eng., 1920.
Ferrar, Max and Bertha. *Burma*. London, 1900.
Francklin, William. *Tracts, Political, Geographical, and Commercial; on the Dominions of Ava, and the North Western Parts of Hindustaun*. London, 1811.
Furnivall, J. S. *Colonial Policy and Practice*. 2d ed. New York, 1956.
———. *The Fashioning of Leviathan: The Beginnings of British Rule in Burma*. Rangoon, 1939.
———. "Industrial Agriculture." *Journal of the Burma Research Society* 48, no. 1 (June 1965): 87–97.
———. *An Introduction to the Political Economy of Burma*. 3d ed. Rangoon, 1957.
———. "Land as a Free Gift of Nature." *Economic Journal* 19 (1909): 552–62.
——. "The Political Economy of the Tropical Far East." *Journal of the Royal Central Asian Society* 29, nos. 3, 4 (1942): 195–210.
——. "Safety First—A Study in the Economic History of Burma." *Journal of the Burma Research Society* 40, no. 1 (June 1957): 24–38.
——. "Some Historical Documents." *Journal of the Burma Research Society* 6, no. 3 (December 1916): 213–23; 8, no. 1 (April 1918): 40–52; 9, no. 1 (April 1919): 33–52.
Fytche, Albert. *Burma Past and Present*. 2 vols. London, 1878.
Gordon, Robert. *The Irrawaddy River*. London, 1885.
Guyot, James. "Bureaucratic Transformation in Burma." In *Asian Bureaucratic Systems Emergent from the British Imperial Tradition*, edited by Ralph Braibanti. Durham, N.C., 1966.
Hall, D. G. E. *Burma*. London, 1950.
———. *A History of South-East Asia*. London, 1964.
Halliday, Robert. *The Talaings*. Rangoon, 1917.
Harvey, G. E. *British Rule in Burma, 1824–1942*. London, 1946.
———. *History of Burma from the Earliest Times to 10 March 1824, The Beginning of the English Conquest*. 2d ed. London, 1967.

Hendry, D. "Rice in Burma." *Tropical Agriculture* 5, no. 1 (January–March 1928): 12–15, 34–36, 51–53.

Htin Aung, U. *Epistles Written on the Eve of the Anglo-Burmese War.* The Hague, 1968.

——. *The Stricken Peacock: Anglo-Burmese Relations 1752–1948.* The Hague, 1965.

Ireland, A. *The Province of Burma.* 2 vols. Boston, 1907.

Leach, F. B. "The Rice Industry of Burma." *Journal of the Burma Research Society* 27, no. 1 (April 1937): 61–73.

Luce, G. H. "The Economic Life of the Early Burman." In *Fiftieth Anniversary Publication of the Burma Research Society.* Rangoon, 1960.

McMahon, A. R. *The Karens of the Golden Chersonese.* London, 1876.

Marshall, H. I. *The Karen People of Burma.* Columbus, Ohio, 1922.

Mason, F. *Burmah, Its People and Natural Productions, or Notes on the Nations, Fauna, Flora, and Minerals of Tenasserim, Pegu and Burmah.* Rangoon, 1860.

Moscotti, A. D. "British Policy in Burma, 1917–1937." Ph.D. diss., Yale University, 1950.

Mya Maung, U. "Cultural Value and Economic Change in Burma." *Asian Survey* 4 (March 1964): 757–64.

——. "The Genesis of Economic Development in Burma: The Plural Society." Ph.D. diss., Catholic University of America, 1962.

Mya Sein, Daw. *Administration of Burma: Sir Charles Crosthwaite and the Consolidation of Burma.* Rangoon, 1938.

Nash, Manning. "Burmese Buddhism in Every Day Life." *American Anthropologist* 65, no. 2 (April 1963): 285–95.

———. *The Golden Road to Modernity.* New York, 1965.

———, and June. "Marriage, Family and Population Growth in Upper Burma." *Southwestern Journal of Anthropology* 19, no. 3 (Autumn, 1963): 251–66.

Nisbet, John. *Burma under British Rule and Before.* 2 vols. London, 1901.

Pearn, B. R. *History of Rangoon.* Rangoon, 1939.

———. *The Indian in Burma.* Ledbury, Eng., 1946.

Pfanner, David E. "Rice and Religion in a Burmese Village." Ph.D. diss., Cornell University, 1962.

———, and Ingersoll, Jasper. "Theravada Buddhism and Village Economic Behavior: A Burmese and Thai Comparison." *Journal of Asian Studies* 21, no. 3 (May 1962): 341–62.

Phayre, Arthur. *History of Burma.* London, 1883.

Rafi, M. *The Problem of Indian Settlers in Burma.* New Delhi, 1946.

Rangoon Gazette, 1929-38.

Rutledge, Guy. "Some Notes on the Burma Census." *Journal of the Burma Research Society* 2, no. 2 (1912): 153–60.

Sarkisyanz, E. *Buddhist Backgrounds of the Burmese Revolution.* The Hague, 1965.

Schmitt, Hans O. "Decolonization and Development in Burma." *Journal of Development Studies* 4, no. 1 (October 1967): 97–108.

Scott, J. G. (Shway Yoe, pseudonym). *The Burman: His Life and Notions.* New York, 1963.
Shein, U. *Burma's Transport and Foreign Trade, 1885–1914.* Rangoon, 1964.
Smith, D. E. *Religion and Politics in Burma.* Princeton, 1965.
Spate, O. H. K. "Beginnings of Industrialization in Burma." *Economic Geography* 17, no. 1 (January 1941): 75–92.
———. "The Burmese Village." *Geographical Review* 35 (1945): 523–43.
———, and Trueblood, L. W. "Rangoon: A Study in Urban Geography." *Geographical Review* 32 (1942): 56–73.
Spiro, Melford. "Buddhism and Economic Action in Burma." *American Anthropologist* 68, no. 3 (October 1966): 1163–73.
Stamp, L. D. "Burma: An Underdeveloped Monsoon Country." *Geographical Review* 20, no. 1 (January 1930): 86–109.
———. *Vegetation of Burma.* Rangoon, 1926.
Than Tun, U. "Agriculture in Burma: A.D.1000–1300." Typed ms. India Office Library, London, Eng.
Thein Maung, U. *Immigration Problem of Burma.* Rangoon, 1939.
Traeger, Frank N. *Furnivall of Burma: An Annotated Bibliography of the Works of John S. Furnivall.* New Haven, Conn., 1963.
Tun Wai, U. *Currency and Credit in Burma.* Bombay, 1953.
———. *Economic Development of Burma.* Rangoon, 1961.
Vadja, E. H. "Burmese Urban Characteristics." Ph.D. diss., University of Chicago, 1960.
Walinsky, L. J. *Economic Development of Burma, 1951–1960.* New York, 1962.
Woodman, Dorothy. *The Making of Burma.* London, 1962.

SECONDARY SOURCES, INDIA AND GENERAL

Aitchison, C. U., comp. *A Collection of Treaties, Engagements and Sanads Relating to India and Neighboring Countries.* Vol. 12. Calcutta, 1931.
Baden-Powell, B. H. *Land Systems of British India.* 3 vols. London, 1892.
Bauer, P. T., and Yamey, B. S. *The Economics of Under-developed Countries.* Chicago, 1957.
Beaglehole, T. H. *Thomas Munro and the Development of Administrative Policy in Madras, 1792–1818.* Cambridge, Eng., 1966.
Bearce, George D. *British Attitudes Towards India, 1784–1858.* Oxford, 1961.
Beidelman, Thomas O. *A Comparative Analysis of the Hindu Jajmani System.* Locust Valley, N.Y., 1959.
Benedict, Burton. "Stratification in Plural Societies." *American Anthropologist* 64, no. 4 (December 1962): 1235–47.
Bernadelli, H. "New Zealand and Asiatic Migration." *Population Studies* 6, no. 1 (July 1952): 39–54.
Bhatia, B. M. *Famines in India, 1860–1965.* London, 1967.
Blyn, George. *Agricultural Trends in India, 1891–1947: Output, Availability, and Productivity.* Philadelphia, 1966.

Boeke, J. H. *Economics and Economic Policy of Dual Societies.* New York, 1953.
Boserup, Ester. *The Conditions of Agricultural Growth.* Chicago, 1965.
Boyd, M. F. *Malariology.* 2 vols. Philadelphia, 1949.
Braithwaite, Lloyd. "Social Stratification and Cultural Pluralism." *Annals of the New York Academy of Sciences* 83 (January 1957): 816–31.
Bryce-Laporte, R. S. "M. G. Smith's Version of Pluralism—The Questions It Raises." *Comparative Studies in Society and History* 10, no. 1 (October 1967): 114–20.
Burridge, Kenhelm. *New Heaven, New Earth.* New York, 1969.
Cotter, Michael. "Towards a Social History of the Vietnamese Southward Movement." *Journal of Southeast Asian History* 9, no. 1 (March 1968): 12–24.
Davis, Kingsley. *The Population of India and Pakistan.* Princeton, N.J., 1951.
Depres, Leo. *Cultural Pluralism and Nationalist Politics in British Guiana.* Chicago, 1967.
———. "The Implications of Nationalist Politics in British Guiana for the Development of Cultural Theory." *American Anthropologist* 66, no. 5 (1964): 1051–77.
Desai, W. S. *India and Burma: A Study.* Bombay, 1954.
Dewey, Alice. "Trade and Social Control in Java." *The Journal of the Royal Anthropological Institute of Great Britain and Ireland* 92, nos. 1, 2 (January–December 1962): 177–90.
Dotson, Floyd and Lillian. *The Indian Minority of Zambia, Rhodesia and Malawi.* New Haven, Conn., 1968.
Elliot, C. M. "Agriculture and economic development in Africa: theory and experience 1880–1914." In *Agrarian Change and Economic Development,* edited by E. L. Jones and S. J. Woolf. London, 1969.
Farmer, B. H. *Ceylon: A Divided Nation.* London, 1963.
Firth, Raymond, and Yamey, B. S., eds. *Capital Saving and Credit in Peasant Societies.* London, 1964.
Foster, G. M. "Peasant Society and the Image of the Limited Good." *American Anthropologist* 67, no. 2 (April 1965): 293–315.
Freedman, Maurice. "The Growth of a Plural Society in Malaya." *Pacific Affairs* 33, no. 2 (1960): 158–68.
Gallagher, J., and Robinson, R. "The Imperialism of Free Trade." *The Economic History Review.* 2d ser., 4, no. 1 (August 1953): 1–15.
Gangulee, N. *Indians in the Empire Overseas.* London, 1947.
Geertz, Clifford. *Agricultural Involution.* Berkeley, Calif., 1966.
———. *The Social History of an Indonesian Town.* Cambridge, Mass., 1965.
Ginsburg, Norton. *Atlas of Economic Development.* Chicago, 1961.
———, and Roberts, Chester. *Malaya.* Seattle, Wash., 1958.
Gourou, Pierre. *L'utilisation du sol en Indochine Française.* Paris, 1940.
Hardgraves, R. L. *The Nadars of Tamilnad.* Berkeley, Calif., 1969.
Higgins, Benjamin. *Economic Development: Problems, Principles and Policies.* New York, 1959.

Hill, Polly. *Migrant Cocoa Farmers of Southern Ghana.* Cambridge, Eng., 1963.
Hla Myint, U. *The Economics of the Developing Countries.* New York, 1964.
Hobsbawm, E. J. "The General Crisis of the European Economy in the 17th Century." *Past and Present* 5 (May 1954): 33–53.
Hoetinck, H. "The Concept of Pluralism as Envisaged by M. G. Smith." *Caribbean Studies* 7, no. 1 (April 1967): 36–43.
———. *The Two Variants in Caribbean Race Relations: A Contribution to the Sociology of Segmented Societies.* London, 1967.
Hunter, W. W. *The Marquess of Dalhousie.* Oxford, 1890.
Indian Emigrant. 6 vols, Madras, 1914–19.
Ingram, James. *Economic Change in Thailand Since 1850.* Stanford, Calif., 1954.
Isaacs, Harold R. *India's Ex-Untouchables.* Bombay, 1965.
Iyer, G. S. *Some Economic Aspects of British Rule in India.* Madras, 1903.
Karve, Irawati. *Hindu Society–an Interpretation.* Poona, 1961.
Keyfitz, Nathan. "Urbanization in South and Southeast Asia." In *The Study of Urbanization,* edited by P. M. Hauser and L. F. Schnore. New York, 1965.
Kondapi, C. *Indians Overseas, 1839–1949.* New Delhi, 1951.
Kumar, Dharma. *Land and Caste in South India.* Cambridge, Eng., 1965.
Kumar, Ravinder. *Western India in the Nineteenth Century.* London, 1968.
Kuper, Leo. "Plural Societies: Perspectives and Problems." In *Pluralism in Africa,* edited by Kuper and Smith. Berkeley, Calif., 1969.
———, and Smith, M. G., eds. *Pluralism in Africa.* Berkeley, Calif., 1969.
Kuznets, Simon et al. *Population Distribution and Economic Growth–United States, 1870–1950.* 3 vols. Philadelphia, 1957, 1960, 1964.
Landes, David S. *The Unbound Prometheus, Technological Change and Industrial Development in Western Europe from 1750 to the Present.* Cambridge, Eng., 1969.
LeBar, F. M. et al. *Ethnic Groups of Mainland Southeast Asia.* New Haven, Conn., 1964.
Le Thanh Khoi. *Le Viet-Nam: histoire et civilisation.* Paris, 1955.
Levin, Jonathan. *The Export Economies.* Cambridge, Mass., 1960.
Ludowyk, E. F. C. *The Story of Ceylon.* London, 1962.
McKenzie, H. I. "The Plural Society Debate: Some Comments on a Recent Contribution." *Social and Economic Studies* 15, no. 1 (March 1966): 53–60.
Mahajani, Usha. *The Role of the Indian Minorities in Burma and Malaya.* Bombay, 1960.
Morris, H. S. *The Indians in Uganda, Caste and Sect in a Plural Society.* London, 1968.
———. "The Plural Society." *Man* 57, no. 148 (1957): 124–25.
———. "Some Aspects of the Concept Plural Society." *Man,* n.s., 2, no. 2 (1967): 169–84.
Morris, Morris David. "Towards a Reinterpretation of Nineteenth-Century

Indian Economic History." *Journal of Economic History* 23, no. 4 (December 1963): 606–18.

———. "Trends and Tendencies in Indian Economic History," *Indian Social and Economic History Review* 5 (December 1968): 319–88.

Mukherjee, Nilmani, and Frykenberg, Robert Eric. "The Ryotwari System and Social Organization in the Madras Presidency." In *Land Control and Social Structure in Indian History*, edited by Frykenberg. Madison, Wis., 1969.

Nadel, S. F. *The Foundations of Social Anthropology*. London, 1951.

Neale, Walter C. *Economic Change in Rural India: Land Tenure and Reform in Uttar Pradesh*. New Haven, Conn., 1962.

———. "Land is to Rule." In *Land Control and Social Structure in Indian History*, edited by Robert Eric Frykenberg. Madison, Wis., 1969.

Pares, Richard. "The Economic Factors in the History of Empire." *Economic History Review* 3 no. 2 (May 1937): 119–44.

Rao, A. V. Raman. *Economic Development of Andhra Pradesh, 1766–1957*. Bombay, 1958.

Rau, C. H. "The Banking Caste of Southern India." *Indian Review* (Madras), 8, no. 8 (August 1907): 593–95.

Ravenstein, E. G. "The Laws of Migration." *Journal of the Royal Statistical Society of London* 48 (June 1885): 167–227, 52 (June 1889): 241–301.

Rogers, E. M., and Shoemaker, F. F. *Communication of Innovations*. New York, 1971.

Rudolph, Lloyd I. and Susanne H. *The Modernity of Tradition*. Chicago, 1967.

Sadli, M. "Reflections on Boeke's Theory of Dualistic Economies." In *The Economy of Indonesia: Selected Readings*, edited by Bruce Glassburner. Ithaca, N.Y., 1971.

Sandhu, K. Singh. *Indians in Malaya: Immigration and Settlement, 1786–1957*. Cambridge, Eng., 1969.

Sansom, R. L. *The Economics of Insurgency in the Mekong Delta of Vietnam*. Cambridge, Mass., 1970.

Schrieke, B. "The Causes and Effects of Communism on the West Coast of Sumatra." *Indonesian Sociological Studies*. Vol. 1. The Hague, 1966.

Schultz, Theodore. *Transforming Traditional Agriculture*. New Haven, Conn., 1964.

Schumpeter, J. A. *The Theory of Economic Development*. Cambridge, Mass., 1961.

Siegelman, Philip. "Colonial Development and the Chettiar: A Study in the Ecology of Modern Burma, 1850–1941." Ph.D. diss., University of Minnesota, 1962.

Sjaastad, L. A. "The Costs and Returns of Human Migration." *Journal of Political Economy* 70, no. 5, pt. 2 (October 1962): 80–93.

Skinner, G. William. "The Chinese Minority." In *Indonesia*, edited by Ruth T. McVey. New Haven, Conn., 1963.

———. *Chinese Society in Thailand: An Analytical History*. Ithaca, N.Y., 1957.

Smith, M. G. "Institutional and Political Conditions of Pluralism." In *Pluralism in Africa,* edited by Leo Kuper and M. G. Smith. Berkeley, Calif., 1969.

———. *Plural Society in the West Indies.* Berkeley, Calif., 1965.

———. "Some Developments in the Analytic Framework of Pluralism." In *Pluralism in Africa,* edited by Leo Kuper and M. G. Smith. Berkeley, Calif., 1969.

Smith, R. T. "Review of *Social and Cultural Pluralism in the Caribbean.*" *American Anthropologist* 63, no. 1 (February 1961): 155–57.

Steward, Julian. "Levels of Socio-Cultural Integration: An Operational Concept." *Southwest Journal of Anthropology* 5, no. 7 (1951): 374–90.

Stokes, Eric. *The English Utilitarians and India.* Oxford, 1959.

Thurston, Edgar. *Tribes and Castes of South India.* 7 vols. Madras, 1909.

Tiwari, S. G. *Economic Prosperity of the United Provinces, A Study in the Provincial Income Its Distribution and Working Conditions, 1921–39.* Bombay, 1951.

Van den Berghe, Pierre L. "Pluralism and the Polity: A Theoretical Explanation." In *Pluralism in Africa,* edited by Leo Kuper and M. G. Smith. Berkeley, Calif., 1969.

———. *Race and Racism: A Comparative Perspective.* New York, 1967.

———. "Towards a Sociology of Africa." *Social Forces* 43 (October 1964): 11–18.

Wales, H. G. Q. *Ancient Siamese Government and Administration.* London, 1934.

Whitcombe, Elizabeth. *Agrarian Conditions in Northern India: The United Provinces under British Rule.* Vol. 1. Berkeley, Calif., 1972.

Wickberg, Edgar. *The Chinese in Philippine Life, 1850–1898.* New Haven, Conn., 1965.

Winder, R. B. "The Lebanese in West Africa." *Comparative Studies in Society and History* 4 (1961–62): 292–333.

Wiser, William H. *The Hindu Jajmani System.* Lucknow, 1936.

Zachariah, K. C. *A Historical Study of Internal Migration in the Indian Sub-Continent, 1901–1931.* Bombay, 1964.

INDEX

NEW PERSPECTIVES IN SOUTHEAST ASIAN STUDIES

The Burma Delta: Economic Development and Social Change on an Asian Rice Frontier, 1852–1941
Michael Adas

From Rebellion to Riots: Collective Violence on Indonesian Borneo
Jamie S. Davidson

The Floracrats: State-Sponsored Science and the Failure of the Enlightenment in Indonesia
Andrew Goss

Revolution Interrupted: Farmers, Students, Law, and Violence in Northern Thailand
Tyrell Haberkorn

Amazons of the Huk Rebellion: Gender, Sex, and Revolution in the Philippines
Vina A. Lanzona

Policing America's Empire: The United States, the Philippines, and the Rise of the Surveillance State
Alfred W. McCoy

An Anarchy of Families: State and Family in the Philippines
Edited by Alfred W. McCoy

The Hispanization of the Philippines: Spanish Aims and Filipino Responses, 1565–1700
John Leddy Phelan

Pretext for Mass Murder: The September 30th Movement and Suharto's Coup d'État in Indonesia
John Roosa

The Social World of Batavia: Europeans and Eurasians in Colonial Indonesia, second edition
Jean Gelman Taylor

Việt Nam: Borderless Histories
Edited by Nhung Tuyet Tran and Anthony Reid

Modern Noise, Fluid Genres: Popular Music in Indonesia, 1997–2001
Jeremy Wallach